Criminological Theory

Third Edition

Stephen G. Tibbetts dedicates this book to his daughter, Rian Sage,
who has been really cool to hang out with watching SpongeBob
over the past decade; Rian has been the best daughter anyone could ask for.

Criminological Theory

The Essentials

Third Edition

Stephen G. Tibbetts
California State University, San Bernardino

Los Angeles | London | New Delhi
Singapore | Washington DC | Melbourne

FOR INFORMATION:

SAGE Publications, Inc.
2455 Teller Road
Thousand Oaks, California 91320
E-mail: order@sagepub.com

SAGE Publications Ltd.
1 Oliver's Yard
55 City Road
London EC1Y 1SP
United Kingdom

SAGE Publications India Pvt. Ltd.
B 1/I 1 Mohan Cooperative Industrial Area
Mathura Road, New Delhi 110 044
India

SAGE Publications Asia-Pacific Pte. Ltd.
3 Church Street
#10-04 Samsung Hub
Singapore 049483

Printed in the United States of America

Library of Congress Cataloging-in-Publication Data

Names: Tibbetts, Stephen G., author.

Title: Criminological theory : the essentials / Stephen G. Tibbetts, California State University, San Bernardino.

Description: Third Edition. | Thousand Oaks : SAGE Publications, [2018] | Revised edition of the author's Criminological theory, [2015] | Includes bibliographical references and index.

Identifiers: LCCN 2017036278 | ISBN 9781506367897 (pbk. : alk. paper)

Subjects: LCSH: Criminology. | Crime.

Classification: LCC HV6018 .T53 2018 | DDC 364.01—dc23
LC record available at https://lccn.loc.gov/2017036278

This book is printed on acid-free paper.

Acquisitions Editor: Jessica Miller
Editorial Assistant: Rebecca Lee
Production Editor: Laureen Gleason
Copy Editor: Megan Markanich
Typesetter: C&M Digitals (P) Ltd.
Proofreader: Scott Oney
Indexer: Michael Ferreira
Cover Designer: Janet Kiesel
Marketing Manager: Jillian Oelsen

18 19 20 21 22 10 9 8 7 6 5 4 3 2

Brief Contents

Detailed Contents

CHAPTER 9. Social Reaction and Critical Models of Crime — 187

CHAPTER 10. Feminist Models of Crime — 199

CHAPTER 11. Life-Course Perspectives of Criminality — 215

Preface

This textbook is intended to cover the essential topics of criminological theory in a more brief and efficient manner than other larger, more comprehensive texts on this topic. The third edition of *Criminological Theories: The Essentials* presents a comprehensive overview of the major concepts and perspectives of virtually all major theories in the evolution of criminological theory, reviewing some of the most recent empirical research on each theory that is currently available. Furthermore, in each chapter, as well as an entire concluding chapter, this book examines the various policy implications that can be derived from each type of criminological theory in addition to what can possibly be done but has not yet been tested.

A number of excellent criminology theory textbooks are available to students and professors, so why this one? This book can serve as the primary text for an introductory undergraduate course in criminological theory or as the primary text for a graduate course, given the depth and comprehensive nature of the discussion of virtually all theories in the historic and modern criminological literature. It is important to note that the book provides a comprehensive, yet concise, survey of the current state of existing scientific literature in virtually all areas of criminological theory as well as giving a history of how we got to this point regarding each theoretical model and topic area. A key feature of this text is a section in each chapter that examines various policy implications that have resulted from most of the dominant theories in the discipline in addition to results from empirical evaluation studies of programs based on theories presented in each chapter.

Structure of the Book

This book uses a rather typical outline for criminological theory textbook topics or chapters, beginning with an introduction of the definitions of *crime* and *criminology* and measuring crime as well as what such measures of crime reveal regarding the various characteristics that are most associated with higher offending rates. This is a very important aspect of the book, because each theory or model must be judged by how well it explains the distribution of crime rates among these various characteristics. In the Introduction, the criteria that are required for determining causality are also discussed, including an examination of how extremely difficult (often impossible) this is to do in criminological research because we can't randomly assign individuals to bad parenting, unemployment, low IQ, and so on.

This book presents 12 chapters that chronologically trace the history and development of criminological theory with an emphasis on when such perspectives became popular among theorists and mainstream society. Thus, we will start with the earliest models (Preclassical and Classical School) of criminal theorizing in the 18th century. Then, we will examine the evolution of the Positive School perspective of the 19th century, which began with biological theories of crime. Next, the book will present the various other positive theories that were proposed in the early 20th century, which include social structure models and social process theories that were presented in the early or mid-1900s. Then, we will explore theoretical models that were presented in the latter 20th century, such as social

CRIMINOLOGICAL THEORY: THE ESSENTIALS

conflict and Marxist and feminist models of criminality. Chapters 10, 11, and 12 then present the more contemporary theoretical explanations of criminality, which include developmental and life-course models, integrated theories of crime, and a separate chapter regarding feminist perspectives of crime, which we are very proud to present. This book is divided into 12 chapters that mirror the chapters in a typical criminology textbook, each dealing with a particular type or category of theories in criminology. Each of the chapters concludes with an evaluation of the empirical support for the theories and policy implications derivable. These chapters are as follows:

1. Introduction to the Book: An Overview of Issues in Criminological Theory

We first provide an introductory chapter that deals with what criminological theory is as well as examining the concepts of crime and the criteria used to determine whether a theory is adequate for explaining behavior. This chapter introduces the facts and criteria by which all of the theoretical models presented in the following chapters will be evaluated. We also include a discussion of the criteria involved in determining whether a given factor or variable actually causes criminal behavior.

2. Preclassical and Classical Theories of Crime

In this chapter, we examine the types of theories that were dominant before logical theories of crime were presented, namely supernatural or demonic theories of crime. Then we examine how the Age of Enlightenment led to more rational approaches to explaining criminal behavior, such as that of the Classical School and neoclassical theory. We also discuss at length the major model that evolved from the Classical School: deterrence theory. We describe studies that have empirically tested deterrence theory.

3. Modern Applications of the Classical Perspective: Deterrence, Rational Choice, and Routine Activities or Lifestyle Theories of Crime

In this chapter, we review more contemporary theoretical models and empirical findings regarding explanations of crime that focus on deterrence and other recent perspectives—such as rational choice theory, routine activities theory, and the lifestyle perspective—that are based on the assumption that individuals rationally choose their behavior or targets. Some of these perspectives focus more on the perceived costs or benefits of a given act to the individual who carries it out, whereas other models focus on the types of locations that people choose to commit crime or the daily activities or lifestyles that predispose them to certain criminal behavior.

4. Early Positive School Perspectives of Criminality

This chapter will examine the early development of theoretical models proposing that certain individuals or groups are predisposed to criminal offending. The earliest theories in the 19th century proposed that certain physical traits are associated with criminal behavior, whereas perspectives in the early 20th century proposed that such criminality is due to level of intelligence. This chapter also examines body type theory, which proposes that the physical body type of an individual has an effect on criminality. We will also examine modern applications of this perspective and review the empirical support such theoretical models have received in modern times.

5. Modern Biosocial Perspectives of Criminal Behavior

In this chapter, we will review the various forms of modern studies that investigate the link between physiology and criminality, including family studies, twin and adoption studies, cytogenetic studies, and studies on hormones and neurotransmitters. We will examine some of the primary methods used to explore this link as well as discuss the findings of more rational and recent empirical studies, which show a relatively consistent link between physiological factors and criminal behavior.

6. Early Social Structure and Strain Theories of Crime

This chapter reviews the development of the social structure perspective, which originated in the 19th century and culminated with Merton's theory of strain in the early 20th century. A variety of perspectives based on Merton's strain theory will be examined, but all of these models have a primary emphasis on how the social structure produces criminal behavior. We examine the many empirical studies that have tested the validity of these early social structure theories as well as discussing policy implications that these models suggested.

7. The Chicago School and Cultural and Subcultural Theories of Crime

In this chapter, we examine the evolution and propositions of the scholars at the University of Chicago, the most advanced form of criminological theorizing of the early 20th century. In addition to discussing the evolution of the Chicago School and its application of ecological theory to criminal behavior, we examine the more modern applications of this theoretical framework for explaining criminal behavior among residents of certain neighborhoods. Finally, we discuss several theoretical models that examine cultural or subcultural groups that differ drastically from conventional norms.

8. Social Process and Learning Theories of Crime

This chapter examines the many perspectives that have proposed that criminal behavior is the result of being taught by significant others to commit crime. When these theories were first presented, they were considered quite novel. We examine the evolution of various theories of social learning, starting with the earliest, which were based on somewhat outdated forms of learning theory, and then progressing to more modern theories that incorporate contemporary learning models. We also examine the most recent versions of this theoretical perspective, which incorporates all forms of social learning in explaining criminal behavior.

9. Social Reaction and Critical Models of Crime

In this chapter, we examine a large range of theories, with the common assumption that the reason for criminal behavior is factors outside of the traditional criminal justice system. Many social reaction theories, for example, are based on labeling theory, which proposes that it is not the individual offender who is to blame, but rather the societal reaction to such early antisocial behavior. Furthermore, this chapter examines the critical perspective, which blames the existing legal and economical structure for the "criminal" label that is used against most offenders.

10. Feminist Models of Crime

This chapter examines the various theoretical feminist perspectives of crime. Feminist criminology evolved when various assumptions and stereotypes about women in criminal justice were being questioned. Such questions included women as both offenders and victims. We discuss the importance of research regarding female offending, which was largely neglected in nearly all previous research before the late 19th century, and then discuss the extant literature that has been produced in recent years. This chapter discusses how important it is to examine the research that has been done on female offending and how key it is to understanding why women are so much less likely to commit serious violent offenses than males—and perhaps to using that understanding to reduce male chronic offending in society.

11. Life-Course Perspectives of Criminality

This chapter examines the various theoretical perspectives that emphasize the predisposition and influences present among individuals who begin committing crime at early versus later ages. We also examine the various stages of life that tend to have a high influence on an individual's state of criminality (e.g., marriage) as well as the empirical studies that have examined these types of transitions in life. Finally, we examine the various types of offenders and the kinds of transitions and trajectories that tend to influence their future behavior, along with various policy implications that can be suggested by such models of criminality.

12. Integrated Theoretical Models and New Perspectives of Crime

In this chapter, we present the general theoretical framework for integrated models. Then, we introduce criticisms of such integration of traditional theoretical models. In addition, we present several integrated models of criminality, some of which are based on micro-level factors and others that are based on macro-level factors. Finally, we examine the weaknesses and strengths of these various models based on empirical studies that have tested their validity.

New to This Edition

- A new chapter dedicated entirely to feminist perspectives (see Chapter 10) examines the feminist models of crime and underscores the importance of examining research related to female offending.

- Case studies that examine offender motives help students apply the theories discussed.

- Coverage of policy is now further integrated into each chapter as opposed to having a stand-alone chapter on this topic.

- Coverage of critical topics, such as the influence of employment on criminal behavior, the success of school programs to reduce delinquent behavior, and federal sentencing guidelines in regard to crack versus powder cocaine have been expanded throughout.

- Statistics, graphs, and tables have all been updated to demonstrate the most recent trends in criminology.

Digital Resources

To enhance the use of this text and to assist those using this book as a core text, we have developed high-quality digital resources for instructors.

Instructor Teaching Site. A password-protected site, available at **study.sagepub.com/tibbetts3e,** features resources that have been designed to help instructors plan and teach their courses. These materials include an extensive test bank, chapter-specific PowerPoint slides, lecture notes, sample course syllabi, web resources, and links to SAGE journal articles.

Acknowledgments

I would first of all like to thank executive editor Jessica Miller. Jessica's faith in and commitment to the project is greatly appreciated, and she has provided excellent guidance in making this new edition much better than the previous versions of this text. I also owe much gratitude to my very able production editor, Laureen Gleason. They kept up a most useful three-way dialogue among author, publisher, and a parade of excellent reviewers, making this text the best that it could possibly be. My copy editor, Megan Markanich, spotted every errant comma, dangling participle, and missing reference in the manuscript, for which I am truly thankful. Thank you one and all. I would like to express our great appreciation for Jerry Westby, the editor for the first two editions of this text. Jerry remains a very close friend. Jerry, I wish you well in the next stage of your life!

I also would like to thank the various individuals who helped me complete this book. First, I would like to thank the professors I had as an undergraduate at the University of Florida, who first exposed me to criminological theory. These professors include Ronald Akers and Lonn Lanza-Kaduce, with a special thanks to Donna Bishop, who was the instructor in my first criminological theory course. I would also like to thank the influential professors I had at the University of Maryland, including Denise Gottfredson, Colin Loftin, David McDowell, Lawrence Sherman, and Charles Wellford. I give a very special acknowledgment to Raymond Paternoster, who was my primary mentor and adviser and exerted an influence words can't describe. Ray and his wife, Ronet Bachman, provided rare support as surrogate parents when I was in graduate school. Ray also introduced me to the passion for criminological theory that I hope is reflected in this book.

I would like to thank Alex Piquero, also at the University of Maryland, with whom I had the great luck of sharing a graduate student office in the mid-1990s and who is now a professor at the university. Without the many collaborations and discussions about theory that I had with Alex, this book would be quite different and would likely not exist. Alex and his wife, Nicole Leeper Piquero, have consistently been key influences on my perspective on and understanding of theories of crimes, especially contemporary models (and the works of both of the Piqueros are represented in this book).

In addition, I would like to thank several colleagues who have helped me subsequent to my education. First, I would like to thank John Paul Wright at the University of Cincinnati and Chris Gibson at the University of Florida for inspiring me to further explore biosocial and developmental areas of criminality. Also, I would like to thank Donna Derbish and Matthew Logan at California State University, San Bernardino (CSUSB), who provided much help in the compilation of materials for this book. In addition, I would like to especially thank Pamela Schram and Larry Gaines, fellow professors at CSUSB, who have provided the highest possible level of support and guidance during my career. Furthermore, it should be noted that Pamela Schram provided key insights and materials that aided in the writing of several chapters of this book. Finally, I would like to thank Jose Rivera, an award-winning lecturer at CSUSB, for sharing his experiences in his more than eight years of being a prisoner in California State prisons and providing material for this and other books and articles; he is a true friend and colleague.

My mother and father, Jane and Steve Tibbetts Sr., have been the key to all of my accomplishments. We don't get to choose our parents, but I won the lottery by having them to guide me through life.

I owe the most gratitude to my wife, Kim, who has patiently put up with me typing away for the past few years while working on various versions of this book. Her constant support and companionship are what keep me going; she is the most supportive companion anyone could ask for.

I am grateful to the many reviewers who spent considerable time reading early drafts of my work and who provided helpful suggestions for improving both the textual material and the edited readings. Trying to please so many individuals is a challenge but one that is ultimately satisfying and undoubtedly made the book better than it would otherwise have been. Heartfelt thanks to the following experts:

Stuart Agnew, University of Suffolk

Shannon Barton-Bellessa, Indiana State University

Deborah Baskin, Loyola University–Chicago

Michael L. Benson, University of Cincinnati

Robert Brame, University of South Carolina

Tammy Castle, University of West Florida

James Chriss, Cleveland State University

Ellen G. Cohn, Florida International University

Toni DuPont-Morales, Pennsylvania State University

Joshua D. Freilich, John Jay College

Randy Gainey, Old Dominion University

Julie L. Globokar, PhD, Kent State University

Evan Gorelick, Germanna Community College

Robert Hanser, Kaplan University

Jay Healey, Simon Fraser University

Heath Hoffman, College of Charleston

Thomas Holt, University of North Carolina, Charlotte

Rebecca Katz, Morehead State University

Dennis Longmire, Sam Houston State University

Gina Luby, DePaul University

Michael J. Lynch, University of South Florida

J. Mitchell Miller, University of Texas, San Antonio

Michelle Hughes Miller, Southern Illinois University, Carbondale

Jake Phillips, Sheffield Hallam University

Travis Pratt, Arizona State University

Lois Presser, University of Tennessee

Aqeel Saeid, Humber Institute of Technology and Advanced Learning

Robert Sarver, University of Texas, Arlington

Martin S. Schwartz, Ohio University

Joseph Scimecca, George Mason University

Victoria Silverwood, Cardiff University

Ira Sommers, California State University, Los Angeles

Amy Thistlethwaite, Northern Kentucky University

Kimberly Tobin, Westfield State College

Adam Trahan, University of North Texas

Michael Turner, University of North Carolina, Charlotte

Scott Vollum, James Madison University

Courtney Waid, North Dakota State University

Barbara Warner, Georgia State University

Mary G. Wilson, Kent State University Trumbull Campus

James Windle, University of East London

Sarah Yercich, Northern Arizona University

CHAPTER 1

Introduction to the Book
An Overview of Issues in Criminological Theory

Welcome to the world of criminological theory! It is an exciting and complex endeavor that explains why certain individuals and groups commit crimes and why other people do not. This book will explore the conceptual history of this endeavor as well as current theories. Most of us can relate directly to many of these theories; we may know friends or family members who fit dominant models of criminal behavior.

This introduction begins by describing what criminology is; what distinguishes it from other perspectives of crime, such as religion, journalism, and philosophy; and how definitions of crime vary across time and place. Then it examines some of the major issues used to classify different theories of criminology. After exploring the various paradigms and categories of criminological theory, we discuss what characteristics help to make a theory a good one—in criminology or in any scientific field. In addition, we review the specific criteria for proving causality—for showing which predictors or variables actually cause criminal behavior. We also explain why—for logistic and ethical reasons—few theories in criminology will ever meet the strict criteria required to prove that key factors actually cause criminal behavior. Finally, we look at the strengths and weaknesses of the various measures of crime, which are used to test the validity of all criminological theories, and what those measures reveal about how crime is distributed across various individuals and groups. Although the discussion of crime distribution, as shown by various measures of criminality, may seem removed from our primary discussion regarding theories of why certain individuals and groups commit more crime than others, nothing could be further from the truth. Ultimately, all theories of criminal behavior will be judged based on how much each theory can explain the observed rates of crime shown by the measures of criminality among individuals and groups.

What Is Criminology, and How Does It Differ from Other Examinations of Crime?

Criminology is the scientific study of crime—and especially of why people commit crime. Although many textbooks have more complex definitions of crime, the word *scientific* separates our definition from other perspectives and examinations of crime.[1] Philosophical and legal examinations of crime are based on logic and deductive reasoning, for example, by developing propositions for what makes logical sense. Journalists play a vital role in

---

[1]Stephen Brown, Finn Esbensen, and Gilbert Geis, *Criminology*, 8th ed. (Cincinnati, OH: Anderson, 2013).

examinations of crime by exploring what is happening in criminal justice and revealing injustices and new forms of crime; however, they tend to examine anecdotes or examples of crime as opposed to objective measures of criminality.

Taken together, philosophical, legal, and journalistic perspectives of crime are not scientific because they do not involve the use of the **scientific method**. Specifically, they do not develop specific predictions, known scientifically as **hypotheses**, which are based on prior knowledge and studies, and then go out and test these predictions through observation. Criminology is based on this scientific method, whereas other examinations of crime are not.

Instead, philosophers and journalists tend to examine a specific case, make conclusions based on that one example of a crime incident, and then leave it at that. Experts in these nonscientific disciplines do not typically examine a multitude of stories similar to the one they are considering, nor do they apply the elements of their story to an existing theoretical framework that offers specific predictions or hypotheses. Further, they do not test those predictions by observation. The method of testing predictions through observation and then applying the findings to a larger body of knowledge, as established by theoretical models, is solely the domain of criminologists, and it separates criminology from other fields. The use of the scientific method is a distinguishing criterion for many studies of human behavior, such as psychology, economics, sociology, and anthropology, which is why these disciplines are generally classified as **social sciences**; criminology is one of them.

To look at another perspective on crime, religious accounts are almost entirely based on dogmatic, authoritarian, or reasoning principles, meaning that they are typically based on what some authority (e.g., the Pope or the Bible, the Torah, or the Koran) has to say about the primary causes of crime and the best ways to deal with such violations. These ideas are not based on observations. A science like criminology is based not on authority or anecdotes but on empirical research—even if that research is conducted by a 15-year-old who performs a methodologically sound study. In other words, the authority of the scientist performing the study does not matter; rather, the observed evidence and the soundness of the methodology—how the study was performed—are of utmost importance. Criminology is based on science, and its work is accomplished through direct observation and testing of hypotheses, even if those findings do not fit neatly into logical principles or the general feelings of the public.

What Is Theory?

Theory can be defined as a set of concepts linked together by a series of statements to explain why an event or phenomenon occurs. A simple way of thinking about theories is that they provide explanations of why the world works the way it does. In other words, a theory is a model of the phenomenon that is being discussed, which in this case is criminal behavior. Sometimes, perhaps quite often, theories are simply wrong, even if the predictions they give are highly accurate.

For example, in the early Middle Ages, most people, including expert scientists, believed Earth was the center of the universe because everything seemed to rotate and revolve around our home planet. If we wake up day after day and see the sun (or moon) rise and set in close to the same place, it appears that these celestial bodies are revolving around Earth, especially considering the fact that we don't feel the world around us moving. Furthermore, calendars predicting the change of seasons, as well as the location and phases of these celestial bodies (such as the moon), were quite accurate. However, although the experts were able to predict the movements of celestial objects quite well and develop extremely accurate calendars, they had absolutely no understanding of what was actually happening. Later, when some individuals tried to convince the majority that they were wrong, specifically that Earth was not the center of the universe, they were condemned as heretics and persecuted, even though their theoretical models were correct.

The same type of argument could be made about Earth being flat; at one time, observations and all existing models seemed to claim it as proven and true. Some disagreed and decided to test their own predictions, which is how America was discovered by European explorers. Still, many who believed Earth was round were persecuted or cast out of mainstream society in Europe at the time.

Two things should be clear: Theories can be erroneous, and accurate predictions can be made (e.g., early calendars and moon and star charts) using them, even though there is no true understanding of what is actually happening. One way to address both of these issues is to base knowledge and theories on scientific observation and testing. All respected theories of crime in the modern era are based on science; thus, we try to avoid buying into and applying theories that are inaccurate, and we continuously refine and improve our theories (based on findings from scientific testing) to gain a better understanding of what causes people to commit crime. Criminology, as a science, always allows and even welcomes criticism of its existing theoretical models. There is no emphasis on authority but rather on the scientific method and the quality of the observations that take place in testing the predictions. All scientific theories can be improved, and they are improved only through observation and empirical testing.

▲ **Image 1.1**   Earth seen from the surface of the moon. Theories of Earth as the center of the universe were dominant for many centuries, and scientists who proposed that Earth was not the center of the universe were often persecuted. Over time, the theory was proved false.

SOURCE: © istockphoto.com / RomoloTavani

Case Study: Burke and Hare

During the 1820s, Edinburgh, Scotland, was a major center for those pursuing an education in medicine. Almost 60 years prior to Jack the Ripper, the first serial murderers, William Burke and William Hare, captured media attention. During a 12-month period, Burke and Hare killed 16 people in Edinburgh before being arrested in November 1828. What made these killings so sordid was that Burke and Hare committed them for the sole purpose of selling the cadavers to medical schools for dissection and medical research. They were assisted by Burke's companion, Helen M'Dougal, and Hare's wife, Margaret. Burke and Hare would lure their victims with alcohol. Then, they would suffocate their inebriated victims by lying on their chests and holding their mouths and nostrils closed. Subsequently, Burke and Hare would sell these cadavers, "no questions asked," to Dr. Robert Knox, a promising anatomist.

What made these killings so sordid was that Burke and Hare committed them for the sole purpose of selling the cadavers to medical schools for dissection and medical research.

(Continued)

(Continued)

During the trial, Hare was granted immunity in return for testifying against Burke. Burke was found guilty and sentenced to death by hanging. He was hanged on January 28, 1829. Ironically, the next day, Burke's cadaver was donated to the University of Edinburgh, where Professor Alexander Monro conducted the dissection in the anatomical theater.[2] In fact, the University of Edinburgh Anatomical Museum has an exhibit of William Burke's skeletal remains. A description of the exhibit ends with a 19th-century children's rhyme:

Up the close and down the stair

In the house with Burke and Hare

Burke's the butcher

Hare's the thief

Knox the boy who buys the beef.[3]

In January 2016, Arthur and Elizabeth Rathburn from Grosse Pointe Park, Michigan (6 miles outside of Detroit), were indicted for running a black-market body part business. The Rathburns obtained most of the cadavers from two Chicago-area body donation labs. Many of the families who donated the bodies of their loved ones did so with the belief that they would go to science. A number of these cadavers were infected with HIV, hepatitis B, and other diseases. The Rathburns would use chainsaws, band saws, and reciprocating saws to butcher these cadavers for body parts. The Rathburns stored body parts from more than 1,000 people inside a warehouse. Subsequently, they would sell these butchered body parts to medical and dental trainees. However, they sometimes did not disclose to their customers that these body parts were infected with disease.[4]

More than 180 years separate these two cases; the technological expertise needed to carry out these crimes significantly changed during this time. However, one consistent theme that links these two cases is motive—monetary gain. This is one of the most fascinating aspects to studying crime—although technology may have changed how crimes are committed (e.g., Internet fraud), have the explanations changed? Studying motives and factors (e.g., poverty, peer influences, low self-control) that cause such motives is the primary topic of this book.

What Is Crime?

Definitions of crime vary drastically. For example, some take a **legalistic approach** to defining crime, including only acts that are specifically prohibited in the legal codes of a given jurisdiction. The problem with such a definition is that what is a crime in one jurisdiction is not necessarily a crime in other jurisdictions. To clarify, some acts,

---

[2]Lisa Rosner, *Anatomy Murders: Being the True and Spectacular History of Edinburgh's Notorious Burke and Hare and of the Man of Science Who Abetted Them in the Commission of Their Most Heinous Crimes* (Philadelphia: University of Pennsylvania Press, 2011), 240–244.

[3]The University of Edinburgh, Biomedical-Sciences/Anatomy, "William Burke," March 22, 2016, http://www.ed.ac.uk/biomedical-sciences/anatomy/anatomymuseum/exhibits/burke.

[4]Meg Wagner, "Detroit Couple Accused of Hacking Donated Corpses with Chainsaw, Selling Diseased Body Parts to Unwitting Medical Students," *New York Daily News*, January 30, 2016, http://www.nydailynews.com/news/crime/body-part-dealer-rented-infected-cadavers-students-article-1.2514657.

such as murder and armed robbery, are against the law in virtually all countries and all regions of the United States, across time and culture. These are known as acts of ***mala in se***, literally meaning *evil in itself*.[5] Typically, these crimes involve serious violence and shock the society in which they occur.

Other crimes are known as acts of ***mala prohibita***, which has the literal meaning of *evil because prohibited*. This term acknowledges that these crimes are not inherently evil acts; they are bad only because the law says so.[6] A good example is prostitution, which is illegal in most of the United States but is quite legal and even licensed in most counties of Nevada. The same can be said about gambling and drug possession or use.

▲ **Image 1.2**　Prostitution is considered a *mala prohibita* offense because it is not inherently evil and is even legal in many jurisdictions around the world.

SOURCE: © istockphoto.com / stevanovicigor

These are just examples of acts that are criminal only in certain places or at certain times and thus are not agreed upon by most members of a given community.

This book examines both *mala in se* and *mala prohibita* types of offenses, as well as other acts of **deviance**, which are not against the law in many places but are statistically atypical and may be considered more immoral than illegal. For example, in Nevada in the 1990s, a young man watched his friend (who was later criminally prosecuted) kill a young girl in the bathroom at a casino, but he told no one. Although most people would claim that this was highly immoral, at that time, the Nevada state laws did not require people who witnessed a killing to report it to authorities. (Note: As a result of this event, Nevada made withholding such information a criminal act.) Therefore, this act was deviant because most people would find it immoral, but it was not criminal because it was not technically against the laws in the jurisdiction at that time.

Other acts of deviance are not necessarily immoral but are certainly statistically unusual and violate social norms, such as purposely "passing gas" at a formal dinner. Such activities are relevant for our discussion, even if they are not defined as criminal by the law, because they show a disposition toward antisocial behavior, which is often found in individuals who are likely to become criminal offenders. Furthermore, some acts are moving from deviant to illegal all the time, such as using cell phones while driving or smoking cigarettes in public; many jurisdictions are moving to have these behaviors made illegal and have been quite successful to date, especially in New York and California.

Most *mala in se* activities (e.g., murder) are highly deviant, too, meaning they are not typically found in society, but many, if not most, *mala prohibita* acts are not deviant because they are committed by most people at some point. Speeding on a highway is a good example of a *mala prohibita* act that is illegal but not deviant. This book will examine theories for all of these types of activities, even those that do not violate the law in a given jurisdiction at the present time.

[5]Brown, Esbensen, and Geis, *Criminology*.

[6]Ibid.

How Are Criminological Theories Classified? The Major Theoretical Paradigms

Scientific theories of crime can be categorized based on several important concepts, assumptions, and characteristics. To begin, most criminological theories are classified by the paradigm they emphasize. **Paradigms** are distinctive theoretical models or perspectives; in the case of crime, they vary based largely on opposing assumptions of human behavior. There are four major paradigms.[7]

The first of these, deterrence or rational choice theories, commonly referred to as the **Classical School** perspective, will be discussed at length later in this book. It assumes that individuals have free will and choose to commit crimes based on rational, hedonistic decisions; they weigh out the potential costs and benefits of offending and then choose what will maximize their pleasure and minimize their pain. The distinguishing characteristic of these theories is that they emphasize the free choice individuals have in committing crime. The other paradigms are based on the influence of factors other than free will or rational decision making—for example, biology, culture, parenting, and economics.

Another category of theories is positivism, which is somewhat the opposite of rational choice theories. These theories argue that individuals do not have free will or rationality in making decisions to commit crime. Rather, the **Positive School** perspective assumes that individuals are passive subjects of determinism, which means that people do not freely choose their behavior. Instead, their behavior is determined by factors outside of their free will, such as genetics, IQ, education, employment, peer influences, parenting, and economics.[8] Most of the highly respected and scientifically validated criminological theories of the modern era fall into this category.[9]

Another group of criminological theories belongs to the conflict or critical perspective, which emphasizes the use of law as a reaction or tool to enforce restraint on others by those in power or authority; it also involves how society reacts when a person (often a juvenile) is caught doing something wrong. These theories emphasize group behavior over individual behavior: Groups that are in power use the criminal codes as a tool in keeping people who have limited power restrained or confined.

Finally, over the past few decades, a new category has emerged, namely the integrated theoretical models, which attempt to combine the best aspects of explanatory models into a single, better theoretical framework for understanding crime. These models tend to suffer from the logical inconsistencies inherent in integrating theoretical models that have opposing assumptions or propositions. All of these categories will become clearer as we progress through this book.

Additional Ways to Classify Criminological Theories

Although the major paradigms are the primary way criminological theories are classified, there are several other ways that they can be categorized. Specifically, theoretical models can be classified based on whether they focus on individuals or groups as their primary units of examination. For instance, some theories emphasize why certain individuals do or do not commit crime. This level of investigation, in which the focus is on the individual, is often referred to as the **micro level of analysis**, much as microeconomics is the study of economics on the individual (person) level. When your instructors score each student on an exam, this is a micro-level analysis.

On the other hand, many theories emphasize primarily the group or **macro level of analysis**, much as macroeconomics is the study of economic principles at the aggregate or group level. In this book, some chapters are

---

[7]Thomas J. Bernard, Jeffrey B. Snipes, and Alexander L. Gerould, *Vold's Theoretical Criminology*, 6th ed. (Oxford: Oxford University Press, 2010).

[8]Ibid.

[9]Lee Ellis and Anthony Walsh, "Criminologists' Opinions about Causes and Theories of Crime and Delinquency," *The Criminologist* 24 (1999): 1–4.

separated by whether the individual or the group level of analysis is emphasized. For example, social process theories tend to be more micro-level oriented, whereas social structure theories are more macro-level oriented. Here's a good example: If instructors compare the mean score (or average) of one class to the mean score of another, this is a comparison of group rates, regardless of the performance of any individual in either class. Ultimately, a great theory would explain both the micro and macro levels of analysis, but we will see that very few attempt to explain or account for both levels.

Criminological theories can also be classified by their general perspective on how laws are made. Some theories assume that laws are made to define acts as criminal to the extent that they violate rights of individuals, and thus, virtually everyone agrees that such acts are immoral. This type of perspective is considered a **consensual perspective** (or nonconflict model). On the other hand, many modern forms of criminological theories fall into an opposite category, commonly known as the **conflict theories**, which assume that different groups disagree about the fairness of laws and that laws are used as a tool by those in power to keep down other, lower-power groups. There are many forms of both consensual and conflict theoretical models, and both will be specifically noted as we progress through the book.

A final, but perhaps most important, way to classify theories is in terms of their assumptions regarding human nature. Some theories assume that people are born good (giving, benevolent, etc.) and are corrupted by social or other developmental influences that lead them to crime. A good example is strain theory, which claims that people are born innocent and with good intentions but that society causes them to commit crime. On the other hand, many of the most popular current theories claim that virtually all individuals are born with a disposition toward being bad (selfish, greedy, etc.) and must be socialized or restrained from following their inherent propensities for engaging in crime.[10] A good example of this is control theory, which assumes that all individuals have a predisposition to be greedy, selfish, violent, and so on (i.e., they are criminally disposed) and therefore that people need to be controlled or prevented from acting on their natural, inherent disposition toward selfish and aggressive behaviors.

A variation of these theories is often referred to as *tabula rasa*, literally translated as blank slate. This assumes that people are born with no leaning toward good or bad but are simply influenced by the balance of positive or negative influences that are introduced socially during their development. A good example of this perspective is differential association or reinforcement theory, which assumes that all individuals are born with a blank slate and that they learn whether to be good or bad based on what they experience.

Although the dominant assumption tends to vary across these three models from time to time, the most popular theories today (which are self- and social-control theories) seem to imply the second option, specifically that people are born selfish and greedy and must be socialized and trained to be good and conforming.[11] There are other ways that criminological theories can be classified, but the various characteristics we have discussed in this chapter summarize the most important factors.

Characteristics of Good Theories

Respected scientific theories in any field, whether it be chemistry, physics, or criminology, tend to have the same characteristics. After all, the same scientific review process (i.e., blind peer review by experts) is used in all sciences to determine which studies and theoretical works are of high quality. The criteria that characterize a good theory in chemistry are the same as those used to judge a criminological theory. Such characteristics include parsimony,

---

[10]Ibid.

[11]Ibid.

scope, logical consistency, testability, empirical validity, and policy implications.[12] Each of these characteristics is examined here. (It should be noted that our discussion and many of the examples provided for the characteristics are taken from Akers and Sellers, 2012.[13])

Parsimony is achieved by explaining a given phenomenon—in our case criminal activity—in the simplest way possible. Other characteristics being equal, the simpler a theory, the better. The problem with criminal behavior is that it is highly complex. However, that has not stopped some criminologists from attempting to explain this convoluted phenomenon in highly simple ways. For example, one of the most recent and most popular theories (as indicated by the amount of related research and by which theories the experts believe are most important) is the theory of low self-control (which we discuss later in this book). This very simple model holds that one personality factor—low self-control—is responsible for all criminal activity. The originators of this theory, Michael Gottfredson and Travis Hirschi, asserted that every single act of crime and deviance is caused by this same factor: low self-control.[14] Everything from speeding, smoking tobacco, not wearing a seat belt while driving, and having numerous sex partners to committing serious crimes such as murder and armed robbery are caused by low self-control.

Although this theory has been disputed by much of the subsequent research on this model, it remains one of the most popular and accepted models of the modern era.[15] Furthermore, despite the criticisms of this theory, many notable criminologists still believe that this is the best single model of offending that has been presented to date. In addition, there is little doubt that this model has become the most researched theoretical model over the last two decades.[16]

Perhaps the most important reason why so much attention has been given to this theory is its simplicity, putting all of the focus on a single factor. Virtually all other theoretical models have proposed multiple factors that may play major parts in determining why individuals commit crime. After all, how can low self-control explain white-collar crime? Some self-control is required to obtain a white-collar position of employment. It is true that a simple theory is better than a more complex one, as long as other characteristics are equivalent. However, given a complex behavior like criminal behavior, it is unlikely that a simple explanation, such as naming one factor to account for everything, will prove adequate.

Scope, the next characteristic of a theory, indicates how much of a given phenomenon the theory seeks to explain. This is somewhat related to parsimony in the sense that some theories, like the theory of low self-control, seek to explain all crimes and all deviant acts as well. Thus, the theory of low self-control has a very wide scope. Other theories of crime, such as some versions of strain theory, may seek to explain only property crime or drug use. However, the wider the scope of what a theory can explain, the better the theory, assuming other characteristics are equal.

Logical consistency is the extent to which a theory makes sense in terms of its concepts and propositions. It is easier to show what we mean by logical consistency if we give examples of what does not fit this criterion. Some theories simply don't make sense because of the face value of their propositions. For example, Cesare Lombroso, called the father of criminology, claimed that the most serious offenders are "born criminals," biological throwbacks to an earlier stage of evolutionary development who can be identified by their physical features.[17] Lombroso, who is discussed at more length later in this book, claimed that tattoos were one of the physical features that identified these born criminals. This doesn't make sense, however, because tattoos are not biological physical features—no

---

[12]Ronald Akers and Christine Sellers, *Criminological Theories*, 6th ed. (Oxford: Oxford University Press, 2012).

[13]Ibid., 4–19.

[14]Michael Gottfredson and Travis Hirschi, *A General Theory of Crime* (Palo Alto, CA: Stanford University Press, 1990).

[15]Ellis and Walsh, "Criminologists' Opinions," 3–4.

[16]Anthony Walsh and Lee Ellis, "Political Ideology and American Criminologists' Explanations for Criminal Behavior," *The Criminologist* 24 (1999): 1, 14.

[17]Cesare Lombroso, *The Criminal Man* (Milan: Hoepli, 1876).

baby has ever been born with a tattoo. This criticism will make even more sense when we discuss the criteria for determining causality later in this chapter.

Another prominent example of theories that lack logical consistency is the work of early feminist theorists, such as Freda Adler, who argued that, as females gain educational and employment opportunities, their rates of crime will be more likely to converge with those of males.[18] Such hypotheses were logically inconsistent with the data available at the time they were presented and are even more inconsistent with the data available today; the facts show that females who are given the most opportunities commit the fewest crimes, while females who have not been given these benefits commit the most crimes.

These are just two examples of how past theories were logically inconsistent with the data available at the time they were created, not to mention inconsistent with future research findings, which have completely dismissed their hypotheses.

Testability is the extent to which a theory can be put to empirical, scientific testing. Some theories simply cannot be tested. A good example is Sigmund Freud's theory of the psyche. Freud described three domains of the psyche—the conscious ego, the subconscious id, and the superego—but none of these domains can be observed or tested.[19] Although some theories can be quite influential without being testable (as was Freud's theory), other things being equal, it is a considerable disadvantage for a theoretical model to be untestable and unobservable. Fortunately, most established criminological theories can be examined through empirical testing.

Empirical validity is the extent to which a theoretical model is supported by scientific research. Obviously, this is highly related to the previous characteristic of testability. However, while virtually all accepted modern criminological theories are testable, that does not mean they are equal in terms of empirical validity. Although some integrated models (meaning two or more traditional theories that have been merged together; these will be examined later in this book) have gained a large amount of empirical validity, these models "cheat" because they merge the best of two or more models, even when the assumptions of these models are not compatible. The independent theoretical model that has garnered the most empirical validity is differential reinforcement theory, which has been strongly supported for various crime types (from tobacco usage to violence) among a wide variety of populations (from young children to elderly subjects).[20]

Ultimately, empirical validity is perhaps one of the most important characteristics used in determining how good a theory is at explaining a given phenomenon or behavior. If a theory has good empirical validity, it is an accurate explanation of behavior; if it does not have good empirical validity, it should be revised or dismissed because it is simply not true.

Policy implications refer to the extent to which a theory can create realistic and useful guidance for changing the way society deals with a given phenomenon. In our case, this means providing a useful model for informing authorities of how to deal with crime. An example is the broken windows theory, which says that to reduce serious crimes, authorities should focus on the minor incivilities that occur in a given area. This theory has been used successfully by many police agencies (most notably by New York City police, who reduced their homicide rate by more than 75% in the past decade). Other theories may not be as useful in terms of reducing crime because they are

---

[18]Freda Adler, *Sisters in Crime* (New York: McGraw-Hill, 1975).

[19]See Stephen G. Tibbetts, *Criminological Theory: The Essentials* (Thousand Oaks, CA: Sage, 2015), 8.

[20]See Ronald Akers and Gang Lee, "A Longitudinal Test of Social Learning Theory: Adolescent Smoking," *Journal of Drug Issues* 26 (1996): 317–43; Ronald Akers and Gang Lee, "Age, Social Learning, and Social Bonding in Adolescent Substance Abuse," *Deviant Behavior* 19 (1999): 1–25; Ronald Akers and Anthony J. La Greca, "Alcohol Use among the Elderly: Social Learning, Community Context, and Life Events," in *Society, Culture, and Drinking Patterns Re-examined*, ed. David J. Pittman and Helene Raskin White (New Brunswick, NJ: Rutgers Center of Alcohol Studies, 1991), 242–62; Sunghyun Hwang, *Substance Use in a Sample of South Korean Adolescents: A Test of Alternative Theories* (Ann Arbor, MI: University Microfilms, 2000); and Sunghyun Hwang and Ronald Akers, "Adolescent Substance Use in South Korea: A Cross-Cultural Test of Three Theories," in *Social Learning Theory and the Explanation of Crime: A Guide for the New Century*, ed. Ronald Akers and Gary F. Jensen (New Brunswick, NJ: Transaction, 2003).

too abstract or propose changes that are far too costly or impossible to implement, such as theories that emphasize changing family structure or the chromosomal makeup of individuals. So, other things being equal, a theory that has readily available policy implications would be more advantageous than theories that do not.

Criteria for Determining Causality

There are several criteria for determining whether a certain variable causes another variable to change—in other words, causality. For this discussion, we will be using standard scientific notation to designate an independent or predictor variable (X) that results in a dependent or explanatory variable (Y). Such criteria are used for all scientific disciplines, whether chemistry, physics, biology, or criminology. In this book, we are discussing crime, so we will concentrate on examples that relate to this goal, but some examples will be given that are not crime related. Unfortunately, we will also see that, given the nature of our field, there are important problems with determining causality, largely because we are dealing with human beings as opposed to a chemical element or biological molecule.

The three criteria that are needed to show causality are (1) temporal ordering; (2) correlation, or covariation; and (3) accounting for spuriousness.

Temporal ordering requires that the predictor variable (X) precede the explanatory variable (Y) if we are to determine that X causes Y. Although this seems like a no-brainer, it is sometimes violated in criminological theories. For example, you'll remember that Lombroso claimed born criminals could be identified by tattoos, which obviously goes against this principle.

A more recent scientific debate has focused on whether delinquency is an outcome variable (Y) due to associations with delinquent peers and associates (X) or whether delinquency (X) causes associations with delinquent peers and associates (Y), which then leads to even more delinquency. This can be seen as the argument of which came first, the chicken or the egg. Studies show that both processes are often taking place, meaning that delinquency and associations with delinquent peers are likely to be both predictor and explanatory variables in most cases, and this forms a reciprocal or feedback loop that encourages both causal paths.[21] Thus, temporal ordering is an important question, and often it is quite complex and must be examined fully before causal order can be understood.

▲ **Image 1.3**   Early theories identified criminals by whether they had tattoos; at that time, this might have been true. In contemporary times, many individuals have tattoos, so this would not apply.

SOURCE: © istockphoto.com / Rawpixel Ltd

Correlation, or **covariation**, is the extent to which a change in the predictor (X) is associated with a change (either higher or lower) in the explanatory variable (Y). In other words, a change in X leads to a change in Y. For example, a rise in unemployment (X) in a given location is likely to lead to a rise in crime rates (Y) in the same area; this would be a positive

---

[21] Terence Thornberry, "Toward an Interactional Theory of Delinquency," *Criminology* 25 (1987): 863–87.

association because both increased. Similarly, an increase in employment (X) is likely to lead to a decrease in crime rates (Y) in that area; this would be a negative, or inverse, association, because one decreased and the other increased. The criterion of covariance is not met when a change in X does not produce any change in Y. That is, if a statistically significant change in X does not lead to a statistically significant change in Y, then this criterion is not met.

However, correlation alone does not mean that X causes Y. For example, if ice cream sales (X) tend to be highly associated with crime rates (Y), this does not mean that ice cream sales cause higher crime rates. Rather, other factors—in this case, warm weather—lead to increases in both sales of ice cream and the number of people who are outdoors in public areas and interacting, which naturally leads to greater opportunities and tendencies to engage in criminal activity. This brings us to the final criterion for determining causality.

Accounting for **spuriousness** is a complicated way of saying that, to determine that X causes Y, other factors (typically called Z factors) that could be causing the observed association must be accounted for before we can be sure that it is actually X that is causing Y. In other words, it is often a third factor (Z) that causes two events to occur together in time and place. A good example of a spurious association would be the observation that a greater number of firefighters at the scene of a fire is correlated with more damage. If only the first two criteria of causality were followed, this would lead to the conclusion that an increased number of fire officers (X) causes the heavier fire damage (Y). This conclusion meets the temporal ordering and covariance criteria. However, a third Z variable or factor is causing both X and Y to appear together. This Z variable is the size of the fire, which is causing more officers to show up and also causing more damage. Once this Z factor is accounted for, the effect of X on Y becomes nonexistent.

Using the Lombroso example, tattoos may have predicted criminality at the time he wrote (although criminals weren't born with them). However, Lombroso did not account for an important Z factor—namely, associates or friends who also had tattoos. This Z factor caused the simultaneous occurrence of both other factors. To clarify, individuals who had friends or associates with tattoos tended to get tattoos, and (especially at that time in the 1800s) friends or associates who had tattoos also tended to commit more crime. In that era, pirates and incarcerated individuals were most likely to get tattoos. Therefore, had Lombroso controlled for the number of tattooed associates of the criminals he studied, he likely would have found no causal effect on crime from body art.

Ultimately, researchers in criminology are fairly good at determining the first two criteria of causality: temporal ordering and covariance or correlation. Most scientists can perform classical experiments that randomly assign subjects either to receive or not to receive the experimental manipulation to examine the effect on outcomes. However, the dilemma for criminologists is that the factors that appear to be important (according to police officers, parole agents, and corrections officers) are family variables, personality traits, employment variables, intelligence, and other similar characteristics that cannot be experimentally manipulated to control for possible Z factors. After all, how can we randomly assign certain people or groups to bad parents or bad educations, no jobs, low IQs, bad genetics, or delinquent peers? Even if we could manage such manipulations, ethical constraints would prohibit them.

Thus, as criminologists, we may never be able to meet all the criteria of causality, so we are essentially stuck with building a case for the factors we think are causing crime by amassing as much support as we can in terms of temporal ordering and covariance or correlation, and perhaps accounting for other factors in advanced statistical models. Ultimately, social science, especially criminology, is a difficult field in terms of establishing causality, and we shall see that the empirical validity of various criminological theories is hindered by such issues.

Measures of Crime

Crime can be measured in an infinite number of ways. To some extent, readers have measured crime by observing what has been happening in their own neighborhoods or reading or watching the news every day. However, some measures of crime go beyond these anecdotal or personal experiences, and these more exacting measures are what criminologists commonly use to gauge rates of crime across time and place.

Specifically, three major categories of crime measures are used by social scientists to examine crime. The first and most used measure is the **Uniform Crime Report (UCR)**. Police send reports about certain crimes and arrests to the Federal Bureau of Investigation (FBI), which combines the many thousands of reports they receive from across the nation and publishes the UCR annually.

The second measure is the **National Crime Victimization Survey** (**NCVS**; prior to the early 1990s, it was known as the National Crime Survey [NCS]). Like the UCR, this report is issued by the U.S. Department of Justice (DOJ), but the data are collected in an entirely different way. Specifically, interviews are conducted with a large, random sample of U.S. households, asking how much crime they have experienced in half-year intervals. The NCVS is collected by the research branch of the DOJ, called the Bureau of Justice Statistics (BJS), in conjunction with the U.S. Census Bureau, which was one of the earliest agencies to collect information about citizens and thus is the most experienced at such endeavors.

The third measure, which is perhaps the most important for purposes of this book, is **self-report data (SRD)**, which are primarily collected by independent academic scientists or think tank agencies, such as the RAND Corporation. Participating in surveys or interviews, individuals report crimes against themselves or crimes they have committed. This measure is the most important for the purposes of this book because the UCR and NCVS do not provide in-depth information on the offenders or the victims, such as personality, biology or physiology, family life, and economic information. These factors are of the utmost importance for our purposes because there is a broad consensus that they cause people to commit crime, yet they are missing from the most commonly used measures of crime. SRD are the best, and in most cases the only, measure for figuring out why some people offend and others do not. However, like the other measures, self-reports have numerous weaknesses as well as strengths.

Each of these three measures is briefly examined here. Although the measures are not the primary emphasis of this book, it is important to understand their strengths and weaknesses.

The Uniform Crime Report

The UCR is the oldest and most used measure of crime rates in the United States for purposes of examining trends and distribution of crime. It was first published in the early 1930s, and although changes have been made along the way, it is relatively stable in terms of comparing various years and decades. As mentioned before, the data are collected by many thousands of independent police agencies at federal, state, and local levels. These thousands of agencies send their reports of crimes and arrests to their respective state capitals, which then forward their synthesized reports to FBI headquarters, where all reports are combined to provide an overview of crime in the nation.

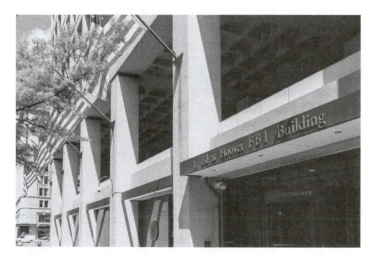

▲ **Image 1.4**   The annual UCRs are produced by the FBI. Local, county, and state criminal justice agencies send their annual crime data to the J. Edgar Hoover Building in Washington, DC. UCR data are, by their nature, incomplete, as many crimes are never reported to the police at all. This dark figure of crime might be as high as 90% of all crime incidents.

SOURCE: © istockphoto.com / mixmotive

FBI definitions of crimes often differ from state categorizations, and how crimes are differentiated will be important in future discussions in this chapter. The FBI concentrates on eight (four violent and four property) **index offenses**, or Part I offenses. The four violent crimes are murder and nonnegligent manslaughter, forcible (not statutory) rape, robbery, and aggravated assault (which involves intentions of serious injury to the victim). The four property offenses are burglary (which includes a breaking and entering or trespass), motor vehicle theft, larceny (which does not involve a trespass; e.g., shoplifting), and arson (which was added to the crime index count in the late 1970s). All reports to police for these eight offenses are included in the crime index, whether or not they resulted in an arrest. This information is often referred to as crimes known to police (CKP).

The UCR also includes about two dozen other offenses known as **nonindex offenses**, or Part II offenses, which are reported only if an arrest is made. These offenses range from violent crimes (such as simple assault), to embezzlement and fraud, to offenses that are considered violations of the law only if an individual is under 18 years of age (such as running away from home). The major problem with the estimates of these nonindex offenses is that the likelihood of arresting someone for such crimes is less than 10% of the actual occurrence, so the data regarding nonindex offenses are highly inaccurate. The official count from the FBI is missing at least 90% of the actual offenses that take place in the United States. Therefore, we will primarily concentrate on index offenses for the purposes of our discussion.

Even the count of index offenses has numerous problems. The most important and chronic problem with using the UCR as a measure of crime is that, most of the time, victims fail to report crimes—yes, even aggravated assault, forcible rape, robbery, burglary, and larceny. Recent studies estimate that about 70% to 80% of these serious crimes are not reported to police. Criminologists call this missing amount of crime the **dark figure** because it never shows up in the police reports that get sent to the FBI.

There are many reasons why victims do not report these serious crimes to the police. One of the most important is that they consider it a personal matter. Many times, the offense is committed by a family member, a close friend, or an acquaintance. For instance, police are rarely informed about aggravated assaults among siblings. Rape victims are often assaulted on a date or by someone they know; they may feel that they contributed to their attack by choosing to go out with the offender, or they may believe that police won't take such a claim seriously. Regardless of the reason, many crime victims prefer to handle it informally and not involve the police.

Another major reason why police are not called is that victims don't feel the crime is important enough to report. For example, a thief may steal a small item that the victim won't miss, so she or he may not see the need to report what the police or FBI would consider a serious crime. This is likely related to another major reason why people do not report crime to the police: They have no confidence that reporting the case to law enforcement will do any good. Many people, often residents of neighborhoods that are the most crime-ridden, are likely to feel that the police are not competent or will not seriously investigate their charges.

There are many other reasons why people do not report their victimizations to police. Some may fear retaliation, for example, in cases involving gang activity; many cities, especially those with many gangs, have seen this occur even more in recent years. The victims may also fail to report a crime for fear that their own illegal activities will be exposed; an example is a prostitute who has been brutally beaten by her pimp. In U.S. society, much crime is committed against businesses, but those businesses may be very reluctant to report crimes because they don't want a reputation for being a hot spot for criminal activity. Sometimes when victims do call the police or 911, they leave the scene if the police fail to show up in a reasonable amount of time. This has become a chronic problem despite efforts by police departments to prioritize calls.

Perhaps the most chronic, most important reason for failure to report crimes—but one that is often ignored—can be traced to U.S. school systems. Most studies of crime and victimization in schools show that many and maybe even most juvenile crimes occur in schools, but these offenses almost never get reported to police, even when school resource officers (SROs) are assigned to the school. Schools—and especially private schools—have a vested interest in not reporting crimes that occur on their premises to the police. After all, no school (or school system) wants to become known as crime-ridden.

Schools are predisposed to being crime-ridden because the most likely offenders and the most likely victims—young people—interact there in close quarters for most of the day. The school is much happier, however, if teachers and administrators deal informally with the parties involved in an on-campus fight; the school doesn't want these activities reported to and by the media. In addition, the student parties involved in the fight don't want to be formally arrested and charged with the offense, so they are also happy with the case being handled informally. Finally, the parents of the students are also generally pleased with the informal process because they don't want their children involved in a formal legal case.

Even universities and colleges follow this model of not reporting crimes when they occur on campus. A good example can be seen on the websites of most major colleges, which are required by federal law to report crimes on campus. Official reports of crimes, ranging from rapes to liquor law violations, are often in the single digits each year for campuses housing many thousands of students. Of course, some crimes may not be reported to the school, and others may be dealt with administratively rather than by calling police. The absence of school data is a big weakness of the UCR.

Besides the dark figure, there are many other criticisms of the UCR as a measure of crime. For example, the way that crimes are counted can be misleading. Specifically, the UCR counts only the most serious crime that is committed in a given incident. For example, if a person or persons rob, rape, and murder a victim, only the murder will show up in the UCR; the robbery and rape will not be recorded. Furthermore, there are inconsistencies in how the UCR counts the incidents; for example, if a person walks into a bar and assaults eight people there, it is counted as eight assaults, but if the same person walks into the bar and robs every person of wallets and purses, it is counted as one robbery. This makes little sense, but it is the official count policy used by the UCR.

Other, more important criticisms of the UCR involve political considerations, such as the fact that many police departments (such as in Philadelphia and New York City) have systematically altered the way that crimes are defined, for example, by manipulating the way that classifications and counts of crimes are recorded (e.g., aggravated assault [an index crime] vs. simple assault [a nonindex crime]). Thus, official estimates can make it seem as if major crimes have decreased in the city when in fact they may have actually increased.

It is also important to note the strengths of the UCR. First, it was introduced in 1930, making it the longest-lasting systematic measure of crime in the United States. This is a very important advantage when we want to examine trends in crime over most of the 20th century. We will see later that there have been extremely high crime rates at certain times (such as during the 1930s and the 1970s to 1980) and very low crime rates at other times (such as the early 1940s and recent years [late 1990s to the present]). Other measures, such as the NCVS and national SRD, did not come into use until much later, so the UCR is important for the fact that it started so early.

Another important strength of this measure is that two of the offenses that the UCR concentrates on are almost always reported and therefore overcome the weakness of the dark figure, or lack of reporting to police. These two offenses are murder or nonnegligent manslaughter and motor vehicle theft. Murder is almost always reported because a dead body is found; very few murders go unreported to authorities. Although a few may elude official recording—for example, if the body is transported elsewhere or carefully hidden—almost all murders are recorded. Similarly, motor vehicle thefts, a property crime, are almost always reported because any insurance claims must provide a police report. Most cars are worth thousands (or at least many hundreds) of dollars, so victims tend to report when their vehicle(s) have been stolen; this provides a rather valid estimate of property crime in specific areas. The rest of the offenses (yes, even the other index crimes) counted by the UCR are far less reliable. If someone is doing a study on homicide or motor vehicle theft, the UCR is likely the best source of data, but for any other crime, researchers should probably look elsewhere.

This is even further advised for studies examining nonindex offenses, which the UCR counts only when someone is arrested for a given offense. The vast majority of nonindex offenses do not result in an arrest. To shed some light on how much actual nonindex crime is not reported to police, it is useful to examine the **clearance rate** of the index offenses in the UCR, our best indicator of solving crimes. Even for the crimes that the FBI considers most serious, the clearance rate is about 21% of crimes reported to police ("reported to police" meaning that police made a report of the crime). Of course, the more violent offenses have higher clearance rates because (outside of murder) they inherently have a witness, namely the victim, and because police place a higher priority on solving violent crimes. However, for some of the index crimes, especially serious property offenses, the clearance rates are very low. Furthermore, it should be noted that the clearance rate of serious index crimes has not improved at all over the past few decades despite much more advanced resources and technology, such as DNA testing, fingerprints, and faster cars. These data on the clearance rates are only for the most serious, or index, crimes; thus, the reporting of the UCR regarding nonindex crimes is even more inaccurate because there is even less reporting (i.e., the dark figure) and less clearance of these less serious offenses. In other words, the data provided by the UCR regarding nonindex offenses are totally invalid and thus for the most part completely worthless.

Ultimately, the UCR is good for (a) measuring the overall crime rate in the United States over time, (b) examining what crime was like prior to the 1970s, and (c) investigating murder and motor vehicle theft. Outside of these offenses, the UCR has serious problems, and fortunately, we have better measures for examining crime rates in the United States.

The National Crime Victimization Survey

Another commonly used measure of crime is the NCVS (the NCS until the early 1990s), which is distinguished from other key measures of crime because it concentrates on the victims of crime, whereas other measures tend to emphasize the offenders. In fact, that is the key reason why this measure was started in 1973 after several years of preparation and pretesting. To clarify, one of the key recommendations of Lyndon Johnson's President's Commission on Law Enforcement and Administration of Justice in the late 1960s was to learn more about the characteristics of victims of crime; at that time, virtually no studies had been done on the subject, whereas much research had been done on criminal offenders. The efforts of this commission set into motion the creation of the NCVS.

Since it began, the NCVS has been designed and collected by two agencies: the U.S. Census Bureau and the BJS, which is one of the key research branches of the DOJ. The NCVS is collected in a completely different way from the other commonly used measures of crimes; the researchers select tens of thousands of U.S. households, and each member of the household who is over 12 years of age is interviewed every 6 months about crime that occurred in the previous 6-month period (each selected household remains in the survey for 3 years, resulting in seven collection periods, including the initial interview). Although the selection of households is to some extent random, the way the sampling is designed guarantees that a certain proportion of the selected households have certain characteristics. For example, before the households are selected, they are first categorized according to factors such as region of the country, type of area (urban, suburban, rural), income level, and racial or ethnic composition. This type of sampling, called a multistage, stratified cluster sampling design, ensures that enough households are included in the survey to permit conclusions regarding these important characteristics. As you will see later in this chapter, some of the most victimized groups (by rate) in the United States do not make up a large portion of the population or households. So, if the sampling design were not set up to select a certain number of people from certain groups, it is quite likely the researchers would not obtain enough cases to draw conclusions about them.

The data gathered from this sample are then adjusted, and statistical estimates are made about crime across the United States, with the NCVS estimates showing about 3 times more crime than the UCR rates. Some may doubt the ability of this selected sample to represent crime in the nation, but most studies find that its estimates are far more accurate than those provided by the UCR (with the exception of homicide and maybe motor vehicle theft). This is largely due to the expertise and professionalism of the agencies that collect and analyze the data, as well as the carefully thought out and well-administered survey design, as indicated by interview completion rates (which are typically more than 90% higher than those of virtually all other crime and victimization surveys).

One of the biggest strengths of the NCVS is that it directly addresses the worst problem with the previously discussed measure, the UCR. Specifically, the greatest weakness of the UCR is the dark figure, or the crimes that victims fail to report, which happens most of the time (except in cases of homicide or motor vehicle theft). The NCVS interviews victims about crimes that happened to them, even those that were not reported to police. Thus, the NCVS captures far more crime events than the UCR, especially crimes that are highly personal (such as rape). The extent to which the NCVS captures much of this dark figure of crime is its greatest strength.

Despite this important strength, the NCVS, like the other measures of crime, has numerous weaknesses. Probably the biggest problem is that two of the most victimized groups in U.S. society are systematically not included in the NCVS. Specifically, homeless people are completely left out because they do not have a home and the participants are contacted through households, yet they remain one of the most victimized groups per capita in our society. Another highly victimized group in our society that is systematically not included in the NCVS is young children. Studies consistently show that the younger a person is, the more likely she or he is to be victimized. Infants in particular, especially in their first hours or days of life, face great risk of death and other sorts of victimization, typically from parents or caregivers. This is not very surprising, especially in light of the fact that very young children cannot defend themselves or run away. They can't even tell anyone until they are old enough to speak, and then most are too afraid to do so or are not given an opportunity. Although, to some extent, it is understandable to exempt young children from such sensitive questions, the loss of this group is huge in terms of estimating victimization in the United States.

The NCVS also misses the crimes suffered by American businesses, which cumulatively constitute an enormous amount of crime. In the early years of the NCVS, businesses were also sampled, but that practice was discontinued in the late 1970s. Had it continued, it would have provided invaluable information for social scientists and policy makers, not to mention the businesses that are losing billions of dollars each year as a result of crimes committed against them.

Many find it surprising that the NCVS does not collect data on homicide, which most people and agencies consider the most serious and important crime. Researchers studying murder cannot get information from the NCVS but must rely on the UCR, which is most accurate in its reporting for this crime type.

The NCVS also has issues with people accurately reporting the victimization that has occurred to them in the previous 6 months. However, studies show that their reports are surprisingly accurate most of the time. Often when participants report incidents inaccurately, they make unknowing mistakes rather than intentionally lying. Obviously, victims sometimes forget incidents that have occurred, probably because, most of the time, they know or are related to the person committing the offense against them, so they never think of it as a crime per se but rather as a personal disagreement. When asked if they were victims of theft, they may not think to report the time that a brother or uncle borrowed a tool without asking and never returned it.

Although NCVS researchers go to great lengths to prevent it, a common phenomenon known as **telescoping** tends to occur, which leads to overreporting of incidents. Telescoping is the human tendency to perceive events as having occurred more recently than they actually did. This is one of the key reasons why NCVS researchers interview household subjects every 6 months, but telescoping still happens. For instance, a larceny may have occurred 8 months ago, but it seems as if it happened just a few months ago to the participant, so it is reported to the researchers as occurring in the past 6 months when it really didn't. Telescoping thus inflates national crime rate estimates for a given interval.

As mentioned before, an additional weakness is that the NCVS did not start until 1973, so it cannot provide any estimates of victimization prior to that time. A study of national crime rates prior to the 1970s has little choice but to use the UCR. Still, for most crimes, the NCVS has provided a more accurate estimate over the past three decades. Since the NCVS was created, the crime trends it has revealed have tended to be highly consistent with those shown by the UCR. For example, both measures show violent crime rates peaking at the same time (about 1980), and both agree on when the rates increased (the 1970s) and decreased (the late 1990s to the present) most. This is very good, because if they did not agree, that would mean at least one of them was wrong. Before we discuss the national trends in crime rates, however, we will examine the strengths and weaknesses of a third measure of crime.

Self-Report Studies of Crime

The final measure of crime consists of various self-report studies of crime, in which individuals report (in either a written survey or an interview) the extent of their own past criminal offending or victimization and other information. There is no one systematic study providing a yearly estimate of crime in the United States; rather, self-report studies tend to be conducted by independent researchers or institutes. Even when they do involve a national sample (such as the National Youth Survey [NYS]), they almost never use such data to make estimates of the extent of crime or victimization across the nation.

This lack of a long-term, systematic study that can be used to estimate national crime rates may be the greatest weakness of self-report studies; however, this very weakness—not having a universal consistency in collection—is also its greatest strength. To clarify, researchers can develop their questionnaires to best fit the exact purposes of their study. For example, if researchers are doing a study on the relationship between a given personality trait (e.g., narcissism) and criminal offending, they can simply give participants a questionnaire that contains a narcissism scale and items that ask about past criminal behavior. Of course, these scales and items must be checked for their reliability and validity, but this is a relatively easy way to directly measure and test the hypotheses the researcher is most concerned about.

Some question the accuracy of SRD because they believe participants typically lie, but most studies have concluded that participants generally tell the truth. Specifically, researchers have compared self-reported offenses to lie detector machine results, readministered the same survey to the same individuals to see if they answer the same way each time (called test–retest reliability), and cross-checked self-reported arrests with police arrest data. All of these methods have shown that most people tend to be quite truthful when answering surveys.[22]

The most important aspect of self-report surveys is that they are the only available source of data for determining the social and psychological reasons people commit crime. The UCR and NCVS have virtually no data on the personality, family life, biological development, or other characteristics of criminal offenders, which are generally considered key factors in the development of criminality. Therefore, although we examine the findings of all three measures in the next chapter, the vast majority of the content we cover in this book will be based on findings from self-report studies.

What Do the Measures of Crime Show regarding the Distribution of Crime?

It is important to examine the most aggregated trends of crime, namely the ups and downs of overall crime rates in the United States across different decades. We will start with crime in the early 1900s—largely because the best data started being collected during this era and also because the 20th century (especially the most recent decades) is most relevant to our understanding of the reasons for our current crime rates. However, most experts believe that the U.S. crime rate, whether in terms of violence or property offending, used to be far higher prior to the 20th century; historians have arrived at this conclusion based on sporadic, poorly recorded documentation from the 18th and 19th centuries. By virtually all accounts, crime per capita (especially homicide) was far higher in the 1700s and 1800s than at any point after 1900, which is likely due to many factors but perhaps most importantly because formal agencies of justice, such as police and corrections (i.e., prisons, parole), did not exist in most of the United States until the middle or end of the 1800s. Up to that time, it was up to individual communities or vigilantes to deal with offenders.

---

[22]Michael Hindelang, Travis Hirschi, and J. Weis, *Measuring Delinquency* (Beverly Hills, CA: Sage, 1981).

▲ **Image 1.5** Group portrait of a police department liquor squad posing with cases of confiscated alcohol and distilling equipment during Prohibition.

SOURCE: © Getty Images / Archive Photos / Archive Photos

Therefore, there was little ability to investigate or apprehend criminals and no means to imprison them. But, as industrialization increased, the need to establish formal police agencies and correctional facilities evolved as a way to deal with people who offended in modern cities. By 1900, most existing states had formed police and prison systems, which is where our discussion will begin. See Figure 1.1.

The level of crime in the United States, particularly homicide, was relatively low at the beginning of the 20th century, perhaps because of the formal justice agencies that had been created during the 19th century. For example, the first metropolitan U.S. police departments were formed in Boston and then New York during the 1830s; in the same decade but a bit earlier, the first state police department, the Texas Rangers, had been established, and the U.S. Marshals Service had

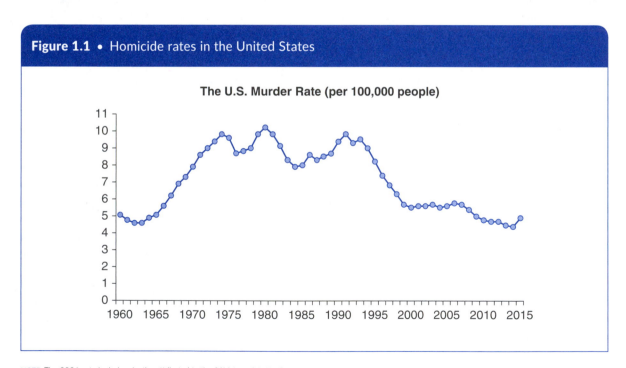

Figure 1.1 • Homicide rates in the United States

The U.S. Murder Rate (per 100,000 people)

NOTE: The 2001 rate includes deaths attributed to the 9/11 terrorist attacks.

SOURCE: FBI.

been founded still earlier. Although prisons started in the late 1790s, they did not begin to resemble their modern form or proliferate rapidly until the mid-1800s. The first juvenile court was formed in the Chicago area in 1899. The development of these formal law enforcement and justice agencies may have contributed to the low levels of crime and homicide in the very early 1900s. (Note: Our discussion of the crime rate in the early 1900s will primarily deal with homicide, because murder records constitute the only valid records of crime from that time; the UCR did not start until the 1930s. Most people consider homicide the most serious crime, and its frequency typically reflects the overall crime rate.)

The effects of the creation of these formal agencies did not persist long into the 20th century. Looking at the level of homicides that occurred in the United States, it is obvious that large increases took place between 1910 and 1920, likely because of extremely high increases in industrialization as the U.S. economy moved from an agricultural to an industrial emphasis. More important, population growth was rapid as a result of urbanization. Whenever high numbers of people move into an area (in this case, cities) and form a far more dense population (think of New York City at that time or Las Vegas in current times), it creates a crime problem. This is likely due to there being more opportunities to commit crimes against others; after all, when people are crammed together, it creates a situation in which there are far more potential offenders in close proximity to far more potential victims. A good modern example of this is high schools, which studies show have higher crime rates than city subways or other crime-ridden areas, largely because they densely pack people together, and in such conditions, opportunities for crime are readily available. Thus, the rapid industrialization and urbanization of the early 1900s is probably the most important reason for the increase in homicide and crime in general in the United States at that time.

The largest increases in U.S. homicide in the early 1900s occurred during the 1920s and early 1930s, with the peak level of homicide coming in the early 1930s. Criminologists and historians have concluded that this huge increase in the homicide rate was primarily due to two factors beyond the industrialization and urbanization that explained the increase prior to the 1920s. First, the U.S. Congress passed a constitutional amendment that banned the distribution and consumption of alcohol beginning in 1920. The period that followed is known as Prohibition. This legal action proved to be a disaster, at least in terms of crime, and Congress later agreed—but not until the 1930s—by passing another amendment to do away with the previous amendment that banned alcohol. For about 14 years, which notably recorded the highest U.S. rates of homicide and crime before 1950, the government attempted to stop people from drinking.

Prior to Prohibition, gangsters had been relatively passive and had not held much power. However, the ban on alcohol gave the black market a lot of potential in terms of monetary profit and reasons for killing off competition. Some of the greatest massacres of rival gangs of organized crime syndicates (e.g., the Italian Mafia) occurred during the Prohibition era. The impact on crime was likely only one of the many problems with Prohibition, but it was a very important and deadly one for our purposes. Once Prohibition ended in the early 1930s, homicide and crime rates decreased significantly, which may have implications for modern drug policies. According to studies, many banned substances today are less violence producing than alcohol, which studies show is the most violence-causing substance. For example, most criminologists believe that the current war on drugs may actually be causing far more crime than it seeks to prevent (even if it may be lowering the number of drug addicts) due to the black market it creates for drugs that are in demand, much like the case with alcohol during Prohibition.

Another major reason why the homicide rate and overall crime levels increased so much during the early 1930s was the Great Depression, which sent the United States into an unprecedented state of economic upheaval. Most historians and criminologists agree that the stock market crash of the late 1920s was a primary contributor to the large numbers of homicides in the early 1930s. We will return to this subject later when we examine the strain theory of crime, which emphasizes economic structure and poverty as the primary causes of crime.

Although the homicide and crime rate experienced a significant drop after Prohibition was eliminated, another reason for this decrease was likely the social policies of the New Deal, which was implemented by President Franklin D. Roosevelt. Such policies included those that created new jobs for people hit hardest by the Depression through programs such as Job Corps and the Tennessee Valley Authority, both of which still exist today. Although such programs likely aided economic (and thus crime) recovery in the United States, world events of the early 1940s provided the greatest reasons for the huge decreases that were seen at that time.

The entry of the United States into World War II was probably the biggest contributor to decreasing U.S. crime in the early 20th century. As you will notice, homicides decreased dramatically during the 4 years (1941–1945) that hundreds of thousands of young men (the most likely offenders and victims) were sent overseas to fight on two fronts, Europe and the South Pacific. Anytime a society loses a huge portion of the most common offenders, namely young (teenage to 20s) males, it can expect a drop in crime like the one the United States experienced in the 1940s. However, at the end of 1945, most of these men returned and began making babies, which triggered the greatest increase in babies that U.S. society had ever seen. This generation of babies started what historians call the baby boom, which would have the greatest impact on crime levels that has ever been recorded in U.S. history.

Although crime rates increased after soldiers returned home from overseas in the late 1940s, they did not rise to anywhere near the levels present during Prohibition and the Great Depression. Alcohol was legal, and the economy was doing relatively well after World War II. During the 1950s, the crime level remained relatively low and stable until the early 1960s, when the impact of the baby boom emerged in terms of the crime rate. If a very large share of the population is made up of young people, particularly teenage or early-20s males, the crime rate will almost inevitably go up. This is exactly what occurred in the United States, starting in the early 1960s, and it led to the largest 10-year increase in crime that the country has ever seen.

The Baby Boom Effect

The UCR shows that the greatest single-decade increase in the crime rate occurred between 1965 and 1975. In that time, the overall crime rate more than doubled, an unprecedented increase. Notably, this increase occurred during the War on Poverty, which was set into motion by President Lyndon B. Johnson in a program he termed the Great Society; the crime increase thus turned many people and policy makers against having the government address economic issues to better society. However, the demographic factor that these individuals did not take into account was that this was the era in which most people in society belonged to young age groups, which predisposed the nation to the high crime rates experienced at this time. In contrast, the following generation, called Generation X, which includes those individuals born between 1965 and 1978, had a very low birth rate, which may have contributed to the low crime rates observed in recent years.

The high numbers of young people in society were not the only societal trend going on during the late 1960s and early 1970s that would lead to higher crime rates. For example, a large number of people were being arrested as a result of their participation in the civil rights movement, the women's rights movement, and anti–Vietnam War activities. Perhaps most important, the 1970s showed the highest levels of drug usage and favorable attitudes toward drugs since accurate national studies had first been conducted. Virtually all measures of drug usage peaked during the 1970s or early 1980s.

So, ultimately, many things came together between the mid-1960s and the late 1970s to usher in the greatest increase in the crime rate that the United States has ever seen, culminating in the peak of crime and homicide in 1980. All of our measures agree that crime, especially homicide, reached its highest level about that year. Although other periods, such as the early 1990s, showed similar increases in crime, largely due to juvenile offending, no other period showed higher rates than the 1980 period, most likely due to the coming of age of many baby boomers and their high drug usage.

Crime levels declined somewhat in the early 1980s and then rose again in the late 1980s and early 1990s, but the crime and homicide rate never exceeded the 1980 peak. Furthermore, after 1994, the crime rate decreased drastically every year for about a decade, to the point that it dropped as low as it had been in the early 1960s. The U.S. crime rate is currently around where it was about 50 years ago.

There are many reasons for this huge decrease over the past two decades. One of the biggest reasons is that the population has a relatively smaller proportion of young people than it did during the 1960s and 1970s, but obviously there is more to the picture. Drug usage, as well as favorable attitudes toward drugs, has dropped a lot in recent years. Furthermore, the incarceration rate of prisoners is about 400% to 500% of what it was in the early 1970s. Although many experts have claimed that locking up criminals does not reduce crime levels in a society, it is hard to deny that imprisoning 5 times more people will not result in catching many, if not most, of the habitual offenders. It makes sense: By rate, the United States currently locks up more citizens in prison than virtually any other developed country.

Almost all crime tends to be nonrandom. Consistent with this, the crime measures show a number of trends in which crime occurs among certain types of people, in certain places, at certain times, and so on. We turn to an examination of such concentrations of crime, starting with large, macro differences in crime rates across regions of the United States.

Rates of Crime

Regional and City Differences

Crime tends to be higher in certain regions of the country. According to the UCR, the United States is separated into four regions: Northeast, Midwest, South, and West. For the past few decades, crime rates (based on crime per capita) have been significantly higher in two of these regions: the South and the West. These two regions consistently have higher rates than the other regions, with one or the other having the highest rates for violence or property offenses or both each year. Some studies have found that, when poverty levels are accounted for, much of the regional difference is explained away. Although this is a very simple conclusion, the studies seem to be consistent in tying regional differences to variations in social factors, notably socioeconomic levels.

Regardless of the region, there seems to be extreme variation from high to low crime rates across states and cities within each of these large regions. For example, crime measures consistently show that certain U.S. states and jurisdictions have consistently high crime rates. The two standouts are Louisiana and the District of Columbia, with the latter having an extremely high rate—typically more than 8 times the national average for homicide. It is quite ironic that arguably the most powerful city in the world has an extremely serious crime problem, certainly one of the worst in our nation.

Another question is why crime rates in states or jurisdictions, or in cities and counties, vary drastically from one region to the next. For instance, Camden, New Jersey, one of the cities in the lower-rate Northeast region according to the UCR, had the highest rate of crime among all U.S. cities in the years 2004 and 2005. Detroit, Michigan, was second worst for both of these years; it used to be number one before Camden outdid it. At the same time, however, New Jersey had some of the safest cities in the nation for these years—2 of the 10 safest cities are in New Jersey, which shows how much crime can vary from place to place, even those in relatively close proximity. Notably, in the most recent estimates from the FBI, the cities of St. Louis and New Orleans exhibited the highest rates of serious violent crimes in 2006 and 2007, respectively. An important factor for New Orleans was the devastation of the city's infrastructure after Hurricane Katrina, which essentially wiped out the city's criminal justice system and resources.

Crime has also been found to cluster within a given city, whether the overall city is relatively low crime or high crime. Virtually every area (whether urban, suburban, or rural) has what are known as **hot spots**, or places that have high levels of crime activity. Such places are often bars or liquor stores or other types of businesses, such as bus stops and depots, convenience stores, shopping malls, motels and hotels, fast-food restaurants, check-cashing businesses, tattoo parlors, or discount stores (such as dollar stores). However, hot spots can also be residential places, such as homes that police are constantly called to for domestic violence or apartment complexes that are crime-ridden—something often seen in subsidized housing areas.

Even the nicest of cities and areas have hot spots, and even the worst cities and areas also tend to have most of their police calls coming from specific addresses or businesses. This is one of the best examples of how crime does not tend to be random. Many police agencies have begun using spatial software on computer systems to analyze where the hot spots in a given city are and to predict where certain crimes are likely to occur in the future. This allows more preventive patrols and proactive strategies in such zones. One criminological theory, routine activities theory, is largely based on explaining why hot spots exist.

Rates of Crime according to Time of Day and Time of Year

Another way that crime is known to cluster is by time of day. This varies greatly depending on the type of group being examined. For example, juvenile delinquency and victimization, especially for violence, tends to peak sharply at 3:00 p.m. on school days (about half of the days of the year for children), which is the time that youths are most likely to lack supervision (i.e., children are let out of school and are often not supervised by adults until they get home). On the other hand, adult crime and victimization, especially for violence, tends to peak much later on, at about 11:00 p.m. on almost all days, which is a sharp contrast to the juvenile peak in midafternoon. These estimates are primarily based on FBI and UCR data.

To some extent, the peak hour for juveniles is misleading; other non-police-based estimates show that just as much crime is going on during school, but schools tend not to report it. As stated previously, this widespread lack of reporting by schools occurs because none of the parties involved wants a formal police report taken. Typically, the youth doesn't want to be arrested; the child's parents don't want their daughter or son to be formally processed by police; and most important, no school wants to become known as a dangerous place. Thus, the police are typically called only in extreme cases—for example, if a student pulls a gun on another student or actually uses a weapon.

This underreporting also occurs in colleges and universities, because such institutions depend largely on tuition for funding, and this goes down if enrollment levels decline. After all, no parents want to send their teenagers to a college that is high in crime. Federal law now requires virtually all colleges to report their crime levels to the public, so there is a lot at stake if police take formal reports on crime events. Thus, most colleges, like K–12 school systems, have an informal process in place so that even violent crimes can often be handled informally.

Crimes tend to peak significantly during the summer. Studies show that criminals tend to be highly opportunistic, meaning that they happen to be going about their normal activities when they see an opportunity to commit a crime, as compared to a more hydraulic model, in which an offender actually goes out looking to commit a crime. Because criminals are like everyone else in most ways, they tend to be out and about more in the summer, so they are more likely to see opportunities at that time. Furthermore, youths are typically out of school during the summer, so they are often bored and not supervised by adults as much as during the traditional school year. Burglary tends to rise 300% during the summer, an increase that may be linked to the fact that people go on vacation and leave their homes vacant for weeks or months at a time. All of these factors come together to produce much higher rates in the summer than in any other season.

A couple of crimes, such as murder and robbery, tend to have a second peak in the winter, which most experts believe is due to high emotions during the holidays, additional social interaction (and often the drinking of alcohol) during the holidays, and an increase in wanting money or goods for gift giving, which would explain robbery increases at that time. These offenses are the exception, however, not the rule. Most offenses, including murder and robbery, tend to have their highest peaks during warmer summer months.

Rates of Crime according to Age and Gender

Age is perhaps the most important way that crime and victimization tend to cluster in certain groups. Almost no individual gets arrested before the age of 10; if one does, it is a huge predictor that the child is likely to become a habitual, chronic offender. However, between the ages of 10 and 17, the offending rate for all serious street crimes (i.e., FBI index crimes) goes up drastically, peaking at an average age of 17. Then the offending rates begin decreasing significantly, such that by the time people reach the age of 20, the likelihood of being arrested has fallen in half as compared to the midteenage years. This offending level continues to decline throughout life for all of the serious index crimes, although other crimes, such as white-collar crimes, tax evasion, and gambling, are likely to be committed more often at later ages.

The extraordinarily high levels of offending in the teenage years have implications for how we prevent and deal with juvenile delinquency and help explain why we are so bad at preventing habitual offenders from committing so many crimes. We are often good at predicting who the most chronic, serious offenders are by the time they are in their 20s, but that does little good because most offenders have committed most of their crimes before they hit 20 years old.

Another characteristic important in the way crime clusters is gender. In every society, at every time in recorded history, males have committed far more serious street crimes (both violent and property) than females. It appears there is almost no closing of this gap in offending—at least for FBI index crimes. Even in the most recent years, males have been the offenders in 80% to 98% of all serious violent crimes (murder, robbery, aggravated assault, forcible rape) and have made up the vast majority of offenders in property index crimes (burglary, motor vehicle theft, arson, and larceny). The fact that the last offense is committed more frequently by males often surprises people because the most common type of larceny is shoplifting, which people often perceive as being done mostly by women. All studies show that men commit most of the larcenies in the United States. It is important to realize that males in all societies throughout the world commit the vast majority of offenses, and the more violent and serious the crimes are, the more men are represented.

However, there are a few nonindex crimes that females commit as much as, or more than, males. Specifically, in terms of property crimes, embezzlement and fraud are two offenses that females commit at rates comparable to those for men, which likely has to do with enhanced opportunities to commit such crimes. Most of the workforce is now female, which wasn't true in past decades, and many women work in banking and other businesses that tempt employees by having large amounts of money available for embezzling. In terms of public disorder, prostitution arrests tend to be mostly female, which is not too surprising.

The only other offense in which females are well represented is running away from home, which is a status offense (illegal for juveniles only). However, virtually all sources and studies of offending rates (e.g., self-report studies) show that male juveniles run away far more than females, but because of societal norms and values, females get arrested far more than males. Feminist theories of the patriarchal model (in short, men are in charge and dominate or control females) and the chivalry model (females are treated differently because they are seen as more innocent) argue that females are protected as a type of property. This may be important in light of the opposing findings regarding female and male rates of running away versus female and male rates of being arrested for running away. The bottom line is that families are more likely to report missing girls than missing boys and more likely to press law enforcement agencies to pursue girls who have run away than boys who have done so. We will explore explanations for such differences in later chapters, particularly in the chapter in which we cover conflict and feminist theories of crime.

Rates of Crime according to Population Density

Victimization and offending rates are also clustered according to the density of a given area. All sources of crime data show that rates of offending and victimization are far higher per capita in urban areas than in suburban and rural regions. Furthermore, this trend is linear: The more rural an area, the lower the rates for crime and victimization. To clarify, urban areas have, by far, the highest rates for offending, followed by suburban areas; the least amount of crime and victimization is found in rural (e.g., farming) areas. This trend has been shown for many decades and is undisputed. Keep in mind that such rates are based on population in such areas, so this trend holds true even per capita for citizens in a given region. This is likely due to enhanced opportunities to commit crime in urban and even suburban areas, as well as the fact that rural communities tend to have stronger **informal controls**, such as family, church, and community ties. Studies consistently show that informal controls are far more effective in preventing and solving crimes than are the **formal controls** of justice, which include all official aspects of law enforcement and justice, such as police, courts, and corrections (i.e., prisons, probation, parole).

A good example of the effectiveness of informal sanctions can be seen in the early formation of the U.S. colonies, such as the Massachusetts Bay Colony. In the early 1600s, crime per capita was at an all-time low in what would become the United States. It may surprise many that police and prisons did not exist then; rather, the low crime rate was due to high levels of informal controls: When people committed crimes, they were banished from the society or were shunned.

As in Nathaniel Hawthorne's novel *The Scarlet Letter*, even for what would now be considered a relatively minor offense (adultery), people were forced to wear a large letter (such as an *A* for adultery or a *T* for theft), and they were shunned by all others in their social world. Such punishments were (and still are) highly effective deterrents for offenders, but they work only in communities with high levels of informal controls. Studies have shown that, in such societies, crime tends to be extremely low—in fact, so low that such communities may "invent" serious crimes so that they can have an identifiable group on which to blame societal problems. We saw this occur in the Massachusetts Bay Colony with the creation of a new offense, witchcraft, for which hundreds of people were put on trial and many were executed.

Such issues will be raised again later when we discuss the sociological theories of Émile Durkheim. Nevertheless, it is interesting to note that some judges and communities have gone back to public-shaming punishments, such as making people carry signs of their offenses or putting the names of offenders in local newspapers. But the conclusion at this point is that rural communities tend to have far higher informal controls, which keep their crime rates low. On the other hand, urban (especially inner-city) areas tend to have very low levels of informal controls, which lead to few attempts by the community to police itself.

Crime also tends to cluster according to social class, with the lower classes experiencing far more violent offending and victimization. This is now undisputed and consistently shown across all sources of data regarding criminal offending. Interestingly, the characteristics associated with offending tend to be a mirror image of those associated with victimization. To clarify, young, poor urban males tend to have the highest rates of criminal offending—and this group also has the highest rates of victimization as a result of violent offending. This mirror image phenomenon is often referred to as the **equivalency hypothesis**. However, the equivalency hypothesis does not characterize the relationship between social class and property crimes. Specifically, members of middle- to upper-class households tend to experience just as much and often more victimization for property crimes than do lower-class households, but the most likely offenders in most property crimes are from the lower class. This makes sense; offenders will tend to steal from the people and places that have the most property or money to steal. This tendency has been found since criminological data were first collected, even back to the early 1800s, and it is often found in present times, although it is not consistently shown each year (e.g., in NCVS data). Nevertheless, the equivalency hypothesis holds true for violent crimes: Lower-class individuals, especially those who are young, inner-city males, commit more violent crimes, and they are victimized more as a result of such violent crimes.

Rates of Crime according to Race or Ethnicity

Another important way crimes are clustered in U.S. society is by race or ethnicity. In terms of violent crimes, the most victimized group by far in the United States is Native Americans or American Indians. According to NCVS data, Native Americans are victimized at almost twice the rate of any other racial or ethnic group. This is likely due to the extreme levels of poverty, unemployment, and so on that exist on virtually all American Indian reservations.

Although some Indian tribes have recently gained profits from operating gaming casinos on their lands, the vast majority of tribes in most states are not involved in such endeavors, so deprivation and poverty are still the norm.

Although there is little offending data for this group (the UCR does not adequately measure this group in its arrest data), it is generally assumed that Native Americans have the highest rates of offending as well. This is a fairly safe assumption, because research has clearly shown that the vast majority of criminal offending and victimization are **intraracial**. This means that crime tends to occur within a race or ethnicity (e.g., Whites offending against Whites) as opposed to being **interracial** or across races or ethnicities (e.g., Whites offending against Blacks).

Another major group that experiences an extremely high rate of victimization, particularly for homicide, is Blacks. (The term *Black* is used here, as

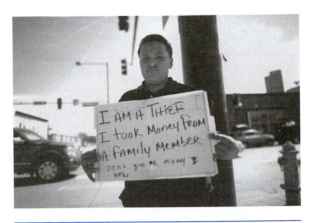

▲ **Image 1.6** Offenders being forced to hold signs as part of their punishment is becoming a more popular informal sanction that shames individuals in their communities.

SOURCE: © Joe Amon / Denver Post / Getty Images

opposed to *African American*, because this is what most measures [e.g., the UCR and NCVS] use and because many African Americans are not Black [e.g., many citizens from Egypt or South Africa]). According to UCR data for homicide, which the NCVS does not report, Blacks have by far the highest rates of victimization and offending. Again, this is likely due to the extreme levels of poverty experienced by this group as well as the high levels of single-headed households among this population (which likely explains much of the poverty).

A good example of the high levels of homicide rates among Blacks, in terms of both offending and victimization, can be seen in certain U.S. cities. Washington, DC, New Orleans, St. Louis, and Detroit have some of the highest murder rates among U.S. cities. They also have some of the highest proportions of Black residents as compared to other U.S. cities. Notably, studies have shown that when researchers control for poverty rates and single-headed households, the racial and ethnicity effects seem to disappear.

For example, data show that Washington, DC, and the state of Louisiana are the top two jurisdictions for high rates of poverty, with most of the poor being children or teenagers, the latter of whom are most prone to committing crimes, especially violent offenses (such as murder). Thus, the two racial and ethnic groups rated highest for violent crime, both as victims and offenders—Native Americans and Blacks—also tend to have the highest rates in the nation for poverty and broken families. It should be noted that Hispanics, a common ethnic group in the United States, also have relatively high offending and victimization rates as compared to Whites and other minorities, such as Asians, who tend to experience low rates.

Policy Implications

One of the key elements of a good theory is that it can help inform policy makers in making decisions about how to reduce crime. This theme will be reviewed at the end of each chapter in this book. After all, a criminological theory is only truly useful in the real world if it helps to reduce criminal offending. Many theories have been used as the basis of such changes in policy, and we will present examples of how the theories of crime discussed in each chapter have guided policy making. We will also examine empirical evidence for such policies, specifically to determine whether or not such policies have been successful (and many have not).

Conclusion

Although there are numerous other ways that crime tends to be clustered in our society, we have covered most of the major variables in this chapter. The rest of this book will examine the various theories of why crime tends to occur in such groups and individuals, and the way that we determine the accuracy of these theories will directly relate to how well they explain the high rates of crime in the groups that we have discussed.

/// CHAPTER SUMMARY

- Criminology is the scientific study of crime. It involves the use of the scientific method and testing hypotheses, which distinguishes it from other perspectives of crime (e.g., journalistic, religious, legal) because these fields are not based on science.

- Criminological theory seeks to do more than simply predict criminal behavior; rather, the goal is to more fully understand the reasons why certain individuals offend and others do not.

- Definitions of crime vary drastically across time and place; most criminologists tend to focus on deviant behaviors whether or not they violate criminal codes.

- There are various paradigms, or unique perspectives, pertaining to crime, which have contrasting assumptions and propositions. The Classical School of criminological theory assumes free will and choice among individuals, whereas the Positive School focuses on biological, social, and psychological factors that negate the notion of choice among criminal offenders. Other theoretical paradigms, such as conflict, critical, and integrated models of offending, also exist.

- Criminological theories can be classified by their fundamental assumptions as well as other factors, such as the unit of measure on which they focus—the individual or the group (micro or macro, respectively)—or the assumptions they make regarding basic human nature: good, bad, or blank slate.

- There are more than a handful of characteristics that good criminological theories should have and that bad criminological theories do not have.

- Three criteria are required for determining causality and thus are essential in determining whether or not an independent (predictive) variable (X) actually affects a dependent (consequent) variable (Y).

- This introduction also discussed the primary measures that are used for estimating the crime committed in the United States; these primary measures are police reports (e.g., the UCR), victimization surveys (e.g., the NCVS), and offenders' self-reports of the crimes they have committed.

- We also discussed in this chapter what the measures of crime have shown regarding the distribution of criminal offending according to region, race and ethnicity, time of day, time of year, age, gender, socioeconomic status, and period of history. It is important to note that various theories presented in this book will be tested on the extent to which they can explain the clustering of crime among certain individuals and groups.

KEY TERMS

Classical School 6

clearance rate 14

conflict theories 7

consensual perspective 7

correlation, or covariation 10

criminology 1

dark figure 13

deviance 5

empirical validity 9

equivalency hypothesis 24

formal controls 24

hot spots 21

hypotheses 2

index offenses 13

informal controls 24

interracial 25

intraracial 25

legalistic approach 4

logical consistency 8

macro level of analysis 6

mala in se 5

mala prohibita 5

micro level of analysis 6

National Crime Victimization Survey (NCVS) 12

nonindex offenses 13

paradigms 6

parsimony 8

policy implications 9

Positive School 6

scientific method 2

scope 8

self-report data (SRD) 12

social sciences 2

spuriousness 11

telescoping 16

temporal ordering 10

testability 9

theory 2

Uniform Crime Report (UCR) 12

DISCUSSION QUESTIONS

1. How does criminology differ from other perspectives of crime?

2. How does a good theoretical explanation of crime go beyond simply predicting crime?

3. Should criminologists emphasize only crimes made illegal by law, or should they also study acts that are deviant but not illegal? Explain why you feel this way.

4. Even though you haven't been exposed to all the theories in this book, do you favor classical or positive assumptions regarding criminal behavior? Explain why.

5. Which types of theories do you think are most important: those that explain individual behavior (micro) or those that explain criminality among groups (macro)? Explain your decision.

6. Do you tend to favor the idea that human beings are born bad, good, or a blank slate? Discuss your decision, and provide an example.

7. Which characteristics of a good theory do you find most important? Which are least important? Make sure to explain why you feel that way.

8. Of the three criteria for determining causality between a predictor variable and a consequent variable, which do you think is easiest to show, and which is hardest to show? Why?

9. Which of the measures of crime do you think is the best estimate of crime in the United States? Why? Also, which measure is the best for determining associations between crime and personality traits? Why?

10. Looking at what the measures of crime show, which finding surprises you the most? Explain why.

11. What types of policies do you feel reduce crime the most? Which do you think have little or no effect in reducing crime?

WEB RESOURCES

Measures of Crime

http://criminal-justice.iresearchnet.com/criminology/theories
https://ucr.fbi.gov/crime-in-the-u.s/2015/crime-in-the-u.s.-2015
http://www.bjs.gov/index.cfm?ty=dcdetail&iid=245

CHAPTER 2

Preclassical and Classical Theories of Crime

This chapter will examine the earliest logical theories of rule breaking—namely, explanations of criminal conduct that emphasize free will and the ability of individuals to make rational decisions regarding the consequences of their behavior. The natural capabilities of human beings to make decisions based on expected costs and benefits were acknowledged during the **Age of Enlightenment** in the 17th and 18th centuries. This understanding of human capabilities led to what is considered the first rational theory of criminal activity, **deterrence theory**. This theory has had a more profound impact on justice systems in the United States than any other perspective to date. Furthermore, virtually all criminal justice systems (e.g., policing, courts, corrections) are based on this theoretical model even today.

Such theories of human rationality were in stark contrast to the theories focusing on religious or supernatural causes of crime, which had prevailed through most of human civilization up to the Age of Enlightenment. In addition, the Classical School theories of crime are distinguished from theories in subsequent chapters of this book by their emphasis on the free will and rational decision making of individuals, which modern theories of crime tend to ignore. The theoretical perspectives discussed in this chapter all focus on the ability of human beings to choose their own behavior and destinies, whereas paradigms that existed before and after this period tend to emphasize the inability of individuals to control their behavior due to external factors. Therefore, the Classical School is perhaps the paradigm best suited for analysis of what types of calculations are going on in someone's head before he or she commits a crime.

The different Classical School theories presented in this chapter vary in many ways, most notably in what they propose as the primary constructs and processes individuals use to determine whether they are going to commit a crime. For example, some Classical School theories emphasize the potential negative consequences of their actions, whereas others focus on the possible benefits of such activity. Still others concentrate on the opportunities and existing situations that predispose people to engage in criminal activity. Regardless of their differences, all of the theories examined in this chapter emphasize a common theme: Individuals commit crime because they identify certain situations and acts as beneficial due to the perceived lack of punishment and the perceived likelihood of profits, such as money or peer status. In other words, the potential offender weighs out the possible costs and pleasures of committing a given act and then behaves in a rational way based on this analysis.

The most important distinction of these Classical School theories, as opposed to those discussed in future chapters, is that they emphasize individuals making their own decisions regardless of extraneous influences, such as the economy or bonding with society. Although many extraneous factors may influence the ability of an individual to rationally consider offending situations, the Classical School assumes that the individual takes all these influences into account when making the decision about whether or not to engage in criminal behavior. Given the focus placed on individual responsibility, it is not surprising that Classical School theories are used as the basis for U.S. policies on punishment for criminal activity. The Classical School theories are highly compatible and consistent with the conservative, get-tough movement that has existed since the mid-1970s. Thus, the Classical School still retains the highest importance in terms of policy and pragmatic punishment in the United States as well as throughout all countries in the Western world.

As you will see, the Classical School theoretical paradigm was presented as early as the mid-1700s, and its prominence as a model of offending behavior in criminal justice systems is still dominant. Scientific and academic circles, however, have dismissed many of the claims of this perspective. For reasons we shall explore in this chapter, the assumptions and primary propositions of Classical School theories have been neglected by most recent theoretical models of criminologists. This dismissal is likely premature, given the impact that this perspective has had on understanding human nature, as well as the profound influence it has had on most criminal justice systems, especially in the United States.

Preclassical Perspectives of Crime and Punishment

Over the long course of human civilization, people have mostly believed that criminal activity is caused by supernatural causes or religious factors. It has been documented that some primitive societies believed that crime increased during major thunderstorms or major droughts. Most primitive cultures believed that when a person engaged in behavior that violated the tribe's or clan's rules, the devil or evil spirits were making him or her do it.[1] For example, in many societies, if someone committed criminal activity, it was common to perform exorcisms or primitive surgery, such as breaking open the skull of the perpetrator to allow the demons to leave his or her head. Of course, this almost always resulted in the death of the accused person, but it was seen as a liberating experience for the offender.

This was just one form of dealing with criminal behavior, but it epitomizes how primitive cultures understood the causes of crime. As the movie *The Exorcist* revealed, exorcisms were still being performed on offenders by representatives of a number of religions, including Catholicism, in the 21st century to get the devil out of them. In June 2005, a Romanian monk and four nuns acknowledged engaging in an exorcism that led to the death of the victim, who was crucified, a towel stuffed in her mouth, and left without food for many days.[2] When the monk and nuns were asked to explain why they did this, they defiantly said they were trying to take the devils out of the 23-year-old woman. Although they were prosecuted by Romanian authorities, many governments might not have done so because many societies around the world still believe in and condone such practices.

Readers may be surprised to learn that the Roman Catholic Church still authorizes college-level courses on how to perform exorcisms. Specifically, news reports revealed that a Vatican-recognized university was offering a course in exorcism and demonic possession for a second year because of its concern about the "devil's lure."[3] In fact, Pope Benedict XVI welcomed a large group of Italian exorcists who visited the Vatican in September 2005

---

[1]Stephen E. Brown, Finn-Aage Esbensen, and Gilbert Geis, *Criminology: Explaining Crime and Its Context*, 8th ed. (Cincinnati, OH: Anderson, 2012).

[2]Associated Press, "Romanian Priest Jailed for Killing Young Nun Who Was Crucified during Botched Exorcism Ritual," *Daily Mail*, June 24, 2005, http://www.dailymail.co.uk/news/article-2692892/Romanian-priest-jailed-killing-young-nun-CRUCIFIED-botched-exorcism-ritual.html.

[3]Associated Press, "University Offering Course on Exorcism," *Telegraph*, July 9, 2005, http://www.telegraph.co.uk/news/worldnews/europe/italy/1480798/Vatican-offers-course-in-Satanism-and-exorcism.html.

and encouraged them to carry on their work for the Catholic Church.[4] Furthermore, in 1999, the Roman Catholic Church issued revised guidelines for conducting exorcisms, which recommend consulting physicians when exorcisms are performed; it also provides an 84-page description of the language (in Latin) to be used in such rituals. It should be noted that the use of such exorcisms is quite rare, especially in more developed nations. However, U.S. Catholic bishops recently (in November 2010) cited the need for more trained exorcists and even held a conference in Baltimore, Maryland, on how to conduct exorcisms. This two-day training session instructed clergy on evaluating evil possession as well as reviewing the rituals that comprise an exorcism. More than 50 bishops and 60 priests attended this training session, despite the tendency for exorcists in U.S. dioceses to keep a very low profile.[5]

One of the most common supernatural beliefs in primitive cultures was that the full moon caused criminal activity. Then, as now, there was much truth to the full-moon theory. In primitive times, people believed that crime was related to the influence of higher powers, including the destructive influence of the moon itself. Modern studies have shown, however, that the increase in crime is primarily due to a Classical School theoretical model: There are simply more opportunities to commit crime when the moon is full because there is more light at night, which results in more people being out on the streets. In any case, nighttime is well established as a high-risk period for adult crimes, such as sexual assault.

Although some primitive theories had some validity in determining when crime would be more common, virtually

▲ **Image 2.1** Although more common in ancient times, exorcisms are still approved and carried out by certain groups in attempts to remove evil spirits from individuals.

SOURCE: © iStockphoto.com/KatarzynaBialasiewicz

none of them accurately predicted who would commit the offenses. During the Middle Ages, just about everyone was from the lower classes, and only a minority of that group engaged in offending against the normative society. So, for most of human civilization, there was virtually no rational theoretical understanding of why individuals violate the laws of society; instead, people believed crime was caused by supernatural or religious factors of the devil-made-me-do-it variety.

Consistent with these views, the punishments related to offending during this period were quite harsh by modern standards. Given the assumption that evil spirits drove the motivations for criminal activity, the punishments for criminal acts—especially those deemed particularly offensive to the norms of a given society—were often quite inhumane. Common punishments at that time were being beheaded; being tortured; being burned alive at the stake; and being drowned, stoned, or quartered. Good discussions of such harsh examples of punishment, such as quartering, can be found in Brown et al.'s discussion of punishment.[6]

[4]Reuters, "Pope Benedict XVI Warmly Greets Exorcist Convention," September 17, 2005. https://www.usatoday.com/story/news/world/2013/05/21/pope-francis-exorcism/2347197.

[5]Rachel Zoll, "Catholic Bishops: More Exorcists Needed," *Seattle Times,* November 12, 2010.

[6]Brown et al., *Criminology,* 170–184.

Although many would find the primitive forms of punishment and execution to be quite barbaric, some modern societies still practice them. For example, Islamic court systems, as well as other religious and ethnic cultures, are often allowed to carry out executions and other forms of corporal punishment. Fifteen individuals were whipped with a cane for gambling in Aceh, Indonesia, a highly conservative Muslim region. The caning was held in public and outside a mosque.[7] In the United States, gambling is a relatively minor crime—when it is not totally legal, as in many places in the United States. It is interesting to note, however, that a relatively recent Gallup poll regarding the use of caning (i.e., public whipping) of convicted individuals was supported by most of the American public.[8]

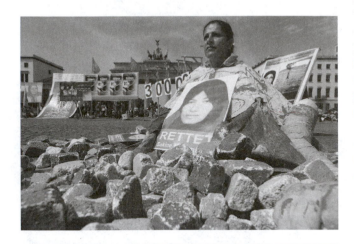

▲ **Image 2.2** A woman protesting the frequent use of stoning to punish individuals, in this case a woman in Iran who was convicted of adultery. Public stoning and caning are still used as punishment by certain societies around the world.

SOURCE: © Getty Images / Sean Gallup / Staff

Compared to U.S. standards, the more extreme forms of corporal punishment, particularly public executions carried out by many religious courts and countries, are drawn out and very painful. An example is stoning, in which people are buried up to the waist and local citizens throw small stones at them until they die (large stones are not allowed because they would lead to death too quickly). In most of the Western world, such brutal forms of punishment and execution were done away with in the 1700s due to the impact of the Age of Enlightenment.

The Age of Enlightenment

In the midst of the extremely draconian times of the mid-1600s, Thomas Hobbes, in his book *Leviathan* (1651), proposed a rational theory of why people are motivated to form democratic states of governance.[9] Hobbes started with the basic framework that all individuals are in a constant state of warfare with all other individuals. He used the extreme examples of primitive tribes and sects. He argued that the primitive state of man is selfish and greedy, so people live in a constant state of fear of everyone else. However, Hobbes also proclaimed that people are also rational, so they will rationally organize sound forms of governance, which can create rules to avoid this constant state of fear. Interestingly, once a government is created, the state of warfare mutates from one waged among individuals or families to one waged between nations. This can be seen in modern times; after all, it is quite rare that a person or family declares war against another (although gangs may be an exception), but we often hear of governments declaring war.

Hobbes stated that the primitive state of fear—of constant warfare of everyone against everyone else—was the motivation for entering into a contract with others to create a common authority. At the same time, Hobbes specified that it was this exact emotion—fear—that was needed to make citizens conform to the given rules or laws in

---

[7]Irwan Firdaus, "15 Caned in Muslim Indonesia for Gaming," *StarNews*, June 25, 2005.

[8]Philip Shenon, "U.S. Youth in Singapore Loses Appeal on Flogging," *New York Times*, April 1, 1994.

[9]Thomas Hobbes, *Leviathan* (1651; repr. New York: Library of Liberal Arts, 1958).

society. Strangely, it appears that the very emotion that inspires people to enter into an agreement to form a government is the same emotion that inspires these same individuals to follow the rules of the government that is created. It is ironic, but it is quite true.

Given the social conditions during the 1600s, this model appears somewhat accurate; there was little sense of community in terms of working toward progress as a group. It had not been that long since the Middle Ages, when one third of the world's population had died from sickness, and many cultures were severely deprived or in an extreme state of poverty. Prior to the 1600s, the feudal system had been the dominant model of governance in most of the Western world. During this feudal era, a very small group of aristocrats (less than 1% of the population) owned and operated the largely agricultural economy that existed. Virtually no rights were afforded to individuals in the Middle Ages or at the time Hobbes wrote his book. Most people had no individual rights in terms of criminal justice, let alone a say in the existing governments of the time. Hobbes's book clearly took issue with this lack of say in the government, which had profound implications for the justice systems of that time.

Hobbes clearly stated that until the citizens were entitled to a certain degree of respect from their governing bodies as well as their justice systems they would never fully buy into the authority of government or the system of justice. Hobbes proposed a number of extraordinary ideas that came to define the Age of Enlightenment. He presented a drastic paradigm shift for social structure, which had extreme implications for justice systems throughout the world.

Hobbes explicitly declared that people are rational beings who choose their destinies by creating societies. Hobbes further proposed that individuals in such societies democratically create rules of conduct that all members of that society must follow. These rules, which all citizens decide upon, become laws, and the result of not following the laws is punishment determined by the democratically instituted government. It is clear from Hobbes's statements that the government, as instructed by the citizens, not only has the authority to punish individuals who violate the rules of the society but, more important, has a duty to punish them. When such an authority fails to fulfill this duty, breakdown in the social order can quickly result.

The arrangement of citizens promising to abide by the rules or laws set forth by a given society in return for protection is commonly referred to as the **social contract**. Hobbes introduced this idea, but it was also emphasized by all other Enlightenment theorists after him, such as Jean-Jacques Rousseau, John Locke, Voltaire, and Baron Charles Montesquieu. The idea of the social contract is an extraordinarily important part of Enlightenment philosophy. Although Enlightenment philosophers had significant differences in what they believed, the one thing they had in common was the belief in the social contract: the idea that people invest in the laws of their society with the guarantee that they will be protected from others who violate such rules.

Another shared belief among Enlightenment philosophers was that the people should be given a say in the government, especially the justice system. All of them emphasized fairness in determining who was guilty as well as appropriate punishments or sentences. During the time in which Enlightenment philosophers wrote, individuals who stole a loaf of bread to feed their families were sentenced to death, whereas upper-class individuals who stole large sums of money or committed murder were pardoned. This goes against common sense; moreover, it violates the social contract. If citizens observe people being excused for violating the law, then their belief in the social contract breaks down. This same feeling can be applied to modern times. When the Los Angeles police officers who were filmed beating suspect Rodney King were acquitted of criminal charges in 1992, a massive riot erupted among the citizens of the community. This is a good example of the social contract breaking down when people realize that the government is failing to punish members of the community (in this case, ironically, and significantly, police officers) who have violated its rules.[10]

The concept of the social contract was likely the most important contribution of Enlightenment philosophers, but there were others. Another key concept of Enlightenment philosophers focused on democracy, emphasizing that

---

[10]Ruben Castaneda, "Rodney King Rewind: L.A. Riots, Crips, Armed Koreans and Two Heroes," *Baltimore Post-Examiner*, May 1, 2012, http://baltimore postexaminer.com/rodney-king-rewind-l-a-riots-crips-armed-koreans-and-two-heroes/2012/05/01.

every person in society should have a say via the government; specifically, they promoted the ideal of "one person, one vote." Granted, at the time they wrote, this meant one vote for each White, landowning male, and not for women, minorities, or the poor, but it was a step in the right direction. Until then, no individuals outside of the aristocracy had had any say in government or the justice system.

The Enlightenment philosophers also talked about each individual's right to life, liberty, and the pursuit of happiness. This probably sounds familiar because it is contained in the U.S. Declaration of Independence. Until the Enlightenment, individuals were not considered to have these rights; rather, they were seen as instruments for serving totalitarian governments. Although most citizens of the Western world take these rights for granted, they did not exist prior to the Age of Enlightenment.

Perhaps the most relevant concept that Enlightenment philosophers emphasized, as mentioned previously, was the idea that human beings are rational and therefore have free will. The philosophers of this age focused on the ability of individuals to consider the consequences of their actions, and they assumed that people freely choose their behavior (or lack thereof), especially in regard to criminal activity. Beccaria, the father of criminal justice, made this assumption in his formulation of what is considered to be the first bona fide theory of why people commit crime, described next.

The Classical School of Criminology

The foundation of the Classical School of criminological theorizing is typically traced to the Enlightenment philosophers, but the specific origin of the Classical School is considered to be the 1764 publication of *On Crimes and Punishments* by Italian scholar Cesare Bonesana, Marchese Beccaria (1738–1794), commonly known as Cesare Beccaria. Amazingly, he wrote this book at the age of 26 and published it anonymously, but its almost instant popularity persuaded him to come forward as the author. Due to this significant work, most experts consider Beccaria the father of criminal justice and the father of the Classical School of criminology but perhaps most importantly, the father of deterrence theory. This chapter provides a comprehensive survey of the ideas and impact of Cesare Beccaria and the Classical School.

Influences on Beccaria and His Writings

The Enlightenment philosophers had a profound impact on the social and political climate of the late 1600s and 1700s. Growing up in this time period, Beccaria was a child of the Enlightenment, and as such, he was highly influenced by the concepts and propositions that these great thinkers proposed. The Enlightenment philosophy is readily evident in Beccaria's essay, and he incorporates many of its assumptions into his work. As a student of law, Beccaria had a good background for determining what was and was not rational in legal policy. But his loyalty to the Enlightenment ideal was ever present throughout his work.

Beccaria emphasized the concept of the social contract and incorporated the idea that citizens give up certain rights in exchange for the state's or government's protection. He also asserted that acts or punishments by the government that violate the overall sense of unity will not be accepted by the populace, largely due to the need for the social contract to be a fair deal. Beccaria explicitly stated that laws are compacts of free individuals in a society. In addition, he specifically noted his appeal to the ideal of the greatest happiness shared by the greatest number, which is otherwise known as **utilitarianism**. This, too, was a focus of Enlightenment philosophers. Finally, the emphasis on free will and individual choice is key to his propositions and theorizing. Indeed, as we shall see, Enlightenment philosophy is present in virtually all of his propositions; he directly cited Hobbes, Montesquieu, and other Enlightenment thinkers in his work.[11]

---

[11]Hobbes, *Leviathan*; Charles Louis de Secondat, Baron de la Brède et de Montesquieu, *The Spirit of the Laws* (1748; New York: Library of Liberal Arts, 1949).

Beccaria's Proposed Reforms and Ideas of Justice

When Beccaria wrote, authoritarian governments ruled the justice systems, which were actually quite unjust during that time. For example, it was not uncommon for a person who stole a loaf of bread in order to feed his or her family to be imprisoned for life or executed. A good example of this is seen in the story of Victor Hugo's *Les Misérables*: The protagonist, Jean Valjean, gets a lengthy prison sentence for stealing food for his starving loved ones. On the other hand, a judge might excuse a person who had committed several murders because the confessed killer was from a prominent family.

Beccaria sought to rid the justice system of such arbitrary acts on the part of individual judges. Specifically, Beccaria claimed in his essay that "only laws can decree punishments for crimes . . . judges in criminal cases cannot have the authority to interpret laws."[12] Rather, he believed that legislatures, elected by the citizens, must define crimes and the specific punishment for each criminal offense. One of his main goals was to prevent a single person from assigning an overly harsh sentence to a defendant and allowing another defendant in a similar case to walk free for the same criminal act, which was quite common at that time. Thus, Beccaria's writings call for a set punishment for a given offense without consideration of the presiding judge's personal attitudes or the defendant's background.

Beccaria believed that "the true measure of crimes is namely the harm done to society."[13] Thus, anyone at all who committed a given act against the society should face the same consequence. He was very clear that the law should impose a specific punishment for a given act, regardless of the circumstances. One aspect of this principle was that it ignored the intent the offender had in committing the crime. Obviously, this principle is not followed in most modern justice systems; intent often plays a key role in the charges and sentencing of defendants in many types of crimes. Most notably, the different degrees of homicide in most U.S. jurisdictions include first-degree murder, which requires proof of planning or *malice aforethought*; second-degree murder, which typically involves no evidence of planning but rather a spontaneous act of killing; and various degrees of manslaughter, which generally include some level of provocation on the part of the victim. This is just one example of the importance of intent, legally known as ***mens rea*** (literally, guilty mind), in most modern justice systems. Many types of offending are graded by degree of intent as opposed to being categorized based only on the act itself, known legally as ***actus reus*** (literally, guilty act). Beccaria's propositions focus on only the *actus reus* because he claimed that an act against society was just as harmful, regardless of the intent, or *mens rea*. Despite his recommendations, most societies factor in the intent of the offender in criminal activity. Still, his proposal that *a given act should always receive the same punishment* certainly seemed to represent a significant improvement over the arbitrary punishments handed out by the regimes and justice systems of the 1700s.

▲ **Image 2.3**   Cesare Beccaria (1738–1794).

---

[12]Cesare Beccaria, *On Crimes and Punishments*, trans. Henry Paolucci (New York: MacMillan, 1963), 14.

[13]Ibid., 64.

Another important reform that Beccaria proposed was to do away with practices that were common in "justice" systems of the time (the word *justice* is in quotation marks because they were largely systems of injustice). Specifically, Beccaria claimed that secret accusations should not be permitted; rather, defendants should be able to confront and cross-examine witnesses. Writing about secret accusations, he said, "Their customary use makes men false and deceptive"; he asked, "Who can defend himself against calumny when it comes armed with tyranny's strongest shield, *secrecy*?"[14] Although some modern countries still accept and use secret accusations and disallow the cross-examination of witnesses, Beccaria set the standard in guaranteeing such rights to defendants in the United States and most Western societies.

In addition, Beccaria argued that torture should not be used against defendants:

A cruelty consecrated by the practice of most nations is torture of the accused . . . either to make him confess the crime or to clear up contradictory statements, or to discover accomplices . . . to discover other crimes of which he might be guilty but of which he is not accused.[15]

Although some countries, such as Israel and Mexico, currently allow the use of torture for eliciting information or confessions, most countries abstain from the practice. There has been wide discussion about a memo, written by former U.S. attorney general Alberto Gonzales when he was President George W. Bush's lead counsel at the White House, claiming that the U.S. military could use torture against terrorist suspects. However, at least in terms of domestic criminal defendants, the United States has traditionally agreed with Beccaria, who believed that any information or oaths obtained under torture are relatively worthless. Beccaria's belief in the worthlessness of torture is further seen in his statement that "it is useless to reveal the author of a crime that lies deeply buried in darkness."[16]

It is likely that Beccaria believed the use of torture was one of the worst aspects of the criminal justice systems of his time and a horrible manifestation of the barbarousness common in the Middle Ages. This is seen in his further elaboration of torture:

This infamous crucible of truth is a still-standing memorial of the ancient and barbarous legislation of a time when trials by fire and by boiling water, as well as the uncertain outcomes of duels, were called "judgments of God."[17]

Beccaria also expressed his doubt of the relevance of any information received via torture:

Thus the impression of pain may become so great that, filling the entire sensory capacity of the tortured person, it leaves him free only to choose what for the moment is the shortest way of escape from pain.[18]

As Beccaria saw it, the policy implications from such use of torture are that "of two men, equally innocent or equally guilty, the strong and courageous will be acquitted, the weak and timid condemned."[19]

---

[14]Ibid., 25–26.

[15]Ibid., 30.

[16]Ibid., 30–31.

[17]Ibid., 31.

[18]Ibid., 32.

[19]Ibid.

Beccaria also claimed that defendants should be tried by fellow citizens or peers, not by judges:

> I consider an excellent law that which assigns popular jurors, taken by lot, to assist the chief judge . . . each man ought to be judged by his peers.[20]

It is clear that Beccaria felt that the responsibility of determining the facts of a case should be placed in the hands of more than one person, a belief driven by his Enlightenment beliefs about democratic philosophy—namely, that citizens of the society should have a voice in judging the facts and deciding the verdicts of criminal cases. This proposition is representative of Beccaria's overall leaning toward fairness and democratic processes, which Enlightenment philosophers shared.

Today, U.S. citizens often take for granted the right to have a trial by a jury of their peers. It may surprise some readers to know that some modern, developed countries have not provided this right. For example, in the 1990s, Russia held jury trials for the first time in 85 years. When Vladimir Lenin was in charge of Russia, he had banished jury trials. Over the course of several decades, the bench trials in Russia produced a 99.6% rate of convictions. This means that virtually every person in Russia who was accused of a crime was found guilty. Given the relatively high percentage of defendants found to be innocent of crimes in the United States—not to mention the numerous people who have been released from death row after DNA analysis showed that they were not guilty—it is rather frightening to think of how many falsely accused individuals have been convicted and unjustly sentenced in Russia over the past century.

Another important aspect of Beccaria's reforms involved making the justice system, particularly its laws and decisions, more public and better understood. This fits the Enlightenment assumption that individuals are rational: If people know the consequences of their actions, they will act accordingly. Beccaria stated that "when the number of those who can understand the sacred code of laws and hold it in their hands increases, the frequency of crimes will be found to decrease."[21] At the time, the laws were often unknown to the populace, in part because of widespread illiteracy but perhaps more as a result of the failure to publicly declare what the laws were. Even when laws were posted, they were often in languages that the citizens did not read or speak (e.g., Latin). Thus, Beccaria stressed the need for society to ensure that its citizens be educated about what the laws are; he believed that this alone would lead to a significant decrease in law violations.

Furthermore, Beccaria believed that the important stages and decision-making processes of any justice system should be made public knowledge rather than being held in secret or carried out behind closed doors. He stated, "Punishment . . . must be essentially public."[22] This has a highly democratic and Enlightenment ring to it, in the sense that citizens of a society are assumed to have the right to know what vital judgments are being made. After all, in a democratic society, citizens give the government the profound responsibility of distributing punishment for crimes against the society. The citizens are entitled to know what decisions their government officials are making, particularly regarding justice. Besides providing knowledge and understanding of what is going on, this sets in place a form of checks and balances on what is happening. Furthermore, the public nature of trials and punishments inherently produces a form of deterrence for those individuals who may be considering criminal activity.

One of Beccaria's most profound and important proposed reforms is one of the least noted. Beccaria said, "The surest but most difficult way to prevent crimes is by perfecting education."[23] We know of no other review of his work that notes this hypothesis, which is quite amazing, because most of the reviews are done for an educational

---

[20]Ibid., 21.

[21]Ibid., 17.

[22]Ibid., 99.

[23]Ibid., 98.

audience. Furthermore, this emphasis on education makes sense, given Beccaria's focus on knowledge of laws and consequences of criminal activity as well as his focus on deterrence.

Beccaria's Ideas regarding the Death Penalty

Another primary area of Beccaria's reforms dealt with the use—and, in his day, the abuse—of the death penalty. First, let it be said that Beccaria was against the use of capital punishment. (Interestingly, he was not against corporal punishment, which he explicitly stated was appropriate for violent offenders.) Perhaps this was due to the times in which he wrote, in which a large number of people were put to death, often by harsh methods. Still, Beccaria had several rational reasons for why he felt the death penalty was not an efficient and effective punishment.

First, Beccaria argued that the use of capital punishment inherently violated the social contract:

Is it conceivable that the least sacrifice of each person's liberty should include sacrifice of the greatest of all goods, life? . . . The punishment of death, therefore, is not a right, for I have demonstrated that it cannot be such; but it is the war of a nation against a citizen whose destruction it judges to be necessary or useful.[24]

The second reason that Beccaria felt that the death penalty was an inappropriate form of punishment was along the same lines: If the government endorsed the death of a citizen, it would provide a negative example to the rest of society. He said, "The death penalty cannot be useful, because of the example of barbarity it gives men."[25] Although some studies show some evidence that use of the death penalty in the United States deters crime,[26] most studies show no effect or even a positive effect on homicides.[27] Researchers have called this increase of homicides after executions the **brutalization effect**, and a similar phenomenon can be seen at numerous sporting events (boxing matches, hockey games, soccer or football games, etc.) when violence breaks out among spectators. There have even been incidents in recent years at youth sporting events.

To further complicate the possibly contradictory effects of capital punishment, some analyses show that both deterrence and brutalization occur at the same time for different types of murder or crime, depending on the level of planning or spontaneity of a given act. For example, a sophisticated analysis of homicide data from California

---

[24]Ibid., 45.

[25]Ibid., 50.

[26]For a review and analysis, respectively, showing deterrent effects of capital punishment, see Charles F. Manski and John V. Pepper, "Deterrence and the Death Penalty: Partial Identification Analysis Using Repeated Cross Sections," *Journal of Quantitative Criminology* 29 (2013): 123–41; and Steven Stack, "The Effect of Publicized Executions on Homicides in California," *Journal of Crime and Justice* 21 (1998): 1–16. See also Isaac Ehrlich, "Capital Punishment and Deterrence," *Journal of Political Economy* 85 (1977): 741–88; Isaac Ehrlich, "The Deterrent Effect of Capital Punishment: A Question of Life and Death," *American Economic Review* 65 (1975): 397–417; Stephen K. Layson, "Homicide and Deterrence: A Reexamination of United States Time-Series Evidence," *Southern Economic Journal* 52 (1985): 68–89; David P. Phillips, "The Deterrent Effect of Capital Punishment: Evidence on an Old Controversy," *American Journal of Sociology* 86 (1980): 139–48; Steven Stack, "Execution Publicity and Homicide in South Carolina," *Sociological Quarterly* 31 (1990): 599–611; Steven Stack, "The Impact of Publicized Executions on Homicide," *Criminal Justice and Behavior* 22 (1995): 172–86; and Steven Stack, "Publicized Executions and Homicide, 1950–1980," *American Sociological Review* 52 (1987): 532–40.

[27]William C. Bailey, "The Deterrent Effect of the Death Penalty for Murder in California," *Southern California Law Review* 52 (1979): 743–64; William C. Bailey and Ruth D. Peterson, "Murder and Capital Punishment: A Monthly Time Series Analysis of Execution Publicity," *American Sociological Review* 54 (1989): 722–43; William J. Bowers, "The Effect of Execution Is Brutalization, Not Deterrence," *Capital Punishment: Legal and Social Science Approaches*, ed. Kenneth C. Haas and James A. Inciardi (Newbury Park, CA: Sage, 1988), 49–89; John K. Cochran, Mitchell Chamlin, and Mark Seth, "Deterrence or Brutalization? An Impact Assessment of Oklahoma's Return to Capital Punishment," *Criminology* 32 (1994): 107–34; James A. Fox and Michael L. Radelet, "Persistent Flaws in Econometric Studies of the Deterrent Effect of the Death Penalty," *Loyola of Los Angeles Law Review* 23 (1990): 29–44; David Lester, "The Deterrent Effect of Execution on Homicide," *Psychological Reports* 64 (1989): 306–14. For a review, see William C. Bailey and Ruth D. Peterson, "Capital Punishment, Homicide, and Deterrence: An Assessment of the Evidence," in *Studying and Preventing Homicide*, ed. M. Dwayne Smith and Margaret A. Zahn (Thousand Oaks, CA: Sage, 1999), 223–45.

examined the effects of a high-profile execution in 1992, largely because it was the first one in the state in 25 years.[28] As predicted, the authors found that nonstranger felony murders, which typically involve some planning, significantly decreased after the high-profile execution, whereas the level of argument-based, stranger murders, which are typically more spontaneous, significantly increased during the same period. Thus, both deterrence and brutalization effects were observed at the same time and location following a given execution.

Another primary reason that Beccaria was against the use of capital punishment was that he believed it was an ineffective deterrent. Specifically, he thought that a punishment that was quick, such as the death penalty, could not be as effective a deterrent as a drawn-out penalty. He stated, "It is not the intensity of punishment that has the greatest effect on the human spirit, but its duration."[29] It is likely that many readers can relate to this type of argument, not that they necessarily agree with it; the idea of spending the rest of one's life in a cell is a very scary concept to most people. To many people, such a concept is more frightening than death, which supports Beccaria's idea that the duration of the punishment may be more of a deterrent than the short, albeit extremely intense, punishment of execution.

Beccaria's Concept of Deterrence and the Three Key Elements of Punishment

Beccaria is generally considered the father of deterrence theory for good reason. Beccaria was the first known scholar to write a work that summarized such extravagant ideas regarding the direction of human behavior toward choice as opposed to fate or destiny. Prior to his work, the common wisdom on the issue of human destiny was that it was chosen by the gods or God. At that time, governments and societies generally believed that people are born either good or bad. Beccaria, as a child of the Enlightenment, defied this belief in proclaiming that people freely choose their destinies and thus their decisions to commit or not commit criminal behavior.

Beccaria suggested three characteristics of punishment that make a significant difference in whether an individual decides to commit a criminal act: celerity (swiftness), certainty, and severity.

Swiftness

The first of these characteristics was celerity, which we will refer to as **swiftness of punishment**. Beccaria saw two reasons why swiftness of punishment is important. At the time he wrote, some defendants were spending many years awaiting trial. Often, this was a longer time than they would have been locked up as punishment for their alleged offenses, even if the maximum penalty had been imposed. As Beccaria stated, "The more promptly and the more closely punishment follows upon the commission of a crime, the more just and useful will it be."[30] Thus, the first reason that Beccaria recommended swiftness of punishment was to reform a system that was slow to respond to offenders.

The second reason that Beccaria emphasized swift sentencing was related to the deterrence aspect of punishment. A swift trial and swift punishment were important, Beccaria said, "because of privation of liberty, being itself a punishment, should not precede the sentence."[31] He felt that this "privation of liberty" was not only unjust, in the sense that some of these defendants would not have been incarcerated for such a long period even if they had been convicted and sentenced to the maximum for the charges they were accused of committing, but also detrimental because the individual would not link the sanction with the violation(s) committed. Specifically,

---

[28]John K. Cochran and Mitchell B. Chamlin, "Deterrence and Brutalization: The Dual Effects of Executions," *Justice Quarterly* (2000): 685–706; Eric G. Lambert et al., "The Impact of Information on Death Penalty Support, Revisited," *Crime and Delinquency* 57 (2011): 572–99.

[29]Beccaria, *Crimes and Punishments*, 46–47.

[30]Ibid., 55.

[31]Ibid., 55.

Beccaria believed that people build an association between the pains of punishment and their criminal acts. He asserted the following:

> Promptness of punishments is more useful because when the length of time that passes between the punishment and the misdeed is less, so much the stronger and more lasting in the human mind is the association of these two ideas, crime and punishment; they then come insensibly to be considered, one as the cause, the other as the necessary inevitable effect. It has been demonstrated that the association of ideas is the cement that forms the entire fabric of the human intellect.[32]

An analogy can be made to training animals or children; you have to catch them in the act, or soon after, or the punishment doesn't matter because the offender doesn't know why he or she is being punished. Ultimately, Beccaria argued that, for both reform and deterrence reasons, punishment should occur quickly after the act. Despite the commonsense aspects of making punishments swift, this has not been examined by modern empirical research and therefore is the most neglected of the three elements of punishment Beccaria emphasized.

Case Study: Deborah Jeane Palfrey

▲ **Image 2.4**   Deborah Jeane Palfrey, known as the "DC Madam," committed suicide in jail before being sentenced. Her case reveals the potentially powerful effects of formal sanctions on individuals' decision making.

SOURCE: © Jacquelyn Martin / ASSOCIATED PRESS

Deborah Jeane Palfrey, known as the "DC Madam," was brought up on charges of racketeering and money laundering related to running a prostitution ring in Washington, DC, and surrounding suburbs in Maryland and Virginia. The clientele of this prostitution ring included some notable politicians, such as state senators and other elected officials. Palfrey faced a maximum of 55 years in prison but likely would have received far less time had she not committed suicide before her sentencing. Her body was found in a storage facility at her mother's home in Tarpon Springs, Florida.

News reports revealed that she had served time before (for prostitution). Author Dan Moldea told *Time* magazine that she had contacted him for a book he was working on and told him "she had done time once before . . . and it damned near killed her. She said there was enormous stress—it made her sick, she couldn't take it, and she wasn't going to let that happen again."[33] The situation could have been worsened by the heightened media attention this case received; while most prostitution cases are handled by local or state courts, this one was handled by federal courts because it concerned Washington, DC.

---

[32] Ibid., 56.

[33] Adam Zagorin, "D.C. Madam: Suicide before Prison," *Time*, May 1, 2008, http://www.time.com/time/nation/article/0,8599,1736687,00.html.

It is quite likely that the impending maximum prison sentence led her to take her own life, given what she had said to Moldea. This shows the type of deterrent effect that jail or prison can have on an individual—in this case, possibly leading her to choose death over serving time. Ironically, Palfrey had commented to the press, after the suicide of a former employee in her prostitution network—Brandy Britton, who hanged herself before going to trial—"I guess I'm made of something that Brandy Britton wasn't made of."[34] It seems that Palfrey had the same concerns as Britton, and she ended up contradicting her bold statement when she ended her own life.

> *"She had done time once before . . . and it damned near killed her. She said there was enormous stress—it made her sick, she couldn't take it, and she wasn't going to let that happen again."*

This case study provides an example of the profound effects legal sanctions can have on individuals. Legal sanctions are not meant to inspire offenders to end their lives, but this case does illustrate the potential deterrent effects of facing punishment from the legal system. We can see this on a smaller scale when a speeding driver's heart rate increases at the sight of a highway patrol or other police vehicle (which studies show happens to most drivers). Even though this offense would result in only a fine, it is a good example of deterrence in our everyday lives. We will revisit the Palfrey case at the conclusion of this chapter, after you have had a chance to review some of the theoretical propositions and concepts that make up deterrence theory.

On a related note, a special report from the U.S. Department of Justice (DOJ), Bureau of Justice Statistics (BJS), concludes that the suicide rate has been far higher among jail inmates than among prison inmates.[35] Specifically, suicides in jails have tended over the past few decades to occur 300% (or 3 times) more often than among prison inmates.

A likely reason for this phenomenon is that many persons arrested and/or awaiting trial (which is generally the status of those in jail) have more to lose, such as their relationships with family, friends, and employers, than do the typical chronic offenders that end up in prison. Specifically, many of the individuals picked up for prostitution and other relatively minor, albeit embarrassing, offenses are of the middle- and upper-class mentality and, thus, are ill equipped to face the real-world consequences of their arrest. The good news is, this same DOJ report showed that suicides in both jails and prisons have decreased during the past few decades, likely due to better policies in correctional settings regarding persons considered at "high risk" for suicide.

Think About It

1. Do you think that some of the clientele (e.g., notable politicians) should have also been charged for a criminal offense?

2. Do you think it made a difference that this case was handled by federal courts rather than local or state courts?

3. Do you think prostitution should be legal?

---

[34] Ibid.

[35] Christopher J. Mumola, *Suicide and Homicide in State Prisons and Local Jails* (Washington, DC: U.S. Department of Justice, Office of Justice Programs, August 2005). http://bjs.gov/content/pub/pdf/shsplj.pdf.

Certainty

The second characteristic that Beccaria felt was vital to the effectiveness of deterrence was **certainty of punishment**. Beccaria considered this the most important quality of punishment: "Even the least of evils, when they are certain, always terrify men's minds."[36] He also said, "The certainty of punishment, even if it be moderate, will always make a stronger impression than the fear of another which is more terrible but combined with the hope of impunity."[37] As scientific studies later showed, Beccaria was accurate in his assumption that perceived certainty or risk of punishment was the most important aspect of deterrence.[38]

It is interesting to note that certainty is the least likely characteristic of punishment to be enhanced in modern criminal justice policy. Over the past few decades, the likelihood that criminals will be caught and arrested has not increased. Law enforcement officials have been able to clear only about 21% of known felonies. Such clearance rates are based on the rate at which known suspects are apprehended for crimes reported to police. Law enforcement officials are no better at solving serious crimes known to police (CKP) than they were in past decades, despite increased knowledge and resources put toward solving such crimes.

Severity

The third characteristic that Beccaria emphasized was **severity of punishment**. Specifically, Beccaria claimed that, for a punishment to be effective, the possible penalty must outweigh the potential benefits (e.g., financial payoff) of a given crime. However, this criterion came with a caveat. This aspect of punishment was perhaps the most complicated part of Beccaria's philosophy, primarily because he thought that too much severity would lead to more crime, but the punishment must exceed any benefits expected from the crime. Beccaria said the following:

> For a punishment to attain its end, the evil which it inflicts has only to exceed the advantage derivable from the crime; in this excess of evil one should include the . . . loss of the good which the crime might have produced. All beyond this is superfluous and for that reason tyrannical.[39]

Beccaria made clear in this statement that punishments should equal or outweigh any benefits of a crime to deter individuals from engaging in such acts. However, he also explicitly stated that any punishments that largely exceed the reasonable punishment for a given crime are inhumane and may lead to further criminality.

A modern example of how punishments can be taken to an extreme and thereby cause more crime rather than deter it is the current three-strikes-you're-out approach to sentencing. Such laws have become common in many states, such as California. In such jurisdictions, individuals who have committed two prior felonies can be sentenced to life imprisonment for committing a crime, even a nonviolent crime, that the state statutes consider a *serious felony*. Such laws have been known to drive some relatively minor property offenders to become violent when they know that they will be incarcerated for life when they are caught. A number of offenders have even wounded or killed people to avoid apprehension, knowing that they would face life imprisonment even for a relatively minor property offense. In a recent study, the authors analyzed the impact of three-strikes laws in 188 large cities in the 25 states

---

[36]Beccaria, *Crimes and Punishments*, 58.

[37]Ibid., 58.

[38]For a good recent review, see Bruce Jacobs and Alex R. Piquero, "Boundary-Crossing in Perceptual Deterrence: Investigating the Linkages between Sanction Severity, Sanction Certainty, and Offending," *International Journal of Offender Therapy & Comparative Criminology* 57 (2013): 792–812.

[39]Beccaria, *Crimes and Punishments*, 43.

that have such laws and concluded that there was no significant reduction in crime rates as a result. Furthermore, the areas with three-strikes laws typically had higher rates of homicide.[40]

Ultimately, Beccaria's philosophy on the three characteristics of good punishment in terms of deterrence—swiftness, certainty, and severity—is still highly respected and followed in most Western criminal justice systems. Despite its contemporary flaws and caveats, perhaps no other traditional framework is so widely adopted. With only one exception—namely, his proposal that a given act should always be punished in exactly the same way (see the next chapter)—Beccaria's concepts and propositions are still considered the ideal in virtually all Western criminal justice systems.

Beccaria's Conceptualization of Specific and General Deterrence

Beccaria also defined two identifiable forms of deterrence: specific and general. Although these two forms of deterrence tend to overlap in most sentences given by judges, they can be distinguished in terms of the intended target of the punishment. Sometimes the emphasis is clearly on one or the other, as Beccaria noted in his work.

Although Beccaria did not coin the terms *specific deterrence* and *general deterrence*, he clearly made the case that both are important. Regarding punishment, he said, "The purpose can only be to prevent the criminal from inflicting new injuries on its citizens and to deter others from similar acts."[41] The first portion of this statement—preventing the criminal from reoffending—focuses on the defendant and the defendant alone, regardless of any possible offending by others. Punishments that focus primarily on the individual are considered specific deterrence, also referred to as special or individual deterrence. This concept is appropriately labeled because the emphasis is on the specific individual who offended. On the other hand, the latter portion of Beccaria's quotation emphasizes the deterrence of others, regardless of whether the individual criminal is deterred. Punishments that focus primarily on other potential criminals and not on the actual criminal are referred to as general deterrence.

Readers may wonder how a punishment would not be inherently both a specific and general deterrent. After all, in today's society, virtually all criminal punishments given to individuals (i.e., specific deterrence) are prescribed in court, a public venue, so people are somewhat aware of the sanctions (i.e., general deterrence). However, when Beccaria wrote in the 18th century, much if not most sentencing was done behind closed doors and was not known to the public and had no way to deter other potential offenders. Therefore, Beccaria saw much utility in letting the public know what punishments were handed out for given crimes. This fulfilled the goal of general deterrence, which was essentially scaring others into not committing such criminal acts, while it also furthered his reforms by letting the public know whether fair and balanced justice was being administered.

Despite the obvious overlap, there are identifiable distinctions between specific and general deterrence seen in modern sentencing strategy. For example, some judges have chosen to hand out punishments to defendants in which they are obligated, as a condition of their probation or parole, to walk along their towns' main streets while wearing signs that say "Convicted Child Molester" or "Convicted Shoplifter." Other cities have implemented policies in which pictures and identifying information of those individuals who are arrested, such as prostitutes or men who solicit them, are put in newspapers or placed on billboards.

These punishment strategies are not likely to be much of a specific deterrent. Having now been labeled, these individuals may actually be psychologically encouraged to engage in doing what the public expects them to do. The specific deterrent effect may not be particularly strong. However, authorities are hoping for a strong general

---

[40]Tomislav V. Kovandzic, John J. Sloan III, and Lynne M. Vieraitis, "'Striking Out' as Crime Reduction Policy: The Impact of 'Three-Strikes' Laws on Crime Rates in the U.S. Cities," *Justice Quarterly* 21 (2004): 207–40. See also Steven N. Durlauf and Daniel S. Nagin, "Imprisonment and Crime: Can Both Be Reduced?," *Criminology and Public Policy* 10 (2011): 13–54.

[41]Ibid., 42.

deterrent effect in most of these cases. They expect that many of the people who see these sign-laden individuals on the streets or in public pictures are going to be frightened away from engaging in similar activity.

There are also numerous diversion programs, particularly for juvenile, first-time, and minor offenders, which seek to punish offenders without engaging them in public hearings or trials. The goal of such programs is to hold the individuals accountable and have them fulfill certain obligations without having them dragged through the system, which is often public. Thus, the goal is obviously to instill specific deterrence without using the person as a poster child for the public, which obviously negates any aspects of general deterrence.

Although most judges invoke both specific and general deterrence in many of the criminal sentences that they hand out, there are notable cases in which either specific or general deterrence is emphasized, sometimes exclusively. Ultimately, Beccaria seemed to emphasize general deterrence and overall crime prevention, as suggested by his statement that "it is better to prevent crimes than to punish them. This is the ultimate end of every good legislation."[42] This claim implies that it is better to deter potential offenders before they offend rather than imposing sanctions on already convicted criminals. Beccaria's emphasis on prevention (over reaction) and general deterrence is also evident in his claim that education is likely the best way to reduce crime. After all, the more educated an individual is regarding the law and potential punishments, as well as public cases in which offenders have been punished, the less likely he or she will be to engage in such activity. Beccaria's identification of the differential emphases in terms of punishment was a key element in his work that continues to be important in modern times.

A Summary of Beccaria's Ideas and His Influence on Policy

Ultimately, Beccaria summarized his ideas on reforms and deterrence with this statement:

> In order for punishment not to be, in every instance, an act of violence of one or of many against a private citizen, it must be essentially public, prompt, necessary, the least possible in the given circumstances, proportionate to the crimes, dictated by the laws.[43]

In this statement, Beccaria is saying that the processing and punishment administered by justice systems must be known to the public, which delegates to the state the authority to make such decisions. Furthermore, he asserted that the punishment must be appropriately swift, certain (i.e., necessary), and appropriately severe, which fits his concept of deterrence. Finally, he reiterated the need to administer the same punishment every time for a given criminal act, as opposed to having arbitrary punishments imposed by one judge. These are just some of many ideas that Beccaria proposed, but he apparently saw these points as being the most important.

Although we, as U.S. citizens, take for granted the rights proposed by Beccaria, they were quite unique concepts during the 18th century. In fact, the ideas proposed by Beccaria were so unusual and revolutionary then that he published his book anonymously. It is obvious that Beccaria was considerably worried about being accused of blasphemy by the church and of being persecuted by governments for his views.

Regarding the first claim, Beccaria was right; the Roman Catholic Church excommunicated Beccaria when it became known that he wrote the book. In fact, his book remained on the list of condemned works until relatively recently (the 1960s). On the other hand, government officials of the time surprisingly embraced his work. The Italian government and most European and other world officials, particularly dictators, embraced his work as well. Beccaria was invited to visit many other country capitals, even those of the most authoritarian states at that time, to help reform their criminal justice systems. For example, Beccaria was invited to meet with Catherine the Great, the czarina of Russia, during the late 1700s, to help revise and improve Russia's justice system. Most historical records

---

[42]Beccaria, *Crimes and Punishments*, 93.

[43]Ibid., 99.

suggest that Beccaria was not a great diplomat or representative of his ideas, largely because he was not physically or socially adequate for such endeavors. However, his ideas were strong and stood on their own merit.

Dictators and authoritarian governments may have liked Beccaria's reform framework so much because it explicitly stated that treason was the most serious crime. He said this:

> The first class of crime, which are the gravest because most injurious, are those known as crimes of *lese majesty* [high treason]. . . . Every crime . . . injures society, but it is not every crime that aims at its immediate destruction.[44]

According to Enlightenment philosophy, violations of law are criminal acts not only against the direct victims but also against the entire society because they break the social contract. As Beccaria stated, the most heinous criminal acts are those that directly violate the social contract, which would be treason and espionage. In Beccaria's reform proposals, dictators may have seen a chance to pacify revolutionary citizens who might be aiming to overthrow their governments. In many cases, reforms were only a temporary solution. After all, the American Revolution occurred in the 1770s, the French Revolution occurred in the 1780s, and other revolutions occurred soon after this period.

Governments that tried to apply Beccaria's ideas to the letter experienced problems, but generally, most European (and American) societies that incorporated his ideas had fairer and more democratic justice systems than they'd had before Beccaria. This is why, to this day, he is considered the father of criminal justice.

The Impact of Beccaria's Work on Other Theorists

Beccaria's work had an immediate impact on the political and philosophical state of affairs in the late 18th century. He was invited to many other countries to reform their justice systems, and his propositions and theoretical model of deterrence were incorporated into many of the new constitutions of countries, most of them formed after major revolutions. The most notable of these was the Constitution and Bill of Rights of the United States.

It is quite obvious that the many founding documents constructed before and during the American Revolution in the late 1700s were heavily influenced by Beccaria and other Enlightenment philosophers. Specifically, the concept that the U.S. government is "of the people, by the people, and for the people" makes it clear that the Enlightenment idea of democracy and voice in government is of utmost importance. Another clear example is the emphasis on due process and individual rights in the U.S. Bill of Rights. Among the important concepts derived from Beccaria's work are the right to trial by jury, the right to confront and cross-examine witnesses, the right to a speedy trial, and the right to be informed about decisions of the justice system (charges, pleas, trials, verdicts, sentences, etc.).

The impact of Beccaria's ideas on the working ideology of our system of justice cannot be overstated. The public nature of our justice system comes from Beccaria, as does the emphasis on deterrence. The United States, as well as virtually all Western countries, incorporates in its justice system the certainty and severity of punishment to reduce crime. This system of deterrence remains the dominant model in criminal justice: The goal is to deter potential and previous offenders from committing crime by enforcing punishments that will make them reconsider the next time they think about engaging in such activity. This model assumes a rationally thinking human being, as described by Enlightenment philosophy, who can learn from past experiences or from seeing others punished for offenses that he or she is rationally thinking about committing. Thus, Beccaria's work has had a profound impact on the existing philosophy and workings of most justice systems throughout the world.

Beyond this, Beccaria also had a large impact on further theorizing about human decision making related to committing criminal behavior. One of the more notable theorists inspired by Beccaria's ideas was Jeremy Bentham (1748–1832) of England, who has become a well-known classical theorist in his own right, perhaps because he

---

[44]Ibid., 68.

▲ **Image 2.5**   Jeremy Bentham, often credited as the founder of University College London, insisted that his body be put on display there after his death. You can visit a replica of it today.

SOURCE: © Popperfoto / Popperfoto / Getty Images

helped spread the Enlightenment/Beccarian philosophy to Britain. His influence in the development of classical theorizing is debated, and a number of major texts do not cover his writings at all.[45] Although he did not add a significant amount of theorizing beyond Beccaria's propositions regarding reform and deterrence, Bentham did further refine the ideas presented by previous theorists, and his legacy is well known.

One of the more important contributions of Bentham was the concept of *hedonistic calculus*, which is essentially the weighing of pleasure versus pain. This, of course, is strongly based on the Enlightenment/Beccarian concept of rational choice and utility. After all, if the expected pain outweighs the expected benefit of doing a given act, the rational individual is far less likely to do it. On the other hand, if the expected pleasure outweighs the expected pain, a rational person will engage in the act. Bentham listed a set of criteria that he thought would go into the decision making of a rational individual. An analogy would be an imagined two-sided balance scale on which the pros and cons of crimes are considered, and then the individual makes a rational decision about whether to commit the crime.

Beyond the idea of hedonistic calculus, Bentham's contributions to the overall assumptions of classical theorizing did not significantly revise the theoretical model. Perhaps the most important contribution he made to the Classical School was helping to popularize the framework in Britain. In fact, Bentham became better known for his design of a prison structure, known as the *panopticon*, which was used in several countries and in early Pennsylvania penitentiaries. This model of prisons used a type of wagon wheel design, in which a post at the center allowed 360-degree visual observation of the various "spokes"—that is, hallways that contained all of the inmate cells.

The Neoclassical School of Criminology

A number of governments, including the newly formed United States, incorporated Beccaria's concepts and propositions in the development of their justice systems. The government that most strictly applied Beccaria's ideas—France after the French Revolution of the late 1780s—found that it worked pretty well except for one concept. Beccaria believed that every individual who committed a certain act against the law should be punished the same way. Although equality in punishment sounds like a good philosophy, the French realized very quickly that not everyone should be punished equally for a certain act.

The French system found that giving a first-time offender the same sentence as a repeat offender did not make much sense, especially when the first-time offender was a juvenile. Furthermore, there were many circumstances in which a defendant appeared to be unmalicious in doing an act, such as when he or she had limited mental capacity or acted out of necessity. Perhaps most important, Beccaria's framework specifically

---

[45]See, for example, Thomas J. Bernard, Jeffrey B. Snipes, and Alexander L. Gerould, *Vold's Theoretical Criminology*, 6th ed. (Oxford: Oxford University Press, 2009).

dismissed the intent (i.e., *mens rea*) of criminal offenders while focusing only on the harm done to society by a given act (i.e., *actus reus*). French society, as well as most modern societies such as the United States, deviated from Beccaria's framework in taking the intent of offenders into account, often in a very important way, such as in determining what type of charges should be filed against those accused of homicide. Therefore, a new school of thought regarding the classical or deterrence model developed, which became known as the **Neoclassical School** of criminology.

The only significant difference between the Neoclassical School and the Classical School of criminology is that the Neoclassical (*neo* means "new") School takes into account contextual circumstances of the individual or situation, allowing for increases or decreases in the punishment. For example, would a society want to punish a 12-year-old first-time offender the same way they would punish a 35-year-old who shoplifted the same item a second time? Does a society want to punish a mentally challenged person for stealing a car once as much as they would punish a person without disabilities who has been convicted of stealing more than a dozen cars? The answer is probably not—or at least, that is what most modern criminal justice authorities have decided, including those in the United States.

▲ **Image 2.6**   Charles Darwin (1809–1882), author of evolutionary theory.

SOURCE: © Getty Images / Hulton Archive / Stringer

This was also the conclusion of French society, which quickly realized that, in this respect, Beccaria's system was neither fair nor effective in terms of deterrence. They came to acknowledge that circumstantial factors play an important part in how malicious or guilty a certain defendant is in committing a given crime. The French revised their laws to take into account both mitigating and aggravating circumstances. This neoclassical concept became the standard in all Western justice systems.

The United States also followed this model and considers contextual factors in virtually all of its charges and sentencing decisions. For example, juvenile defendants are actually processed in completely different courts. Furthermore, defendants who are first-time offenders are generally given options for diversion programs or probation as long as their offenses are not serious.

While the Neoclassical School added an important caveat to the previously important Classical School, it assumes virtually all other concepts and propositions of the Classical School: The social contract, due process rights, and the idea that rational beings will be deterred by the certainty, swiftness, and severity of punishment. This neoclassical framework had, and continues to have, an extremely important impact on the world.

Loss of Dominance of Classical and Neoclassical Theory

For about 100 years after Beccaria wrote his book, the Classical and Neoclassical Schools were dominant in criminological theorizing. During this time, most governments—especially those in the Western world—shifted their justice frameworks toward the neoclassical model. This has not changed even in modern times. For example, when officials attempt to reduce certain illegal behaviors, they increase the punishments or put more effort into catching relevant offenders.

However, the classical and neoclassical frameworks lost dominance among academics and scientists in the 19th century and especially after Darwin's publication in 1859 of *The Origin of Species*, which introduced the concept of evolution and natural selection. This perspective shed new light on other influences on human behavior beyond free will and rational choice (e.g., genetics, psychological deficits). Despite this shift in emphasis among academic and scientific circles, the actual workings of the justice systems of most Western societies still retain the framework of classical and neoclassical models as their model of justice.

Three-strikes laws are an example; others include police department gang units and injunctions that condemn any observed loitering by or gathering among gang members in a specified region. Furthermore, some jurisdictions, such as California, have created gang enhancements for sentencing; after the jury decides whether the defendant is guilty of a given crime, it then considers whether the person is a gang member. If a jury in California decides that the defendant is a gang member, which is usually determined by evidence provided by local police gang units, it automatically adds more time to any sentence the judge gives. These are just some examples of how Western justice systems still rely primarily on deterrence of criminal activity through increased enforcement and enhanced sentencing. The bottom line is that modern justice systems still base most of their policies on classical or neoclassical theoretical frameworks that fell out of favor among scientists and philosophers in the late 1800s.

Policy Implications

Many policies are based on deterrence theory: the premise that increasing the certainty and/or severity of sanctions will deter crime.[46] This is seen throughout our system of law enforcement, courts, and corrections. This is rather interesting, given the fact that classical deterrence theory has not been the dominant explanatory model among criminologists for decades. In fact, a recent poll of close to 400 criminologists in the nation ranked classical theory 22nd out of 24 theories in terms of being the most valid explanation of serious and persistent offending.[47] Still, given the dominance of classical deterrence theory in most criminal justice policies, it is very important to discuss the most common strategies, as well as those that do not appear to be effective, or in some cases are detrimental.

First, the death penalty is used as a general deterrent for committing crime in most U.S. state jurisdictions. As the father of deterrence theory predicted, most studies show that capital punishment has a negligible effect on criminality. A recent review of the extant literature concluded that "the death penalty does not deter crime."[48] In fact, some studies show evidence for a brutalization effect, an increase in homicides after a high-profile execution.[49] Although the evidence is somewhat mixed, it is safe to say that the death penalty is not a consistent deterrent.

Another policy flowing from classical and neoclassical models is adding more police officers to deter crime in a given area. A recent review of the existing literature concluded that simply "adding more police officers will not reduce crime."[50] Rather, it is generally up to communities to police themselves via informal factors of control (family, church, community ties, etc.). However, this same review did find that police engagement in problem-solving activities at a specific location can sometimes reduce crime, but at that point the strategy is not based on deterrence.[51] Furthermore, a recent report concluded that proactive arrests for drunk driving have consistently been found to

[46]Stephen G. Tibbetts, *Criminological Theory: The Essentials* (Thousand Oaks, CA: Sage, 2012), 46–48.

[47]Lee Ellis, Jonathan Cooper, and Anthony Walsh, "Criminologists' Opinions about Causes and Theories of Crime and Delinquency: A Follow-up," *The Criminologist* 33 (2008): 23–26.

[48]Samuel Walker, *Sense and Nonsense about Crime and Drugs*, 7th ed. (Stamford, CT: Cengage, 2010).

[49]Bowers, "Effect of Execution."

[50]Walker, *Sense and Nonsense*.

[51]Ibid.

reduce such behavior, as does arresting offenders for domestic violence, but only if these measures are employed consistently.[52]

One example of court and correctional strategies is the "scared straight" approach that became popular several decades ago.[53] These programs essentially sought to scare or deter juvenile offenders into going "straight" by showing them the harshness and realities of prison life. However, nearly all evaluations of these programs showed that they were ineffective, and some evaluations indicated that these programs led to higher rates of recidivism.[54] There seem to be few successful deterrent policies in the court and corrections components of the criminal justice system. One recent review found that one of the court-mandated policies that seems promising is the provision of protection orders for battered women.[55] Another review in 2017 by David Weisburd, David Farrington, and Charlotte Gill of the systematic reviews and meta-analyses in the extant literature on the effects of court-imposed sanctions concluded that some of the programs showing effectiveness included mental health courts, as well as noncustodial sentences or interventions (such as ignition interlock devices for preventing drunk driving). However, this review concluded that interventions relating to the severity of the sentence and general deterrence had no evidence of effectiveness, and that studies have consistently shown that scared straight programs for juvenile offenders "did more harm than good."[56]

The policies, programs, and strategies based on classical deterrence theory will be examined more thoroughly in the final chapter of this book. To sum up, however, most of these strategies don't seem to work consistently to deter. This is because such a model assumes that people are rational and think carefully before choosing their behavior, whereas most research findings suggest that people often carry out behaviors that they know are irrational or without engaging in rational decision making,[57] which criminologists often refer to as *bounded rationality.*[58] Therefore, it is not surprising that many attempts by police and other criminal justice authorities to deter potential offenders do not seem to have much effect in preventing crime. This explanation will be more fully discussed in the final chapter of the book.

Conclusion

This chapter examined the earliest period of theorizing about criminological theory. The Classical School of criminology evolved out of ideas from the Enlightenment era in the mid- to late 18th century. This school of thought emphasized free will and rational choices that individuals make, from the perspective that people make choices regarding criminal behavior based on the potential costs and benefits that could result from such behavior. This chapter also explored the concepts and propositions of the father of the Classical School, which built the framework on which deterrence theory is based. We also discussed the various reforms that Beccaria proposed, many of which

---

[52]Lawrence Sherman et al., *Preventing Crime: What Works, What Doesn't, What's Promising: A Report to the United States Congress* (Washington, DC: U.S. Department of Justice, 1997).

[53]For a review of these programs and evaluations of them, see Richard Lundman, *Prevention and Control of Juvenile Delinquency*, 3rd ed. (Oxford: Oxford University Press, 2001).

[54]Ibid. Also see David Weisburd, David P. Farrington, and Charlotte Gill, "What Works in Crime Prevention and Rehabilitation: An Assessment of Systematic Reviews," *Criminology & Public Policy* 16 (2017): 415–49.

[55]Sherman et al., *Preventing Crime.*

[56]Weisburd et al., "What Works in Crime Prevention," 424.

[57]For a review of the extant research on this topic, see Alex Piquero and Stephen Tibbetts, *Rational Choice and Criminal Behavior* (New York: Routledge, 2002).

[58]For a more recent discussion on the complexity of developing policies based on deterrence and rational choice models, see Travis Pratt, "Rational Choice Theory, Crime Control Policy, and Criminological Relevance," *Criminology and Public Policy* 7 (2008): 43–52.

were adopted in the formation of the U.S. Constitution and Bill of Rights. The significance of the Classical School in both theorizing about crime and the actual administration of justice in the United States cannot be overestimated. The Classical and Neoclassical Schools of criminology remain to this day the primary framework within which justice is administered, despite the fact that scientific researchers and academics have, for the most part, moved past this perspective to consider social and economic factors.

/// CHAPTER SUMMARY

- The dominant theory of criminal behavior for most of the history of human civilization used demonic, supernatural, or other metaphysical explanations of behavior.

- The Age of Enlightenment was important because it brought a new logic and rationality to understanding human behavior, especially regarding the ability of individual human beings to think for themselves. Hobbes and Rousseau were two of the more important Enlightenment philosophers, and both stressed the importance of the social contract.

- Cesare Beccaria, who is generally considered the father of criminal justice, laid out a series of recommendations for reforming the brutal justice systems that existed throughout the world in the 1700s.

- Beccaria is also widely considered the father of the Classical School or deterrence theory; he based virtually all of his theoretical framework on the work of Enlightenment philosophers, especially their emphasis on humans as rational beings who consider perceived risks and benefits before committing criminal behaviors. This is the fundamental assumption of deterrence models of crime reduction.

- Beccaria discussed three key elements that punishments should have to be effective deterrents: celerity (swiftness), certainty, and severity.

- Specific deterrence involves sanctioning an individual to deter that particular individual from offending in the future. General deterrence involves sanctioning an individual to deter other potential offenders by making an example out of the individual being punished.

- The Neoclassical School was formed because societies found it nearly impossible to punish offenders equally for a given offense. The significant difference between the Classical and Neoclassical Schools is that the neoclassical model takes aggravating and mitigating circumstances into account when an individual is sentenced.

- Jeremy Bentham helped reinforce and popularize Beccaria's ideas in the English-speaking world, and he further developed the theory by proposing the hedonistic calculus, a formula for understanding criminal behavior.

- Despite falling out of favor among most criminologists in the late 1800s, the classical and neoclassical frameworks still constitute the dominant models and philosophies of all modern Western justice systems.

/// KEY TERMS

actus reus 35

Age of Enlightenment 29

brutalization effect 38

certainty of punishment 42

deterrence theory 29

general deterrence 43

mens rea 35

Neoclassical School 47

severity of punishment 42

social contract 33

swiftness of punishment 39

specific deterrence 43

utilitarianism 34

//// DISCUSSION QUESTIONS

1. Do you see any validity to the supernatural or religious explanations of criminal behavior? Provide examples of why you feel the way you do. Is your position supported by scientific research?

2. Which portions of Enlightenment thought do you believe are most valid in modern times? Which portions do you find least valid?

3. Of all of Beccaria's reforms, which do you think made the most significant improvement to modern criminal justice systems and why? Which do you think had the least impact and why?

4. Of the three elements of deterrence that Beccaria described, which do you think has the most important impact on deterring individuals from committing crime? Which of the three do you think has the least impact on deterring potential criminals? Back up your selections with personal experience.

5. Between general and specific deterrence, which do you think is more important for a judge to consider when sentencing a convicted individual? Why do you feel that way?

6. Provide examples of general and specific deterrence in your local community or state. Use the Internet if you can't find examples from your local community. Do you think such deterrence is effective?

7. Given the modern interpretation by the U.S. government of the definition of torture in context with what Beccaria thought about this issue, do you think that the father of criminal justice and deterrence would agree with the interrogation policies of the Bush administration during the Iraq War, which indisputably violated the guidelines set by the Geneva Conventions? Explain your position.

8. Regarding the use of the death penalty, list and explain at least three reasons why the father of criminal justice and deterrence theory felt the way he did. Which of these arguments do you agree with the most? Which argument do you disagree with the most? Ultimately, are you more strongly for or against the death penalty after reading the arguments of Beccaria?

9. Regarding the Neoclassical School, which mitigating factors do you think should reduce the punishment of a criminal defendant the most? Which aggravating circumstances do you think should increase the sentence of a criminal defendant the most? Do you believe that all persons who commit the same act should be punished exactly the same, regardless of age, experience, or gender?

10. What types of policy strategies based on classical and deterrence theory do you support? Which don't you support? Why?

//// WEB RESOURCES

Age of Enlightenment

> http://history-world.org/age_of_enlightenment.htm

Cesare Beccaria

> http://www.constitution.org/cb/beccaria_bio.htm

Demonic Theories of Crime

http://www.ucs.mun.ca/~skenney/courses/3290/3290class4.pdf
http://www.salemweb.com/memorial

Deterrence

http://www.sentencingproject.org/publications/deterrence-in-criminal-justice-evaluating-certainty-vs-severity-of-punishment
http://www.deathpenaltyinfo.org/article.php?scid=12&did=167

Jean-Jacques Rousseau

http://www.philosophypages.com/ph/rous.htm

Jeremy Bentham

http://www.ucl.ac.uk/Bentham-Project/who
http://www.utilitarianism.com/bentham.htm

Neoclassical School

http://study.com/academy/lesson/neoclassical-criminology-school-theory.html

Thomas Hobbes

http://www.philosophypages.com/hy/3x.htm

Modern Applications of the Classical Perspective

Deterrence, Rational Choice, and Routine Activities or Lifestyle Theories of Crime

This chapter will discuss the early aggregate studies of deterrence in the late 1960s, then the perceptual studies of the 1970s, and finally the longitudinal and scenario studies of the 1980s and 1990s to the present. Other policy applications, such as increased penalties for drunk driving, white-collar crime, and so on, will also be examined. This chapter will also discuss the development of rational choice theory in economics and its later application to crime. Finally, it will examine the use of routine activities theory or lifestyle theory as a framework for modern research and applications for reducing criminal activity.

In Chapter 2, we discussed the early development of the Classical and Neoclassical Schools of criminological thought. This theoretical perspective has been the dominant framework used by judges and practitioners in the practice of administering justice and punishment even in current times, but beginning in the late 19th century, criminological researchers dismissed the classical and neoclassical frameworks. Rather, criminological research and theorizing began emphasizing factors other than free will and deterrence. Instead, an emphasis was placed on social, biological, or other factors that go beyond free will and deterrence theory. These theories will be discussed in later chapters, but first we will examine the recent rebirth of classical and neoclassical theory and deterrence.

The Rebirth of Deterrence Theory and Contemporary Research

As just discussed in Chapter 2, the Classical and Neoclassical School frameworks fell out of favor among scientists and philosophers in the late 19th century, largely due to the introduction of Charles Darwin's ideas about evolution and natural selection. However, virtually all Western criminal systems retained the classical and neoclassical frameworks for their model of justice, particularly the United States. Nevertheless, the ideology of Beccaria's work was largely dismissed by academics and theorists after the presentation of Darwin's theory of evolution in the 1860s.

Therefore, the Classical and Neoclassical Schools fell o[...] of criminological theorizing for about 100 years. However, in the 1960s, the Beccarian model o[...]nced a rebirth.

In the late 1960s, several studies using aggregate measure[...]e and punishment were published that used a deterrence model for explaining why individuals engage in criminal behavior. These studies revealed a new interest in the deterrent aspects of criminal behavior and further supported the importance of certainty and severity of punishment in deterring individuals from committing crime, particularly homicide. In particular, evidence was presented that showed that increased risk or certainty of punishment was associated with less crime for most serious offenses. Plus, it is a fact that most offenders who are arrested once never get arrested again, which provides some basic support for deterrence.

Many of these studies used statistical formulas to measure the degree of certainty and severity of punishment in given jurisdictions. One measure used the ratio between crimes reported to police and number of arrests in a given jurisdiction. Another measure of certainty of punishment was the ratio of arrests to convictions, or findings of guilt, in criminal cases. Other measures were also employed. Most of the studies showed the same result: The higher the rate of arrest compared to reports of crime, or the higher the conviction rate compared to the arrest rate, the lower the crime rate in the jurisdiction. On the other hand, the scientific evidence for severity, which such studies generally indicated by the lengths of sentences for comparable crimes or similar measures, did not show much impact on crime.

Additional aggregate studies examined the prevalence and influence of capital punishment on the crime rate in given states.[1] The evidence showed that the states with death penalty statutes also had higher murder rates than non-death-penalty states. Furthermore, the studies showed that murderers in death penalty states who were not executed actually served less time than murderers in non-death-penalty states. Thus, the evidence regarding increased sanctions, including capital punishment, was mixed. Still, a review of the early deterrence studies by the National Academy of Sciences concluded that, overall, there was more evidence for a deterrent effect than against it, although the finding was reported in a tone that lacked confidence, perhaps cautious of what future studies would show.[2]

It was not long before critics noted that studies incorporating aggregate (i.e., macro-level) statistics are not adequate indicators or valid measures of the deterrence theoretical framework, largely because the model emphasizes the perceptions of individuals. Using aggregate or group statistics is flawed because different regions may have higher or lower crime rates than others, thereby creating bias in the ratios for certainty or severity of punishment. Furthermore, the group measures produced by these studies provide virtually no information on the degree to which individuals in those regions perceive sanctions as being certain, severe, or swift. Therefore, the emphasis on the unit of analysis in deterrence research shifted from the aggregate level to a more micro, individual level.

The following phase of deterrence research focused on individual perceptions of certainty and severity of sanctions, primarily drawn at one point in time, known as **cross-sectional studies**. A number of cross-sectional studies of individual perceptions of deterrence showed that perceptions of the risk or certainty of punishment were strongly associated with intentions to commit future crimes, but individual perceptions of the severity of punishments were mixed. Furthermore, it readily became evident that it was not clear whether perceptions were causing changes in behavior or whether behavior was causing changes in perception. This led to the next wave of research—longitudinal

---

[1]Daniel Glaser and Max S. Zeigler, "Use of the Death Penalty v. Outrage at Murder," *Crime and Delinquency* 20 (1974): 333–38; Charles Tittle, Franklin E. Zimring, and Gordon J. Hawkins, *Deterrence: The Legal Threat in Crime Control* (Chicago: University of Chicago Press, 1973); Johannes Andenaes, *Punishment and Deterrence* (Ann Arbor: University of Michigan Press, 1974); Jack P. Gibbs, *Crime, Punishment and Deterrence* (New York: Elsevier, 1975).

[2]Alfred Blumstein, Jacqueline Cohen, and Daniel Nagin, eds., *Deterrence and Incapacitation: Estimating the Effects of Criminal Sanctions on Crime Rates* (Washington, DC: National Academy of Sciences, 1978).

studies of individual perceptions and deterrence—which measured behavior as well as perceptions of risk and severity over time.[3]

One of the primary concepts revealed by longitudinal research was that behavior was influencing perceptions of the risk and severity of punishment more than perceptions were influencing behavior. This was referred to as the **experiential effect**, which is appropriately named because people's previous experience highly influences their expectations regarding their chances of being caught and suffering the resulting penalties.

A common example is that of people who drive under the influence of alcohol (or other substances). Studies show that if you ask people who have never driven drunk how likely they would be to get caught if they drove home drunk, most predict an unrealistically high chance of getting caught. However, if you ask people who have been arrested for driving drunk—even those who have been arrested several times for this offense—they typically predict that the chance is very low. The reason for this is that these chronic drunk drivers have typically been driving under the influence for many years, mostly without being caught. It is estimated that more than 1 million miles are driven collectively by drunk drivers before one person is arrested.[4] If anything, this is likely a conservative estimate. Thus, people who drive drunk—some of whom do so every day—are not likely to be deterred even when they are arrested more than once because they have done so for years. In fact, perhaps the most notable experts on the deterrence of drunk drivers, H. L. Ross and his colleagues, have concluded that drunk drivers who "perceive a severe punishment if caught, but a near-zero chance of being caught, are being rational in ignoring the threat."[5] Thus, even the most respected scholars in this area admit that sanctions against drunk driving are nowhere near certain enough, even if they are growing in severity.

Another common example is seen with white-collar criminals. Some researchers have theorized that being caught by authorities for violating government rules enforced by the U.S. Securities and Exchange Commission (SEC) will make these organizations less likely to commit future offenses.[6] However, business organizations have been in violation of established practices for years by the time they get caught, so it is likely that they will continue to ignore the rules in the future more than organizations that have never violated the rules. Thus, the certainty of punishment for white-collar violations is so low—and many would argue that the severity is also quite low—that it is quite rational for businesses and business professionals to take the risk of engaging in white-collar crime.

It is interesting to note that white-collar criminals and drunk drivers are two types of offenders who are considered more likely to be deterred because they are mostly of the middle- to upper-level socioeconomic class. The extant research on deterrence has shown that individuals who have something to lose are the most likely to be deterred by sanctions. This makes sense: Those who are unemployed or poor or both do not have much to lose, and for them, as well as for some minorities, incarceration may not present a significant departure from the deprived lives that they lead.

The fact that official sanctions have limitations in deterring individuals from drunk driving and white-collar crime is not a good indication of the effectiveness of deterrence-based policies. Their usefulness becomes even more

---

[3]Raymond Paternoster et al., "Perceived Risk and Social Control: Do Sanctions Really Deter?," *Law and Society Review* 17 (1983): 457–80; Raymond Paternoster, "The Deterrent Effect of the Perceived Certainty and Severity of Punishment: A Review of the Evidence and Issues," *Justice Quarterly* 4 (1987): 173–217; Charles F. Manski and John V. Pepper, "Deterrence and the Death Penalty: Partial Identification Analysis Using Repeated Cross Sections," *Journal of Quantitative Criminology* 29 (2013): 123–44.

[4]Benjamin Hansen, "Punishment and Deterrence: Evidence from Drunk Driving" (paper presented at the 7th Annual Conference on Empirical Legal Studies, Stanford University, Stanford, CA, April 2013); H. Laurence Ross, *Deterring the Drunk Driver: Legal Policy and Social Control* (Lexington, KY: Lexington Books, 1982); H. Laurence Ross, *Confronting Drunk Driving: Social Policy for Saving Lives* (New Haven, CT: Yale University Press, 1992); H. Laurence Ross, "Sobriety Checkpoints, American Style," *Journal of Criminal Justice* 22 (1994): 437–44; H. Laurence Ross, Richard McCleary, and Gary LaFree, "Can Mandatory Jail Laws Deter Drunk Driving? The Arizona Case," *Journal of Criminal Law and Criminology* 81 (1990): 156–70.

[5]Ross, "Sobriety Checkpoints," 164.

[6]See the review in Sally Simpson and Christopher S. Koper, "Deterring Corporate Crime," *Criminology* 30 (1992): 347–76.

questionable when other populations are considered, particularly the offenders in most predatory street crimes (robbery, burglary, etc.), in which offenders typically have nothing to lose because they come from poverty-stricken areas and are often unemployed. One recent study showed that being arrested had little effect on perceptions of the certainty of punishment; offending actually corresponded with decreases in such perceptions.[7]

Some people don't see incarceration as that much of a step down in life, given the three meals a day, shelter, and relative stability provided by such punishment. This fact epitomizes one of the most notable paradoxes we have in criminology: The individuals we most want to deter are the least likely to be deterred, primarily because they have nothing to fear. In early Enlightenment thought, Thomas Hobbes asserted that, although fear was the tool used to enforce the social contract, people who weren't afraid of punishment could not effectively be deterred. That remains true in modern days.

Along the same lines, studies have consistently shown that for young male offenders—at higher risk, with low emotional or moral inhibitions, low self-control, and high impulsivity—official deterrence is highly ineffective in preventing crimes with immediate payoffs.[8] Thus, many factors go into the extent to which official sanctions can deter. As we have seen, even among those offenders who are in theory the most deterrable, official sanctions have little impact because their experience of not being caught weakens the value of deterrence.

The identification and understanding of the experiential effect had a profound influence on the interpretation of evidence regarding the impact of deterrence. Researchers saw that, to account for such an experiential effect, any estimation of the influence of perceived certainty or severity of punishment must control for previous experiences of engaging in unlawful behavior. The identification of the experiential effect was the primary contribution of the longitudinal studies of deterrence, but such studies faced even further criticism.

Longitudinal studies of deterrence provided a significant improvement over the cross-sectional studies that preceded this advanced methodology. However, such longitudinal studies typically involved designs in which measures of perceptions of certainty and severity of punishment were collected at points in time that were separated by up to a year, including long stretches between when the crime was committed and when the offenders were asked about their perceptions of punishment. Psychological studies have clearly established that perceptions of the likelihood and severity of sanctions vary significantly from day to day, not to mention month to month and year to year.[9] Therefore, in the late 1980s and early 1990s, a new wave of deterrence research evolved, which asked study

---

[7]Greg Pogarsky, KiDeuk Kim, and Raymond Paternoster, "Perceptual Change in the National Youth Survey: Lessons for Deterrence Theory and Offender Decision-Making," *Justice Quarterly* 22 (2005): 1–29.

[8]For reviews, see Stephen Brown, Finn Esbensen, and Gilbert Geis, *Criminology*, 8th ed. (Cincinnati, OH: Anderson, 2012); Nancy Finley and Harold Grasmick, "Gender Roles and Social Control," *Sociological Spectrum* 5 (1985): 317–30; Harold Grasmick, Robert Bursik, and Karla Kinsey, "Shame and Embarrassment as Deterrents to Noncompliance with the Law: The Case of an Antilittering Campaign," *Environment and Behavior* 23 (1991): 233–51; Harold Grasmick, Brenda Sims Blackwell, and Robert Bursik, "Changes in the Sex Patterning of Perceived Threats of Sanctions," *Law and Society Review* 27 (1993): 679–705; Pamela Richards and Charles Tittle, "Gender and Perceived Chances of Arrest," *Social Forces* 59 (1981): 1182–99; George Loewenstein, Daniel Nagin, and Raymond Paternoster, "The Effect of Sexual Arousal on Expectations of Sexual Forcefulness," *Journal of Research in Crime and Delinquency* 34 (1997): 209–28; Toni Makkai and John Braithwaite, "The Dialects of Corporate Deterrence," *Journal of Research in Crime and Delinquency* 31 (1994): 347–73; Daniel Nagin and Raymond Paternoster, "Enduring Individual Differences and Rational Choice Theories of Crime," *Law and Society Review* 27 (1993): 467–96; Alex Piquero and Stephen Tibbetts, "Specifying the Direct and Indirect Effects of Low Self-Control and Situational Factors in Offenders' Decision Making: Toward a More Complete Model of Rational Offending," *Justice Quarterly* 13 (1996): 481–510; Raymond Paternoster and Sally Simpson, "Sanction Threats and Appeals to Morality: Testing a Rational Choice Model of Corporate Crime," *Law and Society Review* 30 (1996): 549–83; Daniel Nagin and Greg Pogarsky, "Integrating Celerity, Impulsivity, and Extralegal Sanction Threats into a Model of General Deterrence: Theory and Evidence," *Criminology* 39 (2001): 404–30; and Alex Piquero and Greg Pogarsky, "Beyond Stanford and Warr's Reconceptualization of Deterrence: Personal and Vicarious Experiences, Impulsivity, and Offending Behavior," *Journal of Research in Crime and Delinquency* 39 (2002): 153–86. For a recent review and a different explanation of these conclusions, see Greg Pogarsky, "Identifying 'Deterrable' Offenders: Implications for Research on Deterrence," *Justice Quarterly* 19 (2002): 431–52.

[9]Icek Ajzen and Martin Fishbein, *Understanding Attitudes and Predicting Social Behavior* (Englewood Cliffs, NJ: Prentice Hall, 1980); Martin Fishbein and Icek Ajzen, *Belief, Attitude, Intention, and Behavior* (Reading, MA: Addison-Wesley, 1975); Icek Ajzen and Martin Fishbein, "Attitude–Behavior Relations: A Theoretical Analysis and Review of Empirical Research," *Psychological Bulletin* 84 (1977): 888–918. For a recent review, see Pogarsky et al., "Perceptual Change."

participants to estimate their likelihood of committing a criminal act in a given situation as well as their immediate perceptions of the certainty and severity of punishment in the same situation. This wave of research was known as **scenario (vignette) research**.[10]

Scenario research (i.e., vignette design) was created to deal with the limitations of previous methodological strategies for studying the effects of deterrence on criminal offending—specifically, the criticism that individuals' perceptions of the certainty and severity of punishment change drastically from time to time and across different situations. The scenario method dealt with this criticism directly by providing a specific, realistic (albeit hypothetical) situation in which a person engages in a criminal act. Participants in the study are then asked to estimate the chance that they would engage in such activity in the given circumstances and to respond to questions regarding their perceptions of the risk of getting caught (i.e., certainty of punishment) and the degree of severity of punishment they expect.

Another important and valuable aspect of scenario research was that it promoted contemporaneous (i.e., instantaneous) responses about perceptions of risk and the severity of perceived sanctions. In comparison, previous studies (e.g., aggregate, cross-sectional, longitudinal) had always relied on either group or individual measures of perceptions over long periods of time. While some argue that intentions to commit a crime given a hypothetical situation are not accurate measures of what people would do in reality, studies have shown an extremely high correlation between what people report doing in a given scenario and what they would do in real life.[11] A recent review of criticisms of this research method showed that one weakness was that it did not allow respondents to offer their own perceptions of the risk and costs associated with each offense.[12] Despite such criticisms, the scenario method appears to be the most accurate that we have to date to estimate the effects of individuals' perceptions on the likelihood of their engaging in given criminal activity at a given point in time. This is something that the previous waves of deterrence research—aggregate, cross-sectional, and longitudinal studies—could not estimate.

Ultimately, the studies using the scenario method showed that participants were more affected by perceptions of certainty and less so, albeit sometimes significantly, by perceptions of severity. These findings supported previous methods of estimating the effects of *formal* or *official deterrence*, meaning the deterrent effects of three general groups: law enforcement, courts, and corrections (i.e., prisons and probation or parole). Thus, the overall conclusion regarding the effects of official sanctions on individual decision making remained unaltered. However, one of the more interesting aspects of the scenario research method is that it helped solidify the importance of extralegal variables in deterring criminal behavior, variables that had been neglected by previous methods.

---

[10]Loewenstein et al., "The Effect of Sexual Arousal"; Nagin and Paternoster, "Enduring Individual Differences"; Piquero and Tibbetts, "Specifying the Direct"; Paternoster and Simpson, "Sanction Threats"; Stephen G. Tibbetts, "Traits and States of Self-Conscious Emotions in Criminal Decision Making," in *Affect and Cognition in Criminal Decision Making*, ed. Jean-Louis Van Gelder, Henk Elffers, Danielle Reynald, and Daniel Nagin (London: Routledge, 2014), 221–38; Ronet Bachman, Raymond Paternoster, and Sally Ward, "The Rationality of Sexual Offending: Testing a Deterrence/Rational Choice Conception of Sexual Assault," *Law and Society Review* 26 (1992): 343–72; Harold Grasmick and Robert Bursik, "Conscience, Significant Others, and Rational Choice: Extending the Deterrence Model," *Law and Society Review* 24 (1990): 837–61; Harold Grasmick and Donald E. Green, "Legal Punishment, Social Disapproval, and Internalization as Inhibitors of Illegal Behavior," *Journal of Criminal Law and Criminology* 71 (1980): 325–35; Stephen Klepper and Daniel Nagin, "The Deterrent Effects of Perceived Certainty and Severity of Punishment Revisited, *Criminology* 27 (1989): 721–46; Stephen Tibbetts and Denise Herz, "Gender Differences in Students' Rational Decisions to Cheat," *Deviant Behavior* 18 (1996): 393–414; Stephen Tibbetts and David Myers, "Low Self-Control, Rational Choice, and Student Test Cheating," *American Journal of Criminal Justice* 23 (1999): 179–200; Stephen Tibbetts, "Shame and Rational Choice in Offending Decisions," *Criminal Justice and Behavior* 24 (1997): 234–55.

[11]Ajzen and Fishbein, *Understanding Attitudes*; Donald Green, "Measures of Illegal Behavior in Individual Behavior in Individual-Level Deterrence Research," *Journal of Research in Crime and Delinquency* 26 (1989): 253–75; Icek Ajzen, "From Intentions to Actions: A Theory of Planned Behavior," in *Action-Control: From Cognition to Behavior*, ed. Julius Kuhl and Jurgen Beckmann (New York: Springer, 1985), 11–39; Icek Ajzen and Martin Fishbein, "The Prediction of Behavioral Intentions in a Choice Situation," *Journal of Experimental Psychology* 5 (1969): 400–416.

[12]Jeffrey A. Bouffard, "Methodological and Theoretical Implications of Using Subject-Generated Consequences in Tests of Rational Choice Theory," *Justice Quarterly* 19 (2002): 747–71.

These extralegal or informal deterrence variables, which include any factors beyond the formal sanctions of police, courts, and corrections—such as employment, family, friends, or community—are typically known as informal or unofficial sanctions. The scenario research studies helped show that these informal sanctions provided most of the deterrent effect—if there was any. These findings coincided with the advent of a new model of deterrence, which became commonly known as *rational choice theory*.

Rational Choice Theory

Rational choice theory is a perspective that criminologists adapted from economists, who used it to explain a variety of individual decisions regarding a variety of behaviors. This framework emphasizes all the important factors that go into a person's decision to engage or not engage in a particular act. In terms of criminological research, the rational choice model emphasized both official or formal forms of deterrence and also the informal factors that influence individual decisions regarding criminal behavior. This represented a profound advance in the understanding of human behavior. After all, as studies showed, most individuals are more affected by informal factors than they are by official or formal factors.

Although there were several previous attempts to apply the rational choice model to the understanding of criminal activity, the most significant work, which brought rational choice theory into the mainstream of criminological research, was Derek Cornish and Ron Clarke's *The Reasoning Criminal: Rational Choice Perspectives on Offending* in 1986.[13] Furthermore, in 1988, Jack Katz published his work *Seductions of Crime*, which, for the first time, placed an emphasis on the benefits (mostly the inherent physiological pleasure) of committing crime.[14] Before Katz's publication, virtually no attention had been paid to the benefits of offending, let alone the fun that people feel when they engage in criminal behavior. A recent study showed that the publication of Cornish and Clarke's book, as well as the timing of other publications such as Katz's, led to an influx of criminological studies in the late 1980s to mid-1990s based on the rational choice model.[15]

These studies on rational choice showed that while official or formal sanctions tend to have some effect on individuals' decisions to commit crime, they almost always are relatively unimportant compared to extralegal or informal factors.[16] The effects of people's perceptions of how much shame or loss of self-esteem they would experience, even if no one else found out that they committed the crime, was one of the most important variables in determining whether or not they would do so.[17] Additional evidence indicated that females were more influenced by the effects of shame and moral beliefs in this regard than were males.[18] Recent studies have shown that differing

---

[13]Derek Cornish and Ron Clarke, *The Reasoning Criminal: Rational Choice Perspectives on Offending* (New York: Springer-Verlag, 1986).

[14]Jack Katz, *Seductions of Crime* (New York: Basic Books, 1988).

[15]Stephen Tibbetts and Chris Gibson, "Individual Propensities and Rational Decision-Making: Recent Findings and Promising Approaches," in *Rational Choice and Criminal Behavior*, ed. Alex Piquero and Stephen Tibbetts (New York: Routledge, 2002), 3–24. See recent review by Jean-Louis Van Gelder et al. (eds.), *Affect and Cognition in Criminal Decision Making* (London: Routledge, 2014).

[16]For a recent review, see Pamela Schram and Stephen Tibbetts, *Introduction to Criminology: Why Do They Do It?*, 2nd ed. (Thousand Oaks, CA: Sage, 2018), 96–100.

[17]Grasmick and Bursik, "Conscience"; Pogarsky, "Identifying 'Deterrable' Offenders"; Tibbetts, "Shame and Rational Choice"; Nagin and Paternoster, "Enduring Individual Differences"; Tibbetts and Herz, "Gender Differences"; Tibbetts and Myers, "Low Self-Control"; Harold Grasmick, Brenda Sims Blackwell, and Robert Bursik, "Changes over Time in Gender Differences in Perceived Risk of Sanctions," *Law and Society Review* 27 (1993): 679–705; Harold Grasmick, Robert Bursik, and Bruce Arneklev, "Reduction in Drunk Driving as a Response to Increased Threats of Shame, Embarrassment, and Legal Sanctions," *Criminology* 31 (1993): 41–67; Stephen Tibbetts, "Self-Conscious Emotions and Criminal Offending," *Psychological Reports* 93 (2004): 101–31.

[18]Tibbetts and Herz, "Gender Differences"; Grasmick et al., "Changes in the Sex Patterning"; Finley and Grasmick, "Gender Roles"; Pogarsky et al., "Perceptual Change"; Stephen Tibbetts, "Gender Differences in Students' Rational Decisions to Cheat," *Deviant Behavior* 18 (1997): 393–414.

▲ **Image 3.1** There are both formal and informal elements of deterrence that influence decisions of whether or not to commit criminal behavior.

SOURCE: © istockphoto.com / kali9; © istockphoto.com / JackF; © istockphoto.com / IPGGutenbergUKLtd; © istockphoto.com / shironosov; © istockphoto.com / f8grapher; © istockphoto.com / Rklfoto

levels of certain personality traits, especially self-control and empathy, are likely the reason why males and females differ so much in engaging in criminal activity.[19] Finally, the influence of peers has a profound impact on individual perceptions of the pros and cons of offending, because seeing friends get away with crimes significantly decreases the perceived risk of punishment.[20]

Another area of rational choice research dealt with the influence that an individual's behavior would have on those around her or him. A recent review and test of perceived social disapproval showed that this was one of the most important variables in decisions to commit crime.[21] In addition to self-sanctions, such as feelings of shame and embarrassment, the perception of how loved ones, friends, and employers would respond is perhaps the most important factor that goes into a person's decision to engage in criminal activity. These are the people we deal with every day, and some of them are the source of our livelihoods, so it should not be too surprising that our perceptions of how they will react strongly affect how we behave.

Perhaps the most important finding of rational choice research was that the expected benefits—in particular, the pleasure offenders would get from offending—had one of the most significant effects on their decisions to offend. Many other conclusions have been made regarding the influence of extralegal or informal factors on criminal offending, but the ultimate conclusion that can be made is that these informal deterrent variables typically hold more influence on individual decision making regarding deviant activity than the official or formal factors that were emphasized by traditional Classical School models of behavior.

---

[19]Nagin and Paternoster, "Enduring Individual Differences"; Grasmick et al., "Changes over Time"; Tibbetts, "Self-Conscious Emotions"; Tibbetts, "Traits and States."

[20]Pogarsky et al., "Perceptual Change."

[21]Pogarsky, "Identifying 'Deterrable' Offenders."

The rational choice model of criminal offending became the modern framework of deterrence. Official authorities acknowledged the influence of extralegal or informal factors, as seen in modern efforts to incorporate the family, employment, and community in rehabilitation efforts. Such efforts are highly consistent with the current understanding of the Classical School and rational choice frameworks—namely, that individuals are more deterred by the perceived impact of their actions on informal aspects of their lives than they are by the formal punishments they might face if they carry out illegal acts.

Routine Activities Theory

Routine activities theory, or **lifestyle theory**, is another contemporary form of the Classical School framework in the sense that it assumes an offender who makes rational decisions. The general model of routine activities theory was originally presented by Lawrence Cohen and Marcus Felson in 1979.[22] This theoretical framework emphasized the presence of three factors that come together in time and place to create a high likelihood of crime and victimization. These three factors are motivated offender(s), suitable target(s), and lack of guardianship. Overall, the theory is appropriately named in the sense that it assumes that most crime occurs in the daily routine of people who happen to see—and then seize—tempting opportunities to commit crime. Studies tend to support this idea, as opposed to the idea that most offenders leave their home knowing they are going to commit a crime; the latter offenders are called hydraulic and are relatively rare compared to the opportunistic type.

Regarding the first factor noted as being important for increasing the likelihood of criminal activity—a motivated offender—routine activities theory does not provide much insight. Rather, the model simply assumes that some individuals tend to be motivated and leaves it at that. Fortunately, we have many other theories that can fill this notable absence. The strength of routine activities theory lies in its elaboration of the other two aspects of a crime-prone environment: suitable targets and lack of guardianship.

Suitable targets can include a variety of situations. For example, a very suitable target can be a vacant house in the suburbs, which the family has left for summer vacation. Data clearly show that burglaries more than double in the summer when many families are on vacation. Other forms of suitable targets range from an unlocked car to a female alone at a shopping mall carrying a lot of cash and credit cards or purchased goods. Other likely targets are bars or other places that serve alcohol. Offenders have traditionally targeted drunk persons because they are less likely to be able to defend themselves, as illustrated by a history of lawbreakers rolling drunks for their wallets that extends back to the early part of the 20th century. This is only a short list of the many types of suitable targets that are available to motivated offenders in everyday life.

▲ **Image 3.2**   Marcus Felson (1947–), Rutgers University, author of routine activities theory.

SOURCE: Courtesy of Marcus Felson

The third and final aspect of the routine activities model for increased likelihood of criminal activity is the lack of guardianship. Guardianship is often thought of as a police officer or security guard, which is often the case. There

---

[22]Lawrence Cohen and Marcus Felson, "Social Change and Crime Rates: A Routine Activities Approach," *American Sociological Review* 44 (1979): 214–41.

are many other forms of guardianship, however, such as owning a dog to protect a house, which studies demonstrate can be quite effective. Just having a car or house alarm constitutes a form of guardianship. Furthermore, the presence of an adult, neighbor, or teacher can effectively guard an area against crime. In fact, recent studies show that increased lighting in the area can prevent a significant amount of crime, with one study showing a 20% reduction in overall crime in areas randomly chosen to receive improved lighting as compared to control areas that did not.[23] Regardless of the type of guardianship, it is the absence of adequate guardianship that sets the stage for crime; on the other hand, each step taken toward protecting a place or person is likely to deter offenders from choosing the target in relation to others. Locations that have a high convergence of motivated offenders, suitable targets, and lack of guardianship are typically referred to as *hot spots*.[24]

Case Study: The Green River Killer

Gary Leon Ridgway was convicted and sentenced in 2003 after many decades of acting as the Green River Killer; he had stabbed his first victim at age 16 in 1965. He confessed to killing 71 victims (although he was convicted of only 48), virtually all of them women. He appeared to live separate lives. In one aspect of his life in the Seattle area, he was the father of a son and husband to his third wife. The other side involved picking up women, mostly prostitutes and strippers, who were willing to engage in sexual activity with him in remote locations.

He claimed that he would hide or bury the bodies of the victims he really "liked" because he knew he would want to go back and have sex with them later, which he did on occasion. He would also place various objects, such as a fish, bottle, or sausage, at the crime scene to throw off authorities, because these objects didn't match the modus operandi they were expecting to help link the crimes together. So he did appear to plan his crimes, at least in terms of manipulating the crime scenes (whether the primary scene, where the killing took place, or the secondary scene, where the body was dumped).

He also notably said, "I would choke them . . . and I was really good at it." But when asked by an investigator in an official interview where he ranked on a scale of evil from 1 to 5, he said he was a 3. So there appears to be a disconnect between the way he thinks and the way society at large thinks.

▲ **Image 3.3** Gary Leon Ridgway, who was a serial killer, confessed to murdering at least 71 victims.

SOURCE: King County Sheriff's Office, via Wikimedia Commons

Ridgway was caught after DNA from crime scenes was matched to a saliva test he had taken years before, when authorities had suspected him but didn't have enough evidence to make an arrest. So he continued his killing spree for many years, until they finally obtained further evidence linking him to some of the murders. Ridgway is now serving 480 years in prison for 48 life sentences, due to a bargain that got him out of the death penalty.

(Continued)

---

[23]David P. Farrington and Brandon C. Welsh, "Improved Street Lighting and Crime Prevention," *Justice Quarterly* 19 (2002): 313–43; Spiros Kitsinelisa and Georges Zissisa, "A Short Review on Lighting and Security," *Journal of Applied Security Research* 7 (2012): 341–353.

[24]For further discussion and more recent studies, see Schram and Tibbetts, "*Introduction to Criminology*," 100–105.

(Continued)

But why did he do it? Obviously, he has some psychological issues. But he passed the psychological test to determine readiness to stand trial, so he was not ruled legally insane. Virtually all his victims easily fit within his lifestyle, as he traveled around in his truck and picked up women in essentially the same area where he worked and lived. He never went far out of his way. In fact, none of his victims seemed to come from outside the Seattle area. And he would almost always dump or bury the bodies within a relatively limited radius in that region—hence his label, "the Green River Killer."

> *. . . When asked by an investigator in an official interview where he ranked on a scale of evil from 1 to 5, he said he was a 3.*

In one notable instance, he claimed that his son was with him in the truck when he picked up a woman. He had his son stay in the truck while he took the woman a distance away and killed her. But we know that he tended to pick up and kill these women as part of his daily routine, which included working at a truck-painting factory. Thus, this case applies to the routine activities theory and lifestyles perspective covered in this chapter. Also keep in mind that even at the time when he was apprehended for these murders, he had a relatively stable marriage, which is not atypical for serial killers. They often lead separate lives, and both lives can seem fairly routine despite extreme contradictions.

1. What was the Green River Killer's typical method of operation (MO), or how he carried out most of his killings?

2. How is the Green River Killer's case a good example of routine activities theory?

SOURCE: Jeff Jensen and Jonathan Case, *Green River Killer: A True Detective Story* (Milwaukie, OR: Dark Horse Books, 2011).

Perhaps the most supportive evidence for routine activities theory and hot spots was the study of 911 calls for service in Minneapolis, Minnesota.[25] This study examined all serious calls (as well as total calls) to police for a 1-year period. Half of the top 10 places from which police were called were bars or locations where alcohol was served. As mentioned previously, establishments that serve alcohol are often targeted by motivated offenders because of their high proportion of suitable targets. Furthermore, a number of bars tend to have a low level of guardianship in relation to the number of people they serve. Readers of this book may well relate to this situation. Most college towns and cities have certain drinking establishments that are known as being hot spots for crime.

Still, the Minneapolis hot spot study showed other types of establishments that made the top 10 rankings. These included places such as bus depots, convenience stores, run-down motels and hotels, downtown malls, and strip malls. The common theme linking these locations and the bars was the convergence of the three aspects described by routine activities theory as being predictive of criminal activity. Specifically, these places attracted motivated offenders, largely because they have a lot of vulnerable targets and lack sufficient levels of security or guardianship.

---

[25]Lawrence Sherman, Patrick R. Gartin, and Michael Buerger, "Hot Spots of Predatory Crime: Routine Activities and the Criminology of Place," *Criminology* 27 (1989): 27–56.

Figure 3.1 • Routine activities theory

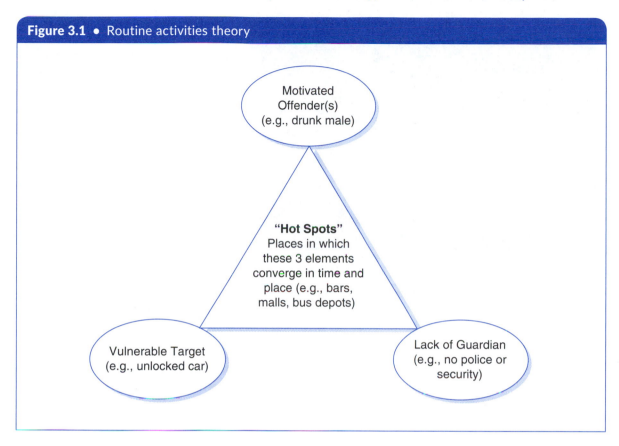

The routine activities framework has been applied in many contexts and places, many of them international.[26] Modern applications of routine activities theory include geographic profiling, which uses satellite positioning systems in perhaps the most attractive and marketable aspect of criminological research in contemporary times. Essentially, such research incorporates computer software for a Global Positioning System (GPS) to identify the exact location of every crime that takes place in a given jurisdiction. Such information has been used to solve or predict various crimes, to the point where serial killers have been caught by triangulating the sites where the victims were found to show the most likely place where the killer lived.

[26]Anthony A. Braga, Andrew V. Papachristos, and David M. Hureau, "The Effects of Hot Spots Policing on Crime: An Updated Systematic Review and Meta-Analysis," *Justice Quarterly* 29 (2012): 1–31; Jon Gunnar Bernburg and Thorolfur Thorlindsson, "Routine Activities in Social Context: A Closer Look at the Role of Opportunity in Deviant Behavior," *Justice Quarterly* 18 (2001): 543–67. See also Richard Bennett, "Routine Activity: A Cross-National Assessment of a Criminological Perspective," *Social Forces* 70 (1991): 147–63; James Hawdon, "Deviant Lifestyles: The Social Control of Routine Activities," *Youth and Society* 28 (1996): 162–88; James L. Massey, Marvin Krohn, and Lisa Bonati, "Property Crime and the Routine Activities of Individuals," *Journal of Research in Crime and Delinquency* 26 (1989): 378–400; Terrance Miethe, Mark Stafford, and J. Scott Long, "Social Differences in Criminological Victimization: A Test of Routine Activities/Lifestyles Theories," *American Sociological Review* 52 (1987): 184–94; Elizabeth Mustaine and Richard Tewksbury, "Predicting Risks of Larceny Theft Victimization: A Routine Activity Analysis Using Refined Lifestyle Measures," *Criminology* 36 (1998): 829–57; D. Wayne Osgood et al., "Routine Activities and Individual Deviant Behavior," *American Sociological Review* 61 (1996): 635–55; Dennis Roncek and Pamela Maier, "Bars, Blocks, and Crimes Revisited: Linking the Theory of Routine Activities to the Empiricism of Hot Spots," *Criminology* 29 (1991): 725–53; and Robert Sampson and John Wooldredge, "Linking the Micro- and Macro-Level Dimensions of Lifestyle-Routine Activity and Opportunity Models of Predatory Victimization," *Journal of Quantitative Criminology* 3 (1987): 371–93.

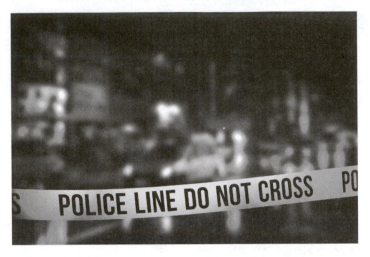

▲ **Image 3.4**   Crimes tend to be concentrated in certain places and certain times and thus are not typically random events. The places that have a high concentration of crimes are referred to as hot spots.

SOURCE: © istockphoto.com / mrtom-uk

Some theorists have proposed a theoretical model based on individuals' lifestyles, which has a large overlap with routine activities theory, as shown in studies previously reviewed.[27] It only makes sense that a person who lives a more risky lifestyle, for example, by frequenting bars or living in a high-crime area, will be at more risk because she or he is close to various hot spots as identified by routine activities theory. Although some criminologists label this phenomenon a lifestyle perspective, it is virtually synonymous with the routine activities model because such lifestyles incorporate the same conceptual and causal factors in routine activities.

Policy Implications

There are numerous policy implications that can be derived from the theories and scientific findings in this chapter. Here, we will concentrate on some of the most important policies. First, we look at the policy of broken windows, which has many assumptions similar to those of the routine activities and rational choice theories. The broken windows perspective emphasizes the need for police to crack down on minor offenses to reduce major crimes.[28] Although many cities (e.g., New York and Los Angeles) have claimed reductions in serious crimes by using this theory, crime was reduced by the same amount across most U.S. cities during the same time (the late 1990s to mid-2000s).

Relatedly, regarding the effectiveness of targeting hot spots of crime—which is based primarily on routine activities theory—according to a 2017 article by David Weisburd, David Farrington, and Charlotte Gill, the most recent systematic reviews and meta-analyses studies have concluded that policing strategies that place focused emphasis on hot spots appear to be effective in reducing crime in those areas.[29] It is also notable that this same extensive recent review of the extant literature found little evidence for displacement of crime out of areas when they are targeted by focused policing efforts.[30] Thus, there appears to be strong support for police strategies in focusing on problematic hot spots in communities. Research by Cory Haberman in 2017 has promoted advancing the examination of spatial crime areas by examining the overlapping nature of hot spots of different crime types.[31]

[27]Hawdon, "Deviant Lifestyles"; Sampson and Wooldredge, "Linking the Micro"; Brown et al., *Criminology*.

[28]James Q. Wilson and George Kelling, "Broken Windows: The Police and Neighborhood Safety," *Atlantic Monthly* (March 1982): 29–38.

[29]David Weisburd, David P. Farrington, and Charlotte Gill, "What Works in Crime Prevention and Rehabilitation: An Assessment of Systematic Reviews," *Criminology & Public Policy* 16 (2017): 415–49.

[30]Ibid.

[31]Cory R. Haberman, "Overlapping Hot Spots? Examination of the Spatial Heterogeneity of Hot Spots of Different Crime Types," *Criminology & Public Policy* 16 (2017): 633–60.

Additionally, a study by Robert Apel and Julie Horney in 2017, based on a routine activities theoretical framework, examined the influence of employment and criminal behavior among a national sample of 717 males.[32] The findings of this study indicated that employment significantly reduced criminal behavior but only when individuals reported a strong level of commitment to their jobs. The authors concluded that for such individuals who had high levels of commitment to their job, their employment reduced the unstructured leisure time that would offer offenders situational inducements or opportunities to commit crime. This certainly supports the routine activities theoretical framework; when individuals are not simply wandering about, but rather are at work, they are less likely to offend because they are not presented with attractive opportunities to commit street crimes.

Other policies derived from the theories in this chapter include the *three strikes, you're out* policy, which assumes that offenders will make a rational choice not to commit future offenses because they could go to prison for life if they commit three felonies; the negatives certainly outweigh the expected benefits for the third crime. Remember Beccaria's view that for deterrence to be extremely effective, punishment must be swift, certain, and severe. Where does the three-strikes policy fall in this equation? The bottom line is that it is much more severe than it is swift or certain. Given Beccaria's philosophy (see Chapter 2), this policy will probably not work because it is not certain or swift. However, it is severe in the sense that a person can be sentenced to life if she or he commits three felony offenses over time.

A controversial three-strikes law was passed by voter initiative in California, and other states have adopted similar types of laws.[33] It sends third-time felons to prison for the rest of their lives regardless of the nature of that third felony. California first requires convictions for two *strikeable* felonies: crimes like murder, rape, aggravated assault, burglary, drug offenses, and so on. Then, any third felony can trigger a life sentence. The stories about people going to prison for the rest of their lives for stealing pieces of pizza or shoplifting DVDs, while rare, are quite true.

The question we are concerned with here is, does the three-strikes policy work? As a specific deterrent, the answer is clearly yes; offenders who are in prison for the rest of their lives cannot commit more crimes on the streets. In that regard, three-strikes works very well. Some people feel, however, that laws like three-strikes need to have a general deterrent effect to be considered successful, meaning that this law should deter everyone from engaging in multiple crimes. So is three-strikes a general deterrent? Unfortunately, there are no easy answers to this question because laws vary from state to state, the laws are used at different rates across the counties in a given state, and so forth.

There is at least some consensus in the literature, however. One study from California suggests that three-strikes has reduced crime,[34] but the remaining studies show that three-strikes either has had no effect on crime or has actually increased crime.[35] How could three-strikes increase crime? The authors attributed the increase in homicide following the enactment of three-strikes laws to the possibility that third-strikers have an incentive to kill victims and any witnesses in an effort to avoid apprehension. Although this argument is tentative, it may be true.[36]

---

[32]Robert Apel and Julie Horney, "How and Why Does Work Matter? Employment Conditions, Routine Activities, and Crime among Adult Male Offenders," *Criminology* 55 (2017): 307–43.

[33]David Shichor and Dale K. Sechrest, eds., *Three Strikes and You're Out: Vengeance as Social Policy* (Thousand Oaks, CA: Sage, 1996).

[34]Joanna M. Shepherd, "Fear of the First Strike: The Full Deterrent Effect of California's Two- and Three-Strikes Legislation," *Journal of Legal Studies* 31 (2002): 159–201.

[35]See Lisa Stolzenberg and Stewart J. D'Alessio, "Three Strikes and You're Out: The Impact of California's New Mandatory Sentencing Law on Serious Crime Rates," *Crime and Delinquency* 43 (1997): 457–69; Mike Males and Dan Macallair, "Striking Out: The Failure of California's 'Three-Strikes and You're Out' Law," *Stanford Law and Policy Review* 11 (1999): 65–72.

[36]Steven N. Durlauf and Daniel S. Nagin, "Imprisonment and Crime: Can Both Be Reduced?," *Criminology and Public Policy* 10 (2011): 13–54; Thomas B. Marvell and Carlisle E. Moody, "The Lethal Effects of Three-Strikes Laws," *Journal of Legal Studies* 30 (2001): 89–106. See also Tomislav Kovandzic, John J. Sloan III, and Lynne M. Vieraitis, "Unintended Consequences of Politically Popular Sentencing Policy: The Homicide-Promoting Effects of 'Three Strikes' in U.S. Cities (1980–1999)," *Criminology and Public Policy* 1 (2002): 399–424. For a review of empirical evaluations of three-strikes laws, see John Worrall, "The Effect of Three-Strikes Legislation on Serious Crime in California," *Journal of Criminal Justice* 32 (2004): 283–96.

This is just one of the many policy implications that can be derived from this chapter. We expect that readers of this book will come up with many more policy implications, but it is vital to examine the empirical literature to determine these policies' usefulness in reducing criminal activity. Other policy implications of the theories and findings described in this chapter will be discussed in the final chapter of this book.

In a strategy that is also strongly based on the rational choice model, a number of judges have started using shaming strategies to deter offenders from recidivating.[37] They have ordered everything from publicly posting pictures of men arrested for soliciting prostitutes to forcing offenders to walk down main streets of towns wearing signs that announce that they've committed crimes. These are just two examples of an increasing trend that emphasizes the informal or community factors required to deter crime. Unfortunately, to date, there have been virtually no empirical evaluations of the effectiveness of such shaming penalties, although studies of expected shame for doing an act consistently show a deterrent effect.[38]

Conclusion

This chapter reviewed the more recent forms of classical and deterrence theory, such as rational choice theory, which emphasizes the effects of informal sanctions (e.g., family, friends, employment) and the benefits and costs of offending, and a framework called routine activities theory, which explains why victimization tends to occur far more often in certain locations (i.e., hot spots) due to the convergence of three key elements in time and place—motivated offender(s), vulnerable target(s), and lack of guardianship—which create attractive opportunities for crime as individuals go about their everyday activities. The common element across all of these perspectives is the underlying assumption that individuals are rational beings who have free will and thus choose their behavior based on assessment of a given situation, such as by weighing possible risks versus potential payoffs. Although the studies examined in this chapter lend support to many of the assumptions and propositions of the classical framework, it is also clear that there is a lot more involved in explaining criminal human behavior than the individual decision making that goes on before a person engages in rule violation. After all, human beings, especially chronic offenders, are often not rational and often do things spontaneously without considering the potential risks beforehand. So, despite the use of the classical and neoclassical models in most systems of justice in the modern world, such theoretical models of criminal activity largely fell out of favor among experts in the mid-19th century, when an entirely new paradigm of human behavior became dominant. This new perspective became known as the Positive School, and we will discuss the origin and development of this paradigm in the following chapter.

//// CHAPTER SUMMARY

- After 100 years of neglect by criminologists, the classical and deterrence models experienced a rebirth in the late 1960s.

- The seminal studies in the late 1960s and early 1970s were largely based on aggregate and group rates of crime as well as group rates of certainty and severity of punishment, which showed that levels of actual punishment and especially certainty of punishment were associated with lower levels of crime.

---

[37] Alex Piquero and Stephen Tibbetts, eds., *Rational Choice and Criminal Behavior* (New York: Routledge, 2002).

[38] Tibbetts, "Gender Differences."

- A subsequent wave of deterrence research, cross-sectional surveys, which were collected at one time, supported previous findings that perceptions of certainty of punishment had a strong, inverse association with offending, whereas findings regarding severity were mixed.

- Longitudinal studies showed that much of the observed association between perceived levels of punishment and offending could be explained by the experiential effect, which is the phenomenon whereby behavior, rather than deterrence, affects perceptions (i.e., as opposed to perceptions affecting behavior).

- Scenario studies addressed the experiential effect by supplying a specific context—that is, through presenting a detailed vignette and then asking what subjects would do in that specific circumstance and what their perceptions of the event were.

- Rational choice theory emphasizes not only the formal and official aspects of criminal sanctions but also the informal or unofficial aspects, such as family and community.

- Whereas traditional classical deterrence theory ignored the benefits of offending, rational choice theory emphasizes them, such as the thrill offending produces, as well as the social benefits of committing crime.

- Routine activities theory provides a theoretical model that explains why certain places have far more crime than others and why some locations have hundreds of calls to police each year, whereas others have none.

- Lifestyle theories of crime reveal that the way people live may predispose them to both crime and victimization.

- Routine activities theory and the lifestyle perspective are becoming key in one of the most modern approaches to predicting and reducing crime and victimization. Specifically, GPS and other forms of geographical mapping of crime events have contributed to an elevated level of research and attention given to these theoretical models, due to their importance in specifically documenting where crime occurs and, in some cases, predicting where future crimes will occur.

- All of the theoretical models and studies reviewed in this chapter were based on classical and deterrence models, which assume that individuals consider the potential benefits and costs of punishment and then make their decisions about whether or not to engage in a criminal act.

/// KEY TERMS

cross-sectional studies 54

experiential effect 55

rational choice theory 58

routine activities theory
(lifestyle theory) 60

scenario (vignette) research 57

/// DISCUSSION QUESTIONS

1. Do you think it was good that the deterrence model was reborn, or do you think it should have been left for dead? Explain why you feel this way.

2. Considering the aggregate level of research in deterrence studies, do you find such studies valid? Explain why or why not.

3. In comparing longitudinal studies to scenario (vignette) studies, which do you think offers the most valid method for examining individual perceptions regarding the costs and benefits of committing offenses? Explain why you feel this way.

4. Can you relate to the experiential effect? If you can't, do you know someone whose behavior seems to resemble that which results from this phenomenon? Make sure to articulate what the experiential effect is.

5. With rational choice theory in mind, consider whether you would rather be subject to formal sanctions if none of your family, friends, or employers found out that you had engaged in shoplifting, or face the informal sanctions but receive no formal punishment (other than being arrested) for such a crime. Explain your decision.

6. As a teenager, did you or family or friends get a rush out of doing things that were deviant or wrong? If so, did that feeling seem to outweigh any legal or informal consequences that might have deterred you or people you knew?

7. With routine activities theory in mind, consider which places, residences, or areas of your hometown fit the idea that certain places have more crime than others (i.e., are hot spots)? Explain how you, friends, or others (including police) in your community deal with such areas. Does it work?

8. Which of the three elements of routine activities theory do you feel is the most important to address in efforts to reduce crime in the hot spots?

9. What lifestyle characteristics lead to the highest offending or victimizing rates? List at least five factors that lead to such propensities.

10. Find at least one study that uses mapping and geographical (GPS) data, and report the conclusions of that study. Do the findings and conclusions fit the routine activities theoretical framework? Why or why not?

11. What types of policy strategies derived from rational choice and routine activities theories do you think would be most effective? Least effective?

/// WEB RESOURCES

Modern Testing of Deterrence

>   http://politics.oxfordre.com/view/10.1093/acrefore/9780190228637.001.0001/
>   acrefore-9780190228637-e-313
>   https://marisluste.files.wordpress.com/2010/11/deterrence-theory.pdf

Rational Choice Theory

>   http://www.academia.edu/12541099/An_Evaluation_of_the_Rational_Choice_Theory_in_Criminology
>   http://www.answers.com/topic/rational-choice-theory-criminology

Routine Activities and Lifestyle Theory

>   http://www.popcenter.org/learning/pam/help/theory.cfm

CHAPTER 4

Early Positive School Perspectives of Criminality

In this chapter, we will discuss the dramatic differences in assumptions between the Classical and Positive Schools of criminological thought. We will also touch on the pre-Darwinian perspectives of human behavior (e.g., phrenology) as well as the influence that Charles Darwin had on the perspectives of all social sciences, particularly criminology. Finally, we will discuss the theories and methods used by early positivists, particularly Cesare Lombroso, IQ theorists, and body type researchers, with an emphasis on the criticisms of these perspectives, methodologies, and resulting policies.

After many decades of dominance by the Classical School (see Chapters 2 and 3), academics and scientists were becoming aware that the deterrence framework did not explain the distribution of crime. Their restlessness led to new explanatory models of crime and behavior. Most of these perspectives focused on the fact that certain individuals or groups tend to offend more than others and the idea that such "inferior" individuals should be controlled or even eliminated. This ideological framework fit a more general stance toward **eugenics**, the study of and policies related to the improvement of the human race via control over reproduction, which as we will see was explicitly mandated for certain groups. Thus, the conclusion was that there must be notable variations across individuals and groups that can help determine who is most at risk of offending.

So, in the early to mid-1800s, several perspectives were offered regarding how to determine which individuals or groups were most likely to commit crime. Many of these theoretical frameworks were made to distinguish the more "superior" individuals or groups from the "inferior" individuals or groups. Such intentions were likely related to the increased use of slavery in the world during the 1800s as well as imperialism's fight to quell rebellions at that time. For example, slavery was at its peak in the United States during this period, and many European countries controlled many dozens of colonies, which they were trying to retain for profit and domain.

Perhaps the first example of this belief was represented by **craniometry**. Craniometry was the belief that the size of the brain or skull represents the superiority or inferiority of certain individuals or ethnic or racial groups.[1] The size of the brain and the skull were considered because, at that time, it was believed that a person's skull perfectly conformed to brain structure; thus, the size of the skull was believed to reflect the size of the brain. Modern science has challenged this assumption, but there actually is a significant correlation between the size of the skull

---

[1] For a review, see Nicole Rafter, "The Murderous Dutch Fiddler," *Theoretical Criminology* 9, no. 1 (2005): 65–96.

and the size of the brain. Still, even according to the assumptions of the craniometrists, it is unlikely that much can be gathered about an individual's intelligence from the overall size of the brain, and certainly the skull, from simple measurements of mass.

The scientists who studied this model, if they were dealing with living subjects, would measure the various sizes or circumferences of the skulls. If they were dealing with recently dead subjects, then they would actually measure the brain weight or volume of the participants. When dealing with subjects who had died long before, craniometrists would measure the volume of skulls by pouring seeds inside and then pouring those that fit into graduated cylinders. Later, when these scientists realized that seeds were not a valid measure of volume, they moved toward using buckshot or ball bearings.

Most studies by the craniometrists tended to show that subjects of White or Western European descent were superior to those of other ethnic groups in terms of brain volume or skull size. Furthermore, the front portion of the brain (i.e., the genu) was thought to be larger in superior individuals or groups, and the hind portion of the brain or skull (i.e., the splenium) was predicted to be larger in inferior individuals or groups. Notably, these researchers typically knew which brains or skulls belonged to which ethnic or racial group before measurements were taken, making for an unethical and improper methodology. Such biased measurements continued throughout the 19th century and into the early 1900s.[2] These examinations were largely done with the intention of furthering the assumptions of eugenics, which aimed to prove under the banner of science that certain individuals and ethnic or racial groups are inferior to others. The fact that this was their intent is underscored by subsequent tests using the same subjects but performed without knowledge of which skulls or brains were from certain ethnic or racial groups; these later studies showed only a small correlation between size of the skull or brain and certain behaviors or personalities.[3]

Furthermore, once some of the early practitioners of craniometry died, their brains were found to have volumes that were less than average or average. The brain of K. F. Gauss, for example, was relatively small but more convoluted, with more gyri and fissures. Craniometrists then switched their postulates to say that more convoluted or complex brain structures, with more fissures and gyri, indicated superior brains.[4] However, this argument was even more tentative and more vague than the former hypotheses of craniometrists and thus did not last long. The same was true of craniometry in general, thanks to its noticeable lack of validity. However, it is important to note that modern studies show that people who have significantly larger brains tend to score higher on intelligence tests.[5]

Despite the failure of craniometry to explain the difference between criminals and noncriminals, scientists were not ready to give up the assumption that criminal behavior could be explained by visual differences in the skull (or brain), and they certainly weren't ready to give up the assumption that certain ethnic or racial groups were superior or inferior to others. Therefore, the experts of the time created **phrenology**. Phrenology was the science of determining human dispositions based on distinctions (e.g., bumps) in the skull, which were believed to conform to the shape of the brain.[6] Readers should keep in mind that much of the theorizing by the phrenologists still aimed

---

[2]For example, compare Robert Bean, "Some Racial Peculiarities of the Negro Brain," *American Journal of Anatomy* 5 (1906): 353–432, which showed a distinct difference in the brains across race when brains were identified by race before comparison, to Franklin P. Mall, "On Several Anatomical Characters of the Human Brain, Said to Vary According to Race and Sex, with Especial Reference to the Weight of the Frontal Lobe," *American Journal of Anatomy* 9 (1909): 1–32, which showed virtually no differences among the same brains when comparisons were made without knowledge of the races of the brains prior to comparison. See discussion in Stephen Jay Gould, *The Mismeasure of Man*, 2nd ed. (New York: Norton, 1996).

[3]See Mall, "On Several Anatomical Characters"; much of the discussion in this section is taken from Gould, *Mismeasure of Man*.

[4]Edward A. Spitska, "A Study of the Brains of Six Eminent Scientists and Scholars Belonging to the Anthropological Society, Together with a Description of the Skull of Professor E. D. Cope," *Transactions of the American Philosophical Society* 21 (1907): 175–308.

[5]Stanley Coren, *The Left-Hander Syndrome* (New York: Vintage, 1993); James Kalat, *Biological Psychology*, 8th ed. (New York: Wadsworth, 2004).

[6]Orson S. Fowler, *Fowler's Practical Phrenology: Giving a Concise Elementary View of Phrenology* (New York: O. S. Fowler, 1842).

to support the assumptions of eugenics and show that certain individuals and groups of people are inferior or superior to others.

It is important to keep in mind that, like the craniometrists, phrenologists assumed that the shape of the skull conformed to the shape of the brain. Thus, a bump or other abnormality on the skull directly related to an abnormality in the brain at that spot. Such assumptions have been refuted by modern scientific evidence, so it is not surprising that phrenology fell out of favor in criminological thought rather quickly.

Like its predecessor, however, phrenology got some things right. Certain parts of the brain are indeed responsible for specific tasks. For example, in the original phrenological map, destructiveness was indicated by abnormalities above the left ear. Modern scientific studies show that the most vital part of the brain in terms of criminality associated with trauma is the left temporal lobe, the area above the left ear.[7] Also, most readers know that specific portions of the brain govern the operation of different physical activities; one area governs the action of our hands, whereas other areas govern our arms, legs, and so on. So, the phrenologists had a few things right, but they were completely wrong about the extent to which bumps on the skull could indicate who would be most disposed to criminal behavior.

Once phrenology fell out of favor among scientists, researchers and society in general did not want to depart from the assumption that certain

▲ **Image 4.1**   Nineteenth-century phrenologists believed that each section of the brain was responsible for a particular human personality trait. If a section was enlarged or shrunken, the personality was assumed to be likewise abnormal. Doctors, particularly those doing entry examinations at American prisons, would examine each new inmate's head for bumps or cavities to develop a criminal profile. For example, if the section of the brain responsible for acquisitiveness was enlarged, the offender was probably a thief. Lombroso and his school combined phrenology with other models that included external physical traits to single out criminals from the general population.

SOURCE: © istockphoto.com / scotspencer

individuals or ethnic groups are inferior to others. Therefore, another discipline, known as **physiognomy**, became popular in the mid-1800s. Physiognomy is the study of facial and other bodily aspects to indicate developmental problems, such as criminality. Not surprisingly, the early physiognomy studies focused on contrasting various racial or ethnic groups to prove that some were superior or inferior to others.[8]

Given modern understandings of science, it is not surprising that physiognomy did not last long as a respected scientific perspective of criminality. At any time other than the late 1800s, their ideas would not have been accepted for long, if at all. However, the theory emerged at an auspicious time. Specifically, Darwin published his work *The Origin of Species* in the late 1800s and made a huge impact on societal views regarding the rank order of groups in societies.

---

[7]For reviews, see Adrian Raine, *The Anatomy of Violence: The Biological Roots of Crime* (New York: Pantheon, 2013), and Adrian Raine, *The Psychopathology of Crime* (San Diego: Academic Press, 1993).

[8]Josiah C. Nott and George R. Gliddon, *Types of Mankind* (Philadelphia: Lippincott/Grambo, 1854); Josiah C. Nott and George R. Gliddon, *Indigenous Races on Earth* (Philadelphia: Lippincott, 1868).

Darwin's model outlined a vague framework suggesting that humans had evolved from more primitive beings and that the human species (like all others) had evolved from a number of adaptations preferred by natural selection. In other words, some species are selected by their ability to adapt to the environment, whereas others do not adapt as well and die off or at least become inferior in terms of dominance. This assumption of Darwin's work, which was quickly and widely accepted by both society and scientists throughout the world, falsely led to an inclination to believe that certain ethnic or racial groups are inferior or superior to other groups. Despite a backlash by many religious authorities, who were likely threatened by the popularity of a theory that promoted natural design as opposed to a higher being or creator, Darwin had created a scientific snowball that spread like wildfire across virtually all scientific disciplines, particularly criminology.

Darwin was not a criminologist, so he is not considered a father or theorist in the field. However, he did set the stage for what followed in criminological thought. Specifically, Darwin's theory laid the groundwork for what would become the first major scientific theory of crime, namely, Lombroso's theory of born criminals, which also tied together the assumptions and propositions of craniometry, phrenology, and physiognomy.

Lombroso's Theory of Atavism and Born Criminals

Basing his work on Darwin's theory of natural selection, Cesare Lombroso (1835–1909) created what is widely considered the first attempt toward scientific theory in criminological thought. Most previous theorists were not scientists; Cesare Beccaria, for example, was trained in law and never tested his propositions. Unlike the craniometrists and phrenologists, Beccaria did not seek to explain levels of criminality. However, Lombroso was trained in medical science, and he aimed to document his observations and use scientific methodology. Furthermore, timing was on his side in the sense that Darwin's theory was published 15 years prior to Lombroso's major work, and in that time, the idea of evolution had become immensely popular with both scientists and the public.

Lombroso's Theory of Crime

The first edition of Lombroso's *The Criminal Man* was published in 1876 and created an immediate response in most Western societies, influencing both their ideas and policies related to crime and justice.[9] In this work, Lombroso outlined a theory of crime that largely brought together the pre-Darwinian theories of craniometry, phrenology, and physiognomy. Furthermore, Lombroso thought that certain groups and individuals were atavistic, and that they likely were born to commit crime. **Atavism** refers to the idea that a person or feature of an individual is a throwback to an earlier stage of evolutionary development. In other words, Lombroso thought serious criminals were lower forms of humanity in terms of evolutionary progression. For example, Lombroso would probably have suggested that chronic offenders are more like earlier stages of humankind—that is, like *missing links*—than they are like modern humans.

Lombroso noted other types of offenders, such as the mentally ill and *criminaloids*, who committed minor offenses due to external or environmental circumstances, but he argued that the *born criminals* should be the target in addressing crime, insisting that they were the most serious and violent criminals in any society. These are what most criminologists now refer to as *chronic offenders*. Furthermore, Lombroso claimed that born criminals cannot be stopped from their natural tendencies to be antisocial.

On the other hand, Lombroso claimed that, although it was their nature to commit crime, born criminals could be stopped, or at least partially deterred, by society. According to Lombroso, societies could identify born criminals,

---

[9]Cesare Lombroso, *The Criminal Man* (L'uomo Delinquente), 1st ed. (Milan: Hoepli, 1876), 2nd ed. (Turin: Bocca, 1878).

even early in life, through their **stigmata**. Stigmata were physical manifestations of the atavism of an individual—that is, features indicating a prior evolutionary stage of development.

Lombroso's List of Stigmata

According to Lombroso, more than five stigmata indicate that an individual is atavistic and inevitably will be a born criminal. Understandably, readers may be wondering what these stigmata are, given their importance. This is a great question, but the answer varies. In the beginning, this list was largely based on Lombroso's work as a physician; it included features such as large eyes and large ears. Lombroso changed this list as he went along, however, even in the last edition of his book published well into the 1900s, which might be considered poor science.

▲ **Image 4.2**   Cesare Lombroso (1837–1909).

SOURCE: Reproduced in "Rassenkunde des jüdischen Volkes" by Hans F. K. Günther 1929, J. F. Lehmanns Verlag, München, via Wikimedia Commons

For the most part, stigmata consisted of facial and bodily features that deviated from the norm, which is almost anything that went outside the bell curve of normal human physical development—in other words, abnormally small or large noses, abnormally small or large ears, abnormally small or large eyes, abnormally small or large jaws. Lombroso also threw in some extraphysiological features, such as tattoos and a family history of epilepsy and other disorders.[10] Although tattoos may be somewhat correlated to crime and delinquency, is it likely that they cause antisocial behavior? Given Lombroso's model that people are born criminal, it is quite unlikely that such factors are causally linked to criminality. How many babies are born with tattoos? Ignoring the illogical nature of many of the stigmata, Lombroso professed that people who had more than five of these physical features were born criminals and that something should be done to prevent their inevitable future offending career.

As a physician working for the Italian army, Lombroso examined the bodies of war criminals who had been captured and brought in for analysis. According to Lombroso, he first came to the realization of the nature of criminals when a particular individual was brought in for him to examine:

> This was not merely an idea, but a flash of inspiration. At the sight of that skull, I seemed to see all of a sudden, lighted up as a vast plain under a flaming sky, the problem of the nature of the criminal—an atavistic being who reproduces in his person the ferocious instincts of primitive humanity and the inferior animals.[11]

This was Lombroso's first exposure to such a criminal, and this account of it was his first acknowledgment of the theory that he created. He expanded on this theory by specifying some of the physical features he observed in this individual:

---

[10]Gould, *Mismeasure of Man*, 153.

[11]Lombroso, *Criminal Man*, as cited and discussed by Ian Taylor, Paul Walton, and Jock Young, *The New Criminology: For a Social Theory of Deviance* (London: Routledge, 1973), 41.

Thus were explained anatomically the enormous jaws, high cheek bones . . . solitary lines in the palms, extreme size of the orbits, handle-shaped ears found in criminals, savages and apes, insensibility to pain, extremely acute sight, tattooing, excessive idleness, love of orgies, and the irresponsible craving of evil for its own sake, the desire not only to extinguish life in the victim, but to mutilate the corpse, tear its flesh and drink its blood.[12]

Although most people may now laugh at his words, at the time he wrote this description, it would have rung true to most readers, which is likely why his book was the dominant text for many decades in the criminological field. In this description, Lombroso incorporates many of the core principles of his theory, including the idea that criminals are atavistic or biological throwbacks from evolution as well as the premise that they can be identified by "stigmata."

A good example of the popular acceptance of Lombroso's "scientific" stigmata was Bram Stoker's use of them in the 1896 novel *Dracula*, which featured a character based on Lombrosian traits of a villain, such as a high-bridged, thin nose; arched nostrils; massive eyebrows; and pointed ears. This novel was published in the late 1800s, when Lombroso's theory was highly dominant in society and in science. Lombroso's ideas became quite popular among academics, scientists, philosophers, fiction writers, and those responsible for criminal justice policy.

Beyond identifying born criminals by their stigmata, Lombroso said he could associate the stigmata with certain types of criminals—anarchists, burglars, murderers, shoplifters, and so on. Of course, his work is quite invalid by modern research standards.

Lombroso as the Father of Criminology and the Father of the Positive School

Lombroso's theory came a decade and a half after Darwin's work had been published and had spread rapidly throughout the Western world. Also, Lombroso's model supported what were then the Western world's views on slavery, deportation, and so on. Due to this timing and the fact that Lombroso became known as the first individual who actually tested his hypotheses through observation, Lombroso is widely considered the father of criminology. This title does not indicate respect for his theory, which has been largely rejected, or for his methods, which are considered highly invalid by modern standards. It is deserved, however, in the sense that he was the first person to gain recognition by testing his theoretical propositions. Furthermore, his theory coincided with political movements that became popular at that time: the Fascism and Nazism of the early 1900s.

Beyond being considered the father of criminology, Lombroso is also considered the father of the Positive School of criminology because he was the first to gain prominence in identifying factors beyond free will and free choice, which the Classical School said were the sole cause of crime. Although previous theorists, such as craniometrists and phrenologists, had presented perspectives that went beyond free will, Lombroso was the first to gain widespread attention. Lombroso's perspective gained almost immediate support in all developed countries of that time, which is the most likely reason why Lombroso is considered the father of the Positive School of criminology.

It is important to understand the assumptions of *positivism*, which most experts consider somewhat synonymous with the term **determinism**. Determinism is the assumption that most human behavior is determined by factors beyond free will and free choice. In other words, determinism (i.e., the Positive School) assumes that human beings do not decide how they will act by logically thinking through the costs and benefits of a given situation. Rather, the Positive School attributes all kinds of behavior, especially crime, to biological, psychological, and sociological variables.

---

[12]Taylor et al., *New Criminology*, 41–42.

Many readers probably feel they chose their career paths and made most other key decisions in their lives. However, scientific evidence shows otherwise. For example, studies clearly show that far more than 90% of the world's population has adopted the religious affiliation (e.g., Baptist, Buddhist, Catholic, Judaist) of their parents or caretakers. Therefore, what most people consider to be an extremely important decision—the choice of beliefs regarding a higher being or force—is almost completely determined by the environment in which they were brought up. Almost no one sits down and studies various religions before deciding which one suits him or her the best. Rather, in almost all cases, religion is determined by culture, and this finding goes against the Classical School's assumption that free will rules. The same type of argument can be made about the clothes we wear, the food we prefer, and the activities that give us pleasure.

Another way to distinguish positivism and determinism from the Classical School lies in the way scientists view human behavior, which can be seen best in an analogy with chemistry. Specifically, a chemist assumes that, if a certain element is subjected to certain temperatures, pressures, or mixtures with other elements, a predicted response will result. In a highly comparable way, a positivist assumes that, when human beings are subjected to poverty, delinquent peers, low intelligence, or other factors, they will react and behave in predictable ways. Therefore, there is virtually no difference in how a chemist feels about particles and elements and how a positivistic scientist feels about how humans react when exposed to biological and social factors.

In Lombroso's case, the deterministic factor was the biological makeup of the individual. However, we shall see in the next several chapters that positivistic theories focus on a large range of variables, from biology to psychology to social aspects. For example, many readers may believe that bad parenting, poverty, and associating with delinquent peers are some of the most important factors in predicting criminality. If you believe that such variables have a significant influence on decisions to commit crime, then you are likely a positive theorist; you believe that crime is caused by factors above and beyond free choice or free will.

Lombroso's Policy Implications

Beyond the theoretical aspects of Lombroso's theory of criminality, it is important to realize that his perspective had profound consequences for policy. Lombroso was called to testify in numerous criminal processes and trials to determine the guilt or innocence of suspects. Under the banner of science (comparable to what we consider DNA or fingerprint analysis in modern times), Lombroso was asked to specify whether or not a suspect had committed a crime.[13] Lombroso based such judgments on the visual stigmata that he could see among suspects.[14] Lombroso documented many of his experiences as an expert witness at criminal trials. Here is one example: "[One suspect] was, in fact, the most perfect type of the born criminal: enormous jaws, frontal sinuses, and zygomata, thin upper lip, huge incisors, unusually large head. . . . [H]e was convicted."[15]

When Lombroso was not available for such "scientific" determinations of the guilty persons, his colleagues or students (often referred to as lieutenants) were often sent. Some of these students, such as Enrico Ferri and Raphael Garrofalo, became quite active in the Fascist regime of Italy in the early 1900s. This model of government, like that of the Nazi Party of Germany, sought to remove the "inferior" groups from society.

Another policy implication in some parts of the world was the identification of young children on the basis of observed stigmata, which often become noticeable in the first 5 to 10 years of life. This led to tracking or isolating of certain children, largely based on physiological features. Although many readers may consider such policies

---

[13]See Gould, *Mismeasure of Man*.

[14]For a review of such identifications, see Gould, *Mismeasure of Man*.

[15]Cesare Lombroso, *Crime: Its Causes and Remedies* (Boston: Little, Brown, 1911), 436.

ridiculous, modern medicine has supported the identification, documentation, and importance of what are termed *minor physical anomalies (MPAs)*, which it holds may indicate high risk of developmental problems. Some of these MPAs include the following:

- Head circumference out of the normal range

- Fine, "electric" hair

- More than one hair whorl

- Epicanthus, which is observed as a fold of skin extending from the lower eyelids to the nose and appears as droopy eyelids

- Hypertelorism (orbital), which represents an increased interorbital distance

- Malformed ears

- Low-set ears

- Excessively large gap between the first and second toes

- Webbing between toes or fingers

- No earlobes

- Curved fifth finger

- Third toe longer than the second toe

- Asymmetrical ears

- Furrowed tongue

- Simian crease[16]

Given that such visible physical aspects are still correlated with developmental problems, including criminality, it is obvious that Lombroso's model of stigmata for predicting antisocial problems has implications to the present day. Such implications are more accepted by modern medical science than they are in the criminological literature. Furthermore, some modern scientific studies have shown that being unattractive predicts criminal offending, which somewhat supports Lombroso's theory of crime.[17]

About three decades after Lombroso's original work was published, and after a long period of dominance, criminologists began to question his theory of atavism and stigmata. Furthermore, it became clear that more was involved in criminality than just the way people looked, such as psychological aspects of individuals. However, scientists and societies were not ready to depart from theories like Lombroso's, which assumed that certain people or groups of people were inferior to others, so they simply chose another factor to emphasize: intelligence or IQ.

---

[16]Taken from Mary Waldrop and Charles Halverson, "Minor Physical Anomalies and Hyperactive Behavior in Young Children," in *Exceptional Infant: Studies in Abnormalities*, ed. Jerome Hellmuth (New York: Brunner/Mazel, 1971), 343–81, as cited and reviewed by Diana Fishbein, *Biobehavioral Perspectives on Criminology* (Belmont, CA: Wadsworth, 2001).

[17]Robert Agnew, "Appearance and Delinquency," *Criminology* 22 (1984): 421–40.

Case Study: Carlton "Stocking Strangler" Gary

Carlton Gary was a significantly violent offender, who was nicknamed "the Stocking Strangler" because he would break into women's homes in Columbus, Georgia, then beat them up, rape them, and use a stocking or scarf to strangle them. He is believed to have killed seven white women aged fifty-five to ninety using this same consistent method.

Gary was a rather handsome man who even worked on local television as a model, and was dating a female deputy sheriff during the time he was committing some of these murders.

One interesting fact is that Gary was a rather handsome man who even worked on local television as a model, and was dating a female deputy sheriff during the time he was committing some of these murders. Additionally, he was a loyal caregiver for his elderly aunt. However, he was not only a murderer but also a drug dealer and pimp.

Gary was clearly sly, perhaps even intelligent, which was how he managed to escape from a prison in Onondaga County, New York, by sawing through bars of his cell; even though he broke his ankle in his jump from the prison wall, he still got away by stealing a bicycle. He also escaped from a South Carolina prison, and in Georgia successfully prolonged his killing career by falsely (and convincingly) accusing another man for one of his murders.

So Gary was a chronic offender who had been in and out of trouble since he was a child. But he also had a high IQ and showed near genius-like levels in his creative attempts to escape authorities numerous times. What explains the offending by this individual?

According to Dr. Adrian Raine at University of Pennsylvania, one of the leading experts on biosocial factors in criminality, many of Gary's problems relate to various biological and social risk factors coming together and creating a type of perfect storm. Specifically, he points out that Carlton Gary never really knew his father, having met him only once when he was twelve. His mother (and her boyfriends) were physically abusive to him when he was very young, and then his mother essentially abandoned him at an early age, so he was passed around to various relatives and acquaintances at least fifteen times before his first arrest as a youth. Gary resorted to living on the streets and, often malnourished, eating out of garbage cans. Beyond the malnutrition, another physiological risk factor was that he was knocked unconscious during school recess at a young age, and was diagnosed with minimal brain dysfunction. Additionally, he had at least five or more minor physical anomalies, such as adherent ear lobes and webbing of his fingers. According to Dr. Raine, the culmination and, more importantly, the interaction among all of these biological and social/environmental factors is very likely the reason why Carlton Gary became such a persistent, predatory killer.

SOURCE: Adrian Raine, *The Anatomy of Violence: The Biological Roots of Crime* (New York: Pantheon, 2013).

The IQ Testing Era

Despite the evidence that was presented against Lombroso, his theorizing remained dominant until the early 1900s, when criminologists realized that stigmata and the idea of born criminals were not valid. However, even at that time, theorists and researchers were not ready to give up on the eugenics assumption that certain ethnic or racial groups were superior or inferior to others. Thus, a new theory emerged based on a more quantified measure that was originated, with benevolent intentions, by Alfred Binet in France. This new measure was IQ, short for *intelligence quotient*. At that time, IQ was calculated as chronological age divided by mental age, which was then multiplied by 100, with the average score being 100. This scale has changed enormously over time, but the basic premise was that the test could be used to determine whether someone was above or below average intelligence (100).

As mentioned previously, Binet had good intentions: He created IQ scores to identify youths who were not performing up to par on academic skills. Binet was explicit in stating that IQ could be changed; the reason he proposed a score to identify slow learners was so that they could be trained to increase their IQs.[18] However, when Binet's work was brought over to the United States, his basic assumptions and propositions were twisted. One of the most prominent individuals who used Binet's IQ test in the United States for purposes of deporting, incapacitating, sterilizing, and otherwise ridding society of low-IQ individuals was H. H. Goddard.

Goddard is generally considered the leading authority on the use and interpretation of IQ testing in the United States.[19] He adapted Binet's model to examine immigrants who were coming into the United States from foreign lands. It is important to note that Goddard proposed quite different assumptions regarding intelligence or IQ than did Binet. Goddard asserted that IQ was static or innate, meaning that such levels could not be changed, even with training. His assumption was that intelligence was inherited from parents and passed from generation to generation.

Goddard labeled low IQ **feeblemindedness**, which in the 1900s actually became a technical, scientific term characterizing those who had significantly below-average levels of intelligence. Of course, being a scientist, Goddard specified certain levels of feeblemindedness, which were ranked based on the degree to which scores were below average. Ranking from the highest to the lowest intelligence, the first group were the *morons*, the second-lowest group were the *imbeciles*, and the lowest-intelligence group were the *idiots*.

According to Goddard, from a eugenics point of view, the biggest threat to the progress of humanity was not the idiots but the morons. In Goddard's words, "The idiot is not our greatest problem. . . . He does not continue the race with a line of children like himself. . . . It is the moron type that makes for us our great problem."[20] That is, the moron is the one group out of the three categories of feebleminded who is smart enough to slip through the cracks and reproduce.

Goddard received many grants to fund his research to identify the feebleminded. Goddard took his research team to the major immigration center at Ellis Island in the early 1900s to identify the feebleminded as they attempted to enter the United States. Many members of his team were women, who he felt were better at distinguishing the feebleminded by sight:

▲ **Image 4.3**   H. H. Goddard (1866–1957).

SOURCE: © Getty Images / Heritage Images / Contributor

The people who are best at this work, and who I believe should do this work, are women. Women seem to have closer observation than men. It was quite impossible for others to see how . . . women could pick out the feeble-minded without the aid of the Binet test at all.[21]

---

[18]Gould, *Mismeasure of Man.*

[19]Again, most of this discussion is taken from Gould, *Mismeasure of Man*, because his review is perhaps the best known in the current literature.

[20]Henry H. Goddard, *The Kallikak Family, a Study of the Heredity of Feeble-Mindedness* (New York: MacMillan, 1912).

[21]Henry H. Goddard, "The Binet Tests in Relation to Immigration," *Journal of Psycho-Asthenics* 18 (1913): 105–7; quote taken from page 106, as cited in Gould, *Mismeasure of Man.*

Goddard was proud of the increase in the deportation of potential immigrants to the United States, enthusiastically reporting that deportations for the reason of mental deficiency increased by 350% in 1913 and 570% in 1914 over the averages of the preceding five years.[22] However, over time, Goddard realized that his policy recommendations of deportation, incarceration, and sterilization were not based on accurate science.

After consistently validating his IQ test on immigrants and mental patients, Goddard finally tested his intelligence scale on a relatively representative cross-section of American citizens, namely draftees for military service during World War I. The results showed that many of these

▲ **Image 4.4** Ellis Island.

recruits would score as feebleminded (i.e., as having a mental age of less than 12) on the IQ test. Therefore, Goddard lowered the criterion for determining feeblemindedness from the mental age of 12 to that of age 8. Although this appears to be a clear admission that his scientific method was inaccurate, Goddard continued to promote his model of the feebleminded for many years, and societies used his ideas.

However, toward the end of his career, Goddard admitted that intelligence could be improved, despite his earlier assumptions that it was innate and static.[23] In fact, Goddard actually claimed that he had "gone over to the enemy."[24] However, despite Goddard's admission that his assumptions and testing were not determinant of individuals' intelligence levels, the snowball had been rolling for too long and had gathered too much strength to fight even the most notable theorists' admonishments.

Sterilization of individuals, mostly females, continued in the United States based on scores of intelligence tests. Often the justification was not a person's own intelligence scores but those of his or her mother or father. Goddard had proclaimed that the *germ-plasm* determining feeblemindedness was passed on from one generation to the next, so it inevitably resulted in offspring being feebleminded as well. Thus, the U.S. government typically sterilized individuals, typically women, based on the IQ scores of their parents.

The case of *Buck v. Bell*, brought to the U.S. Supreme Court in 1927, dealt with the issue of sterilizing individuals who had scored, or whose parents had scored, as mentally deficient on intelligence scales. The majority opinion, written by one of the court's most respected jurists, Oliver Wendell Holmes Jr., stated:

---

[22]Gould, *Mismeasure of Man*, 198.

[23]Henry H. Goddard, "Feeblemindedness: A Question of Definition," *Journal of Psycho-Asthenics* 33 (1928): 219–27, as discussed in Gould, *Mismeasure of Man*.

[24]Ibid., 224.

We have seen more than once that the public welfare may call upon the best citizens for their lives. It would be strange if it could not call upon those who already sap the strength of the state for these lesser sacrifices.... Three generations of imbeciles are enough.[25]

Thus, the highest court in the United States upheld the use of sterilization for the purposes of limiting reproduction among individuals who were deemed feebleminded according to an IQ score. Such sterilizations continued until the 1970s, when the practice was finally halted. Governors of many states, such as North Carolina, Virginia, and California, have given public apologies for what was done. For example, in 2002, the governor of California, Gray Davis, apologized for the state law passed almost a century earlier that had resulted in the sterilization of about 19,000 women in California.

Although this aspect of U.S. history is often hidden from the public, it did occur, and it is important to acknowledge this blot on our nation's history, especially at a time when we were fighting abuses of civil rights by the Nazis and other regimes. Ultimately, the sterilizations, deportations, and incarcerations based on IQ testing are an embarrassing episode in the history of the United States.

For decades, the issue of IQ was not researched or discussed much in the literature. However, in the 1970s, a very important study was published in which Travis Hirschi and Michael Hindelang examined the effect of intelligence on youths' behaviors.[26] Hirschi and Hindelang found that, among youths of the same race and social class, intelligence had a significant effect on delinquency and criminality among individuals. This study, as well as others, showed that the IQ of delinquents or criminals is about 10 points lower than that of noncriminals.[27]

This study led to a rebirth in research regarding intelligence testing within the criminological perspective. A number of recent studies have shown that certain types of intelligence are more important than others. For example, several studies have shown that having low verbal intelligence has the most significant impact on predicting delinquent and criminal behavior.[28]

This tendency makes sense, because verbal skills are important for virtually all aspects of life, from everyday interactions with significant others to filling out forms at work to dealing with people via employment. In contrast, most people do not require advanced math or quantitative skills at their jobs or in day-to-day experiences, let alone spatial and other forms of intelligence that are more abstract. Thus, the fact that low verbal IQ is the type of intelligence that represents the most direct prediction for criminality is most likely due to the general need for verbal skills in routine daily activities. After all, people who lack communication skills will likely find it hard to obtain or retain employment or deal with family and social problems.

This rebirth in studies regarding the link between intelligence and criminality seemed to reach a peak with the publication of Richard Herrnstein and Charles Murray's *The Bell Curve* in 1994.[29] Although this publication changed the terms *moron*, *imbecile*, and *idiot* to relatively benign terms (e.g., *cognitively disadvantaged*), their argument was

---

[25]As quoted in Gould, *Mismeasure of Man*, 365.

[26]Travis Hirschi and Michael Hindelang, "Intelligence and Delinquency: A Revisionist Review," *American Sociological Review* 42 (1977): 571–87.

[27]For a review, see Raymond Paternoster and Ronet Bachman, *Explaining Criminals and Crime* (Los Angeles: Roxbury, 2001). Also see Raine, *Psychopathology*.

[28]See Joshua Isen, "A Meta-Analytic Assessment of Wechsler's P > V Sign in Antisocial Populations," *Clinical Psychology Review* 30 (2010): 423–35; and Chris L. Gibson, Alex R. Piquero, and Stephen G. Tibbetts, "The Contribution of Family Adversity and Verbal IQ to Criminal Behavior," *International Journal of Offender Therapy and Comparative Criminology* 45 (2001): 574–92. See also Hirschi and Hindelang, "Intelligence and Delinquency"; Terrie Moffitt, "The Neuropsychology of Delinquency: A Critical Review of Theory and Research," in *Crime and Justice: An Annual Review of Research*, Vol. 12, ed. Michael Tonry and Norval Morris (Chicago: University of Chicago Press, 1990), 99–169; Terrie Moffitt and Bill Henry, "Neuropsychological Studies of Juvenile Delinquency and Juvenile Violence," in *The Neuropsychology of Aggression*, ed. Joel S. Milner (Boston: Kluwer, 1991), 67–91; and the conclusion by Paternoster and Bachman in *Explaining Criminals*, 51.

[29]Richard J. Herrnstein and Charles Murray, *The Bell Curve: Intelligence and Class Structure in the United States* (New York: Free Press, 1994).

consistent with that of the feeblemindedness researchers of the early 20th century. Herrnstein and Murray argued that people with low IQ scores are somewhat destined to be unsuccessful in school, become unemployed, produce illegitimate children, and commit crime. They also suggest that IQ or intelligence is primarily innate, or genetically determined, and that there is little chance of improving it. These authors also noted that African Americans tended to score lowest, whereas Asians and Jewish people tended to score highest, and they offered results from social indicators supporting their argument that the intelligence levels of the latter resulted in relative success in life in terms of group-level statistics.

This book produced a public outcry, resulting in symposiums at major universities and other venues in which the authors' postulates were largely condemned. As noted by other reviews of the impact of this work, some professors at public institutions were sued in court because they used this book in their classes.[30] The book received blistering reviews from fellow scientists.[31] However, none of these scientific critics has fully addressed the undisputed fact that African Americans consistently score low on intelligence tests and that Asians and Jews score higher on these examinations. Furthermore, none has adequately addressed the issue that—even within these populations—low IQ scores (especially on verbal tests) predict criminality. For example, in samples of African Americans, the group that scores lowest on verbal intelligence consistently commits more crime and is more likely to become delinquent or criminal. So, despite the harsh criticism of *The Bell Curve*, it is apparent that there is some validity to the authors' arguments.

With the popularity of intelligence testing and IQ scores in the early 20th century, it is not surprising that this was also the period when other psychological models of deviance and criminality became popular. However, one of the most popular involved body type theories.

Body Type Theory: Sheldon's Model of Somatotyping

Although there were numerous theories based on body types in the late 1800s and early 1900s, such as Lombroso's and those of others who called themselves criminal anthropologists, none of these perspectives had a more enduring impact than that of William Sheldon. In the mid-1940s, a new theoretical perspective was proposed that merged the concepts of biology and psychology. Sheldon claimed that, in the embryonic and fetal stages of development, individuals tend to have an emphasis on certain tissue layers.[32] According to Sheldon, these varying degrees of emphasis are largely due to heredity and lead to the development of certain body types and temperaments or personalities. This became the best-known body type theory, also known as **somatotyping**.

According to Sheldon, all embryos must develop three distinct tissue layers, and this much is still acknowledged by perinatal medical researchers. The first layer of tissue is the **endoderm**, which is the inner layer of tissues and includes the internal organs, such as the stomach, large intestine, and small intestine. The middle layer of tissue, called the **mesoderm**, includes the muscles, bones, ligaments, and tendons. The **ectoderm** is the outer layer of tissue, which includes the skin, capillaries, and much of the nervous system's sensors.

Sheldon used these medical facts regarding various tissue layers to propose that certain individuals tend to emphasize certain tissue layers relative to others, typically due to inherited dispositions. In turn, Sheldon believed that such emphases lead to certain body types in an individual, such that people who have a focus on their

---

[30]See Stephen E. Brown, Finn-Aage Esbensen, and Gilbert Geis, *Criminology: Explaining Crime and Its Context*, 8th ed. (Cincinnati, OH: Anderson, 2012), 260 (see chap. 2).

[31]J. Blaine Hudson, "Scientific Racism: The Politics of Tests, Race, and Genes," *Black Scholar* 25 (1995): 1–10; David Perkins, *Outsmarting IQ: The Emerging Science of Learnable Intelligence* (New York: Free Press, 1995); Francis Cullen et al., "Crime and the Bell Curve: Lessons from Intelligent Criminology," *Crime and Delinquency* 43 (1997): 387–411; Robert Hauser, "Review of the Bell Curve," *Contemporary Sociology* 24 (1995): 149–53; Howard Taylor, "Book Review, *The Bell Curve*," *Contemporary Sociology* 24 (1995): 153–58; Gould, *Mismeasure of Man*, 367–90.

[32]William Sheldon, E. M. Hartl, and E. McDermott, *Varieties of Delinquent Youth* (New York: Harper, 1949).

▲ **Image 4.5a**   Endomorph. Physical traits: soft body, underdeveloped muscles, round shape, overdeveloped digestive system. Associated personality traits: love of food, tolerance, evenness of emotions, love of comfort, sociability, good humor, relaxed mood, need for affection.

SOURCE: © 2012 Encyclopaedia Britannica, Inc.

▲ **Image 4.5b**   Mesomorph. Physical traits: hard, muscular body; overly mature appearance; rectangular shape; thick skin; upright posture. Associated personality traits: love of adventure, desire for power and dominance, courage, indifference to what others think or want, assertive mien, boldness, zest for physical activity, competitive nature, love of risk and chance.

SOURCE: © 2012 Encyclopaedia Britannica, Inc.

▲ **Image 4.5c**   Ectomorph. Physical traits: thin, flat chest; delicate build; young appearance; light muscling; stooped shoulders; large brain. Associated personality traits: self-consciousness, preference for privacy, introversion, inhibition, social anxiety, artistic inclination, mental intensity, emotional restraint.

SOURCE: © 2012 Encyclopaedia Britannica, Inc.

endoderms in embryonic development will inevitably become **endomorphic**, or obese (see Image 4.5a). According to this theory, individuals who have an emphasis on the middle layer of tissue will typically become **mesomorphic**, or of an athletic or muscular build (see Image 4.5b), while individuals who have an emphasis on the outer layer will end up with an **ectomorphic** build, or thin (see Image 4.5c).

Sheldon and his research team graded each subject on three dimensions corresponding to these body types. Each body type was measured on a scale of 1 to 7, with 7 being the highest score. Obviously, no one could score a 0 for any body type because all tissue layers are needed for survival; we all need our internal organs, bone and muscular structure, and outer systems (skin, capillaries, etc.).

Each somatotype always had the following order: endomorphy, mesomorphy, ectomorphy. Thus, the scores on a typical somatotype might be 3-6-2, which would indicate that this person scored a 3 (a little lower than average) on endomorphy, a 6 (high) on mesomorphy, and a 2 (relatively low) on ectomorphy. According to Sheldon's theory, this hypothetical subject would be a likely candidate for criminality because of the relatively high score on mesomorphy. In fact, the results from his data, as well as all studies that have examined the association of body types with delinquency or criminality, would support this prediction.

Perhaps most important, Sheldon proposed that these body types matched personality traits or temperaments. Individuals who were endomorphic (obese), Sheldon claimed, tended to be more jolly or lazy. The technical term for this temperament is **viscerotonic**. In contrast, people who were mesomorphic (muscular) typically had risk-taking and aggressive temperaments, called **somotonic**. Last, individuals who were ectomorphic (thin) tended to have introverted or shy personalities, which is referred to as **cerebrotonic**. According to Sheldon, members of the middle group, the mesomorphs, obviously had the highest propensity toward criminality because they were disposed toward a risk-taking and aggressive personality.

Interestingly, many politicians were subjects in Sheldon's research. Most entering freshmen at Ivy League schools, especially Harvard, were asked to pose for photos for Sheldon's studies. The Smithsonian Institution still retains a collection of nude photos of George W. Bush, Hillary Rodham Clinton, and many other notable figures.[33]

Sheldon used poor methodology to test his theory. He based his measures of subjects' body types on what he subjectively judged from viewing three perspectives of each subject and often from only three pictures taken of each subject in the three poses. He also had his trained staff view many of the photos and make their determinations of how these individuals scored on each category of body type. The reliability among these scorings has been shown to be weak, meaning that the trained staff did not tend to agree with Sheldon or among themselves on the somatotypes for each participant.

This is not surprising, given the high level of variation in body types and the fact that Sheldon and his colleagues did not employ the technology that is used today, such as caliper tests and submersion in water tanks, which provide the information for which he was searching. People may alter their weights, going from an ectomorphic or mesomorphic build to a more endomorphic form, or vice versa. Presented with the argument that individuals often alter their body types via diet or exercise, Sheldon responded that he could tell what the "natural" body type of each individual was from the three pictures that were taken. Obviously, this position is not a strong one, as demonstrated by the poor interrater reliability shown by his staff. Therefore, Sheldon's methodology is questionable, which casts doubt on the entire theoretical framework.

Despite the problems in his methodology, Sheldon clearly showed that mesomorphs, or individuals who had muscular builds and tended to take more risks, were more delinquent and criminal than individuals who had other body types or temperaments.[34] Furthermore, other researchers, even those who despised Sheldon's theory, found the same associations between mesomorphy and criminality as well as related temperaments (i.e., somotonic) and criminality.[35] Subsequent studies showed that mesomorphic boys were far more likely to have personality traits that predicted criminality, such as aggression, short temper, self-centeredness, and impulsivity.

Recent theorists have also noted the link between an athletic, muscular build and the highly extroverted, aggressive personality that is often associated with this body type.[36] In fact, some recent theorists have gone so far as to claim that chronic offenders, both male and female, can be identified early in life by their relatively V-shaped pelvic structure as opposed to a U-shaped pelvic structure.[37] The V-shaped pelvis is said to indicate relatively high levels of androgens (male hormones, like testosterone) in the system, which predisposes individuals toward crime. On the other hand, a more U-shaped pelvis indicates relatively low levels of such androgens and therefore lower propensity toward aggression and criminality. Using this logic, it may be true that more hair on an individual's arms (whether that person be male or female) is predictive of a high likelihood for committing crime. However, no research exists regarding this factor.

Regarding the use of body types and characteristics in explaining crime, many of the hard-line sociologists who have attempted to examine or replicate Sheldon's results have never been able to refute the association between

---

[33]See discussion in Brown et al., *Criminology*, 246.

[34]Sheldon et al., *Varieties*.

[35]Sheldon Glueck and Eleanor Glueck, *Physique and Delinquency* (New York: Harper & Row, 1956). See also Emil Hartl, *Physique and Delinquent Behavior* (New York: Academic Press, 1982); and Juan Cortes, *Delinquency and Crime* (New York: Seminar Press, 1972). For the most recent applications, see Hans J. Eysenck and G. H. Gudjonsson, *The Causes and Cures of Criminality* (New York: Plenum, 1989).

[36]James Q. Wilson and Richard Herrnstein, *Crime and Human Nature* (New York: Simon & Schuster, 1985).

[37]Eysenck and Gudjonsson, *Causes and Cures*; Raine, *Psychopathology*.

mesomorphs and delinquency or criminality, nor the association between mesomorphy and the somotonic characteristics of risk-taking and aggression.[38] Thus, the association between being muscular or athletically built and engaging in criminal activities is now undisputed and assumed to be true.

Still, sociologists have taken issue with the reasons for this association. Whereas Sheldon claimed it was due to inherited traits for a certain body type, sociologists argue that this association is due to societal expectations: Muscular male youths would be encouraged to engage in risk-taking and aggressive behavior. For example, a young male with an athletic build would be encouraged to join sports teams and engage in high-risk behaviors by peers. Who would gangs most desire as members? More muscular, athletic individuals would be better at fighting and performing acts that require a certain degree of physical strength and stamina.

Ultimately, it is now established that mesomorphs are more likely to commit crime.[39] Furthermore, the personality traits linked to having an athletic or muscular build are dispositions toward risk-taking and aggressiveness, and few scientists dispute this correlation. No matter which theoretical model is adopted—whether the biopsychologists' or the sociologists'—the fact is that mesomorphs are indeed more likely to be risk-taking and aggressive and, thus, to commit more crime than individuals of other body types.

However, whether the cause is biological or sociological is a debate that shows the importance of theory in criminological research. After all, the link between mesomorphy and criminality is now undisputed; the explanation of why this link exists has become a theoretical debate. Readers may make their own determination—if not now, then later.

Our position is that both biology and social environment are likely to interact with one another in explaining this link. Thus, it is most likely that both nature and nurture are at play in this association between mesomorphy and crime, and both Sheldon and his critics may be correct. A middle ground can often be found in theorizing on criminality. It is important to keep in mind that theories in criminology, as a science, are always considered subject to falsification and criticism and can always be improved. Therefore, our stance on the validity and influence of this theory, as well as others, should not be surprising.

Policy Implications

Many policy implications can be derived from the theories presented in this chapter. First, one could propose more thorough medical screening at birth and in early childhood, especially regarding minor physical anomalies (MPAs). The studies reviewed in this chapter obviously implicate numerous MPAs in developmental problems (most of them arising in the womb). These MPAs are a red flag signaling problems, especially in cognitive abilities, which are likely to have a significant impact on propensity for criminal behavior.[40] Recent reviews of such MPAs have been found to be very important in identifying red flags for higher likelihood for criminal behavior, even in children as young as age 3.[41] Furthermore, recent studies have found that a high number of MPAs interact with other social factors.[42] Specifically, MPAs have been found to interact with environmental risk factors, such as family disorder or adversity, consistently in prediction of antisocial or criminal adults.[43]

Other policy implications derived from the theories and findings of this chapter involve having same-sex classes for children in school because they focus on deficiencies that have been shown for both young boys and

---

[38]Cortes, *Delinquency and Crime*; Glueck and Glueck, *Physique and Delinquency*. For a review, see Eysenck and Gudjonsson, *Causes and Cures*.

[39]For a review, see Lee Ellis and Anthony Walsh, *Criminology: A Global Perspective* (Minot: Pyramid Press, 2000), supplemental tables and references.

[40]Fishbein, *Biobehavioral Perspectives*.

[41]Raine, *Anatomy of Violence,* 192–94.

[42]Ibid.

[43]Ibid.

girls. Numerous school districts now have policies that specify same-sex math courses for female children. This same strategy might be considered for male children in English or literature courses because males have a biological disposition for a lower aptitude than females in this area of study. Furthermore, far more screening should be done to determine IQ and aptitude levels of young children in order to identify which children require extra attention because studies show that such early intervention can make a big difference in improving their IQ and aptitude.[44]

A recent report that reviewed the extant literature regarding what types of programs work best for reducing crime noted the importance of diagnosing early head trauma and further concluded that one of the most consistently supported programs for such at-risk children are those that involve weekly infant home visitation.[45] Another obvious policy implication derived from biosocial theory is mandatory health insurance for pregnant mothers and children, which is quite likely the most efficient way to reduce crime in the long term.[46] Finally, all youths should be screened for abnormal levels of hormones, neurotransmitters, and toxins (especially lead).[47]

Conclusion

In this chapter, we discussed the development of the early Positive School of criminology. The Positive School can be seen as the opposite of the Classical School perspective, which we covered in Chapters 2 and 3, because positivism assumes that individuals have virtually no free will; rather, criminal behavior is considered to be the result of determinism, which means that factors other than rational decision making, such as poverty, intelligence, bad parenting, and unemployment, influence us and determine our behavior.

The earliest positivist theories, such as craniometry and phrenology, were developed in the early 1800s but did not become popular outside of scientific circles, likely because they were presented prior to Charles Darwin's theory of evolution. In the 1860s, Darwin's theory became widely accepted, which set the stage for the father of criminology, Lombroso, to propose his theory of born criminals. Lombroso's theory was based on Darwin's theory of evolution and argued that the worst criminals are born that way, being biological throwbacks to an earlier stage of evolution. Unfortunately, Lombroso's theory led to numerous policies that fit the philosophy and politics of Fascism, which found useful a theory proposing that certain people were inferior to others. However, Lombroso and many of his contemporaries became aware that the field should shift to a more multifactorial approach, such as one emphasizing how environment and social factors interact with physiological influences.

We also discussed theories regarding low IQ scores, traditionally known as feeblemindedness. Although most recent studies show that there is a correlation between crime and low IQ, this association is not quite as strong as thought in the early 1900s. Modern studies show consistent evidence that low verbal IQ is related with criminality,[48] especially when coupled with sociological factors, such as weak family structure. This is the state of the criminological field today, and it will be discussed in the next chapter.

Finally, we explored the theories and evidence regarding body types in predisposing an individual toward criminality. Studies have shown that the more athletic or mesomorphic an individual is, the higher the probability that this individual will be involved in criminality. This relationship is likely based on hormonal levels, and this type of association will be explored in the next chapter.

---

[44]John P. Wright, Stephen Tibbetts, and Leah Daigle, *Criminals in the Making: Criminality across the Life Course* (Thousand Oaks, CA: Sage, 2015).

[45]Lawrence Sherman et al., *Preventing Crime: What Works, What Doesn't, What's Promising: A Report to the United States Congress* (Washington, DC: U.S. Department of Justice, 1997) (see chap. 2).

[46]Wright et al., *Criminals in the Making*.

[47]Ibid., 258–63.

[48]Gibson et al., "Contribution of Family Adversity."

Ultimately, we have examined a variety of physiological and psychological factors that predict criminal offending according to empirical research. Still, the existence of such influence is largely conditional—that is, based on environmental and social factors.

/// CHAPTER SUMMARY

- The Positive School of criminology assumes the opposite of the Classical School. Whereas the Classical School assumes that individuals commit crime because they freely choose to act after rationally considering the expected costs and benefits of the behavior, the Positive School assumes that individuals have virtually no free will or choice in the matter; rather, their behavior is determined by factors outside of free will, such as poverty, low intelligence, bad child rearing, and unemployment.

- The earliest positive theories, such as craniometry and phrenology, emphasized measuring the size and shape of the skull and brain. These perspectives did not become very popular because they preceded Darwin's theory of evolution.

- Lombroso, the father of criminology, presented a theoretical model that assumed that the worst criminals are born that way. Highly influenced by Darwin, Lombroso claimed that born criminals are evolutionary throwbacks who are not as highly developed as most people.

- Lombroso claimed that these born criminals could be identified by physical features called stigmata. This led to numerous policy implications that fit with the societal beliefs at that time, such as Fascism.

- In the early 1900s, the IQ test was invented in France and was quickly used by American researchers in their quest to identify the feebleminded. This led to massive numbers of deportations, sterilizations, and institutionalizations across the United States and elsewhere.

- Modern studies support a link between low verbal IQ and criminality, even within a given race, social class, or gender.

- Merging elements of the early physiological and psychological perspectives are body type theories. The best known of these is somatotyping, which was proposed by William Sheldon. Sheldon found that an athletic or muscular build (i.e., mesomorphy) is linked to an aggressive, risk-taking personality, which in turn is associated with higher levels of crime.

- Despite the methodological problems with Sheldon's body type theory, many propositions and associations of the perspective hold true in modern studies.

- The early Positive School theories set the stage for most of the other theories we will be covering in this book because they emphasize use of the scientific method for studying and explaining criminal activity.

/// KEY TERMS

atavism 72

cerebrotonic 83

craniometry 69

determinism 74

ectoderm 81

ectomorphic 82

endoderm 81

endomorphic 82

eugenics 69

feeblemindedness 78

mesoderm 81

mesomorphic 82

minor physical
   anomalies (MPAs) 76

phrenology 70

physiognomy 71

somatotyping 81

somotonic 83

stigmata 73

viscerotonic 82

//// DISCUSSION QUESTIONS

1. What characteristics distinguish the Positive School from the Classical School regarding criminal thought? Which of these schools do you lean toward in your own perspective of crime and why?

2. Name and describe the various early schools of positivistic theories that existed in the early to mid-1800s (pre-Darwin) as well as the influence that they had on later schools of thought regarding criminality. Do you see any validity in these approaches (as modern medical science does)? Why or why not?

3. What were the significant reasons that these early schools of positivistic theories did not gain much momentum in societal popularity? Does this lack of popularity relate to the neglect of biological perspectives of crime in modern times?

4. What portion of Lombroso's theory of criminality do you find least valid? Which do you find most valid?

5. Most readers have taken the equivalent of an IQ test (e.g., SAT or ACT tests). Do you believe that this score is a fair representation of your knowledge as compared to that of others? Why or why not? Do your feelings reflect the criticisms of experts regarding the use of IQ (e.g., as in feeblemindedness theory) in identifying potential offenders?

6. In light of scientific findings that show that verbal IQ is a consistent predictor of criminality among virtually all populations and samples, can you provide evidence from your personal experience for why this occurs?

7. What portion of Sheldon's body type theory do you find most valid? What do you find least valid?

8. If you had to give yourself a somatotype (e.g., 3-6-2), what would it be? Explain why your score would be the one you provide, and note whether this would make you likely to be a criminal in Sheldon's model.

9. Provide somatotypes of five of your family members or best friends. Do the somatotypes have any correlation with criminality according to Sheldon's predictions? Either way, describe your findings.

10. Ultimately, do you believe that some of the positive theoretical perspectives presented in this chapter are valid, or do you think they should be entirely dismissed in terms of understanding or predicting crime? Either way, state your case.

11. What types of policies would you implement if you were in charge, given the theories and findings in this chapter?

//// WEB RESOURCES

Body Type Theories/Somatotyping

   http://www.innerexplorations.com/psytext/shel.htm
   http://www.teachpe.com/gcse_health/somatotypes.php

IQ Testing/Feeblemindedness

http://www.eugenicsarchive.org/html/eugenics/static/themes/12.html

Cesare Lombroso

http://www.historyextra.com/article/feature/born-criminal-lombroso-origins-modern-criminology

Phrenology/Craniometry

http://www.phrenology.org/index.html
http://skepdic.com/cranial.html

CHAPTER 5

Modern Biosocial Perspectives of Criminal Behavior

This chapter will discuss the more modern biological studies of the 20th century. We will begin with studies from the early 1900s—particularly those that sought to emphasize the influence of biological factors on criminality. Virtually all of these studies have shown a significant biological effect in the development of criminal propensities. Then we will examine the influence of a variety of physiological factors, including chromosomal mutations, hormones, neurotransmitters, brain trauma, and other dispositional aspects of individuals' nervous systems. A special emphasis will be placed on showing the consistent evidence that has been found for the interaction between physiological and environmental factors (i.e., biosocial factors).

This chapter will examine a variety of perspectives that deal with interactions between physiological and environmental factors, which is currently the dominant model explaining criminal behavior. First, we will discuss the early studies that attempted to emphasize the biological aspects of offending: family, twin, and adoption studies. All of these studies show that biological influences are more important than social and environmental factors, and most also conclude that when both negative biological and disadvantaged environmental variables are combined, these individuals are by far the most likely to offend in the future, which fully supports the interaction between nature and nurture factors.

Later in this chapter, we will examine other physiological factors, such as hormones and neurotransmitters. We will see that chronic, violent offenders tend to have significantly different levels of hormones and other chemicals in their bodies than do other individuals. Furthermore, we will examine brain trauma and activity among violent offenders, and we will see that habitual violent criminals tend to have slower brain wave patterns and lower anxiety levels than other persons. Ultimately, we will see that numerous physiological distinctions can be made between chronic violent offenders and others but that these differences are most evident when physical factors are combined with being raised in poor, disadvantaged environments.

Nature versus Nurture: Studies Examining the Influence of Genetics and Environment

At the same time that Freud was developing his perspective of psychological deviance, other researchers were busy testing the influence of heredity versus environment to see which of these two components had the strongest effect on predicting criminality. This type of testing produced four waves of research: (1) family studies; (2) twin studies;

(3) adoption studies; and, in recent years, (4) studies of identical twins separated at birth. Each of these waves of research contributed to our understanding of how much criminality is inherited from our parents (or other ancestors) versus how much is due to cultural norms, such as family or community. Ultimately, all of the studies have shown that the interaction between these two aspects—genetics and environment—is what causes crime among individuals and groups in society.

Family Studies

The most notable **family studies** were done in the early 1900s by Richard Dugdale in his study of the Jukes family and the previously discussed researcher Henry Goddard, who studied the Kallikak family.[1] These studies were supposed to test the proposition that criminality is more likely to be found in certain families, which would indicate that crime is inherited. Due to the similarity of the results, we will focus here on Goddard's work on the Kallikak family.

This study showed that a much higher proportion of children from the Kallikak family became criminal. Furthermore, Goddard thought that many of the individuals (often children) from the Kallikak family actually looked like criminals, which fit Cesare Lombroso's theory of stigmata. In fact, Goddard had photographs made of many members of this family to back up these claims. However, follow-up investigations of Goddard's research have shown that many of these photographs were actually altered to make the subjects appear more sinister or evil (fitting Lombroso's stigmata) by altering their facial features—most notably their eyes.[2]

Despite the despicable methodological problems with Goddard's data and subsequent findings, two important conclusions can be made from the family studies that were done in the early 1900s. The first is that criminality is indeed more common in some families; in fact, no study has ever shown otherwise. However, this tendency cannot be shown to be a product of heredity or genetics. After all, individuals from the same family are also products of a similar environment—often a bad one—so this conclusion from the family studies does little to advance knowledge regarding the relative influence of nature versus nurture in terms of predicting criminality.

The second conclusion of family studies was more insightful and interesting. Specifically, they showed that criminality by the mother (or head female caretaker) had a much stronger influence on the future criminality of the children than did the father's criminality. This is likely due to two factors. The first is that the father is often absent most of the time while the children are being raised. Perhaps more important is that it takes much more for a woman to transgress social norms and become a convicted offender, which indicates that the mother is highly antisocial; this gives some (albeit limited) credence to the argument that criminality is somewhat inherited. Despite this conclusion, it should be apparent from the weaknesses in the methodology of family studies that this finding did not hold much weight in the nature versus nurture debate. Thus, a new wave of research soon emerged that did a better job of measuring the influence of genetics versus environment, which was twin studies.

Twin Studies

After family studies, the next wave of tests done to determine the relative influence on criminality between nature and nurture involved **twin studies**, the examination of identical twin pairs versus fraternal twin pairs. Identical twins are also known as **monozygotic (MZ) twins** because they come from a single (hence *mono*) egg (*zygote*). Such twins share 100% of their genotype, meaning they are identical in terms of genetic makeup. Keep in mind that everyone shares approximately 99% of the human genetic makeup, leaving about 1% that can vary over the entire species. On the other hand, fraternal twins are typically referred to as **dizygotic (DZ) twins** because they come

---

[1]Stephen Jay Gould, *The Mismeasure of Man*, 2nd ed. (New York: Norton, 1996) (see chap. 4, n. 2).

[2]Ibid., 198–204, for an excellent discussion of the alteration of Goddard's photographs.

from two (hence *di*) separate eggs. Such DZ twins share 50% of genes that can vary, which is the same amount that any siblings from the same two parents share. DZ twins can be of different genders and may look and behave quite differently, as many readers have probably observed.

The goal of the twin studies was to examine the **concordance rates** between MZ twin pairs and DZ twin pairs regarding delinquency. Concordance is a count based on whether two people (or a twin pair) share a certain trait (or lack of the trait); for our purposes, the trait is criminal offending. Regarding a count of concordance, if one twin is an offender, then we look to see if the other is also an offender. If that person is, then we say there is concordance given the fact that the first twin was a criminal offender. Also, if neither of the twins is an offender, that also is concordant because they both lack the trait.

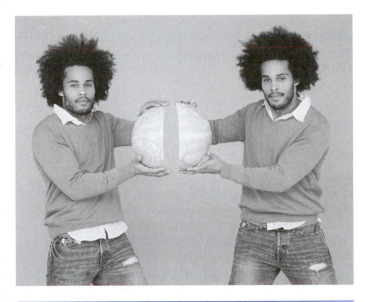

▲ **Image 5.1**   Identical twins.

However, if one twin is a criminal offender and the other twin of the pair is not an offender, then this would be discordant in the sense that one has a trait that the other does not.

Thus, the twin studies focused on comparing the concordance rates of MZ twin pairs versus those of DZ twin pairs with the assumption that any significant difference in concordance could be attributed to the similarity of the genetic makeup of the MZ twins (which is 100%) versus the DZ twins (which is significantly less—that is, 50%). If genetics plays a major role in determining the criminality of individuals, then it would be expected that MZ twins would have a significantly higher concordance rate for being criminal offenders than would DZ twins. In these studies, it was assumed that each twin in each MZ or DZ twin pair had been raised in more or less the same environment as the other twin since each pair had been brought up in the same family at the same time.

A number of studies were performed in the early and mid-1900s that examined the concordance rates between MZ and DZ twin pairs. These studies clearly showed that identical twins had far higher concordance rates than did fraternal twins; most studies showed twice as much concordance or more for MZ twins—even for serious criminality.[3]

However, the studies regarding the comparisons between the twins were strongly criticized for reasons that many readers readily see. Specifically, identical twins, who look almost exactly alike, are typically dressed the same by their parents and treated the same by the public. In addition, they are generally expected to behave the same way. However, this is not true for fraternal twins, who often look very different and quite often are of different genders. Thus, the foundation for criticism of the twin studies was the very valid argument that the higher rate of concordance among MZ twins could have been due to the extremely similar way they were treated or expected to behave

[3]See reviews in Adrian Raine, *The Anatomy of Violence* (New York: Pantheon, 2013); Adrian Raine, *The Psychopathology of Crime* (San Diego: Academic Press, 1993); and John P. Wright, Stephen G. Tibbetts, and Leah Daigle, *Criminals in the Making: Criminality across the Life Course*, 2nd ed. (Thousand Oaks, CA: Sage, 2015) (see chap. 4). See also Juan B. Cortes, *Delinquency and Crime* (New York: Seminar Press, 1972); and Karl O. Christiansen, "Seriousness of Criminality and Concordance among Danish Twins," in *Crime, Criminology, and Public Policy*, ed. Roger Hood (New York: Free Press, 1974).

by society. Another criticism of the early twin studies had to do with the questionable accuracy of determinations of whether twins were fraternal or identical, which was often done by sight in the early tests.[4] Although these criticisms were seemingly valid, the most recent meta-analysis, which examined virtually all of the twin studies done up to the 1990s, concluded that the twin studies showed evidence of a significant hereditary basis for criminality.[5] Still, the criticisms of such studies were quite valid; therefore, in the early to mid-1900s, researchers involved in the nature versus nurture debate attempted to address these valid criticisms by moving on to another methodological approach to examining this debate: adoption studies.

Adoption Studies

Due to the valid criticisms leveled at twin studies in determining the relative influence of nature (biological) or nurture (environmental), researchers in this area moved on to **adoption studies**, which examined the predictive influence of the biological parents versus that of the adoptive parents who raised the children from infancy to adulthood. It is important to realize that, in such studies, the adoptees were typically given up for adoption prior to 6 months of age, meaning that the biological parents had relatively no interaction with their natural children; rather, they were almost completely raised from infancy by the adoptive parents.

Perhaps the most notable of the adoption studies was done by Sarnoff Mednick and his colleagues in which they examined male children born in Copenhagen between 1927 and 1941 who had been adopted early in life.[6] In this study and virtually all others that have examined adoptees in this light, by far the highest predictability for future criminality was found for adopted youths who had *both* a biological parent and an adoptive parent who were convicted criminals. However, the Mednick study also showed that the criminality of biological parent(s) had a far greater predictive effect on future criminality of offspring than did the criminality of adoptive parents. Still, the adopted children who were least likely to become criminal had no parent with a criminal background. In light of this last conclusion, these findings support the major contentions of this book's author in the sense that they fully back up the nature *via* nurture argument as opposed to the nature *versus* nurture argument. They support the idea that both biological *and* environmental factors contribute to the future criminality of youths.

Unfortunately, the researchers who performed these studies focused on the other two groups of youths—those who had either only criminal biological parents or only criminal adoptive parents. Thus, these adoption studies found that the adoptees who had only biological parents who were criminal had a much higher likelihood of becoming criminal compared to the youths who had only adoptive parents who were criminal. Obviously, this finding supports the idea that genetic influence predisposes people toward criminality. However, this methodology was subject to criticism.

Perhaps the most notable criticism of adoption studies was that adoption agencies typically incorporated a policy of **selective placement** in which adoptees were placed with adoptive families similar in terms of demographics and background to their biological parents. Such selective placement could bias the results of adoption studies. However, recent analyses have examined the impact of such bias, concluding that, even after accounting for the influence of selective placement, the ultimate findings of the adoption studies are still somewhat valid.[7] Children's

---

[4]Raine, *Psychopathology of Crime*.

[5]Glenn Walters, "A Meta-Analysis of the Gene–Crime Relationship," *Criminology* 30 (1992): 595–613.

[6]Barry Hutchings and Sarnoff A. Mednick, "Criminality in Adoptees and Their Adoptive and Biological Parents: A Pilot Study," in *Biosocial Bases of Criminal Behavior*, ed. Sarnoff Mednick and Karl O. Christiansen (New York: Gardner Press, 1977), 127–41. See recent review and study by Randi Hjalmarsson and Matthew J. Lindquist, "The Origins of Intergenerational Associations in Crime: Lessons from Swedish Adoption Data," *Labour Economics* 20 (2013): 68–81.

[7]See James Q. Wilson and Richard J. Herrnstein, *Crime and Human Nature* (New York: Simon & Schuster, 1985); and Walters, "Gene–Crime Relationship."

biological parents likely have more influence on their future criminality than the adoptive parents who raise them from infancy to adulthood. Still, the criticism of selective placement was strong enough to encourage a fourth wave of research in the nature versus nurture debate, which became studies on identical twins separated at birth.

Twins Separated at Birth

Until recently, studies of identical twins separated at birth were virtually impossible because it was so difficult to get a high number of identical twins who had indeed been separated early. But since the early 1990s, **twins-separated-at-birth studies** have been possible. Readers should keep in mind that, in many of the identical twin pairs studied for these investigations, the individuals did not even know they had a twin. Furthermore, the environments in which they were raised were often extremely different; one twin might be raised by a very poor family in an urban environment while the other twin was raised by a middle- to upper-class family in a rural environment.

These studies—the most notable having been done at the University of Minnesota—found that the twin pairs often showed extremely similar tendencies for criminality, sometimes more similar than those seen in concordance rates for identical twins raised together.[8] This finding obviously supports the profound influence of genetics and heredity, which is not surprising to most well-read scientists, who now acknowledge the extreme importance of inheritance of physiological and psychological aspects to human behavior. Perhaps more surprising was why separated identical twins, who had never known that they had a twin and were often raised in extremely different circumstances, had just as high or even higher concordance rates than identical twins who were raised together.

The leading theory for this phenomenon is that identical twins who are raised together actually go out of their way to deviate from their natural tendencies to form an identity separate from their identical twin with whom they have spent their entire lives. As for criticisms of this methodology, none have been presented in the scientific literature. Thus, it is somewhat undisputed at this point that the identical-twins-separated-at-birth studies have shown that genetics has a significant impact on human behavior, especially regarding criminal activity.

Ultimately, taking all of the nature versus nurture methodological approaches and subsequent findings together, the best conclusion that can be made is that genetics and heredity both have significant impacts on criminality. Environment simply cannot account for all of the consistent results seen in the comparisons between identical twins and fraternal twins, those of identical twins separated at birth, and those of adoptees with criminal biological parents versus those who did not have such parents. Despite the taboo nature of and controversial response to the findings of such studies, it is quite clear that when nature and nurture are compared, biological rather than environmental factors tend to have the most influence on the criminality of individuals. Still, the author of this book hopes that readers will emphasize the importance of the interaction between nature and nurture (better stated as nature *via* nurture). Ultimately, the author hopes to have shown quite convincingly through scientific study that it is the interplay between biology and the environment that is most important in determining human behavior.

Perhaps in response to this nature versus nurture debate, a new theoretical perspective was offered in the mid-1900s that merged biological and psychological factors in explaining criminality. Although it leaned more toward the nature side of the debate, critics would use this same perspective to promote the nurture side, so this framework was useful in promoting the interaction between biology and sociological factors.

Cytogenetic Studies: The XYY Factor

Beyond the body type theories, another model was proposed in the early 1900s regarding biological conditions that predispose individuals toward crime: **cytogenetic studies**. Cytogenetic studies of crime focus on the

---

[8]Thomas J. Bouchard et al., "Sources of Human Psychological Differences: The Minnesota Study of Twins Reared Apart," *Science* 250 (1990): 223–28. Also see the review in Wright et al., *Criminals in the Making* (chap. 4).

genetic makeup of individuals, with a specific focus on abnormalities in chromosomal makeup, and specifically chromosomal abnormalities that occur randomly in the population. Many of the chromosomal mutations that have been studied (such as XYY) typically result not from heredity but from random mutations in chromosomal formation.

The normal chromosomal makeup for women is XX, which represents an X from the mother and an X from the father. The normal chromosomal makeup for men is XY, which represents an X from the mother and a Y from the father. However, as in many species of animals, there are often genetic mutations, which we see in human beings. Consistent with evolutionary theory, virtually all possible variations of chromosomes that are possible have been found in the human population, such as XXY, XYY, and many others. We will focus our discussion on the chromosomal mutations that have been most strongly linked to criminality.

One of the first chromosomal mutations recognized as a predictor of criminal activity was XYY. In 1965, the first major study showed that this mutation was far more common in a Scottish male population of mental patients than in the general population.[9] Specifically, in the general population, XYY occurs in about 1 of every 1,000 males. The first major study that examined the influence of XYY sampled about 200 men in the mental hospital; one occurrence would have been predicted, assuming what was known about the general population. The study, however, found 13 individuals who were XYY, which suggested that individuals who have mental disorders are more likely to have XYY than those who do not. Males who have XYY have at least 13 times the likelihood (or a 1,300% chance) of having behavioral disorders compared with those who do not have this chromosomal abnormality. Subsequent studies have not been able to dismiss the effect of XYY on criminality, but they have concluded that this mutation is more often linked with property crime than with violent crime.[10]

Would knowing this relationship help in policies regarding crime? Probably not, considering the fact that 90% of the male mental patients were not XYY. Still, this study showed the importance of looking at chromosomal mutations as a predictor of criminal behavior.

Such mutations include numerous chromosomal abnormalities, such as XYY, which is a male who is given an extra Y chromosome, making him more "malelike." These individuals are often very tall but slow in terms of social and intelligence skills. Another type of mutation is XXY, which is otherwise known as Klinefelter's syndrome; it results in more feminine males (homosexuality has been linked to this mutation). Many other types of mutations have been observed, but it is the XYY mutation that has been the primary focus of studies, which is largely due to the higher levels of testosterone produced by this chromosomal mutation (see Figure 5.1).

One study examined the relative criminality and deviance of a group of individuals in each of these groups of chromosomal mutations (see Figure 5.1).[11] This study found that the higher the level of male hormones produced by the chromosomal mutation, the greater the likelihood that people with the mutation would commit criminal and deviant acts. On the other hand, the higher the level of feminine hormones produced by the chromosomal mutation, the lower the likelihood that the individuals would commit criminal activity. Ultimately, all of these variations in chromosomes show that there is a continuum of femaleness and maleness and that the more malelike the individual is in terms of chromosomes, the more likely he is to commit criminal behavior.

Ultimately, the cytogenetic studies showed that somewhat random abnormalities in an individual's genetic makeup can have a profound influence on her or his level of criminality. Whether or not this can or should be used in policy related to crime is another matter, but the point is that genetics does indeed contribute to a disposition to

[9]Patricia A. Jacobs et al., "Aggressive Behavior, Mental Sub-normality, and the XYY Male," *Nature* 208 (1965): 1351–52.

[10]See review in Raymond Paternoster and Ronet Bachman, *Explaining Criminals and Crime* (Los Angeles: Roxbury, 2001), 53.

[11]Anthony Walsh, "Genetic and Cytogenetic Intersex Anomalies: Can They Help Us to Understand Gender Differences in Deviant Behavior?" *International Journal of Offender Therapy and Comparative Criminology* 39 (1995): 151–66. See also Kristine Stochholm et al., "Criminality in Men with Klinefelter's Syndrome and XYY Syndrome: A Cohort Study," *British Medical Journal Open* 2 (2012).

Figure 5.1 • Hypothetical scattergram relating masculinity/androgen level (designated by karyotype) to deviance

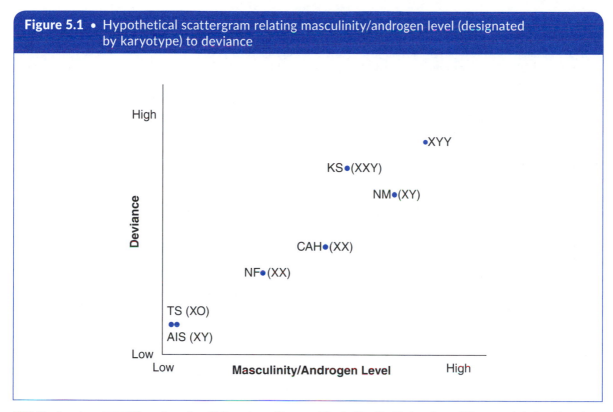

NOTE: TS = Turner's syndrome; AIS = androgen insensitivity syndrome; NF = normal female; KS = Klinefelter's syndrome; CAH = congenital adrenal hyperplasia; NM = normal male; XYY = Jacob's (supermale) syndrome.

SOURCE: Anthony Walsh, "Genetic and Cytogenetic Intersex Anomalies: Can They Help Us to Understand Gender Differences in Deviant Behavior?" *International Journal of Offender Therapy and Comparative Criminology* 39 (1995): 151–66. Copyright © 1995 SAGE Publications, Inc. Reprinted by permission of SAGE Publications, Inc.

commit criminal acts. The extent to which male hormones or androgens are increased by the mutation is an important predictor of criminal traits.

Hormones and Neurotransmitters: Chemicals That Determine Criminal Behavior

Various chemicals in the brain and the rest of the body determine how we think, perceive, and react to various stimuli. Hormones, such as testosterone and estrogen, carry chemical signals to the body as they are released from certain glands and structures. Some studies have shown that a relatively excessive amount of testosterone in the body is consistently linked to criminal or aggressive behavior; most studies show a moderate relationship.[12] This

---

[12]Alan Booth and D. Wayne Osgood, "The Influence of Testosterone on Deviance in Adulthood: Assessing and Explaining the Relationship," *Criminology* 31 (1993): 93–117; Richard Ronay and William von Hippel, "Power, Testosterone, and Risk-Taking," *Journal of Behavioral Decision Making* 23 (2010): 473–82; Hosanna Soler, P. Vinayak, and David Quadagno, "Biosocial Aspects of Domestic Violence," *Psychoneuroendocrinology* 25 (2000): 721–73. For a review, see Lee Ellis and Anthony Walsh, *Criminology: A Global Perspective* (Boston: Allyn & Bacon, 2000). See also Raine, *Anatomy of Violence*.

relationship is seen even in the early years of life.[13] On the other side of the coin, studies have also shown that hormonal changes in females can cause criminal behavior. Specifically, studies have shown that a high proportion of the women in prison for violent crimes committed their crimes during their premenstrual cycle at which time women experience a high level of hormones that make them more malelike due to relatively low levels of estrogen compared to progesterone.[14]

Anyone who doubts the impact of hormones on behavior should examine the scientific literature regarding performance on intelligence tests at different times of day. Virtually everyone performs better on spatial and mathematical tests early in the day, when people have relatively higher levels of testosterone and other male hormones in their bodies; on the other hand, virtually everyone performs better on verbal tasks in the afternoon or evening, when people have relatively higher levels of estrogen or other female hormones in their systems.[15] Furthermore, studies have shown that individuals who are given shots of androgens (male hormones) before math tests tend to do significantly better on spatial and mathematics tests than they would do otherwise. Scientific studies show that the same is true for people who are given shots of female hormones prior to verbal or reading tests.

It is important to realize that this process of differential levels of hormones begins at a very early age, specifically at about the fifth week after conception. At that time, the Y chromosome of the male tells the developing fetus that it is a male and stimulates production of higher levels of testosterone. So, even during the first few months of gestation, the genes on the Y chromosome significantly alter the course of genital and thus hormonal development.[16]

This level of testosterone alters the genitals of the fetus during gestation as well as prompting later changes in the genital area and produces profound increases in testosterone in the teenage and early adult years. This produces not only physical differences but also huge personality and behavioral alterations.[17] High levels of testosterone and other androgens tend to "masculinize" the brain toward risk-taking behavior, whereas the lower levels typically found in females tend to result in the default feminine model.[18] High levels of testosterone have numerous consequences, such as lowered sensitivity to pain, enhanced seeking of sensory stimulation, and a right hemisphere shift in brain dominance, which has been linked to higher levels of spatial aptitude but lower levels of verbal reasoning and empathy. These consequences have profound implications for criminal activity and are more likely to occur in males than females.[19]

Ultimately, hormones have a profound effect on how individuals think and perceive their environments. All criminal behavior comes down to cognitive decisions in our 3-pound brains. So, it should not be surprising that hormones play a highly active role in this decision-making process. Nevertheless, hormones are probably secondary compared to levels of **neurotransmitters**, which are chemicals in the brain and body that help transmit electric signals from one neuron to another.

Neurotransmitters can be distinguished from hormones in the sense that hormones carry a signal that is not electric, whereas the signals that neurotransmitters carry are indeed electric. Neurotransmitters are chemicals that

---

[13]Jose R. Sanchez-Martin et al., "Relating Testosterone Levels and Free Play Social Behavior in Male and Female Preschool Children," *Psychoneuroendocrinology* 25 (2000): 773–83.

[14]Diane Halpern, *Sex Differences in Cognitive Abilities* (Mahwah, NJ: Lawrence Erlbaum, 2000).

[15]Ibid.

[16]Lee Ellis, "A Theory Explaining Biological Correlates of Criminality," *European Journal of Criminality* 2 (2005): 287–315.

[17]Ibid.

[18]Chandler Burr, "Homosexuality and Biology," *Atlantic Monthly* 271 (1993): 47–65; Lee Ellis and M. Ashley Ames, "Neurohormonal Functioning and Sexual Orientation: A Theory of Homosexuality-Heterosexuality," *Psychological Bulletin* 101 (1987): 233–58; Ellis, "A Theory."

[19]Martin Reite et al., "Neuropsychological Test Performance and MEG-based Brain Lateralization: Sex Differences," *Brain Research Bulletin* 32 (1993): 325–28; Jorge Moll et al., "The Neural Correlates of Moral Sensitivity: A Functional Magnetic Resonance Imaging Investigation of Basic and Moral Emotions," *Journal of Neuroscience* 22 (2002): 2730–36; Kimberly Badger, Rebecca Simpson Craft, and Larry Jensen, "Age and Gender Differences in Value Orientation among American Adolescents," *Adolescence* 33 (1998): 591–96.

are released when a neuron, the basic unit of the nervous system, wants to send an electric message to one or more neighboring neurons. Sending such a message requires the creation of neural pathways, which means that neurotransmitters must be activated in processing the signal. At any given moment, healthy levels of various neurotransmitters are needed to pass messages from one neuron to the next across gaps between them, called synapses.

Although there are many types of neurotransmitters, the most studied in relation to criminal activity are **dopamine** and **serotonin**. Dopamine is most commonly linked to feeling good. For example, dopamine is the chemical that tells us when we are experiencing good sensations, such as good food, sex, and so on. Most illicit drugs elicit a pleasurable sensation by enhancing the levels of dopamine in our systems. Cocaine and methamphetamine, for example, tell the body to produce more dopamine and inhibit the enzymes that typically mop up the dopamine in our systems after it is used.

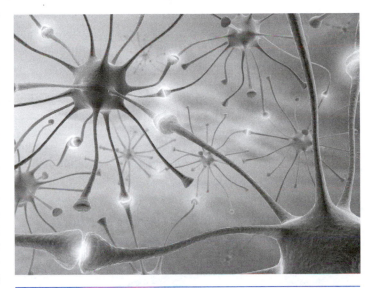

▲ **Image 5.2** Neurons are the basic cells in our nervous system, and they communicate via chemicals called neurotransmitters that aid in sending electric messages across gaps between neurons called synapses.

SOURCE: © istockphoto.com / ktsimage

Although a number of studies show that low levels of dopamine are linked to high rates of criminality, other studies show no association with—or even a positive link to—criminal behavior.[20] However, the relationship between dopamine and criminal behavior is probably curvilinear, such that both extremely high and extremely low levels of dopamine are associated with deviance. Unfortunately, no conclusion can be made at this point due to the lack of scientific evidence regarding this chemical.

On the other hand, a clear conclusion can be made about the other major neurotransmitter that has been implicated in criminal offending: serotonin. Studies have consistently shown that low levels of serotonin are linked with criminal offending.[21] Serotonin is important in virtually all information processing, whether it be learning or emotional; thus, it is vital in most aspects of interacting with the environment. Those who have low levels of serotonin are likely to have problems in everyday communication and life in general. Therefore, it is not surprising that low levels of serotonin are strongly linked to criminal activity.

---

[20]For reviews, see Kevin Beaver, *Biosocial Criminology: A Primer* (Dubuque, IA: Kendall/Hunt, 2008); Raine, *Anatomy of Violence*; and Diana H. Fishbein, *Biobehavioral Perspectives in Criminology* (Belmont, CA: Wadsworth/Thomson Learning, 2001).

[21]For a review, see Ellis, "A Theory." See also Rachel Blumensohn et al., "Reduction in Serotonin 5HT Receptor Binding on Platelets of Delinquent Adolescents," *Psychopharmacology* 118 (1995): 354–56; Emil F. Coccaro et al., "Central Serotonin Activity and Aggression," *American Journal of Psychiatry* 154 (1997): 1430–35; Mairead Dolan et al., "Serotonergic and Cognitive Impairment in Impulsive Aggressive Personality Disordered Offenders: Are There Implications for Treatment?" *Psychological Medicine* 32 (2002): 105–17; and Richard J. Davidson, Katherine M. Putnam, and Christine L. Larson, "Dysfunction in the Neural Circuitry of Emotion Regulation: A Possible Prelude to Violence," *Science* 289 (2000): 591–94.

Brain Injuries

Another area of physiological problems associated with criminal activity is that of trauma to the brain. As mentioned before, the brain weighs only 3 pounds, but it is responsible for every criminal act that an individual commits, so any problems related to this structure have profound implications regarding behavior, especially deviance and criminal activity.

Studies have consistently shown that damage to any part of the brain increases the risk of crime by that individual in the future. However, trauma to certain portions of the brain tends to have more serious consequences than injury to other areas. Specifically, damage to the frontal or **temporal lobes** (particularly those on the left side) appears to have the most consistent associations with criminal offending.[22] These findings make sense primarily because the **frontal lobes** (which include the prefrontal cortex) are the areas of the brain where the realm of higher-level problem solving and "executive" functioning takes place.[23] Thus, the frontal lobes, especially on the left side, process what we are thinking and inhibit us from doing what we are emotionally charged to do. Thus, any moral reasoning relies on this executive area of the brain because it is the region that considers long-term consequences.[24] If people suffer damage to their frontal lobes, they will be far more inclined to act on their emotional urges because they are not receiving any logical inhibitions from this specialized region.

In a similar vein, the temporal lobe region is highly related to memory and emotion. To clarify, the temporal lobes cover and communicate almost directly with certain structures of our brain's limbic systems. Certain limbic structures govern our memories (the hippocampus) and emotions (the amygdala). Any damage to the temporal lobe, which is generally located above the ear, is likely to damage these structures or the effective communication of these structures to other portions of the brain. Therefore, it is understandable why trauma to the temporal region of the brain is linked to future criminality.

▲ **Image 5.3** Harking back to the 19th century, when postmortem examinations of the brains of criminals were a frequent phenomenon, researchers dissected the brain of serial killer John Wayne Gacy after his execution. The attempt to locate an organic explanation for his monstrous behavior was unsuccessful.

SOURCE: © AP Photo/M. Spencer Green

[22]For reviews, see Raine, *Anatomy of Violence*, 80–89; and Raine, *Psychopathology of Crime*, 129–54. See also Joseph M. Tonkonogy, "Violence and Temporal Lobe Lesion: Head CT and MRI Data," *Journal of Neuropsychiatry* 3 (1991): 189–96; and Percy Wright et al., "Brain Density and Symmetry in Pedophilic and Sexually Aggressive Offenders," *Annals of Sex Research* 3 (1990): 319–28.

[23]Ellis, "A Theory," 294. See also Diana Fishbein, "Neuropsychological and Emotional Regulatory Processes in Antisocial Behavior," in *Biosocial Criminology: Challenging Environmentalism's Supremacy*, ed. Anthony Walsh and Lee Ellis (New York: Nova Science, 2003), 185–208.

[24]Bobbi Jo Anderson, Malcolm D. Holmes, and Erik Ostresch, "Male and Female Delinquents' Attachments and Effects of Attachments on Severity of Self-Reported Delinquency," *Criminal Justice and Behavior* 26 (1999): 435–52.

Case Study: Charles Whitman

Charles Whitman's shooting spree is legendary and notorious for many reasons. He killed 15 people and injured 28 others from a landmark university tower at the University of Texas at Austin (UT Austin; the UT flagship campus). But what is almost more fascinating is his life story up until that fateful day.

Whitman was, by most accounts, a great person and a good soldier. He was one of the youngest Eagle Scouts ever to earn the honor. He graduated near the top of his class in high school and then went on to become a stellar member of the U.S. Marine Corps, earning the rating of sharpshooter. He used this skill when he went on his shooting rampage on August 1, 1966. It should be noted that the day before, he killed his wife and mother and left some letters (which will come up later). Then he planned out his attack on the university for the following day.

▲ **Image 5.4**   Charles Whitman shot 43 people from the university clock tower at University of Texas at Austin (UT Austin), killing 15.

SOURCE: ©iStockphoto.com/Gregg Mack

The day after Whitman killed his wife and mother, he proceeded to the main tower at UT Austin, killed the receptionist, ascended the tower, and waited for classes to break; he then opened fire on the crowd of students. It is notable that he had taken with him a variety of materials that imply he was in it for the long haul. These items included toilet paper, spray deodorant, water canteens, gasoline, rope, and binoculars as well as a variety of weapons, such as a machete, a hatchet, a .357 Magnum revolver, a 12-gauge sawed-off shotgun, two rifles (one with a telescopic sight), 700 rounds of ammunition, and other weapons.

Whitman was shooting people on the run and in places only a trained sharpshooter could hit. He shot a pregnant woman, who later gave birth to a stillborn baby. He also shot a person crossing a street 500 yards away. This is the type of shot glorified in *Full Metal Jacket*, a Stanley Kubrick film that examined the Marine boot camps of the late 1960s. There is no doubt that Whitman was an expert sharpshooter and that the Marine Corps trained him well. Unfortunately, in this case his training was used against innocent targets. Whitman continued his mass killing for a couple of hours until several police officers were able to find a way through ground tunnels and then up to the top of the tower, where they shot and killed Whitman.

But why did he do it? The best guess we have, which directly relates to this chapter, began with one of his last letters. He wrote, "After my death, I wish an autopsy on me to be performed to see if there is any mental disorder." An autopsy was performed, and as Whitman sort of predicted, he did not simply have a mental disorder but a large brain tumor (about the size of a golf ball). As we examine how vulnerable our brain functioning can be to trauma, imagine the likely effects of a large tumor on thinking and processing skills.

But why did he do it?

Think About It

1. Do you believe Whitman was insane? Give your reasons why you believe so or not.

2. Given how much planning went into his attack, how much of an effect do you believe his tumor had on him at the time of the attack?

SOURCES: Ronald M. Holmes and Stephen T. Holmes, *Mass Murders in the United States* (Upper Saddle River, NJ: Prentice Hall, 2000); Jo Durden Smith, *100 Most Infamous Criminals* (New York: MetroBooks, 2003).

Central and Autonomic Nervous System Activity

The brain is a key player in two different types of neurological systems that have been linked to criminal activity. The first is the **central nervous system (CNS)**, which involves our brains and spinal columns and governs our voluntary motor activities. For example, the fact that you are reading this sentence means that you are in control of this brain-processing activity. Empirical studies of the influence of CNS functioning on criminality have traditionally focused on brain wave patterns with most using electroencephalograms (EEGs). Although EEGs do not do a good job of describing which areas of the brain are active or inactive, they do reveal how much the brain as an entire organ is performing at certain times.

Studies have compared brain wave patterns of known chronic offenders (e.g., psychopaths, repeat violent offenders) to those of "normal" people (i.e., those who have never been charged with a crime).[25] These studies consistently show that the brain wave patterns of chronic offenders are abnormal compared to those of the normal population with most studies showing slower brain wave patterns in psychopaths.[26] Four types of brain wave patterns are found, from slowest to fastest: delta, theta, alpha, and beta.[27] Delta waves are often seen when people sleep, whereas theta waves are typically observed in lower levels of wakefulness, such as drowsiness. Alpha waves (which tend to be divided into slow and fast wave patterns, as are beta waves) are usually related to a more relaxed wakefulness, and beta waves are observed with high levels of wakefulness, such as in times of extreme alertness and particularly in times of excited activity.

The studies that have compared brain wave patterns among chronic offenders and normals have shown significant differences. Psychopaths tend to have more activity in the theta (and sometimes slow alpha) patterns, whereas normals tend to show more activity in the fast alpha or beta waves. These consistent findings reveal that the cortical arousal of chronic offenders tends to be significantly slower than that of people who do not typically commit crimes. Thus, it is likely that chronic offenders typically do not have the mental functioning that would dispose them toward accurate assessments regarding the consequences of committing criminal behavior.

The second area of the nervous system that has been most linked to criminal behavior is the **autonomic nervous system (ANS)**, which is primarily responsible for involuntary motor activities, such as heart rate, dilation of pupils, and electric conductivity in the skin. This is the type of physiological activity that is measured by polygraph measures, or lie detector tests. Such measures capitalize on the inability of individuals to control physiological responses to anxiety, which occurs in most normal persons when they lie, especially regarding illegal behavior. However, such measures are not infallible because the individuals who are most at risk of being serious, violent offenders are the most likely to pass such tests even when they are lying. See Figure 5.2.

---

[25]Adrian Raine and Peter H. Venables, "Enhanced P3 Evoked Potentials and Longer P3 Recovery Times in Psychopaths," *Psychophysiology* 25 (1988): 30–38; Lance O. Bauer and Victor M. Hesselbrock, "Frontal P300 Decrements, Childhood Conduct Disorder, Family History, and the Prediction of Relapse among Abstinent Cocaine Abusers," *Drug and Alcohol Dependence* 44 (1997): 1–10. For a review, see Ellis, "A Theory."

[26]For a review, see Raine, *Psychopathology of Crime*, 174–78. See also Robert D. Hare, *Psychopathy: Theory and Practice* (New York: Wiley, 1970); Jan Volavka, "Electroencephalogram among Criminals," in *The Causes of Crime: New Biological Approaches*, ed. Sarnoff A. Mednick, Terrie E. Moffitt, and Susan Stack (Cambridge: Cambridge University Press, 1987), 137–45; Peter H. Venables, "Psychophysiology and Crime: Theory and Data," in *Biological Contributions to Crime Causation*, ed. Terrie E. Moffitt and Sarnoff A. Mednick (Dordrecht: Martinus Nijhoff, 1988); and Peter H. Venables and Adrian Raine, "Biological Theory," in *Applying Psychology to Imprisonment: Theory and Practice*, ed. Barry McGurk, David Thornton, and Mark Williams (London: Her Majesty's Stationery Office, 1987), 3–28.

[27]For further discussion and explanation, see Raine, *Psychopathology of Crime*, 174–77.

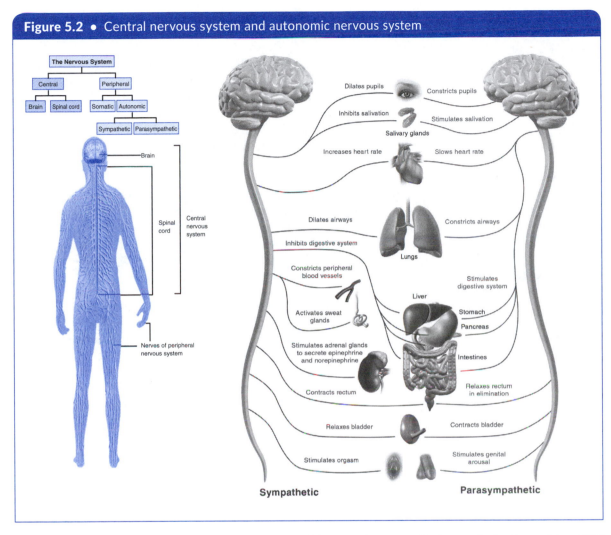

Figure 5.2 • Central nervous system and autonomic nervous system

SOURCE: Bob Garrett, *Brain and Behavior: An Introduction to Biological Psychology.* Copyright © SAGE Publications, Inc. Reprinted by permission of SAGE Publications, Inc.

Consistent with the findings regarding CNS arousal levels, studies have consistently shown that individuals who have significantly low levels of ANS functioning are far more likely to commit criminal acts.[28] For example, studies consistently show that chronic violent offenders tend to have much slower resting heartbeats than normal people;

[28]For a review, see Raine, *Psychopathology of Crime*, 159–73. See also the following reviews and studies: Peter H. Venables, "Childhood Markers for Adult Disorders," *Journal of Child Psychology and Psychiatry and Allied Disciplines* 30 (1989): 347–64; Adrian Raine and Peter H. Venables, "Skin Conductance Responsivity in Psychopaths to Orienting, Defensive, and Consonant-Vowel Stimuli," *Journal of Psychophysiology* 2 (1988): 221–25; and Traci Bice, "Cognitive and Psychophysiological Differences in Proactive and Reactive Aggressive Boys" (doctoral dissertation, Department of Psychology, University of Southern California, 1993).

a number of studies estimate this difference to be as much as 10 beats per minute slower for the offenders.[29] This is a highly significant gap that cannot be explained away by alternative theories—for example, the explanation that offenders are just less excited in laboratory tests.

Furthermore, people who have such low levels of ANS arousal tend to experience what is known in the psychological literature as *stimulus hunger*. Stimulus hunger means that individuals with such a low level of ANS arousal may constantly seek out experiences and stimuli that are risky and thus often illegal. Readers may recall children they have known who can never seem to get enough attention, with some even seeming to enjoy being spanked or other forms of harsh punishment. In addition, people with a low level of ANS arousal may feel no anxiety about punishment, even corporal punishment, and thus they may not adequately learn right from wrong through normal forms of discipline. This is perhaps one of the reasons why children who are diagnosed with attention deficit hyperactivity disorder (ADHD) have a higher likelihood of becoming criminals than their peers.

Because people who are accurately diagnosed with ADHD have a neurological abnormality—a significantly low functioning ANS level of arousal—doctors prescribe stimulants (e.g., Ritalin) for such youths. It may seem counterintuitive to prescribe a hyperactive person a stimulant; however, the medication boosts the individual's ANS functioning to a normal level of arousal. This makes such individuals experience a healthy level of anxiety, which they would not normally experience from wrongdoing. Assuming that the medication is properly prescribed and at the correct dosage, children who are treated tend to become more attuned to the discipline that they face if they engage in rule violation.

Children who do not fear punishment at all—in fact, some of them do not feel anxiety even when being physically punished (e.g., spanking)—are likely to have lower-than-average levels of ANS functioning. Such individuals are likely to become chronic offenders if this disorder is not addressed, because they will not respond to discipline or consider the long-term consequences of their risky behavior. If people don't fear punishment or negative consequences from their behavior, they may be more likely to engage in selfish, greedy behavior. Thus, it is important to address this issue when it becomes evident. On the other hand, children will be children, and ADHD and other disorders have been overly diagnosed in recent years. A well-trained physician should investigate thoroughly to decide whether an individual has such a low level of ANS functioning that medication or therapy is required to curb deviant behavior.

Individuals who have significantly lower ANS arousal are likely to pass lie detector tests because they feel virtually no or little anxiety when they lie; many of them lie all the time. Thus, it is ironic, but the very people whom lie-detecting measures are meant to capture are the most likely to pass such tests, which is probably why they are typically not allowed to be used in court. Only through medication or cognitive behavioral therapy can such individuals learn to consider the long-term consequences of the decisions they make regarding their behavior.

Individuals with low levels of ANS functioning are not always destined to become chronic offenders. Some evidence has shown that people with low ANS arousal often become successful corporate executives, decorated military soldiers, world-champion athletes, and high-level politicians. Most of these occupations require people who constantly seek out exciting, risky behaviors, and others require constant and convincing forms of lying to others. So there are many legal outlets and productive ways for people with low levels of ANS functioning to use their natural tendencies. These individuals could perhaps be steered toward such occupations and opportunities when they present themselves. This is clearly a better option than committing antisocial acts against others in society.

---

[29]See Enrico Mezzacappa et al., "Anxiety, Antisocial Behavior, and Heart Rate Regulation in Adolescent Males," *Journal of Psychiatry* 38 (1997): 457–69; Graham A. Rogeness et al., "Differences in Heart Rate and Blood Pressure in Children with Conduct Disorder, Major Depression, and Separation Anxiety," *Psychiatry Research* 33 (1990): 199–206; and Daniel J. Kindlon et al., "Longitudinal Patterns of Heart Rate and Fighting Behavior in 9- through 12-Year-Old Boys," *Journal of the American Academy of Child and Adolescent Psychiatry* 34 (1995): 371–77.

Ultimately, low levels of cortical arousal in both the CNS and ANS are clearly linked to a predisposition toward criminal activity. However, modern medical research and societal opportunities exist to help such individuals divert their tendencies toward more prosocial outlets.

Biosocial Approaches to Explaining Criminal Behavior

Perhaps the most important and most recent perspective of how criminality is formed is that of biosocial approaches to explaining crime. Specifically, if there is any conclusion that can be made regarding the previous theories and research in this chapter, it is that both genetics and environment influence behavior, particularly the interaction between the two. Even the most fundamental aspects of life can be explained by these two groups of factors.

For example, if we look at the height of individuals, we can predict with a great amount of accuracy how tall a person will be by looking at the individual's parents and other ancestors because much of height is determined by a person's genotype. However, even for something as physiological as height, the environment plays a large role. As many readers will observe, individuals who are raised in poor, underdeveloped areas (e.g., Mexico, Asia) are shorter than children raised in the United States. However, individuals who descend from parents and relatives in these underdeveloped areas but are raised in the United States tend to be just as tall (if not taller) than children born here. This is largely due to diet, which obviously is an environmental factor.

In other words, our genotype provides a certain range or window that determines the height of an individual based on ancestral factors. But the extent to which individuals grow to the maximum or minimum, or somewhere in between, is largely dependent on what occurs in the environment as they develop. This is why biologists make a distinction between genotype, which is directly due to genetics, and **phenotype**, which is a manifestation of genetics interacting with the environment. The same type of biosocial effect is seen for criminal behavior.

Furthermore, over the past decades, a number of empirical investigations have examined the extent to which physiological variables interact with environmental variables, and the findings of these studies have shown consistent predictions regarding criminality. Such studies have been more accurate than those that rely on either physiological and genetic variables or environmental factors separately. For example, findings from a cohort study in Philadelphia showed that individuals who had low birth weights were more likely to commit crime, but that was true primarily if they were raised in a lower-income family or a family with a weak social structure.[30] Those who were raised in a relatively high-income household or a strong family structure were unlikely to become criminals. It was the coupling of both a physiological deficiency (i.e., low birth weight) and an environmental deficit (i.e., weak family structure or income) that had a profound effect on propensity for criminal behavior.

In addition, recent studies have shown that when incarcerated juveniles were assigned to diets with limited levels of simple carbohydrates (e.g., sugars), their reported levels of violations during incarceration declined by almost half (45%).[31] Furthermore, other studies have reported that various food additives and dyes, such as those commonly found in processed foods, can also have a significant influence on criminal behavior. Thus, the old saying "you are what you eat" appears to have some scientific weight behind it—at least regarding criminal behavior. Additional studies have found that high levels of certain toxins, particularly lead and manganese, can have profound effects on behavior, including criminality. Recent studies have found a consistent, strong effect of high lead levels in predicting criminal behavior. Unfortunately, medical studies have also found many subtle sources of high lead levels, such as the fake jewelry that many children wear as toys. Also unfortunate is that the individuals who are most vulnerable to high levels of lead (like virtually every other toxin) are children, yet they are the most likely to

[30]Stephen Tibbetts and Alex Piquero, "The Influence of Gender, Low Birth Weight, and Disadvantaged Environment in Predicting Early Onset of Offending: A Test of Moffitt's Interactional Hypothesis," *Criminology* 37 (1999): 843–78.

[31]Stephen J. Shoenthaler, *Improve Your Child's IQ and Behavior* (London: BBC Books, 1991).

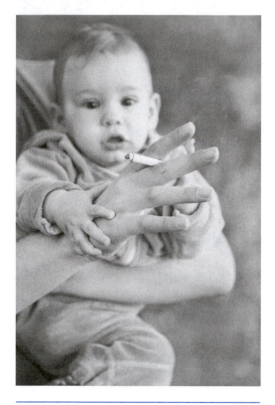

▲ **Image 5.5**   Young children are particularly vulnerable when exposed to dangerous toxins.

be exposed. Even more unfortunate is that the populations most susceptible to biosocial interactions (e.g., poor, urban) are most likely to experience high levels of lead, largely due to old paint, which often contains lead, and other household products that contain dangerous toxins.[32]

Consistently, other studies have shown that prenatal and perinatal problems alone do not predict violence very well. However, when such perinatal problems are considered along with environmental deficits, such as weak family structure, this biosocial relationship often predicts violent rather than property crime.[33] Other studies have shown the effects on criminality of a biosocial interaction between the impact of physiological factors within the first minute of life, called Apgar scores, and environmental factors, including exposure to nicotine.[34] Additional studies have also found that the interaction between maternal cigarette smoking and the father's absence from the household is associated with criminal behavior, especially early in life, which is one of the biggest predictors of chronic offending in the future.[35] One of the most revealing studies showed that, although only 4% of a sample of 4,269 individuals had both birth complications and maternal rejection, this relatively small group of people accounted for more than 18% of the total violent crimes committed by the whole sample.[36] To quote a recent review of literature, Adrian Raine stated, "Almost wherever you go in the world, you find the same effect. The combination of birth complications and adverse home environments appears to be a useful biosocial key that can open the lock on the causes of violence." So studies have clearly shown that the interaction between biological factors and environmental deficiencies has the most consistent effect on future criminality.

Policy Implications

The theories in this chapter have plenty of policy implications; a few of the primary interventions are discussed here. First, there should be universal, funded preschool for all children. This early life stage is important not only for developing academic skills but also for fostering healthy social and disciplinary skills, which children who do

---

[32]Wright et al., *Criminals in the Making*.

[33]Alex Piquero and Stephen Tibbetts, "The Impact of Pre/Perinatal Disturbances and Disadvantaged Familial Environment in Predicting Criminal Offending," *Studies on Crime and Crime Prevention* 8 (1999): 52–71.

[34]For example, Chris Gibson and Stephen Tibbetts, "Interaction between Maternal Cigarette Smoking and Apgar Scores in Predicting Offending," *Psychological Reports* 83 (1998): 579–86. For a review, see Stephen G. Tibbetts, "Birth Complications and the Development of Criminality: A Biosocial Perspective," in Kevin Beaver and Anthony Walsh, *The Ashgate Research Companion to Biosocial Theories of Crime* (Burlington, VT: Ashgate, 2012), 273–90.

[35]Chris Gibson and Stephen Tibbetts, "A Biosocial Interaction in Predicting Early Onset of Offending," *Psychological Reports* 86 (2000): 509–18.

[36]Adrian Raine, Pauline A. Brennan, and Sarnoff A. Mednick, "Birth Complications Combined with Early Maternal Rejection at Age 1 Year Predispose to Violent Crime at Age 18 Years," *Archives of General Psychiatry* 51 (1994): 984–88.

not attend preschool often fail to develop.[37] In addition, there should be funded mental health and drug counseling for all young children and adolescents who exhibit symptoms of mental disorders or drug problems.[38] There should also be universal funding for health care for all expectant mothers, especially those who have risk factors (poverty, inner-city residence, etc.).

Perhaps most important, there should be far more thorough examinations of children's physiological makeup in terms of hormones, neurotransmitters, brain formation and functioning, and genetic design so that earlier interventions can take place. It has been shown empirically that the earlier that interventions take place, the better the outcomes.[39] A review of the extant literature, hereafter referred to as the Maryland Report (because all key authors of the report were professors at the University of Maryland), emphasized the importance of identifying and quickly treating any head and bodily trauma early in development among infants and toddlers, concluding that some of the most consistently supported early intervention programs for such physiological problems are those that involve weekly infant home visitation, typically by nurses or neonatal experts.[40]

Conclusion

This chapter has examined a large range of explanations of criminal behavior that place most of the blame on biological and psychological factors, which are typically intertwined. These types of explanations were primarily popular in the early years of the development of criminology as a science, but they have also been shown in recent years to be quite valid as significant factors in individual decisions to commit crime. This chapter examined the influence of genetics and environment in family studies, twin studies, adoption studies, and studies of identical twins separated at birth. These studies have ultimately shown the consistent influence of inheritance and genetics in predisposing individuals toward criminal activity. This is supported by the influence of hormones (e.g., testosterone) in human behavior as well as the influence of variations in chromosomal mutations (e.g., XYY). Recent research has supported both of these theories in showing that people with high levels of male androgens are far more likely to commit crimes than those who do not have high levels of these hormones.

The link between brain trauma and crime was also discussed, emphasizing the consistent association between damage to the left or frontal parts of the brain. We also examined theories regarding variations in levels of CNS and ANS functioning; nearly all empirical studies have shown that low levels of functioning of these systems have links to criminality. Finally, we explored the extent to which the interaction between physiological factors and environmental variables contributes to the most consistent prediction of criminal offending. Ultimately, it is interesting that the very theories that were key in the early years of the development of criminology as a science are now showing strong support in studies for being primary influences on criminal behavior.

Ultimately, despite the neglect that biosocial models of crime receive in terms of both recognition and policy implications, there is no doubt that this area is crucial if we hope to advance our understanding and create more efficient policies regarding criminal behavior. It is time that all criminologists recognize the degree to which human behavior results from physiological disorders. We all have brains, each about 3 pounds in weight, that determine the choices we make. Criminologists must acknowledge the influence of biological or physiological factors that influence this vital organ, or the discipline will be behind the curve in terms of understanding why people commit (or do not commit) criminal offenses.

---

[37]Wright et al., *Criminals in the Making*.

[38]Ibid.

[39]Samuel S. Wu et al., "Risk Factors for Infant Maltreatment: A Population-Based Study," *Child Abuse and Neglect* 28 (2004): 1253–64.

[40]Lawrence Sherman et al., *Preventing Crime: What Works, What Doesn't, What's Promising: A Report to the United States Congress* (Washington, DC: U.S. Department of Justice, 1997) (see chap. 2).

//// CHAPTER SUMMARY

- Early studies that examined the influence of biology focused on case studies of certain families. These studies showed that criminality was indeed clustered among certain families, but such studies did not separate biology from environment.

- The next stage of studies examined the concordance rates of identical twins versus nonidentical twins. These studies led to the conclusion that genetic makeup was very important, but critics called these conclusions into question.

- The following stage of research examined adoptees to determine which parents (biological or adoptive) had more influence in their future criminal behavior. These studies revealed that biological parents (whom the adoptees never knew) had far more influence than the adoptive parents who raised them. However, there were criticisms of these studies, so the findings were questioned.

- The final stage of the biology versus environment debate was that of identical twins separated at birth as compared to identical twins raised together. These studies showed that the twins who were separated at birth were just as similar, if not more so, than the twins who were reared together. To date, there are no criticisms of this method of study. Thus, it appears that all four waves of study are consistent in showing that biological influences are vitally important in explaining the criminality of individuals.

- This chapter also examined chromosomal mutations, such as the XYY mutation, which has consistently shown associations with criminality. Much, if not most, of this link is believed to be due to the increased male androgens (e.g., testosterone) produced by individuals who have the XYY chromosomal mutation.

- Studies have consistently shown that individuals with higher levels of testosterone and other androgens are more disposed toward criminality; for example, normal males are far more likely than normal females to engage in violent crimes.

- This chapter reviewed findings from studies that show that people with abnormal levels of certain neurotransmitters, such as serotonin, are far more likely to engage in crime than those who have normal levels of these chemicals in their brains or bodies.

- Studies show that criminality is more likely among individuals who have experienced brain trauma or have lower levels of brain functioning, especially in certain regions of the brain, such as the frontal and temporal lobes, which are the regions that largely govern higher-level, problem-solving functions.

- This chapter also reviewed the dispositions of individuals regarding two aspects of the nervous system, specifically the CNS and ANS. Those who have significantly slower brain waves and lower anxiety levels are far more likely to commit crimes.

//// KEY TERMS

adoption studies 92

autonomic nervous system (ANS) 100

central nervous system (CNS) 100

concordance rates 91

cytogenetic studies 93

dizygotic (DZ) twins 90

dopamine 97

family studies 90

frontal lobes 98

monozygotic (MZ) twins 90

neurotransmitters 96

/// DISCUSSION QUESTIONS

1. Is there any validity to family studies in determining the role of genetics in criminal behavior? Explain why or why not.

2. Explain the rationale of studies that compare the concordance rates of identical twins and fraternal twins who are raised together. What do most of these studies show regarding the influence of genetics on criminal behavior? What are the criticisms of these studies?

3. Explain the rationale of studies that examine the biological and adoptive parents of adopted children. What do most of these studies show regarding the influence of genetics on criminal behavior? What are the criticisms of these studies?

4. What are the general findings in identical twins who are separated at birth? What implications do these findings have for the importance of genetics or heritability regarding criminal behavior? Can you find a criticism for such findings?

5. Explain what cytogenetic disorders are, and describe the related disorder that is most linked to criminal behavior. What characteristics of this type of disorder seem to drive the higher propensity for criminal behavior?

6. What types of hormones have been shown by scientific studies to be linked to criminal activity? Give specific examples that show this link to be true.

7. Explain what neurotransmitters are, and describe which neurotransmitters are key in predicting criminal offending. Provide support from previous scientific studies.

8. Which areas of the brain, given trauma, have shown the greatest vulnerability regarding criminal offending? Does the lack of healthy functioning in these areas make sense? Why?

9. How do brain wave patterns differ between chronic, violent criminals and "normal" people? Does this make sense in biosocial models of criminality?

10. How does the ANS differ between chronic, violent criminals and "normal" people? Does this make sense in biosocial models of criminality?

11. What types of policy implications would you support based on the information provided by empirical studies reviewed in this chapter?

/// WEB RESOURCES

Autonomic Nervous System and Central Nervous System

http://www.merckmanuals.com/home/brain,-spinal-cord,-and-nerve-disorders/autonomic-nervous-system-disorders/overview-of-the-autonomic-nervous-system

https://www.ncbi.nlm.nih.gov/pubmedhealth/PMHT0024762/http://www.emedicinehealth.com/anatomy_of_the_central_nervous_system/article_em.htm

Brain Trauma and Crime

http://www.traumaticbraininjury.net/does-brain-injury-contribute-to-criminal-behavior
https://www.ncbi.nlm.nih.gov/pubmed/19996251

Cytogenetic Studies

http://www.jcdr.net/articles/PDF/615/771.pdf
https://www.ncbi.nlm.nih.gov/pmc/articles/PMC3356148
http://bmjopen.bmj.com/content/2/1/e000650

Family, Twin, or Adoption Studies

http://www.bookrags.com/research/twin-studies-wog
http://law.jrank.org/pages/784/Crime-Causation-Biological-Theories-Genetic-epidemiological-studies.html

Hormones and Neurotransmitters

http://serendip.brynmawr.edu/biology/b103/f02/web1/kamlin.html
http://www.gender.org.uk/about/06encrn/63faggrs.htm
https://www.ncbi.nlm.nih.gov/pmc/articles/PMC2612120

CHAPTER 6

Early Social Structure and Strain Theories of Crime

This chapter will review the development of **anomie** or **strain theory**, starting with early social structure theorists, such as Émile Durkheim, then Robert K. Merton, and on to the most modern versions (e.g., general strain theory). We will also examine the empirical research findings on this perspective, which remains one of the dominant theoretical explanations of criminal behavior today. We will finish by discussing the policy implications of this research.

We'll begin with a review of explanations of criminal conduct that emphasize the differences among varying groups in societies, particularly in the United States. Such differences are easy to see in everyday life, and many theoretical models place the blame for crime on observed inequalities and cultural differences between groups. In contrast to the theories presented in previous chapters, social structure theories disregard any biological or psychological variations across individuals. Instead, social structure theories assume that crime is caused by the way societies are structurally organized.

These social structure theories vary in many ways—most notably in what they propose as the primary constructs and processes responsible for causing criminal activity. For example, some structural models emphasize variations in economic or academic success, whereas others focus on differences in cultural norms and values. Still others concentrate on the actual breakdown of the social structure in certain neighborhoods and the resulting social disorganization that occurs from this process, a topic we will reserve for Chapter 7. Regardless of their differences, all of the theories examined in this chapter emphasize a common theme: Certain groups of individuals are more likely to break the law because of disadvantages or cultural differences resulting from the way a society is structured.

The most important distinction between these theories and those discussed in previous chapters is that they emphasize group differences instead of individual differences. Structural models tend to focus on the macro level of analysis as opposed to the micro level. Therefore, it is not surprising that social structure theories are commonly used to explain the propensity of certain racial or ethnic groups for committing crime as well as the overrepresentation of the lower class in criminal activity.

As you will see, these theoretical frameworks were presented as early as the 1800s and reached prominence in the early to mid-1900s, when the political, cultural, and economic climate of society was most conducive to such explanations. Although social structural models of crime have diminished in popularity in recent decades,[1] there is much validity to their propositions in numerous applications to contemporary society.

Early Theories of Social Structure: Early to Mid-1800s

Most criminological and sociological historians trace the origin of social structure theories to the research done in the early to mid-1800s by a number of European researchers—the most important including Auguste Comte, André-Michel Guerry, and Adolphe Quetelet.[2] It is important to understand why structural theories developed in 19th-century Europe. The Industrial Revolution, defined by most historians as beginning in the mid-1700s and ending in the mid-1800s, was in full swing at the turn of the century, so societies were quickly transitioning from primarily agriculturally based economies to industrial based economies. This transition inevitably brought people from rural farmlands to dense urban cities, resulting in an enormous increase in social problems. These social problems ranged from failure to properly dispose of waste and garbage, to constantly losing children and not being able to find them, to much higher rates of crime (which urban areas continue to show today, as compared to suburban and rural areas).

The problems associated with such fast urbanization, as well as the shift in economics, led to drastic changes in the basic social structures in Europe as well as the United States. At the same time, other types of revolutions were also having an effect. Both the American (1776) and French (1789) Revolutions occurred in the last quarter of the 18th century. These two revolutions, inspired by the Enlightenment movement (see Chapter 2), shared an ideology that rejected tyranny and insisted that people should have a voice in how they were governed. Along with the Industrial Revolution, these political revolutions affected intellectual theorizing on social structures, as well as on crime, throughout the 1800s.

Auguste Comte

One of the first important theorists in the area of social structure theory was Auguste Comte (1798–1857), who is widely credited with coining the term *sociology*.[3] Comte distinguished the concepts of **social statics** and **social dynamics.** Social statics are aspects of society that relate to stability and social order; they allow societies to continue and endure. Social dynamics are aspects of social life that alter how societies are structured and pattern the development of societal institutions. Although such conceptualization seems elementary by today's standards, it had a significant influence on sociological thinking at the time. Furthermore, the distinction between static and dynamic societal factors was incorporated into several criminological theories in decades to come.

Between 1851 and 1854, Comte published a four-volume work titled *A System of Positive Polity* that encouraged the use of scientific methods to observe and measure societal factors.[4] Although we tend to take this for granted in modern times, the idea of applying such methods to help explain social processes was rather profound at the time; probably for this reason, Comte is generally considered the founder or father of sociology. Comte's work set the

---

[1]Anthony Walsh and Lee Ellis, "Political Ideology and American Criminologists' Explanations for Criminal Behavior," *The Criminologist* 24, no. 6 (1999): 1, 4; Lee Ellis and Anthony Walsh, "Criminologists' Opinions about Causes and Theories of Crime and Delinquency," *The Criminologist* 24, no. 4 (1999): 1–4.

[2]Much of the discussion of the development of structural theories of the 19th century is drawn from James W. Vander Zanden, *Sociology: The Core*, 2nd ed. (New York: McGraw-Hill, 1990), 8–14.

[3]Vander Zanden, *Sociology: The Core*, 8–9.

[4]Auguste Comte, *A System of Positive Polity*, trans. John Henry Bridges (New York: Franklin, 1875).

stage for the positivistic perspective, which emphasized social determinism and rejected the notion of free will and individual choice that had been common up until that time.

André-Michel Guerry and Adolphe Quetelet

After the first modern national crime statistics were published in France in the early 1800s, a French lawyer named André-Michel Guerry (1802–1866) published a report that examined these statistics and concluded that property crimes were higher in wealthy areas, but violent crime was much higher in poor areas.[5] Some experts have claimed that this report likely represents the first study of scientific criminology[6]; it was later expanded and published as a book, titled *Essay on the Moral Statistics of France*, in 1833. Ultimately, Guerry concluded that the explanation was opportunity: The wealthy had more to steal, and that is the primary cause of property crime. Interestingly, this conclusion is supported by recent U.S. Department of Justice (DOJ) statistics, which show that, compared to lower-class households, property crime is just as common—and maybe more so—in middle- to upper-class households, but violent crime is not.[7] As Guerry stated centuries ago, there is more to steal in wealthier areas, and poor individuals take the opportunity to steal goods and currency from these households and establishments.

Adolphe Quetelet (1796–1874) was a Belgian researcher who, like Guerry, examined French statistics in the mid-1800s. Besides showing relative stability in the trends of crime rates in France, such as in age distribution and female-to-male ratios of offending, Quetelet also showed that certain types of individuals were more likely to commit crime.[8] Specifically, young, male, poor, uneducated, and unemployed individuals were more likely to commit crime than their counterparts,[9] a finding also supported by modern research. Like Guerry, Quetelet concluded that opportunities, in addition to demographic characteristics, had a lot to do with where crime was concentrated.

However, Quetelet added a special component: Greater inequality or gaps between wealth and poverty in the same place

▲ **Image 6.1** Lambert Adolphe Quetelet (1796–1874), the Belgian astronomer and sociologist, circa 1860.

SOURCE: © Getty Images / Popperfoto / Contributor

---

[5]For more thorough discussions of Guerry and Quetelet, see the sources from which I have drawn the information presented here: Piers Beirne, *Inventing Criminology* (Albany: SUNY Press, 1993); Thomas J. Bernard, Jeffrey B. Snipes, and Alexander L. Gerould, *Vold's Theoretical Criminology*, 6th ed. (Oxford: Oxford University Press, 2010) (see chap. 2).

[6]Terrence Morris, *The Criminal Area* (New York: Routledge, 1957), 42–53, as cited in Bernard et al., *Vold's Theoretical Criminology*, 22.

[7]U.S. Department of Justice, Bureau of Justice Statistics, *Sourcebook of Criminal Justice Statistics, 2000, NCJ-190251* (Washington, DC: USGPO, 2001), Table 3.26, 202; Table 3.13, 194.

[8]Beirne, *Inventing Criminology*, 78–81.

[9]Bernard et al., *Vold's Theoretical Criminology*, 23–26.

tend to excite temptations and passions. This is a concept referred to as **relative deprivation**, a condition quite distinct from simple poverty.

For example, a number of deprived areas in the United States do not have high rates of crime—likely because virtually everyone is poor—so people are generally content with their lives relative to their neighbors. However, in areas of the country where very poor people live in close proximity to very wealthy people, animosity and feelings of being deprived develop. Studies have supported this hypothesis.[10] It may well explain why Washington, DC, perhaps the most powerful city in the world and one with many neighborhoods that are severely run-down and poor, has a higher crime rate than any other jurisdiction in the country.[11] Modern studies have also shown a clear linear association between higher crime rates and relative deprivation. For example, David Sang-Yoon Lee found that crime rates were far higher in cities that had wider gaps in income: The larger the gap between the 10th and 90th percentiles, the greater the crime levels.[12]

In addition to the concept of relative deprivation, Quetelet also showed that areas with the most rapidly changing economic conditions have high crime rates. He is perhaps best known for commenting that "the crimes . . . committed seem to be a necessary result of our social organization. . . . Society prepares the crime, and the guilty are only the instruments by which it is executed."[13] This statement makes it clear that crime is a result of societal structure and not the result of individual propensities or personal decision making. Thus, it is not surprising that Quetelet's position was controversial at the time in which he wrote, and he was rigorously attacked by critics for removing all decision-making capabilities from his model of behavior. In response, Quetelet argued that his model could help lower crime rates by leading to social reforms that address the inequalities due to the social structure.[14]

One of the essential points of Guerry's and Quetelet's work is the positivistic nature of their conclusions: that the distribution of crime is not random but rather the result of certain types of people committing certain types of crimes in particular places, largely due to the way society is structured and the way it distributes resources. This perspective of criminality strongly supports the tendency of crime to be clustered in certain neighborhoods as well as among certain people. Such findings support a structural, positivistic perspective of criminality, in which criminality is seen as being deterministic and, thus, caused by factors outside of an individual's control. In some ways, early structural theories were a response to the failure of the classical approach to crime control. As the 19th century drew to a close, classical and deterrence-based perspectives of crime fell out of favor, while social structure theories and other positivist theories of crime, such as the structural models of Guerry and Quetelet, attracted far more attention.

Durkheim and the Concept of Anomie

Although influenced by earlier theorists (e.g., Comte, Guerry, and Quetelet), Durkheim (1858–1916) was perhaps the most influential theorist in the area of modern structural perspectives on criminality.[15] Like most other social theorists of the 19th century, he was strongly affected by the American and French Revolutions and the Industrial

---

[10]Velmer Burton and Frank Cullen, "The Empirical Status of Strain Theory," *Journal of Crime and Justice* 15 (1992): 1–30; Nikos Passas, "Continuities in the Anomie Tradition," in *Advances in Criminological Theory, Vol. 6: The Legacy of Anomie Theory*, ed. Freda Adler and William S. Laufer (New Brunswick, NJ: Transaction Press, 1995); Nikos Passas, "Anomie, Reference Groups, and Relative Deprivation," in *The Future of Anomie Theory*, ed. Nikos Passas and Robert Agnew (Boston: Northeastern University Press, 1997).

[11]U.S. Department of Justice, Bureau of Justice Statistics, *Sourcebook*, Table 3.124, 290.

[12]David Sang-Yoon Lee, "An Empirical Investigation of the Economic Incentives for Criminal Behavior" (bachelor's thesis in economics) (Boston: Harvard University, 1993), as cited in Richard B. Freeman, "The Labor Market," in *Crime*, ed. James Q. Wilson and Joan Petersilia (San Francisco: ICS Press, 1995), 171–92.

[13]Beirne, *Inventing Criminology*, 88, as cited in Bernard et al., *Vold's Theoretical Criminology*, 25.

[14]Bernard et al., *Vold's Theoretical Criminology*, 25–26.

[15]Much of this discussion of Durkheim is taken from Bernard et al., *Vold's Theoretical Criminology*, 100–116 as well as Vander Zanden, *Sociology: The Core*, 11–13.

Figure 6.1 • Durkheim's continuum of development from mechanical to organic societies

Mechanical Societies	Organic Societies
→	Industrialization →
Primitive	Modern
Rural	Urban
Agricultural-based economy	Industrial-based economy
Simple division of labor (few divisions)	Complex division of labor (many specialized divisions)
Law used to enforce conformity	Law used to regulate interactions among divisions
Typically stronger collective conscience	Typically weaker collective conscience

Revolution. In his doctoral dissertation (1893) at the University of Paris, the first sociological dissertation at that institution, Durkheim developed a general model of societal development largely based on economic and labor distribution in which societies are seen as evolving from a simplistic, mechanical society toward a multilayered, organic society (see Figure 6.1).

As outlined in this dissertation, titled *The Division of Labor in Society*, in primitive **mechanical societies**, all members essentially perform the same functions, such as hunting (typically done by males) and gathering (typically done by females). Although there are a few anomalies (e.g., medicine men), virtually everyone experiences essentially the same daily routine. Such similarities in work, as well as constant interaction with like members of the society, leads to a strong uniformity in values, which Durkheim called the **collective conscience**. The collective conscience is the degree to which individuals of a society think alike, or as Durkheim put it, the totality of social likenesses. The similar norms and values among people in these primitive, mechanical societies create *mechanical solidarity*, a very simple social structure with a very strong collective conscience. In mechanical societies, law functions to enforce the **conformity** of the group.

However, as societies progress toward more modern, **organic societies** in the industrial age, the distribution of labor becomes more highly specified. An *organic solidarity* arises in which people tend to depend on other groups because of the highly specified division of labor, and laws have the primary function of regulating interactions and maintaining solidarity among the groups.

For example, modern researchers at universities in the United States tend to be trained in extremely narrow topics—one might be an expert on something as specific as the antennae of certain species of ants. On the other hand, some individuals are still gathering trash from the cans on the same streets every single day. The antennae experts probably have little in common with the garbage collectors and not much interaction with them other than when they pay them. According to Durkheim, moving from the universally shared roles of mechanical societies to the extremely specific roles of organic societal organization results in huge cultural differences and giant contrasts in normative values and attitudes across groups. Thus, the collective conscience in such societies is weak, largely because there is little agreement on moral beliefs or opinions. The preexisting solidarity among members breaks down and the bonds are weakened, which creates a climate for antisocial behavior.

Durkheim was clear in stating that crime is not only normal but necessary in all societies. As a result, his theory is often considered a good representation of structural functionalism. He claimed that all social behaviors, especially crime, provide essential functions in a society. Durkheim thought crime serves several functions. First, it defines the moral boundaries of societies. Few people know or realize what is against societal laws until they see someone punished for a violation. This reinforces their understanding of both what the rules are and what it means to break

▲ **Image 6.2**   Émile Durkheim (1858–1917).

them. Furthermore, the identification of rule breakers creates a bond among the other members of the society, perhaps through a common sense of self-righteousness or superiority.

In later works, Durkheim said the resultant bonding is what makes crime so necessary in a society. Given a community that has no law violators, he thought, society will change the legal definitions of what constitutes a crime to define some of its members as criminals. Examples of this are prevalent, but perhaps the most convincing is that of the Salem witch trials wherein hundreds of individuals were accused and tried for an almost laughable offense and more than a dozen were executed. Durkheim would say this was inevitable because crime was so low in the Massachusetts Bay Colony, as historical records confirm, that society had to come up with a fabricated criterion for defining certain members of the population as offenders.

Other examples are common in everyday life. The fastest way to have a group of strangers bond is to give them a common enemy, which often means forming into cliques and ganging up on others in the group. In a group of three or more college roommates, for example, two or more of the individuals will quickly join together and complain about the others. This is an inevitable phenomenon of human interaction and group dynamics that has always existed throughout the world across time and place. As Durkheim said, even in "a society of saints . . . crimes . . . will there be unknown; but faults which appear venial to the layman will create there the same scandal that the ordinary offense does in ordinary consciousnesses. . . . This society . . . will define these acts as criminal and will treat them as such."[16]

Law enforcement should always be cautious in cracking down on gangs, especially during relatively inactive periods, because it may make the gang stronger. Like all societal groups, when a common enemy appears, gang members—even those who do not typically get along—will come together and "circle the wagons" to protect themselves via strength in numbers. This very powerful bonding effect is one that many sociologists, and especially gang researchers, have consistently observed.[17]

Traditional, mostly mechanical societies could count on relative consensus about moral values and norms, and this sometimes led to too much control and a stagnation of creative thought. Durkheim thought that progress in society typically depends on deviating from established moral boundaries, especially if the society is in the mechanical stage. Some of the many examples include virtually all religious icons. Jesus, Buddha, and Mohammed were persecuted as criminals for deviating from societal norms in the times they preached. Political heroes have also been prosecuted and incarcerated as criminals, such as Gandhi in India, Mandela in South Africa, and Dr. King in the United States. In one of the most compelling cases, scientist and astronomer Galileo proposed a theory that Earth was not the center of the universe. Even though he was right, he was persecuted for his belief in a society that

[16]Émile Durkheim, *The Rules of the Sociological Method*, ed. George E. G. Catlin, trans. Sarah A. Solovay and John H. Mueller (New York: Free Press, 1965), as cited in Bernard et al., *Vold's Theoretical Criminology*.

[17]See discussion in Malcolm Klein, "Street Gang Cycles," in *Crime*, ed. James Q. Wilson and Joan Petersilia (San Francisco: ICS Press, 2002), 217–36.

strictly adhered to its beliefs. Durkheim was clearly accurate in saying that the normative structure in some societies is so strong that it hinders progress and that crime is the price societies pay for progress.

In contrast to mechanical societies, modern societies do not have such extreme restraint against deviations from established norms. Rather, almost the opposite is true; there are too many differences across groups because the division of labor is highly specialized. Thus, the varying roles in society, such as farmers versus scientific researchers, lead to extreme differences in the cultural values and norms of each group. There is a breakdown in the collective conscience because there is really no longer a collective nature in society. Therefore, law focuses not on defining the norms of society but on governing the interactions that take place among the different classes. According to Durkheim, law provides a service in regulating such interactions as societies progress toward more organic (more industrial) forms.

Durkheim emphasized that human beings, unlike other animal species who live according to their spontaneous needs, have no internal mechanism to signal when their needs and desires are satiated. Therefore, the selfish desires of humankind are limitless; the more an individual has, the more he or she wants. People are greedy by nature, and without something to tell them what they need and deserve, they will never feel content.[18] According to Durkheim, society provides the mechanism for limiting this insatiable appetite, having the sole power to create laws that set tangible limits.

Durkheim also noted that in times of rapid change, society fails in this role of regulating desires and expectations. Rapid change can be due to numerous factors, such as war or social movements (like the changes seen in the United States in the 1960s). The transitions Durkheim likely had in mind when he wrote were the American and French Revolutions and the Industrial Revolution. When society's ability to serve as a regulatory mechanism breaks down, the selfish, greedy tendencies of individuals are uncontrolled, causing a state Durkheim called *anomie*, or *normlessness*. Societies in such anomic states experience increases in many social problems, particularly criminal activity.

Durkheim was clear that, whether the rapid change was for good or bad, it would have negative effects on society. For example, whether the U.S. economy was improving, as it did during the late 1960s, or quickly tanking, as it did during the Depression of the 1930s, criminal activity would increase due to the lack of stability in regulating human expectations and desires. Interestingly, these two periods experienced the greatest crime waves of the 20th century, particularly for murder.[19] Another fact that supports Durkheim's predictions is that middle- and upper-class individuals have higher suicide rates than those from lower classes. This is consistent with the idea that it is better to have stability, even if it means always being poor, than it is to have instability at higher levels of income. In his best-known work, *Suicide,* Durkheim took an act that would seem to be the ultimate form of free choice or free will and showed that the decision to take one's own life was largely determined by external social factors. He argued that suicide is a *social fact*, a product of meanings and structural aspects that result from interactions among people.

Durkheim showed that the rate of suicide was significantly lower among individuals who were married, younger, and practiced religions that were more interactive and communal (e.g., Jewish). All of these characteristics boil down to one aspect: The more the social interaction and bonding with the community, the less the suicide. Thus, Durkheim concluded that variations in suicide rates are due to differences in social solidarity or bonding to society. Examples of this are still seen today, as in recent reports of high rates of suicide among people who live in remote areas, like Alaska (which has the highest rate of juvenile suicide), Wyoming, Montana, and the northern portions of Nevada. Another way of looking at the implications of Durkheim's conclusions is that social

---

[18]For more details on these issues, see Émile Durkheim's works: *The Division of Labor in Society* (1893; repr., New York: Free Press, 1965) and *Suicide* (1897; repr., New York: Free Press, 1951).

[19]U.S. Department of Justice, Bureau of Justice Statistics, *Violent Crime in the United States* (Washington, DC: Bureau of Justice Statistics, 1996), as illustrated in Joseph P. Senna and Larry G. Siegel, *Introduction to Criminal Justice*, 8th ed. (Belmont, CA: West/Wadsworth, 1999).

relationships are what make people happy and fulfilled. If they are isolated or have weak bonds to society, they will likely be depressed and discontented with their lives.

Another reason that Durkheim's examination of suicide was important was that he showed that suicide rates increased in times of rapid economic growth or rapid decline. Although researchers later argued that crime rates did not always follow this pattern,[20] Durkheim used quantified measures to test his propositions as the positivistic approach recommended. At the least, Durkheim created a prototype of how theory and empirical research could be combined in testing differences across social groups. This theoretical framework was drawn on heavily for one of the most influential and accepted criminological theories of the 20th century: strain theory.

Strain Theories

All forms of strain theory share an emphasis on frustration as a factor in crime causation, hence the name *strain theories*. Although the theories differ regarding what exactly is causing the frustration—and the way individuals cope (or don't cope) with stress and anger—they all hold that strain is the primary causal factor in the development of criminality. Strain theories all trace their origin to Robert K. Merton's seminal theoretical framework.

Merton's Strain Theory

Working in the 1930s, Merton drew heavily on Durkheim's idea of anomie in developing his own theory of structural strain.[21] Although Merton altered the definition of anomie, Durkheim's theoretical framework was a vital influence in the evolution of strain theory. Combining Durkheimian concepts and propositions with an emphasis on American culture, Merton's structural model became one of the most popular perspectives in criminological thought in the early 1900s and remains one of the most cited theories of crime in the criminological literature.

Cultural Context and Assumptions of Strain Theory

Some have claimed that Merton's seminal piece in 1938 was the most influential theoretical formulation in criminological literature, and it is one of the most frequently cited papers in sociology.[22] Although its popularity is partially due to its strong foundation in previous structural theories, Merton's strain theory also benefited from the timing of its publication. Virtually every theory discussed in this book became popular because it was well suited to the political and social climate of the times, fitting perspectives of how the world worked. Perhaps no other theory better represents this phenomenon than strain theory.

Most historians would agree that, in the United States, the most significant social issue of the 1930s was the economy. The influence of the Great Depression, largely a result of a stock market crash in 1929, affected virtually

---

[20]William J. Chambliss, "Functional and Conflict Theories of Crime," in *Whose Law? What Order?*, ed. William J. Chambliss and Milton Mankoff (New York: Wiley, 1976), 11–16.

[21]For reviews of Merton's theory, see both the original and more recent works by Merton himself: Robert K. Merton, "Social Structure and Anomie," *American Sociological Review* 3 (1938): 672–82; Robert K. Merton, *Social Theory and Social Structure* (New York: Free Press, 1968); and Robert K. Merton, "Opportunity Structure: The Emergence, Diffusion, and Differentiation as Sociological Concept, 1930s–1950s," in *Advances in Criminological Theory: The Legacy of Anomie Theory*, Vol. 6, ed. Freda Adler and William Laufer (New Brunswick, NJ: Transaction Press, 1995). For reviews by others, see Ronald L. Akers and Christine S. Sellers, *Criminological Theories: Introduction, Evaluation, and Application*, 6th ed. (Oxford: Oxford University Press, 2012), 164–68; Stephen E. Brown, Finn-Aage Esbensen, and Gilbert Geis, *Criminology: Explaining Crime and Its Context*, 8th ed. (Cincinnati: Anderson, 2013), 297–307; Marshall B. Clinard, "The Theoretical Implications of Anomie and Deviant Behavior," in *Anomie and Deviant Behavior*, ed. Marshall B. Clinard (New York: Free Press, 1964), 1–56; and Thomas J. Bernard, "Testing Structural Strain Theories," *Journal of Research in Crime and Delinquency* 24 (1987): 262–80.

[22]Clinard, "Theoretical Implications." See also the discussion in Brown et al., *Criminology*, 297.

every aspect of life in the United States. Unemployment and extreme poverty soared, along with suicide rates and crime rates, particularly murder rates.[23] American society was fertile ground for a theory of crime that placed virtually all of the blame on the U.S. economic structure.

On the other side of the coin, Merton was highly influenced by what he saw happening to the country during the Depression and how much the economic institution impacted almost all other social factors, particularly crime. He watched how the breakdown of the economic structure drove people to kill themselves or others, not to mention the rise in property crimes such as theft. Many once-successful individuals were now poor, and some felt driven to crime for survival. Notably, Durkheim's hypotheses regarding crime and suicide were supported during this time of rapid change, and Merton apparently realized that the framework simply had to be brought up-to-date and supplemented.

One of the key assumptions that distinguishes strain theory from Durkheim's perspective is that Merton altered his version of what anomie means. Merton focused on the nearly universal socialization of the American Dream in U.S. society—the idea that as long as people work very hard and pay their dues they will achieve their goals in the end. According to Merton, the socialized image of the goal is material wealth, whereas the socialized concept of the means of achieving the goal is hard work (e.g., education, labor). The conventional model of the American Dream was consistent with the Protestant work ethic, which called for working hard for a long time, knowing that you will be paid off in the distant future.

Furthermore, Merton thought that nearly everyone was socialized to believe in the American Dream no matter what economic class he or she was raised in as a child. There is some empirical support for this belief, and it makes sense. Virtually all parents, even if they are poor, want to give their children hope for the future if they are willing to work hard in school and at a job. Parents and society usually use celebrities as examples of this process—individuals who started off poor and rose to become wealthy. Modern examples include former secretary of state Colin Powell, owner of the NBA Dallas Mavericks Mark Cuban, Oscar-winning actress Hilary Swank, and Hollywood director and screenwriter Quentin Tarantino, not to mention Arnold Schwarzenegger and his amazing rise from teenage immigrant to Mr. Olympia and California governor.

These stories epitomize the American Dream, but parents and society do not also teach the reality of the situation. As Merton pointed out, a small percentage of people rise from the lower class to become materially successful, but the vast majority of poor children don't have much chance of ever obtaining such wealth. This near-universal socialization of the American Dream—which turns out not to be true for most people—causes most of the strain and frustration in American society, Merton said. Furthermore, he thought that most of the strain and frustration was due not to the failure to achieve conventional goals (i.e., wealth) but rather to the differential emphasis placed on material goals and the de-emphasizing of the importance of conventional means.

Merton's Concept of Anomie and Strain

Merton claimed that, in an ideal society, there would be an equal emphasis on conventional goals and means. However, in many societies, one is emphasized more than the other. Merton thought the United States epitomized the type of society that emphasized the goals far more than the means. The disequilibrium in emphasis between the goals and means of societies is what Merton called anomie. So, like Durkheim, Merton saw anomie as a negative state of society; however, the two men had very different ideas of how this state of society was caused. Whereas Durkheim believed that anomie was primarily caused by a society's transitioning too fast to maintain its regulatory control over its members, for Merton, anomie represented too much focus on the goals of wealth in the United States at the expense of conventional means.

---

[23]Larry J. Siegel, *Introduction to Criminal Justice*, 12th ed. (Belmont, CA: Wadsworth, 2010), 44.

Hypothetical situations can be used to illustrate Merton's view: Which of the following two men would be more respected by youths (or even adults) in our society: (1) John, who has his PhD in physics and lives in a one-bedroom apartment because his job as a postdoctoral student pays $25,000 a year; or (2) Joe, who is a relatively successful drug dealer and owns a four-bedroom home, drives a Hummer, dropped out of school in the 10th grade, and makes about $90,000 a year? In years of asking such a question to our classes, we have found that the answer is usually Joe, the drug dealer. After all, he appears to have obtained the American Dream, and little emphasis is placed on how he achieved it.

Still another way of supporting Merton's idea that America is too focused on the goal of material success is to ask you, the reader, to think about why you are taking the time to read this book or to attend college. Specifically, the question for you is this: If you knew that studying this book—or earning a college degree— would not lead to a better employment position, would you read it anyway just to increase your own knowledge? In over a decade of putting this question to about 10,000 students in various university courses, the author of this book has found that only about 5% (usually fewer) of respondents say yes. Interestingly, when asked why they put all of this work into attending classes, many of them say it's for the partying or social life. Ultimately, it seems that most college students would not be engaging in the hard work it takes to educate themselves if it weren't for some payoff at the end of the task. In some ways, this supports Merton's claim that there is an emphasis on the goals and little or no intrinsic value placed on the work itself (i.e., the means). This phenomenon is not meant to be a disheartening or a negative statement; it is meant only to exhibit the reality of American culture. It is quite common in our society to emphasize the goal of financial success as opposed to hard work or education.

Merton thought that individuals, particularly those in the lower class, eventually realize that the ideal of the American Dream is a lie or at least a false illusion for the vast majority. This revelation will likely take place when people are in their late teens to mid-20s, and according to Merton, this is when the frustration or strain is evident. That is consistent with the age–crime peak of offending at the approximate age of 17. Learning that hard work won't necessarily provide rewards, some individuals begin to innovate ways that they can achieve material success without the conventional means of getting it. Obviously, this is often through criminal activity. However, not all individuals deal with strain in this way; most people who are poor do not resort to crime. To Merton's credit, he explained that individuals deal with the limited economic structure of society in different ways. He referred to these variations as **adaptations to strain**.

▲ **Image 6.3**   Robert K. Merton (1910–2003), the sociologist who first proposed strain theory in the 1930s.

Adaptations to Strain

According to Merton, there are five adaptations to strain. The first of these is conformity, in which people buy into the conventional goals of society and the conventional means of working hard in school or at their labor.[24] Like conformists, most readers of this book would probably like to achieve material success and are willing to use conventional means of achieving success through educational efforts and doing a good job at work. Another adaptation to strain is **ritualism**. Ritualists do not pursue the goal of material success—probably because they know they don't have a realistic chance of obtaining it. However, they do buy into the conventional means in the sense that they like to do their jobs or are happy with just making ends meet through their current positions. For example, studies have shown that some of the most contented and happy people in society are those who don't hope to become rich; are quite content with their blue-collar jobs; and often have a strong sense of pride in their work, even if it is sometimes quite menial. To these people, work is a type of ritual, performed without a goal in mind; rather, it is a form of intrinsic goal in and of itself. Ultimately, conformists and ritualists tend to be at low risk for offending, which is in contrast to the other adaptations to strain.

The other three adaptations to strain are far more likely to be associated with criminal offending: **innovation**, **retreatism**, and **rebellion**. Perhaps most likely to become predatory street criminals are the innovators, who Merton claimed greatly desire the conventional goals of material success but are not willing to engage in conventional means. Obviously, drug dealers and professional auto thieves, as well as many other variations of chronic property criminals (bank robbers, etc.), would fit this category. They are innovating ways to achieve the goals without the hard work that is usually required. However, innovators are not always criminals. In fact, many of them are the most respected individuals in our society. For example, some entrepreneurs have used the capitalistic system of our society to produce useful products and services (e.g., the men who designed Google for the Internet) and have made a fortune at a very young age without advanced college education or years of work at a company. Other examples are successful athletes who sign multimillion-dollar contracts at age 18. So, it should be clear that not all innovators are criminals.

The fourth adaptation to strain is retreatism. Retreatists do not seek to achieve the goals of society, and they also do not buy into the idea of conventional hard work. There are many varieties of this adaptation: for example, people who become homeless by choice or who isolate themselves in desolate places without human contact. A good example of a retreatist is Ted Kaczynski, the Unabomber, who left a good position as a professor at the University of California, Berkeley, to live in an isolated cabin in Montana that had no running water or electricity; he did not interact with humans for many months at a time. Other types of retreatists, perhaps the most likely to be criminal, are those who are heavy drug users who actively disengage from social life and try to escape via mind-altering drugs. All of these forms of retreatists seek to drop out of society altogether, thus not buying into its means or goals.

Finally, the last adaptation to strain, according to Merton, is rebellion, which is the most complex of the five adaptations. Interestingly, rebels buy into the idea of societal goals and means, but they do not buy into those currently in place. Most true rebels are criminals by definition, largely because they are trying to overthrow the current societal structure. For example, the founders of the United States were all rebels because they actively fought the governing state—English rule—and clearly committed treason in the process. Had they lost or been caught during the American Revolution, they would have been executed as the criminals they were by law. However, because they won the war, they became heroes and presidents. Another example is Karl Marx. He bought into the idea of goals and means of society—just not those of capitalistic societies. Rather, he proposed socialism or communism as a means to the goal of utopia. So, there are many contexts in which rebels can be criminals, but sometimes they end up being heroes.

Merton also noted that one individual can represent more than one adaptation. Perhaps the best example is that of the Unabomber, who obviously started out as a conformist in that he was a respected professor at the University of California, Berkeley, who was well on his way to tenure and promotion. He then seemed to shift to retreatism in that

---

[24]Merton, *Social Theory.*

he isolated himself from society. Later, he became a rebel who bombed innocent people in his quest to implement his own goals and means as described in his manifesto, which he coerced several national newspapers to publish. This subsequently resulted in his apprehension when his brother read it and informed authorities that he thought his brother was the author.

Finally, some have applied a sports analogy to these adaptations.[25] Assuming a basketball game is taking place, conformists will play to win, and they will always play by the rules and won't cheat. Ritualists will play the game just because they like to play; they don't care about winning. Innovators will play to win, and they will break any rules they can to triumph in the game. Retreatists don't like to play and obviously don't care about winning. Finally, rebels won't like the rules on the court, so they will try to steal the ball and go play by their own rules on another court. Although this is a somewhat simplistic analogy, it is likely to help readers remember the adaptations and perhaps enable them to apply these ways of dealing with strain to everyday situations, such as criminal activity.

Case Study: The Black Binder Bandit

A recent news story reported on a jobless man who was arrested for committing a dozen bank robberies across the Phoenix valley. The man, Cristian Alfredo Urquijo, 39, told authorities that he did it to survive and that "desperation was a great motivator." He was accused of robbing at least a dozen banks between 2010 and 2011. The criminal complaint noted that he had been laid off from work, was unable to find employment, and robbed the Phoenix-area banks to survive. He went on to say, "It's pretty simple. It's black and white. I don't have a job, I had to work, and I rob to survive." During his crime spree, authorities called him the "Black Binder Bandit" because he typically hid a revolver in a black binder and also would usually place the stolen money in this binder.

Urquijo pleaded guilty to nine counts of bank robbery, three counts of armed bank robbery, and one count of use of a firearm in a crime of violence, which carries an enhanced sentence. He had originally been charged with 16 counts of bank robbery, but as often happens in plea negotiations, the counts were reduced. He did admit that he had robbed at least 12 banks and also that he had obtained more than $49,000 from these bank robberies.

It is obvious that this man committed these crimes because he wanted to provide for himself in an economic recession. This is just one of many examples of individuals who are strongly motivated to commit crimes—even the major federal crime of bank robbery—to deal with the economic strain or frustration of not being able to "get ahead" or achieve the American Dream of success. This chapter discusses the evolution of theories that address this concept of trying to provide for oneself or succeed while dealing with societal and economic dynamics in American society. Specifically, this chapter reviews the development of anomie or strain theory, starting with its origins among early social structure theorists, such as Durkheim, and moving to its further development by Merton. The chapter also examines the development of various strain models of offending as well as the most modern versions of strain theory (e.g., general strain theory). We will also examine the empirical research findings on this perspective, which reveal that this framework remains one of the dominant theoretical explanations of criminal behavior in modern times. We will finish this chapter by examining the policy implications suggested by this perspective for explaining criminal behavior, and we will further discuss the case of the Black Binder Bandit toward the end of this chapter.

"It's pretty simple. It's black and white. I don't have a job, I had to work, and I rob to survive."

[25]Bernard et al., *Vold's Theoretical Criminology*, 140.

It should be noted that the Federal Bureau of Investigation (FBI) typically assigns nicknames (such as the Black Binder Bandit) to serial bank robbers. The FBI does so for a very important reason: The public is more likely to take note of serial bank robbers when there is a catchy moniker or nickname attached to them. Apparently, this strategy is useful, because bank robbery actually has a much higher clearance rate than other types of robbery. Other notable nicknames of serial bank robbers in the past few years are the "Mesh-Mask Bandit" (still at large in Texas; wears a mesh mask), the "Geezer Bandit" (still at large in Southern California; authorities believe that the offender may be a young person disguising himself as an elderly person), and the "Michael Jackson Bandit" (still at large in Southern California; wears one glove during robberies). Although all these bank robbery suspects are still at large, many others have been caught as a result of making their nicknames notable to the public.

Think About It

1. Can you articulate why the Black Binder Bandit seems to be a good example of Merton's strain theory?

2. Based on what he said to the police and his behavior, what adaptation of strain would you say best fits him?

3. Outside of the nicknames already listed in this discussion, do you know of any other robbers the authorities have nicknamed and the reason(s) the robbers were given their monikers?

▲ **Image 6.4** As surveillance photos show, Urquijo typically carried into the bank a black binder in which he hid a revolver and the money he acquired from the bank robbery.

SOURCE: azcentral.com

Evidence and Criticisms of Merton's Strain Theory

Merton's framework, which emphasized the importance of economic structure, had a high degree of face validity during the Great Depression; however, many later scientific studies showed mixed support for strain theory. Although research that examined the effects of poverty on violence and official rates of various crimes has found relatively consistent support for Merton's views (albeit with weaker effects than strain theory implies), a series of studies of self-reported delinquent behavior found little or no relationship between social class and criminality.[26] Furthermore, the idea that unemployment drives people to commit crime has received little support.[27]

[26]For examples and reviews of this research, see F. Ivan Nye, *Family Relationships and Delinquent Behavior* (New York: Wiley, 1958); Ronald L. Akers, "Socio-Economic Status and Delinquent Behavior: A Retest," *Journal of Research in Crime and Delinquency* 1 (1964): 38–46; Charles R. Tittle and Wayne J. Villemez, "Social Class and Criminality," *Social Forces* 56 (1977): 474–503; Charles R. Tittle, Wayne J. Villemez, and Douglas A. Smith, "The Myth of Social Class and Criminality: An Empirical Assessment of the Empirical Evidence," *American Sociological Review* 43 (1978): 643–56; Michael J. Hindelang, Travis Hirschi, and Joseph C. Weis, "Correlates of Delinquency: The Illusion of Discrepancy between Self-Report and Official Measures," *American Sociological Review* 44 (1979): 995–1014; Michael J. Hindelang, *Measuring Delinquency* (Beverly Hills, CA: Sage, 1980); Terence P. Thornberry and Margaret Farnworth, "Social Correlates of Criminal Involvement," *American Sociological Review* 47 (1982): 505–17; and Gregory R. Dunaway et al., "The Myth of Social Class and Crime Revisited: An Examination of Class and Adult Criminality," *Criminology* 38 (2000): 589–632. For one of the most thorough reviews, see Charles R. Tittle and Robert F. Meier, "Specifying the SES/Delinquency Relationship," *Criminology* 28 (1990): 271–99.

[27]Gary Kleck and Ted Chiricos, "Unemployment and Property Crime: A Target-Specific Assessment of Opportunity and Motivation as Mediating Factors," *Criminology* 40 (2000): 649–680.

On the other hand, some experts have argued that Merton's strain theory is primarily a structural model of crime that is more a theory of societal groups, not individual motivations.[28] Therefore, some modern studies have used aggregated group rates (i.e., macro-level measures) to test the effects of deprivation as opposed to using individual (micro-level) rates of inequality and crime. Most of these studies provide some support for the hypothesis that social groups and regions with higher rates of deprivation and inequality have higher rates of criminal activity.[29] In sum, there appears to be some support for Merton's strain theory at the macro level of analysis when official measures are being used to indicate criminality.

However, many critics have claimed that these studies do not directly measure perceptions or feelings of strain, so they are only indirect examinations of Merton's theory. In light of these criticisms, some researchers focused on the disparity between what individuals aspire to in various aspects of life (e.g., school, occupation, social life) and what they realistically expect to achieve.[30] The rationale behind these studies was that if an individual has high aspirations (i.e., goals) but a low expectation of actually achieving the goals due to structural barriers, then that individual is more likely to experience feelings of frustration and strain. Furthermore, it was predicted that the larger the gap between aspirations and expectations, the stronger the sense of strain. Of the studies that examined discrepancies between aspirations and expectations, most did not find evidence to link a large gap between these two levels with criminal activity. In fact, several studies found that for most antisocial respondents there was virtually no gap between aspirations and expectations. Rather, most of the subjects who reported the highest levels of criminal activity (typically young males) tended to report low levels of both aspirations and expectations.

Surprisingly, when aspirations were high, it seemed to inhibit offending, even when expectations to achieve those goals were low. One interpretation of these findings is that individuals who have high goals will not jeopardize their chances even if they are slim. On the other hand, individuals who don't have high goals are likely to be indifferent to their future and, in a sense, have nothing to lose. So, without a stake in conventional society, this predisposes them to crime. While this conclusion supports social control theories, it does not provide support for strain theory.

Some critics have argued that most studies on the discrepancies between aspirations and expectations have not been done correctly. For example, Margaret Farnworth and Michael J. Leiber claimed that it was a mistake to examine differences between educational goals and expectations or differences between occupational goals and expectations, which is what most of these studies did.[31] Rather, they proposed testing the gap between economic aspirations (i.e., goals) and educational expectations (i.e., means of achieving the goals). This makes sense, and Farnworth and Leiber found support for a gap between these two factors and criminality. However, they also found that people who reported low economic aspirations were more likely to be delinquent, which supports the previous studies that they criticized. Another criticism of this type of strain theory study is that simply reporting a gap between expectations and aspirations may not mean that the individuals actually feel strain; rather,

[28]Bernard, "Testing Structural Strain Theories"; Steven F. Messner, "Merton's 'Social Structure and Anomie': The Road Not Taken," *Deviant Behavior* 9 (1988): 33–53. See also discussion in Burton and Cullen, "Empirical Status."

[29]For a review of these studies, see Kenneth C. Land, Patricia L. McCall, and Lawrence E. Cohen, "Structural Covariates of Homicide Rates: Are There Any Invariances across Time and Social Space?" *American Journal of Sociology* 95 (1990): 922–63.

[30]For examples and reviews of these types of studies, see Travis Hirschi, *Causes of Delinquency* (Berkeley: University of California Press, 1969), 4–10; Allen E. Liska, "Aspirations, Expectations, and Delinquency: Stress and Additive Models," *Sociological Quarterly* 12 (1971): 99–107; Margaret Farnworth and Michael J. Leiber, "Strain Theory Revisited: Economic Goals, Educational Means, and Delinquency," *American Sociological Review* 54 (1989): 263–74; Burton and Cullen, "Empirical Status"; Velmer S. Burton et al., "Reconsidering Strain Theory: Operationalization, Rival Theories, and Adult Criminality," *Journal of Quantitative Criminology* 10 (1994): 213–39; and Robert F. Agnew et al., "A New Test of Classic Strain Theory," *Justice Quarterly* 13 (1996): 681–704. See also discussion of this issue in Akers and Sellers, *Criminological Theories*, 173–75.

[31]Farnworth and Leiber, "Strain Theory."

researchers have simply, and perhaps wrongfully, assumed that a gap between the two measures indicates feelings of frustration.[32]

Other criticisms of Merton's strain theory include historical evidence and the theory's failure to explain the age–crime curve. Regarding the historical evidence, it is hard to understand why some of the largest increases in crime took place during a period of relative economic prosperity, namely the late 1960s. Between 1965 and 1973, which were generally good economic years in the United States, crime increased more than it had ever done since recording crime rates began. Therefore, if strain theory is presented as the primary explanation for criminal activity, it would probably have a hard time explaining this historical era. On the other hand, the growth in the economy in the 1960s and early 1970s may have caused more disparity between the rich and the poor, thereby producing more relative deprivation.

The other major criticism of strain theory is that it does not explain one of the most established facts in the field: the age–crime curve. In virtually every society in the world, across time and place, predatory street crimes (robbery, rape, murder, burglary, larceny, etc.) tend to peak sharply in the teenage years to early 20s and then drop off very quickly, certainly before age 30. However, most studies show that feelings of stress and frustration tend not to follow this pattern. For example, suicide rates tend to be just as high or higher as one gets older, with middle-aged and elderly people having much higher rates of suicide than those in their teens or early 20s.

On the other hand, it can be argued that crime rates go down even though strain can continue or even increase with age because individuals develop coping mechanisms for dealing with the frustrations they feel. But even if this is true regarding criminal behavior, apparently this doesn't seem to prevent suicidal tendencies. General strain theory emphasized this concept. However, before we cover general strain theory, we will discuss two other variations of Merton's theory that were both developed between 1955 and 1960 to explain gang formation and behavior using a structural strain framework.

Variations of Merton's Strain Theory: Cohen's Model and Cloward and Ohlin's Theory

Cohen's Theory of Lower-Class Status Frustration and Gang Formation

In 1955, Albert Cohen presented a theory of gang formation that used Merton's strain theory as a basis for why individuals resort to such group behavior.[33] In Cohen's model, young, lower-class males are at a disadvantage in school because they lack the normal interaction, socialization, and discipline instituted by educated parents of the middle class. This is in line with Merton's original framework identifying a disadvantage for underclass youth. According to Cohen, such youths are likely to experience failure in school because they are unprepared to conform with middle-class values and fail to meet the middle-class measuring rod, which emphasizes motivation, accountability, responsibility, deferred gratification, long-term planning, respect for authority and property, controlling emotions, and so on.

Like Merton, Cohen emphasized the youths' internalization of the American Dream and the idea that they had a fair chance of success, which would mean that failure to be successful according to this middle-class standard would be very frustrating for them. The strain felt as a result of failure in school performance and lack of respect among peers is often referred to as *status frustration*. It leads youth to develop a system of values opposed to middle-class standards and values. Some have claimed that this represents a Freudian defense mechanism known as **reaction formation**, which involves adopting attitudes or committing behaviors that are opposite of what is expected as a

---

[32]Agnew et al., "A New Test."

[33]Albert Cohen, *Delinquent Boys: The Culture of the Gang* (New York: Free Press, 1955).

form of defiance so as to feel less guilty for not living up to unachievable standards. Specifically, instead of abiding by middle-class norms of obedience to authority, school achievement, and respect for authority, these youths change their normative beliefs to value the opposite characteristics: malicious, negativistic, and nonutilitarian delinquent activity.

Delinquent youths will begin to value destruction of property and skipping school not because these behaviors lead to a payoff or success in the conventional world but simply because they defy the conventional order. In other words, they turn middle-class values upside down and consider activity that violates the conventional norms and laws good, thereby psychologically and physically rejecting the cultural system that has been imposed on them without preparation and fair distribution of resources. Furthermore, Cohen claimed that while these behaviors do not appear to have much utility or value, they are quite valuable and important from the perspective of the strained youths. Specifically, they do these acts to gain respect from their peers.

Cohen stated that he believed that this tendency to reject middle-class values is the primary cause of gangs, a classic example of "birds of a feather flock together." Not all lower-class males resort to crime and join a gang in response to this structural disadvantage. Other variations, beyond that of the **delinquent boy** described previously, include the **college boy** and the **corner boy.** The college boy responds to his disadvantaged situation by dedicating himself to overcoming the odds and competing in middle-class schools despite his unlikely chances for success. The corner boy responds to the situation by accepting his place as a lower-class individual who will somewhat passively make the best of life at the bottom of the social order.

When compared to Merton's original adaptations, Cohen's delinquent boy is probably best seen as similar to a rebel because he rejects the means and goals of conventional society (i.e., middle-class values and success in school), substituting new means and goals (negativistic behaviors and peer respect in the gang). Some would argue that delinquent boys should be seen as innovators because their goals are ultimately the same: peer respect. However, the actual peers involved completely change, so we argue that, through the reaction formation process, the delinquent boy actually creates his own goals and means that go against the conventional, middle-class goals and means. Regarding the college boy, the adaptation that seems to fit the best is that of conformity, because the college boy continues to believe in the conventional goals (i.e., financial success and achievement) and means (hard work via education or labor) of middle-class society. Finally, the corner boy probably best fits the adaptation of ritualism because he knows that he likely will never achieve the goals of society but resigns himself to not obtaining financial success; at the same time, he does not resort to predatory street crime but rather holds a stable, blue-collar job or makes ends meet in other typical, legal ways. Some corner boys end up simply collecting welfare and give up working altogether; they may actually become more like the adaptation of retreatism because they have virtually given up on the conventional means of society (hard work) as well as the goals.

At the time that Cohen developed his theory, official statistics showed that virtually all gang violence, and most violence for that matter, was concentrated among lower-class male youth. However, with the development of self-report studies in the 1960s, Cohen's theory was shown to be somewhat overstated: Middle-class youth were well represented among those who committed delinquent acts.[34] Other studies have also been critical of Cohen's theory, particularly the portions that deal with his proposition that crime rates will increase after youths drop out of school and join gangs. Although the findings are mixed, many studies have found that delinquency is often higher before youths drop out of school and may actually decline once they drop out and

---

[34]Tittle et al., "Myth of Social Class"; Hindelang et al., "Correlates of Delinquency."

become employed.[35] Some critics have pointed out that such findings discredit Cohen's theory, but this is not necessarily true. After all, delinquency may peak right before the youths drop out because they feel the most frustrated and strained then, whereas delinquency may decrease after they drop out because some are raising their self-esteem by earning wages and taking pride in having jobs.

Still, studies have clearly shown that lower-class youths are far more likely to have problems in school and that school failure is consistently linked to criminality.[36] Furthermore, there is little dispute that much of delinquency represents malicious, negativistic, and nonutilitarian activity. For example, what do individuals have to gain from destroying mailboxes or spraying graffiti on walls? These acts will never earn much money or any payoff other than peer respect. So, ultimately, it appears that there is some face validity to what Cohen proposed in the sense that some youths engage in behavior that has no value other than earning peer respect, even though that behavior is negativistic and nonutilitarian according to the values of conventional society. Regardless of some criticisms of Cohen's model, he provided an important structural strain theory of the development of gangs and lower-class delinquency.

Cloward and Ohlin's Theory of Differential Opportunity

Five years after Cohen published his theory, Richard Cloward and Lloyd Ohlin presented yet another structural strain theory of gang formation and behavior.[37] Like Merton and Cohen, Cloward and Ohlin assumed in their model that all youths, including those in the lower class, are socialized to believe in the American Dream and that when individuals realize that they are blocked from conventional opportunities they become frustrated and strained. What distinguishes Cloward and Ohlin's theory from that of the previous strain theories is that they identified three different types of gangs based on the characteristics of each neighborhood's social structure. They believed the nature of gangs varied according to the availability of illegal opportunities in the social structure. So, whereas previous strain theories focused only on lack of legal opportunities, Cloward and Ohlin's model emphasized both legal and illegal opportunities; the availability or lack of these opportunities largely determined what type of gang would form in that neighborhood, hence the name *differential opportunity theory*. Furthermore, the authors acknowledged Edwin Sutherland's influence on their theory (see Chapter 8), and it is evident in their focus on the associations made in the neighborhood.

According to differential opportunity theory, the three types of gangs that form are criminal gangs, conflict gangs, and retreatist gangs. **Criminal gangs** form in lower-class neighborhoods that have an organized structure of adult criminal behavior. Such neighborhoods are so organized and stable that criminal networks are often known and accepted by the conventional individuals in the area. In these neighborhoods, the adult gangsters mentor the youth and take them under their wings. This can pay off for the adult criminals, too, because youths can often be used to do the dirty work for the criminal enterprises in the neighborhood without risk of serious punishment if they are caught. The successful adult offenders supply the youths with the motives and techniques for committing

---

[35]See Bernard, "Testing Structural Strain Theories"; Merton, "Opportunity Structure"; Delbert Elliott and Harwin Voss, *Delinquency and Dropout* (Lexington, MA: D. C. Heath, 1974); Terence P. Thornberry, Melanie Moore, and R. L. Christenson, "The Effect of Dropping Out of High School on Subsequent Criminal Behavior," *Criminology* 23 (1985): 3–18; G. Roger Jarjoura, "Does Dropping Out of School Enhance Delinquent Involvement? Results from a Large-Scale National Probability Sample," *Criminology* 31 (1993): 149–72; and G. Roger Jarjoura, "The Conditional Effect of Social Class on the Dropout Delinquency Relationship," *Journal of Research in Crime and Delinquency* 33 (1996): 232–55. See discussion in Donald J. Shoemaker, *Theories of Delinquency*, 6th ed. (New York: Oxford University Press, 2009).

[36]Alexander Liazos, "School, Alienation, and Delinquency," *Crime and Delinquency* 24 (1978): 355–70; Joseph W. Rogers and G. Larry Mays, *Juvenile Delinquency and Juvenile Justice* (New York: Wiley, 1987); Clarence E. Tygart, "Strain Theory and Public School Vandalism: Academic Tracking, School Social Status, and Students' Academic Achievement," *Youth and Society* 20 (1988): 106–18; Hirschi, *Causes of Delinquency*.

[37]Richard A. Cloward and Lloyd E. Ohlin, *Delinquency and Opportunity: A Theory of Delinquent Gangs* (New York: The Free Press, 1960). For a discussion and theoretical critique of the model, see Bernard, "Testing Structural Strain Theories," and Merton, "Opportunity Structure," respectively.

▲ **Image 6.5**   Organized crime syndicates are typically found in neighborhoods with more structured criminal organizations.

SOURCE: © istockphoto.com / mbbirdy

crime. So, while members of criminal gangs are blocked from legal opportunities, they are offered ample opportunities in the illegal realm.

Criminal gangs tend to reflect the strong organization and stability of such neighborhoods. Therefore, criminal gangs primarily commit property or economic crimes with the goal of making a profit through illegal behavior. These crimes can range from running numbers as local bookies to fencing stolen goods to running businesses that are fronts for vice crimes (e.g., prostitution, drug trading). All of these businesses involve making a profit illegally, and there is often a system or structure in which the criminal activity takes place. Furthermore, these criminal gangs most closely follow Merton's adaptation of innovation because the members still want to achieve the goals of conventional society (financial success). Because of their strong organizational structure, these gangs favor members who have self-control and are good at planning over individuals who are highly impulsive or uncontrolled.

Examples of criminal gangs are seen in movies depicting highly organized neighborhoods that often consist primarily of one ethnicity, including *The Godfather*, *The Godfather Part II*, *A Bronx Tale*, *State of Grace*, *Sleepers*, *New Jack City*, *Clockers*, *GoodFellas*, *Better Luck Tomorrow*, and many others that were partially based on real events. All of these depictions involve a highly structured hierarchy of a criminal enterprise, which is largely a manifestation of the organization of the neighborhood. Hollywood motion pictures also produce stories about older criminals taking younger males from the neighborhood under their wings and training them in the ways of criminal networks. Furthermore, virtually all ethnic groups offer examples of this type of gang or neighborhood; the list of movies that was just given includes Italian American, Irish American, African American, and Asian American examples. Thus, criminal gangs can be found across the racial and ethnic spectrum, largely because all groups have certain neighborhoods that exhibit strong organization and stability.

Conflict gangs were another type of gang that Cloward and Ohlin identified. Conflict gangs tend to develop in neighborhoods that have weak stability and little or no organization. In fact, the neighborhood often seems to be in a state of flux with people constantly moving in and out. Because the youths in the neighborhood do not have a solid crime network or adult criminal mentors, they tend to form as relatively disorganized gangs, and they typically lack the skills and knowledge to make a profit through criminal activity. Therefore, the primary illegal activity of conflict gangs is violence, which they use to gain prominence and respect among themselves and the neighborhood. Due to the disorganized nature of the neighborhoods as well as the gangs themselves, conflict gangs never quite achieve the respect and stability that criminal gangs typically achieve. The members of conflict gangs tend to be more impulsive and lack self-control compared to members of criminal gangs, largely because there are no adult criminal mentors to control them.

According to Cloward and Ohlin, conflict gangs are blocked from both legitimate and illegitimate opportunities. In applying Merton's adaptations, conflict gangs would probably fit the category of rebellion, largely because none of the other categories fit well, but it can also be argued that conflict gangs have rejected the goals and means of conventional society and implemented their own values, which emphasize violence. Examples of motion pictures that depict this type of breakdown in community structure and a mostly violent gang culture are *Menace II Society*,

Boyz n the Hood, *A Clockwork Orange*, *Colors*, and *The Outsiders*, which all emphasize the chaos and violence that results when neighborhood and family organization is weak.

Finally, if individuals are double failures in both legitimate and illegitimate worlds, meaning that they can't achieve success in school or status in their local gangs, they join together to form **retreatist gangs**. Because members of retreatist gangs are no good at making a profit from crime or using violence to achieve status, the primary form of offending is usually drug usage. Like individuals who choose Merton's retreatist adaptation to strain, the members of retreatist gangs often want simply to escape from reality. Therefore, the primary activity of the gang when they get together is usually just to get high, which is well represented by Hollywood in such movies as *Trainspotting*, *Drugstore Cowboy*, and *The Panic in Needle Park*. In all of these movies, the only true goal of the gangs is getting stoned to escape from the worlds where they have failed.

There are a number of empirical studies and critiques of Cloward and Ohlin's theory, with the criticisms being similar to those of Merton's strain theory. Specifically, the critics argue that there is little evidence that gaps between what lower-class youths aspire to and what they expect to achieve produce frustration and strain, nor do such gaps appear predictive of gang membership or criminality.[38] Another criticism of Cloward and Ohlin's theory is the inability to find empirical evidence that supports their model of the formation of three types of gangs and their specializations in offending. While some research supports the existence of gangs that appear to specialize in certain forms of offending, many studies find that the observed specializations of gangs do not exactly follow the categories that Cloward and Ohlin proposed.[39] Additional studies have shown that many gangs tend not to specialize but rather to engage in a wider variety of offending behaviors.

Despite the criticisms of Cloward and Ohlin's model of gang formation, their theoretical framework inspired policy, largely due to the influence that their work had on Attorney General Robert Kennedy, who had read their book. In fact, Kennedy asked Ohlin to assist in developing federal policies regarding delinquency,[40] which resulted in the Juvenile Delinquency Prevention and Control Act of 1961. Cloward and Ohlin's theory was a major influence on the Mobilization for Youth project in New York City, which, along with the federal legislation, stressed creating education and work opportunities for youths. Although evaluations of this program showed little effect on reducing delinquency, it was impressive that such theorizing about lower-class male youths could have such a large impact on policy interventions.

Ultimately, the variations presented by Cohen, as well as Cloward and Ohlin, provided additional revisions that seemed at the time to advance the validity of strain theory. However, most of these revisions were based on official statistics that showed that lower-class male youth committed most crime, which were later shown by self-reports to be exaggerated.[41] Once scholars realized that most of the earlier models were not empirically valid for most criminal activity, strain theory became unpopular for several decades. But during the 1980s, another version was devised by Robert Agnew, who rejuvenated interest in strain theory by devising a way to make it more general and applicable to a larger variety of crimes and forms of deviance.

---

[38] James F. Short, "Gang Delinquency and Anomie," in *Anomie and Deviant Behavior*, ed. Marshall B. Clinard (New York: Free Press, 1964), 98–127; James F. Short, Ramon Rivera, and Ray A. Tennyson, "Perceived Opportunities, Gang Membership, and Delinquency," *American Sociological Review* 30 (1965): 56–67; James F. Short and Fred L. Strodtbeck, *Group Processes and Gang Delinquency* (Chicago: University of Chicago Press, 1965); Liska, "Aspirations"; and Hirschi, *Causes of Delinquency*. See discussion in Shoemaker, *Theories of Delinquency*, 121–30.

[39] Irving Spergel, *Racketville, Slumtown, and Haulburg: An Exploratory Study of Delinquent Subcultures* (Chicago: University of Chicago Press, 1964); Short and Strodtbeck, *Group Processes*; Paul E. Tracy, Marvin E. Wolfgang, and Robert M. Figlio, *Delinquency Careers in Two Birth Cohorts* (New York: Plenum, 1990).

[40] Lamar T. Empey, *American Delinquency*, 4th ed. (Belmont, CA: Wadsworth, 1999).

[41] Tittle et al., "Myth of Social Class"; Hindelang et al., "Correlates of Delinquency."

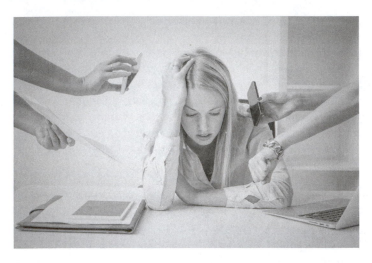

▲ **Image 6.6**   Individuals experience stressors every day, and general strain theory emphasizes the importance of stress and anger in increasing the likelihood of engaging in criminal behavior.

SOURCE: © istockphoto.com / grinvalds

General Strain Theory

In the 1980s, Robert Agnew proposed **general strain theory**, which covers a much larger range of behavior by not concentrating on simply the lower class but providing a model more applicable to the frustrations that all individuals feel in everyday life.[42] Unlike other strain theories, general strain theory does not rely on assumptions about the frustration arising when people realize that the American Dream is a false promise to those of the lower classes. Rather, this theoretical framework assumes that people of all social classes and economic positions deal with frustrations in routine daily life.

Previous strain theories, such as the models proposed by Merton, Cohen, and Cloward and Ohlin, focused on individuals' failure to achieve positively valued goals that they had been socialized to work to obtain. General strain theory also focuses on this source of strain; however, it identifies two additional categories of strain: *presentation of noxious stimuli* and *removal of positively valued stimuli.* In addition to the failure to achieve one's goals, Agnew claimed that the presentation of noxious stimuli (i.e., bad things) in one's life could cause major stress and frustration. Examples of noxious stimuli would include things like an abusive parent, a critical teacher, or an overly demanding boss. These are just some of the many negative factors that can exist in one's life—the number of examples is endless.

The other strain category Agnew identified was the removal of positive stimuli, which is likely the largest cause of frustration. Examples of removal of positively valued stimuli include the loss of a good job, loss of the use of a car for a period of time, or the loss of a loved one. Such losses, like the other two sources of strain, may have varying degrees of influence depending on the individual. One person may not feel much frustration in losing a job or divorcing a spouse, whereas another person may experience severe anxiety or depression from such events.

Ultimately, general strain theory proposes that these three categories of strain (failure to achieve goals, noxious stimuli, and removal of positive stimuli) will lead to stress and that this results in a propensity to feel anger. Anger can be seen as a primary mediating factor in the causal model of the general strain framework. It is predicted that, to the extent that the three sources of strain cause feelings of anger in an individual, he or she will be predisposed to commit crime and deviance. However, Agnew was clear in stating that if an individual can somehow cope with this anger in a positive way, then such feelings do not necessarily have to result in criminal activity. These coping mechanisms vary widely across individuals; different strategies work for some people better than others.

---

[42] For Agnew's works regarding this theory, see Robert Agnew, "A Revised Strain Theory of Delinquency," *Social Forces* 64 (1985): 151–67; Robert Agnew, "Foundation for a General Strain Theory of Crime and Delinquency," *Criminology* 30 (1992): 47–88; Robert Agnew and Helene Raskin White, "An Empirical Test of General Strain Theory," *Criminology* 30 (1992): 475–500; Robert Agnew, "Controlling Delinquency: Recommendations from General Strain Theory," in *Crime and Public Policy: Putting Theory to Work*, ed. Hugh Barlow (Boulder: Westview Press, 1995), 43–70; Agnew et al., "A New Test," 681–704; Robert Agnew, "Building on the Foundation of General Strain Theory: Specifying the Types of Strain Most Likely to Lead to Crime and Delinquency," *Journal of Research in Crime and Delinquency* 38 (2001): 319–61.

For example, some people relieve stress by working out or running, whereas others watch television or a movie. One type of activity that has shown relatively consistent success in relieving stress is laughter, which psychologists are now prescribing as a release of tension. Another is yoga, which includes simple breathing techniques such as taking several deep breaths; it has been shown to physiologically enhance release of stress.

Although Agnew did not originally provide details on how coping mechanisms work or explore the extant psychological research on these strategies, he specifically pointed to such mechanisms for dealing with anger in prosocial ways. The primary prediction regarding coping mechanisms is that individuals who find ways to deal with their stress and anger positively will no longer be predisposed to commit crime, whereas individuals who do not find healthy, positive outlets for their anger and frustrations will be far more likely to commit crime. Obviously, the goal is to reduce the use of antisocial and negative coping mechanisms, such as drug usage or aggression, which either are criminal in themselves or increase the likelihood of offending.

Recent research and theoretical development has more fully examined various coping mechanisms and their effectiveness in reducing anger and, thus, preventing criminal activity. Obviously, in focusing on individuals' perceptions of stress and anger as well as on their personal ability to cope with such feelings, general strain theory places more emphasis on the micro level of analysis. Still, due to its origins in structural strain theory, it is included in this chapter and is typically classified as belonging to the category of strain theories, which include the earlier theories that are more oriented to the macro level. In addition, recent studies and revisions of the theory have attempted to examine the validity of general strain theory propositions at the macro, structural level.[43]

Since it was first proposed in the mid-1980s, there has been a vast amount of research examining various aspects of general strain theory.[44] For the most part, studies have generally supported the model. Most studies find a link between the three categories of strain and higher rates of criminality as well as a link between the sources of strain and feelings of anger or other negative emotions (e.g., anxiety, depression).[45] However, the theory and especially the way it has been tested have also been criticized.

It is important for strain research to measure subjects' perceptions and feelings of frustration, not simply the occurrence of certain events themselves. Unfortunately, some studies have only looked at the latter, and the validity

---

[43]Timothy Brezina, Alex Piquero, and Paul Mazerolle, "Student Anger and Aggressive Behavior in School: An Initial Test of Agnew's Macro-Level Strain Theory," *Journal of Research in Crime and Delinquency* 38 (2001): 362–86.

[44]Agnew and White, "An Empirical Test"; Agnew et al., "A New Test"; Justin W. Patchin and Sameer Hinduja, "Traditional and Nontraditional Bullying among Youth: A Test of General Strain Theory," *Youth and Society* 43 (2011): 727–51; Raymond Paternoster and Paul Mazerolle, "General Strain Theory and Delinquency: A Replication and Extension," *Journal of Research in Crime and Delinquency* 31 (1994): 235–63; Timothy Brezina, "Adapting to Strain: An Examination of Delinquent Coping Responses," *Criminology* 34 (1996): 39–60; John P. Hoffman and Alan S. Miller, "A Latent Variable Analysis of General Strain Theory," *Journal of Quantitative Criminology* 14 (1998): 83–110; John P. Hoffman and Felicia Gray Cerbone, "Stressful Life Events and Delinquency Escalation in Early Adolescence," *Criminology* 37 (1999): 343–74; Paul Mazerolle and Alex Piquero, "Linking Exposure to Strain with Anger: An Investigation of Deviant Adaptations," *Journal of Criminal Justice* 26 (1998): 195–211; Paul Mazerolle, "Gender, General Strain, and Delinquency: An Empirical Examination," *Justice Quarterly* 15 (1998): 65–91; John P. Hoffman and S. Susan Su, "Stressful Life Events and Adolescent Substance Use and Depression: Conditional and Gender Differentiated Effects," *Substance Use and Misuse* 33 (1998): 2219–62; Lisa M. Broidy, "A Test of General Strain Theory," *Criminology* 39 (2001): 9–36; Nicole Leeper Piquero and Miriam Sealock, "Generalizing General Strain Theory: An Examination of an Offending Population," *Justice Quarterly* 17 (2000): 449–84; Paul Mazerolle and Jeff Maahs, "General Strain and Delinquency: An Alternative Examination of Conditioning Influences," *Justice Quarterly* 17 (2000): 753–78; Paul Mazerolle et al., "Strain, Anger, and Delinquent Adaptations: Specifying General Strain Theory," *Journal of Criminal Justice* 28 (2000): 89–101; Stephen W. Baron and Timothy F. Hartnagel, "Street Youth and Labor Market Strain," *Journal of Criminal Justice* 30 (2002): 519–33; Carter Hay, "Family Strain, Gender, and Delinquency," *Sociological Perspectives* 46 (2003): 107–35; Sung Joon Jang and Byron R. Johnson, "Strain, Negative Emotions, and Deviant Coping among African Americans: A Test of General Strain Theory," *Journal of Quantitative Criminology* 19 (2003): 79–105; Paul Mazerolle, Alex Piquero, and George E. Capowich, "Examining the Links between Strain, Situational and Dispositional Anger, and Crime: Further Specifying and Testing General Strain Theory," *Youth and Society* 35 (2003): 131–57; Stephen W. Baron, "General Strain, Street Youth and Crime: A Test of Agnew's Revised Theory," *Criminology* 42 (2004): 457–84.

[45]A recent review of this research can be found in Baron, "General Strain," 457–67.

Figure 6.2 • Model of general strain theory

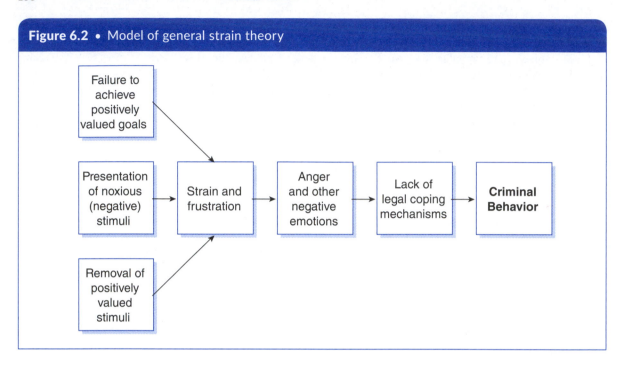

of such findings is questionable.[46] Other studies, however, have directly measured subjective perceptions of frustration as well as personal feelings of anger.[47]

Such studies have found mixed support for the hypothesis that certain events lead to anger[48] but less support for the prediction that anger leads to criminality, and this link is particularly weak for nonviolent offending.[49] On the other hand, the most recent studies have found support for the links between strain and anger as well as anger and criminal behavior, particularly when coping variables are considered.[50] Still, many of the studies that examine the effects of anger use time-stable, trait measures as opposed to incident-specific, state measures that would be more consistent with the situation-specific emphasis of general strain theory.[51] This is similar to the methodological criticism that has been leveled against studies of self-conscious emotions, particularly shame and guilt; when it comes to measuring emotions such as anger and shame, criminologists should choose their measures carefully and make sure the instruments are consistent with the theory they are testing. Thus, future research on general strain theory should employ more effective, subjective measures of straining events and situational states of anger.

---

[46]For examples, see Jean-Louis Van Gelder, Danielle Reynald and Henk Elffers, "Anticipated Emotions and Immediate Affect in Criminal Decision Making: From Shame to Anger," in *Affect and Cognition in Criminal Decision Making*, ed. Jean-Louis Van Gelder, Henk Elffers, Danielle Reynald, and Daniel Nagin (London: Routledge, 2014), 161–78; Paternoster and Mazerolle, "General Strain Theory"; Hoffman and Cerbone, "Stressful Life Events and Delinquency"; and Hoffman and Su, "Stressful Life Events."

[47]Broidy, "A Test"; Baron, "General Strain."

[48]See Brezina, "Adapting to Strain"; Broidy, "A Test"; Mazerolle and Piquero, "Linking Exposure."

[49]Mazerolle and Piquero, "Linking Exposure"; Piquero and Sealock, "Generalizing General Strain Theory"; Mazerolle et al., "Strain, Anger."

[50]Baron, "General Strain"; Mazerolle et al., "Examining the Links."

[51]For examples, see Mazerolle et al., "Strain, Anger"; and Baron, "General Strain." See discussions in Mazerolle et al., "Examining the Links"; and Akers and Sellers, *Criminological Theories*, 180–82.

Regardless of the criticisms of general strain theory, it is hard to deny its face validity. After all, virtually everyone can relate to reacting differently to similar situations based on what kind of day they are having. For example, we all have days in which everything seems to be going great—it's a Friday, you receive accolades at work, and you are looking forward to a nice weekend with your friends or family. If someone says something derogatory to you or cuts you off in traffic, you will probably be inclined to let it go because you're in such a good mood. On the other hand, we also all have days in which everything seems to be going horribly—it's Monday, you get blamed for mishaps at work, and you have a fight with your spouse or significant other. At this time, if someone yells at you or cuts you off in traffic, you may be more inclined to respond aggressively in some way. Or perhaps you will overreact and snap at a loved one or friend when he or she really didn't do much to deserve it; this is often a form of displacement in which a cumulative buildup of stressors results in taking frustration out on another individual. In many ways, this type of behavior, which is prevalent and easy to see in everyday life, supports general strain theory.

Summary of Strain Theories

The common assumption found across all variations of strain theory is that crime is far more common among individuals who are under a great degree of stress and frustration, especially those who can't cope with stress in a positive way. The origin of most variations of strain theory can be traced to Durkheim's and Merton's concepts of anomie, which essentially means a state of chaos, or normlessness, in society due to a breakdown in the ability of societal institutions to regulate human desires, thereby resulting in feelings of strain.

Although different types of strain theories were proposed and gained popularity at various periods throughout the 20th century, they all became accepted during eras that were politically and culturally conducive to such perspectives, especially in terms of the differences across the strain models. For example, Merton's formulation of strain in the 1930s emphasized the importance of the economic institution, which was developed and became very popular during the Great Depression. Then, in the late 1950s, two strain theories that focused on gang formation were developed, by Cohen and by Cloward and Ohlin; they became popular among politicians and society due to a focus on official statistics suggesting that most crime at that time was being committed by lower-class, inner-city male youths—many of whom were gang members. Finally, Agnew developed his general strain model in the mid- to late 1980s, during a time in which a number of general theories of crime were being developed (e.g., Michael Gottfredson and Travis Hirschi's low self-control theory and Rob Sampson and John Laub's developmental theory), so such models were popular at that time, particularly those that emphasized personality traits (such as anger) and experiences of individuals. So, all of the variations of strain, like all of the theories discussed in this book, were manifestations of the period in which they were developed and became widely accepted by academics, politicians, and society.

Policy Implications

Although this chapter dealt with a wide range of theories regarding social structure, the most applicable policy implications are those suggested by the most recent theoretical models of this genre. Thus, we will focus on the key policy factors in the most modern versions of this perspective. The factors that are most vital for policy implications regarding social structure theories are those regarding educational and vocational opportunities and programs that help people develop healthy coping mechanisms to deal with stress.

Empirical studies have shown that intervention programs are needed for high-risk youths that focus on educational or vocational training and opportunities, because developing motivation for such endeavors can have a significant impact on reducing their offending rates.[52] Providing an individual with a job, or the preparation for one,

---

[52]John P. Wright, Stephen Tibbetts, and Leah Daigle, *Criminals in the Making: Criminality across the Life Course* (Thousand Oaks, CA: Sage, 2015).

is key to building a more stable life, even if it is not a high-paying position. As a result, the individual is less likely to feel stressed or strained. In modern times, a person is lucky to have a stable job, and this must be communicated to our youths, and hopefully, they will find some intrinsic value in the work they do.

Specifically, in regard to Merton's strain theory, there have been significant attempts to address the more global issues of deprivation that result from poverty in U.S. society. Perhaps the best example is the War on Poverty, a federal program introduced by President Lyndon B. Johnson during the 1960s. Although an enormous amount of money and other resources were spent in trying to aid the poor in order to reduce crime rates in America, crime rates soared during this period. Many experts noted that the federal investment was not efficiently handed out, but the rise in crime during this period still casts doubt on the effectiveness of such a strategy.

Rather, the Maryland Report of "What Works, What Doesn't?" (see Chapter 5) concludes that vocational training for adult male offenders has consistently lowered offending rates, as have intensive residential training programs for at-risk youth (such as Job Corps).[53] This conclusion appears consistent with our previous finding that a focus on certain high-risk individuals is more effective than programs addressing an entire group, such as all types of offenders. Perhaps this is because not all offenders have the target characteristic, but such programs tend to be effective for those who do. For example, some offenders are thrust into drug programs even though they have never used drugs or alcohol. Also, some offenders are coerced into engaging in vocational programs when they already have skills in a certain trade. Thus, it makes sense to focus resources (e.g., vocational programs, drug programs) on the people who are most at risk for the given risk factor.

Another key area of recommendations from this perspective involves developing healthy coping mechanisms. Everyone deals with stress virtually every day. The key is not avoiding stress or strain, because that is inevitable. Rather, the key is to develop healthy, legal ways to cope with such strain. Many programs have been created to train individuals on how to handle stress without resorting to antisocial behavior. There has been some success gained from anger management programs, particularly the ones that take a cognitive behavioral approach and often involve role-playing to teach individuals to think before they act.[54]

Conclusion

This chapter examined the theories that emphasize inequitable social structure as the primary cause of crime. First, we examined early perspectives, which established that societies vary in the extent to which they are stratified, and looked at the consequences of the inequalities in and complexities of such structures as well as a variety of social concepts that early seminal sociologists noted in the 19th century, such as relative deprivation, collective conscience, and anomie. An important part of this theoretical evolution was the proposition that decisions made by individuals that traditionally were thought to be entirely made by the individual, such as suicide, were actually highly predicted by societal factors.

Our examination of strain theories explored theoretical models proposing that individuals and groups who are not offered equal opportunities for achieving success can develop stress and frustration and, in turn, dispositions for committing criminal behavior. We also examined more modern versions of strain, such as general strain theory, which has shown much support in empirical studies. Finally, we examined the policy recommendations suggested by this theoretical model, which include the need to provide individuals with educational and job opportunities and help them develop healthy coping mechanisms.

---

[53]Lawrence Sherman et al., *Preventing Crime: What Works, What Doesn't, What's Promising: A Report to the United States Congress* (Washington, DC: U.S. Department of Justice, 1997).

[54]Patricia Van Voorhis and Emily Salisbury, *Correctional Counseling and Rehabilitation*, 8th ed. (Cincinnati, OH: Anderson, 2013).

- First, we discussed the primary distinction between social structure theories and other types of explanations (e.g., biological or social process theories).

- We examined the importance of the early sociological positivists, particularly Guerry, Quetelet, and Durkheim as well as their contributions to the study of deviance and crime.

- We explored reasons why strain theory was developed and became popular in its time and discussed the primary assumptions and propositions of Merton's strain theory.

- We identified, defined, and examined examples of all five adaptations to strain identified by Merton.

- We discussed the variations of strain theory of groups presented by Cohen as well as by Cloward and Ohlin, who presented models of youth delinquency or gang formation based on a strain perspective.

- Both Cohen and Cloward and Ohlin presented models that had similar categories of offenders based on the ways that individuals deal with the strain or frustration they face; these types of offenders or gangs mimic some of the adaptations that Merton presented in his original strain framework.

- General strain theory was examined with an emphasis on how it is far more robust and general a theory than Merton's original framework, which only focused on economic strain.

- We examined the empirical support of general strain theory, the emphasis that this theory has placed on factors outside of the economy that frustrate individuals, and the importance of coping mechanisms in dealing with such strain.

KEY TERMS

adaptations to strain 118

anomie 109

collective conscience 113

college boy 124

conflict gangs 126

conformity 113

corner boy 124

criminal gangs 125

delinquent boy 124

general strain theory 128

innovation 119

mechanical societies 113

organic societies 113

reaction formation 123

rebellion 119

relative deprivation 112

retreatism 119

retreatist gangs 127

ritualism 119

social dynamics 110

social statics 110

strain theory 109

DISCUSSION QUESTIONS

1. How does sociological positivism differ from biological or psychological positivism?

2. Which of the early sociological positivism theorists do you think contributed most to the evolution of social structure theories of crime? Why? Do you think their ideas still hold up today?

3. Can you think of modern examples of Durkheim's image of mechanical societies? Do you think such societies have more or less crime than modern organic societies?

4. What type of adaptation to strain do you think fits you the best? The least? What adaptation do you think best fits your professor? Your postal delivery worker? Your garbage collector?

5. Do you know school friends who fit Cohen's model of status frustration? What did they do in response to the feelings of strain?

6. How would you describe the neighborhood where you or others you know grew up in terms of Cloward and Ohlin's model of organization or disorganization? Can you relate to the types of gangs they discussed?

 ## WEB RESOURCES

Émile Durkheim

https://kpulawandsociety.wordpress.com/2012/10/22/durkheims-views-crime-as-normal
https://www.thoughtco.com/emile-durkheim-relevance-to-sociology-today-3026482
http://www.azquotes.com/author/4244-Emile_Durkheim

Strain Theory

http://www.umsl.edu/~keelr/200/strain.html
http://www.oxfordbibliographies.com/view/document/obo-9780195396607/obo-9780195396607-0005.xml

CHAPTER 7

The Chicago School and Cultural and Subcultural Theories of Crime

This chapter will examine the origin and evolution of the Chicago or Ecological School theory, otherwise known as the ecological perspective or the theory of social disorganization. We will also discuss modern research on this theory, which assumes that the environments people live in determine their behavior. Finally, we will discuss the assumptions and dynamics of cultural and subcultural theory in society, highlighting differences in certain models emphasizing inner-city subcultures and other modern examples of subcultures (e.g., street gangs). We will finish by reviewing the policy implications that have been suggested by this perspective of crime.

The Chicago School evolved during the late 19th and early 20th centuries when the city of Chicago desperately needed answers for its exponentially growing problem of delinquency and crime. This became a primary focus in Chicago, where total chaos prevailed at the time.

A significant portion of the Chicago perspective focused on the transmission of cultural values to peers and even across generations as the older youths relayed their antisocial values and techniques to the younger children. Thus, the cultural and subcultural perspective is also a key area of this theoretical model. This cultural aspect of the Chicago model is also examined in this chapter, as are other subculture frameworks of offending behaviors.

The Ecological School and the Chicago School of Criminology

Despite the fact that its name specifies one city, the **Chicago School of Criminology** represents one of the most valid and generalizable theories we will discuss in this book in the sense that many of its propositions can be readily applied to the growth and evolution of virtually all cities around the world. The Chicago School, which is often referred to as the **Ecological School** or the theory of **social disorganization**, also represents one of the earliest examples of balancing theorizing with scientific analysis and at the same time guiding important programs and policy implementations that still thrive today. Perhaps most important, the Chicago School of Criminology was the epitome of using theoretical development and scientific testing to help improve conditions in society when it was most needed, which can be appreciated only by understanding the degree of chaos and crime that existed in Chicago in the late 1800s and early 1900s.

▲ **Image 7.1**   Virtually all large cities, like Chicago, New York, and Los Angeles, grew the same predictable way, and the formation of certain zones or types of areas follow ecological principles.

SOURCE: © istockphoto.com / marchello74

Cultural Context: Chicago in the 1800s and Early 1900s

Experts have determined that 19th-century Chicago was the fastest-growing city in U.S. history.[1] Census data show that the population went from about 5,000 in the early 1800s to more than 2 million by 1900; put another way, the population more than doubled every decade during the 19th century.[2] This massive rate of growth—much faster than that seen in other large U.S. cities such as Boston, Baltimore, New York, Philadelphia, and San Francisco—was due to Chicago's central geographic position. It was in many ways landlocked because, although it sits on Lake Michigan, there was no water route to the city from the Atlantic Ocean until the Erie Canal opened in 1825, which provided access to the Great Lakes region for shipping and migration of people. Three years later came the first U.S. passenger train, the Baltimore and Ohio Railroad, whose route extended from the mid-Atlantic to central areas of the country. These two transportation advancements created a continual stream of migration to the Chicago area, which increased again when the transcontinental railroad was completed in 1869, linking both coasts with the U.S. Midwest.[3]

It is important to keep in mind that, in the early to mid-1800s, many large U.S. cities had virtually no formal social agencies to handle the problems of urbanization—no social workers, building inspectors, garbage collectors, or even police officers. Once police agencies were introduced, their duties often included finding lost children and collecting the garbage, primarily because there weren't other agencies to perform these tasks. Therefore, communities were largely responsible for solving their own problems, including crime and delinquency. By the late 1800s, however, Chicago was largely made up of citizens who did not speak a common language and did not share each other's cultural values. This phenomenon is consistent with U.S. Census Bureau data from that era, which show that 70% of Chicago residents were foreign born and another 20% were first-generation Americans. It was almost impossible for these citizens to organize themselves to solve community problems because, in most cases, they could not even understand each other.

This resulted in the type of chaos and normlessness that Émile Durkheim predicted would occur when urbanization and industrialization occurred too rapidly; in fact, Chicago represented the archetype of a society in an anomic state,

---

[1]For an excellent discussion of the early history of Chicago, see Thomas J. Bernard, *The Cycle of Juvenile Justice*, 2nd ed. (New York: Oxford University Press, 2010).

[2]See discussion in Thomas J. Bernard, Jeffrey B. Snipes, and Alexander L. Gerould, *Vold's Theoretical Criminology*, 6th ed. (Oxford: Oxford University Press, 2010), 117–22 (see chap. 1).

[3]These dates were taken from *The World Almanac, 2000*, Millennium Collector's Edition (Mahwah, NJ: Primedia Reference, 2000).

with almost a complete breakdown in control. One of the most notable manifestations of this breakdown in social control was that children were running wild on the streets in gangs, with adults making little attempt to intervene. So, delinquency was soaring, and it appeared that the gangs controlled the streets as much as any other group.

The leaders and people of Chicago needed theoretical guidance to develop solutions to their problems, particularly regarding the high rates of delinquency. This was a key factor in why the Department of Sociology at the University of Chicago became so important and dominant in the early 1900s. Essentially, modern sociology developed in Chicago because this city needed it the most to solve its social problems. Thus, Chicago became a type of laboratory for sociological researchers, and they developed a number of theoretical models of crime and other social ills that are still shown to be empirically valid today.

▲ **Image 7.2**   The American buffalo was introduced to Catalina Island in California and destroyed much of the unique plant life there. This is an example of a foreign element creating chaos, such as crime does in residential areas.

SOURCE: © istockphoto.com / dmbaker

Ecological Principles in City Growth and Concentric Circles

In the 1920s and 1930s, several new perspectives of human behavior and city growth were offered by sociologists at the University of Chicago. The first relevant model was proposed by Robert E. Park, who claimed that much of human behavior, especially the way cities grow, follows the basic principles of ecology that had been documented and applied to wildlife for many years at that point.[4] Ecology is essentially the study of the dynamics and processes through which plants and animals interact with the environment. In an application of Darwinian theory, Park proposed that the growth of cities follows a natural pattern and evolution.

Specifically, Park claimed that cities represent a type of complex organism with a sense of unity composed of the interrelations among its citizens and groups. Park applied the ecological principle of symbiosis to explain the dependency of various citizens and units on each other: Everyone is better off working together as a whole. Furthermore, Park claimed that all cities would contain identifiable clusters, which he called **natural areas**, which would take on a life or organic unity of their own. To clarify, many cities have neighborhoods that are made up of primarily one ethnic group or are distinguished by certain features. For example, New York City's Hell's Kitchen, Times Square, and Harlem represent areas of one city that have each taken on unique identities; however, each of them contributes to the whole makeup and identity of the city. The same can be seen in other cities, such as Baltimore, which in a two-mile area has the Inner Harbor, Little Italy, and Fell's Point, with each area complementing the other zones. From Miami to San Francisco to New Orleans, all cities across America, and throughout the world for that matter, contain these identifiable natural areas.

---

[4]Robert E. Park, "Human Ecology," *American Journal of Sociology* 42 (1936): 158–64; Robert E. Park, *Human Communities* (Glencoe, IL: Free Press, 1952).

▲ **Image 7.3**   The Chicago or Ecological model proposed that as factories invaded and dominated residential areas, the residents who could afford to leave did and those left were the poor and deprived, which increased risk of crime.

SOURCE: © istockphoto.com / shaunl

Applying several other ecological principles, Park also noted that some areas (or species) may invade and dominate adjacent areas (species). The dominated area or species can recede, migrate to another location, or die off. In wildlife, an example is the incredible proliferation of a plant called kudzu, which grows at an amazing pace and has large leaves. It grows on top of other plants, trees, fields, and even houses, seeking to cover everything in its path and steal all the sunlight needed by other plants. Introduced to the United States in the 1800s at a world exposition, this plant was originally used to stop erosion but got out of control, especially in the southeastern region of the United States. Now kudzu costs the government more than $350 million each year because of its destruction of crops and other flora. This is a good example of a species that invades, dominates, and causes the recession of other species in the area.

A similar example can be found in the introduction of bison on Santa Catalina Island off the Southern California coast in the 1930s. About three dozen buffalo were originally imported to the island for a movie shoot, and the producers decided not to spend the money to remove them after the project, so they have remained and multiplied. Had this occurred in other parts of the United States, it would not have caused a problem. However, the largest mammal native to the island before the bison was a 4-pound fox. So, the buffalo—now numbering in the hundreds, to the point where several hundred were recently shipped to their native Western habitat—have destroyed much of the environment, driving to extinction some plants and animals unique to Catalina Island. Like the kudzu, the bison came to dominate the environment; in this case, other species couldn't move off the island and died off.

Park claimed that a similar process occurs in human cities as some areas invade other zones or areas, and the previously dominant area must relocate or die off. This is easy to see in modern times with the growth of what is known as *urban sprawl*. Geographers and urban planners have long acknowledged the detriment to traditionally stable residential areas when businesses move in. Some of the most recent examples involve the battles of longtime homeowners against the introduction of malls, businesses, and other industrial centers in districts previously zoned residential. The media have documented such fights, especially with the proliferation of such establishments as Walmart and Kmart supercenters, which residents perceive, and perhaps rightfully so, as an invasion. Such an invasion can create chaos in a previously stable residential community due to increased traffic; transient populations; and, perhaps most important, crime. Furthermore, some cities are granting power to such development through eminent domain, by which the local government can take land from homeowners to rezone and import businesses.

When Park developed his theory of ecology, he observed a trend in which businesses and factories were invading the traditionally residential areas of Chicago, which caused major chaos and breakdown in the stability of those areas. Readers, especially those who were raised in suburban or rural areas, can likely relate to this; going back to where they grew up, they can often see fast growth. Such development can devastate the informal controls (such as neighborhood networks or family ties) because it promotes invasion by a highly transient group of consumers and residents who do not have strong ties to the area.

This leads to a psychological indifference to the neighborhood in which no one cares about protecting the community any longer. Those who can afford to leave the area do, and those who can't afford to get out remain until they can save enough money to do so. When Park presented his theory of ecology in the 1920s, having factories that moved into the neighborhood often meant having a lot of smoke billowing out of chimneys. No one wanted to live in such a place, particularly at a time when the effects of pollution were not understood and smokestacks had no filters.

▲ **Image 7.4**   Virtually all large cities in the world historically developed and grew with the same basic design of concentric circles.

SOURCE: Zeimusu / Wikimedia Commons

Certain parts of Chicago and other U.S. cities were perpetually covered by the smog these factories created. In highly industrial areas, the constant and vast coverage of smoke and pollutants made it seem to be snowing or overcast most of the time. It is easy to see how such invasions can completely disrupt the previously dominant and stable residential areas of a community.

Park's ideas became even more valid and influential with the complementary perspective offered by Ernest W. Burgess,[5] who proposed a theory of city growth in which cities were seen as growing not simply on the edges but from the inside outward. It is easy to observe cities growing on the edges, as in the example of urban sprawl, but Burgess claimed that the source of growth was in the cities' centers. Growth of the inner city puts pressure on adjacent zones, which in turn begin to grow into the adjacent zones, following the ecological principle of *succession* identified by Park. This type of development is referred to as radial growth, meaning beginning on the inside and rippling outward.[6]

An example of this can be seen by watching a drop of water fall into the center of a bucket filled with water. The waves from the impact will form circles that ripple outward. This is exactly how Burgess claimed that cities grow. Although the growth of cities is most visible on the edges, largely due to development of businesses and homes where only trees or barren land existed before, the reason for growth there is the pressure forming at the very heart of the city. Another good analogy is the domino effect, because pressure from the center leads to growing pressure on the next zone, which leads to pressure on the adjacent zones and so forth.

Burgess also specified the primary zones—five pseudodistinctive natural areas in a constant state of flux due to growth—that all cities appear to have. He depicted these zones as a set of concentric circles. The first, innermost circle was called Zone I, or the central business district. This area of a city contained the large business buildings, modern skyscrapers that are home to banks, chambers of commerce, courthouses, and other essential business, and political centers such as police headquarters and post offices.

Just outside the business district was the unnumbered factory zone. It was perhaps the most significant in terms of fostering crime because it invaded the previously stable residential areas in Zone II, which Burgess identified as the **zone in transition**. Zone II was appropriately named because it was truly in a state of transition from residential to industrial, primarily because this was the area of the city in which businesses and factories were invading residential areas. Zone II was the area that was most significantly subjected to the ecological principles Park suggested: invasion, domination, recession, and succession. Subsequent criminological theorists focused on this zone.

---

[5]Ernest W. Burgess, "The Growth of the City," in *The City*, ed. Robert Park, Ernest W. Burgess, and Roderick D. McKenzie (Chicago: University of Chicago Press, 1928).

[6]See George Vold, *Theoretical Criminology* (New York: Oxford University Press, 1958), 118–21.

According to Burgess's **theory of concentric circles**, Zone III was the workingmen's homes, relatively modest houses and apartment buildings; Zone IV consisted of higher-priced family dwellings and more expensive apartments; and Zone V was the suburban or commuter zone. These outer three zones Burgess identified were of less importance in terms of crime, primarily because, as a general rule, the farther a family could move out of the city, the better the neighborhood was in terms of social organization and the lower the rate of social ills (e.g., poverty, delinquency). The important point of this theory of concentric circles is that the growth of each inner zone puts pressure on the next zone to grow and push into the next adjacent zone.

It is easy for readers to see examples of concentric circles theory. Wherever you live in the United States, any major city provides real-life evidence of the validity of this perspective. For example, whether people drive on Interstate 95 through Baltimore or Interstate 5 through Los Angeles, they will see the same pattern of city structure. As they approach each of the cities, they see suburban wealth in the homes and buildings, often hidden by trees off the highway. Closer to the cities, they see homes and buildings deteriorating in terms of value. Because parts of the highway systems near Baltimore and Los Angeles are somewhat elevated, drivers entering Zone II can easily see the prevalence of factories and the highly deteriorated nature of the areas. Today, many 20th-century factories have been abandoned or have limited use; these factory zones consist of rusted-out or demolished buildings. Zone II is also often the location of subsidized or public housing. Only the people who can't afford to live anywhere else are forced to live in these neighborhoods. Finally, as drivers enter the inner city of skyscrapers, the conditions improve dramatically because the major businesses have invested their money there. Compared to Zone II, this innermost area is a utopia.

This theory applies around the world, and we challenge readers to find any major city throughout the world that did not develop this way. Nowadays, some attempts have been made to plan community development, and other cities have experienced the convergence of several patterns of concentric circles as central business districts (i.e., Zone Is) are developed in what was previously suburbia (i.e., Zone Vs). However, for the most part, the theoretical framework of concentric circles still has a great deal of support. In fact, even cities found in Eastern cultures have evolved this way. Therefore, Park's application appears to be correct: Cities grow in a natural way across time and place, abiding by the natural principles of ecology.

Case Study: Los Angeles Gangs

Although most case studies we review in this book are about individuals, in this case we concentrate on groups, which is fitting for this chapter because virtually all the theories we will cover in this chapter are macro- or group-level theories. A recent scientific study by researchers at the University of California, Los Angeles, showed that when Los Angeles gangs and incidents of gang activities are mapped, the places with the highest frequency of violence are on the borders between two or more rival gangs.[7]

. . . When Los Angeles gangs and incidents of gang activities are mapped, the places with the highest frequency of violence are on the borders between two or more rival gangs.

This 2012 report showed that, contrary to popular belief, the most dangerous places to be in Los Angeles are not the regions deeply within the territory of a dominant gang but rather on the boundaries of gang territories, perhaps due to turf disputes or the increased likelihood of

---

[7]Dennis Romero, "Gang Map Study Shows Crime Happens along Borders between Sets in L.A." *LA Weekly*, June 27, 2010, http://blogs.laweekly.com/informer/2012/06/gang_maps_angeles_murder_attacks_borders_ucla_study.php?print=true. See also actual study: P. Jeffrey Brantingham et al., "The Ecology of Gang Territorial Boundaries," *Criminology* 50, no. 3 (2012): 851–885. doi:10.1111/j.1745-9125.2012.00281.x.

encountering rival factions. We shall see that this recently observed phenomenon among established gang territories was to some extent predicted and explained by Chicago School theories of crime and city growth proposed more than half a century ago. We will follow up on this case study toward the end of this chapter.

Think About It

1. Why do you think the most violent areas of Los Angeles are those on the borders of rival gangs as opposed to the regions that are strongly dominated by a single gang?

▲ **Image 7.5**   It is on the borders of their territories that gang violence is at a high level, as compared to well within their established home turf where the gangs have entrenched dominance in that region.

SOURCE: © Ted Soqui / Corbis Historical Collection / Getty Images

Shaw and McKay's Theory of Social Disorganization

Clifford Shaw and Henry McKay drew heavily on their colleagues at the University of Chicago in devising their theory of social disorganization, which became known as the Chicago School theory of criminology.[8] Shaw had been producing excellent case studies for years on the individual (i.e., micro) level before he took on theorizing on the macro (i.e., structural) level of crime rates.[9] However, once he began working with McKay, he devised perhaps the most enduring and valid model of why certain neighborhoods have more social problems, such as delinquency, than others.

In this model, Shaw and McKay proposed a framework that began with the assumption that certain neighborhoods in all cities have more crime than other parts of the city, most of them located in Burgess's Zone II, which is the zone in transition from residential to industrial due to the invasion of factories. According to Shaw and McKay, the neighborhoods that have the highest rates of crime typically have at least three common problems (see Figure 7.1): physical dilapidation, poverty, and heterogeneity (which is a fancy way of saying a high cultural mix). There were other common characteristics that Shaw and McKay noted, such as a highly transient population, meaning that people constantly move in and out of the area, as well as unemployment among the residents of the neighborhood.

---

[8]Clifford Shaw and Henry D. McKay, *Juvenile Delinquency and Urban Areas* (Chicago: University of Chicago Press, 1942); Clifford Shaw and Henry D. McKay, *Juvenile Delinquency and Urban Areas*, rev. ed. (Chicago: University of Chicago Press, 1969).

[9]Clifford Shaw, *Brothers in Crime* (Chicago: University of Chicago Press, 1938); Clifford Shaw, *The Jackroller* (Chicago: University of Chicago Press, 1930); Clifford Shaw, *The Natural History of a Delinquent Career* (Chicago: University of Chicago Press, 1931).

Figure 7.1 • Model of Shaw and McKay's theory of social disorganization

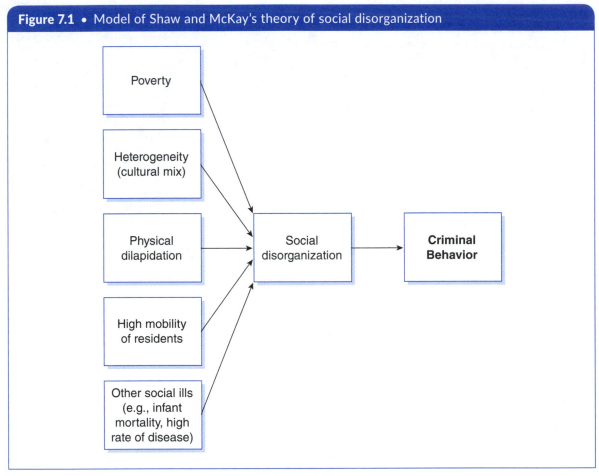

SOURCE: Stephen G. Tibbetts and Craig Hemmens, *Criminological Theory: A Text/Reader*, 2nd ed. (Thousand Oaks, CA: Sage, 2015).

As noted in Figure 7.1, other social ills are included as antecedent factors in the theoretical model. The antecedent social ills tend to lead to a breakdown in social organization, which is why this model is referred to as the theory of social disorganization. Specifically, it is predicted that the antecedent factors of poverty, heterogeneity, and physical dilapidation lead to a state of social disorganization, which in turn leads to crime and delinquency. This means that in a neighborhood that fits the profile of having a high rate of poor, culturally mixed residents in a dilapidated area, people cannot come together to solve problems, such as delinquency among youth.

One of the most significant contributions of Shaw and McKay was that they demonstrated that the prevalence and frequency of various social ills—such as poverty, disease, and low birth weight—tend to overlap with higher delinquency rates. Regardless of what social problem is measured, higher rates are almost always clustered in the zone in transition. Shaw and McKay believed there is a breakdown of informal social controls in these areas and that children begin to learn offending norms from their interactions with peers on the street, through what the researchers call *play activities*.[10] Thus, the breakdown in the conditions of the neighborhood leads to social disorganization, which in turn leads to delinquency in children who learn criminal activities from older youths. Ultimately, the failure of the neighborhood residents to organize themselves allows the older youths to govern the behavior of the younger children. Basically, the older youths in the area provide a system of organization where the neighborhood adults cannot, so younger children follow them.

One of the best things about Shaw and McKay's theoretical model is that they supported their propositions with data from U.S. census and city records, showing that neighborhoods with high rates of poverty and physical dilapidation and high cultural mixes also had the highest rates of delinquency and crime. Furthermore, the high rates of delinquency and other social problems were consistent with Burgess's framework of concentric circles in that the highest rates were observed for the areas that were in Zone II, the zone in transition. There was one exception to the model: The Gold Coast area along the northern coast of Lake Michigan did not have the high rates of social problems, particularly delinquency, even though it was geographically in Zone II according to the otherwise consistent model of concentric circles and neighborhood zones.

Thus, the findings of Shaw and McKay were as predicted in the sense that high delinquency rates occurred in areas where factories were invading residential districts. Furthermore, Shaw and McKay's longitudinal data showed that it did not matter which ethnic groups lived in Zone II; all groups (with the exception of Asians) that lived in that zone had high delinquency rates during their residency. On the other hand, once most of an ethnic group had moved out of Zone II, the delinquency rate among its youths decreased significantly.

This finding rejects the notion of **social Darwinism** because it is clearly not the culture that influences crime and delinquency but rather the criminogenic nature of the environment. If ethnicity or race made a difference, the delinquency rates in Zone II would fluctuate based on who lived there, but the rates continued to be high from one group to the next. Rather, the zone determined the rates of delinquency.

Reaction and Research on Social Disorganization Theory

Over the past few decades, the Chicago School theoretical framework has received an enormous amount of attention from researchers.[11] Virtually all of the research has supported Shaw and McKay's version of social disorganization and the resulting high crime rates in neighborhoods that exhibit such deprived conditions. Modern research has supported the theoretical model proposed by Shaw and McKay, specifically in terms of the high crime rates in disorganized neighborhoods. Also, virtually every city that has an elevated highway (e.g., Richmond, Virginia; Baltimore, Maryland; Los Angeles, California) visually supports Shaw and McKay's model of crime in concentric circles. Drivers entering those cities can see the pattern of dilapidated structures in the zone of transition surrounding the inner-city area. Before and after this layer of dilapidated structures, drivers encounter a layer of houses and residential areas that seem to increase in quality as the driver gets farther away from the inner-city area.

---

[10]Shaw, *Brothers in Crime*, 354–55.

[11]Wouter Steenbeek and John R. Hipp, "A Longitudinal Test of Social Disorganization Theory: Feedback Effects among Cohesion, Social Control, and Disorder," *Criminology* 49 (2011): 833–71; John Laub, "Urbanism, Race, and Crime," *Journal of Research in Crime and Delinquency* 20 (1983): 283–98; Robert Sampson, "Structural Sources of Variation In Race-Age-Specific Rate of Offending across Major U.S. Cities," *Criminology* 23 (1985): 647–73; J. L. Heitgard and Robert J. Bursik, "Extracommunity Dynamics and the Ecology of Delinquency," *American Journal of Sociology* 92 (1987): 775–87; Robert Bursik, "Social Disorganization and Theories of Crime and Delinquency: Problems and Prospects," *Criminology* 26 (1988): 519–51; Ralph Taylor and Jeanette Covington, "Neighborhood Changes in Ecology and Violence," *Criminology* 26 (1988): 553–89; Robert Bursik, "Ecological Stability and the Dynamics of Delinquency," in *Crime and Community*, ed. Albert J. Reiss and Morris H. Tonry (Chicago: University of Chicago Press, 1986), 35–66; Robert Sampson, "Transcending Tradition: New Directions in Community Research, Chicago Style—The American Society of Criminology 2001 Sutherland Address," *Criminology* 40 (2002): 213–30; Robert Sampson, J. D. Morenoff, and T. Gannon-Rowley, "Assessing 'Neighborhood Effects': Social Processes and New Directions in Research," *Annual Review of Sociology* 28 (2002): 443–78; P. O. Wikstrom and Rolf Loeber, "Do Disadvantaged Neighborhoods Cause Well-Adjusted Children to Become Adolescent Delinquents?" *Criminology* 38 (2000): 1109–42.

Figure 7.2 ● Zone map of male delinquents in Chicago, 1925–1933

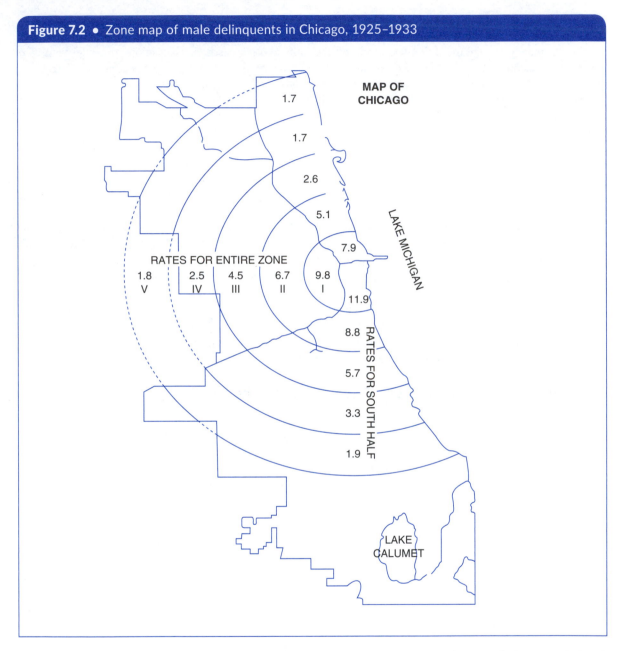

Some critics, however, have raised some valid concerns regarding the original model, arguing that Shaw and McKay's original research did not actually measure their primary construct: social disorganization. Although this criticism is accurate, recent research has shown that the model is valid even when valid measures of social disorganization are included.[12] Such measures of social disorganization include simply asking members of the neighborhood how many neighbors they know by name or how often they observe unsupervised peer groups in the area.

Additional criticisms of Shaw and McKay's formulation of social disorganization focus on the emphasis that the theory places on the macro, or aggregate, level of analysis. Although their theory does a good job of predicting which neighborhoods have higher crime rates, the model does not even attempt to explain why most youths in the worst areas do not become offenders. Furthermore, their model does not attempt to explain why some youths—although a very small number of them—in the best neighborhoods (i.e., in Zone V) choose to commit crime. However, the previously cited case studies completed and published by Shaw, such as *The Jackroller* and *Brothers in Crime,* attempted to address the individual (micro) level of offending.

Also, there was one notable exception to Shaw and McKay's proposition that all ethnic and racial groups have high rates of delinquency and crime while they live in Zone II. Evidence showed that when Japanese Americans made up a large portion of residents in this zone in transition, they had very low rates of delinquency. Thus, as in most theoretical models in social science, there was an exception to the rule.

Perhaps the biggest criticism of Shaw and McKay's theory, one that has yet to be adequately addressed, deals with the fact that they blatantly neglected to propose ways to ameliorate the most problematic source of criminality in Zone II neighborhoods. Although they clearly point to the invasion of factories and businesses into residential areas as a problem, they do not recommend how to slow such invasion. This is likely due to political and financial concerns: Owners of factories and businesses partially financed their research and later were the primary funders of implementation of their policies. Neglect is further represented in their failure to explain the exception of the Gold Coast in their results and conclusions.

Despite the criticisms and weaknesses of the Chicago School perspective of criminology, this theory resulted in one of the largest programs to date in attempting to reduce delinquency rates. Shaw was put in charge of establishing the Chicago Area Project (CAP), which created neighborhood centers in the most crime-ridden parts of Chicago. These centers offered activities for youths and tried to establish ties between parents and officials in the neighborhood. Although this program was never scientifically evaluated, it still exists, and many cities have implemented programs based on this model. For example, Boston implemented a very similar program, which was evaluated by Walter Miller.[13] This evaluation showed that, although the project was effective in establishing relationships and interactions between local gangs and community groups and in providing more educational and vocational opportunities, it seemed to fail in reducing delinquent and criminal behavior. Thus, the overall conclusion made by experts was that the Boston project and other similar programs, like the CAP, typically fail to prevent criminal behavior.[14]

---

[12]Robert Sampson and W. Byron Groves, "Community Structure and Crime: Testing Social Disorganization Theory," *American Journal of Sociology* 94 (1989): 774–802.

[13]Walter B. Miller, "The Impact of a 'Total-Community' Delinquency Control Project," *Social Problems* 10 (1962): 168–91.

[14]For a review, see Richard Lundman, *Prevention and Control of Juvenile Delinquency*, 2nd ed. (New York: Oxford University Press, 1993). See also Bernard et al., *Vold's Theoretical Criminology*, 125–26.

Case Study: Whitey Bulger

▲ **Image 7.6**   Whitey Bulger (1929–) was the head of one of the most notorious organized crime syndicates in Boston until he was apprehended in Southern California in 2011.

SOURCE: United States Marshals Service, United States Department of Justice, via Wikimedia Commons

Whitey Bulger (James Joseph "Whitey" Bulger Jr.) is perhaps the most notorious gangster from the South Boston area, which is saying a lot given the history and tradition of organized crime in "Southie," as they call it. Bulger was a key figure of a criminal organization from the early 1970s to the mid-1990s and head of this organization for much of that time. Under heat from authorities, he fled in 1994, and for 12 years he was on the Federal Bureau of Investigation (FBI) Ten Most Wanted list. Bulger was apprehended with his long-term girlfriend, Catherine Greig, in Santa Monica, California, in 2011. He was sentenced on November 14, 2013, to two terms of life imprisonment, plus 5 years.

Bulger is believed to have been largely in charge of narcotics distribution and extortion rackets in the Southie area during most of the 1980s and early 1990s, along with the violence inherent to such a position. Interestingly, most sources show that he was also an FBI informant during much of this time period, which allowed him to essentially "get away with murder" and his other illegal activities.

Perhaps most related to this chapter, Bulger was seen locally as a type of Robin Hood figure, considered by most people on the streets as a sort of guardian protecting the interests of the neighborhood or local area. After all, Bulger had been a key element of organized crime in that area for many years, and this led to a subcultural or cultural climate placing him as an authority for all that happened in that locale. Furthermore, much of his business dealt with narcotics distribution and extortion, so his motives fit the other theories in this chapter of being largely based on finding criminal opportunities despite the relatively poor and deprived conditions of the South Boston region.

. . . Bulger was seen locally as a type of Robin Hood figure, considered by most people on the streets as a sort of guardian protecting the interests of the neighborhood or local area.

As alluded to before, Bulger likely saw the draw of organized crime as being his only way to accomplish the higher financial and/or social status that could be obtained in the South Boston area. After all, there were not many legitimate opportunities open to him given his early criminal record, not to mention the deprivation and lack of stable employment in that region. Furthermore, he probably also desired to become an important figure in the subculture or culture of that area, and the only likely way to do that was to become a prominent figure in the organized crime syndicates.

Think About It

1. Can you relate to Bulger's local community's attitude toward him as a type of hero?

2. How do you think such a subculture develops in local communities for such prominent gangsters?

SOURCES: Edward MacKenzie Jr. and Phyllis Karas, *Street Soldier: My Life as an Enforcer for "Whitey" Bulger and the Boston Irish Mob* (Hanover, NH: Steerforth, 2004); Kevin Weeks and Phyllis Karas. *Brutal: My Life Inside Whitey Bulger's Irish Mob* (New York: HarperCollins, 2009).

Cultural and Subcultural Theories of Crime

Cultural and subcultural theories of crime assume that there are unique groups in society that socialize their children to believe that certain activities that violate conventional law are good and positive ways to behave. Although it is rather difficult to find large groups of people or classes who fit this definition, it may be that some subcultures or isolated groups of individuals buy into a different set of norms than the conventional, middle-class set of values.

Early Theoretical Developments and Research in Cultural and Subcultural Theory

One of the key developments of cultural theory is the 1967 work of Franco Ferracuti and Marvin Wolfgang, who examined the violent themes of a group of inner-city youths from Philadelphia.[15] Ferracuti and Wolfgang's primary conclusion was that violence is a culturally learned adaptation to deal with negative life circumstances and that learning such norms occurs in an environment that emphasizes violence over other options.[16] These researchers based their conclusion on an analysis of data that showed great differences in the rates of homicide across racial groups. However, Ferracuti and Wolfgang were clear that their theory was based on subcultural norms. Specifically, they proposed that no subculture can be totally different from or totally in conflict with the society of which it is a part.[17] This brings the distinction of culture and subculture to the forefront.

A culture represents a distinct set of norms and values among an identifiable group of people—values that are distinctly different from those of the mainstream culture. For example, communism is distinctly different from capitalism because it emphasizes equality over competition, and it values utopia (i.e., everyone gets to share all profits) over the idea that the best performer gets the most reward. So, it can be said that communists tend to have a different culture than capitalists. There is also a substantial difference between a culture and a subculture, which is typically only a pocket of individuals who may have a set of norms that deviate from conventional values. Therefore, what Ferracuti and Wolfgang developed is not so much a cultural theory as it is a subcultural theory.

This is also seen in the most prominent (sub)culture theory, which was presented by Miller.[18] Miller's theoretical model proposed that the entire lower class had its own cultural value system. According to this model, virtually everyone in the lower class believes in and has been socialized to the values of six **focal concerns**: fate, autonomy, trouble, toughness, excitement, and smartness. Fate means luck, or whatever life has dealt you; it disregards responsibility and accountability for one's actions. Autonomy is the value of independence from authority. Trouble means staying out of legal problems as well as getting into and out of personal difficulties (e.g., pregnancy). Toughness is maintaining your reputation on the street in many ways. Excitement is engagement in activities, some illegal, that help liven up an otherwise mundane existence of being lower class. Smartness emphasizes street smarts or the ability to con others. Miller thought that members of the lower class teach these six focal concerns as a culture or environment (or "milieu," as stated in the title of his work).

A more recent subculture model, proposed by Elijah Anderson, has received a lot of attention in the past few years.[19] This theory focuses on African Americans; because of the very deprived conditions in inner cities, Black Americans who live there feel a sense of hopelessness, isolation, and despair, Anderson asserted. He clearly noted that, although many African Americans believe in middle-class values, these values have no weight on the street,

---

[15]Bernard et al., *Vold's Theoretical Criminology*, 165–69; Frank Schmalleger, *Criminology Today*, 6th ed. (Upper Saddle River: Prentice Hall, 2011).

[16]Franco Ferracuti and Marvin Wolfgang, *The Subculture of Violence: Toward an Integrated Theory of Criminology* (London: Tavistock, 1967).

[17]As quoted in Schmalleger, *Criminology Today*, 230–31.

[18]Walter B. Miller, "Lower Class Culture as a Generating Milieu of Gang Delinquency," *Journal of Social Issues* 14 (1958): 5–19.

[19]Elijah Anderson, *Code of the Street* (New York: W. W. Norton, 2000).

particularly among young urban males. According to Anderson, the "code of the street," which is the appropriate title of his book, is to maintain one's reputation and demand respect. For example, to be treated with disrespect ("dissed") is considered grounds for a physical attack. Masculinity and control of one's immediate environment are treasured characteristics; the immediate environment is perceived as the only thing people can control, given the harsh conditions (e.g., unemployment, poverty) in which they live.

Criticisms of Cultural Theories of Crime

Studies on cultural theories of crime, at least in the United States, find no large groups that blatantly deny the middle-class norms of society. Miller's model of lower-class focal concerns is not consistent across the entire lower class. Studies show that most adults in the lower class attempt to socialize their children to believe in conventional values, such as respect for authority, hard work, and delayed gratification, and not the focal concerns that Miller specified in his model.[20] Ferracuti and Wolfgang admitted that their research findings led them to conclude that their model had more of a subcultural perspective than one emphasizing a distinctly different culture. There may be small groups or gangs who have subcultural normative values, but that doesn't constitute a completely separate culture in society. Perhaps the best subculture theories are those presented by Cohen or Cloward and Ohlin (see Chapter 6) in their variations of strain theory that emphasize the formations of gangs among lower-class male youths. A recent example of a specific group that seems to embrace a different normative code is that of adult male bar fighters, which was presented by Heith Copes and his colleagues.[21] So apparently there are subcultural groups in U.S. society; however, they seem to make up a very small percentage of the population, which somewhat negates the cultural and subcultural perspective of criminality, which claims that crime-fostering subcultures make up a large, distinctive portion of the population. Still, this type of perspective may be important regarding the criminality of select subgroups of offenders, such as street gangs.

Policy Implications

Many of the policy implications suggested by the theoretical models proposed in this chapter are rather ironic. Regarding social disorganization, a paradox exists in the sense that the very neighborhoods most desperately in need of becoming organized to fight crime are the same inner-city ghetto areas where it is, by far, the most difficult to cultivate that organization (e.g., through neighborhood watch or block watch groups). Rather, the neighborhoods that have high levels of organization tend to be those that already have very low levels of crime because the residents naturally police their neighbors' well-being and property; they have a stake in the area's remaining crime free. Although there are some anecdotal examples of success of neighborhood watch programs in high-crime neighborhoods, most of the empirical evidence shows that this approach is "almost uniformly unsupportive" in its ability to reduce crime there.[22] Furthermore, many studies of these neighborhood watch programs find that the groups actually increase the fear of crime in some places, perhaps due to the heightened awareness of crime issues in these areas.[23]

---

[20]Bernard et al., *Vold's Theoretical Criminology.*

[21]Heith Copes, Andy Hochstetler, and Craig Forsyth, "Peaceful Warriors: Codes for Violence among Adult Male Bar Fighters," *Criminology* 51 (2013): 761–94.

[22]John Worrall, *Crime Control in America: What Works?* 2nd ed. (Boston: Allyn & Bacon, 2008), 95.

[23]Ibid.

On the other hand, other types of community crime prevention programs do seem to show some success according to a 2017 systematic review by David Weisburd and his colleagues.[24] Specifically, the study concludes that improving street lighting and adding closed-circuit television cameras can lower crime rates in neighborhoods. The researchers also conclude that the most effective strategies to mobilize communities against crime are programs that involve proactive engagement with the police and other civic partners to enhance social cohension.[25]

Perhaps the most notable programs that resulted from the Chicago School or social disorganization model—the CAP and similar programs—have been dubbed failures in reducing crime rates among the participants. Still, as mentioned previously, there have been some advances in trying to get residents of high-crime areas to become organized in fighting crime. The more specific the goals regarding crime reduction (a specific goal might be careful monitoring of high-level offenders through more intensive supervised probation, repeat victimization prevention programs), the more effective the implementation.[26]

Regarding cultural and subcultural theories, some promising intervention and outreach programs have been suggested by such models. Many programs attempt to build prosocial attitudes among high-risk youths—often young children. For example, a recent evaluation showed that a program called PeaceBuilders, which focuses on children in early grades, was effective in producing gains in conflict resolution, development of prosocial values, and reductions in aggression; a follow-up showed that these attributes were maintained for a long period of time.[27] Another recent anti-aggression training program for boys in foster care showed positive effects in levels of empathy, self-efficacy, and attribution style among boys who had exhibited early-onset aggression.[28] Ultimately, there are effective programs out there that promote prosocial norms and culture. More effort should be given to promoting such programs to help negate the antisocial cultural norms of individuals, especially among high-risk youths.

Conclusion

In this chapter, we examined theoretical perspectives proposing that the lack of social organization in broken-down and dilapidated neighborhoods leads to the inability to contain delinquency and crime. Furthermore, we discussed how this model of crime was linked to processes derived from ecological principles. This type of approach has been tested numerous times, and virtually all studies show that the distribution of delinquents and crime activity is consistent with this model.

We then discussed the ability of cultural and subcultural theories to explain criminal activity. Empirical evidence shows that cultural values make a contribution to criminal behavior but that the existence of an actual alternative culture in our society has not been found. However, some subcultural pockets, particularly inner-city youth gangs, certainly exist and provide some validity for this perspective of crime. Furthermore, the Chicago School perspective plays a role, because these subcultural groups tend to be found in zones of transition.

---

[24]David Weisburd, David P. Farrington, and Charlotte Gill, "What Works in Crime Prevention and Rehabilitation: An Assessment of Systematic Reviews," *Criminology & Public Policy* 16 (2017): 415–49.

[25]Ibid.

[26]Lundman, *Prevention and Control*; Sampson and Groves, "Community Structure"; Bernard et al., *Vold's Theoretical Criminology*; Weisburd et al. "What Works in Crime Prevention."

[27]Daniel J. Flannery, Mark I. Singer, and Kelly L. Wester, "Violence, Coping, and Mental Health in a Community Sample of Adolescence," *Violence and Victims* 18 (2003): 403–18. For a review of this research, see Stephen G. Tibbetts, "Perinatal and Developmental Determinants of Early Onset of Offending: A Biosocial Approach for Explaining the Two Peaks of Early Antisocial Behavior," in *The Development of Persistent Criminality*, ed. Joanne Savage (New York: Oxford University Press, 2009), 179–201.

[28]Karina Weichold, "Evaluation of an Anti-aggressiveness Training with Antisocial Youth," *Gruppendynamik* 35 (2004): 83–105. For a review, see Tibbetts, "Perinatal and Developmental Determinants."

Finally, we examined policy implications suggested by these theoretical models. Regarding social disorganization, we noted that neighborhood crime-fighting groups are hardest to establish in high-crime neighborhoods and easiest to build in those neighborhoods with an already low rate of crime. Nevertheless, there have been some successes. We also looked at intervention and outreach programs based on cultural and subcultural perspectives.

/// CHAPTER SUMMARY

- We examined how principles of ecology were applied to the study of how cities grow, as well as to the study of crime, by researchers at the University of Chicago and how the resultant theories became known as the Chicago (or Ecological) School of Criminology.

- Examples from wildlife were presented as an analogy to illustrate how such ecological principles also apply to criminal elements invading and dominating city areas.

- We learned the history of Chicago and why that history made the city uniquely suited for the development of criminological theory.

- We reviewed the various zones of the concentric circles theory, also a key contribution of the Chicago School of Criminology, and explored which zones are most prone to crime.

- We examined why the findings from the Chicago School of Criminology showed that social Darwinism was not accurate in attributing varying crime rates to ethnicity or race.

- We reviewed much of the empirical evidence regarding the theory of social disorganization and examined the strengths and weaknesses of this theoretical model.

- We discussed the cultural and subcultural model presented by Ferracuti and Wolfgang as well as the cultural model of inner-city urban youths presented by Anderson.

- We discussed Miller's theory of lower-class culture, particularly its six focal concerns.

- We reviewed the strengths and weaknesses of cultural and subcultural theories of crime based on empirical evidence.

/// KEY TERMS

Chicago School of
Criminology 135

cultural and subcultural
theories 147

Ecological School 135

focal concerns 147

natural areas 137

social Darwinism 143

social disorganization 135

theory of concentric circles 140

zone in transition 139

/// DISCUSSION QUESTIONS

1. Identify and discuss an example of the ecological principles of invasion, domination, and succession among animals or plants that was not discussed in this chapter.

2. Can you see examples of the various zones that Shaw and McKay described in the town or city where you live (or the one nearest you)? Try obtaining a map or sketching a plot of this city or town, and then draw the various concentric circles where you think the zones are located.

3. What forms of organization and disorganization have you observed in your own neighborhood? Try to supply examples of both if possible.

4. Can you provide modern-day examples of different cultures and subcultures in the United States? What regions or parts of the country would you say have cultures that are more conducive to crime?

5. Do you know people who believe most or all of Miller's focal concerns? What are their social classes? What are their other demographic features (age, gender, urban vs. rural, etc.)?

6. Do you know individuals who seem to fit either Ferracuti and Wolfgang's cultural theory or Anderson's model of inner-city youths' street code? Why do you believe they actually fit such a model?

//// WEB RESOURCES

Chicago School of Criminology

http://study.com/academy/lesson/the-chicago-schools-social-disorganization-theory.html
http://www.encyclopedia.com/law/legal-and-political-magazines/ecology-crime
http://userpages.umbc.edu/~lutters/pubs/1996_SWLNote96-1_Lutters,Ackerman.pdf

Subcultural Theories

http://study.com/academy/lesson/what-is-subculture-theories-definition-examples.html
http://www.umsl.edu/~keelr/200/subcult.html
https://www.slideshare.net/RSJones/crime-and-deviance-subcultural-approach

CHAPTER 8

Social Process and Learning Theories of Crime

This chapter will discuss Edwin Sutherland's development of differential association theory and how this evolved into Ronald Akers's work of differential reinforcement and other social learning theories, such as techniques of neutralization. Then, the modern state of research on these theories will be presented. We will also discuss the evolution of control theories of crime, emphasizing social bonding and the scientific evidence found regarding the key constructs in Travis Hirschi's control theories, which are two of the most highly regarded perspectives according to criminological experts and their studies.[1] Most of the social process theories assume that criminal behavior is learned behavior, which means that criminal activity is actually learned from others through social interaction, much like riding a bike or playing basketball. Namely, people learn criminal activity from significant others, such as family, peers, or coworkers. However, other social process theories, namely control theories, assume that offending is the result of natural tendencies and thus must be controlled by social processes. Social process theories examine how individuals interact with other individuals and groups and how the learning that takes place in these interactions leads to a propensity for criminal activity. This chapter will explore both of these theoretical frameworks and explain how social processes are vital to both perspectives in determining criminal behavior.

This chapter begins with social process theories known as **learning theories**. Such learning theories attempt to explain how and why individuals learn from significant others to engage in criminal rather than conventional behavior. Next, we discuss **control theories**, which emphasize personal or socialization factors that prevent individuals from engaging in selfish, antisocial behaviors.

Learning Theories

In this chapter, we review theories that emphasize how individuals learn criminal behavior through interacting with significant others, people with whom they typically associate. These learning theories assume that people are born with no tendency toward or away from committing crime. This concept is referred to as **tabula rasa**, or blank slate, meaning that all individuals are completely malleable and will believe what they are told by their significant

---

[1]Anthony Walsh and Lee Ellis, "Political Ideology and American Criminologists' Explanations for Criminal Behavior," *The Criminologist* 24 (1999): 1, 14 (see chap. 1, n. 13).

others and act accordingly. Thus, such theories of learning tend to explain how criminal behavior is learned through cultural norms. One of the main concepts in learning theories is the influence of peers and significant others on an individual's behavior.

Here, three learning theories are discussed: (1) differential association theory, (2) differential identification theory, and (3) differential reinforcement theory. Then we examine techniques of neutralization.

Differential Association Theory

Sutherland introduced his **differential association theory** in the late 1930s.[2] He proposed a theoretical framework that explained how criminal values could be culturally transmitted to individuals from their significant others. Sutherland proposed a theoretical model that included nine principles, but rather than list them all, we will summarize the main points of his theory.

Perhaps the most interesting principle is the first: Criminal behavior is learned. This was a radical departure from previous theories (e.g., Lombroso's "born criminal" theory, Goddard's feeblemindedness theory, Sheldon's body type theory). Sutherland was one of the first to state that criminal behavior is the result of normal social processes, resulting when individuals associate with the wrong type of people, often by no fault on their part. By associating with crime-oriented people, whether parents or peers, an individual will inevitably choose to engage in criminal behavior because that is what he or she has learned, Sutherland thought.

Perhaps the most important of Sutherland's principles, and certainly the most revealing one, was number six in his framework: "A person becomes delinquent because of an excess of definitions favorable to violation of law over definitions unfavorable to violation of law."[3] Sutherland noted that this principle represents the essence of differential association theory. It suggests that people can have associations that favor both criminal and noncriminal behavior patterns. If an individual is receiving more information and values that are pro-crime than anticrime, the individual will inevitably engage in criminal activity. Also, Sutherland claimed that such learning can take place only in interactions with significant others and not via television, movies, radio, or other media.

It is important to understand the cultural context at the time Sutherland was developing his theory. In the early 20th century, most academics, and society for that matter, believed that there was something abnormal or different about criminals. Sheldon's body type theory was popular in the same period, as was the use of IQ to pick out people who were of lower intelligence and supposedly predisposed to crime (both of these theories were covered in Chapter 4). So, the common assumption when Sutherland created the principles of differential association theory was that there was essentially something wrong with individuals who commit crime.

In light of this common assumption, Sutherland's proposal—that criminality is learned just like any conventional activity—was extremely profound. This suggests that any normal person, when exposed to attitudes favorable to crime, will learn criminal activity and that the processes and mechanisms of learning are the same for crime as for most legal, everyday behaviors—namely, social interaction with family and friends and not reading books or watching movies. How many of us learned to play basketball or other sports by reading a book about it? Virtually no one learns how to play sports this way. Rather, we learn the techniques (e.g., how to do a jump shot) and motivations for playing sports (e.g., it is fun or you might be able to earn a scholarship) through our friends, relatives, coaches, and other people close to us. According to Sutherland, crime is learned the same way; our close associates teach us both the techniques (e.g., how to steal a car) and the motivations (e.g., it is fun; you might be able to sell it or its parts). While most criminologists tend to take it for granted that criminal behavior is learned, the idea was rather unique and bold when Sutherland presented his theory of differential association.

---

[2]Edwin H. Sutherland, *Principles of Criminology*, 3rd ed. (Philadelphia: Lippincott, 1939).

[3]Edwin H. Sutherland and Donald R. Cressey, *Principles of Criminology*, 5th ed. (Chicago: Lippincott, 1950), 78.

It is important to keep in mind that differential association theory is just as positivistic as earlier biological and psychological theories. Sutherland clearly believed that if people were receiving more information that breaking the law was good, then they would inevitably commit crimes. There is virtually no allowance for free will and rational decision making in this model of offending. Rather, people's choices to commit crime are determined through their social interactions with those close to them; they do not actually make the decisions to engage (or not engage) in criminal activities. So, differential association can be seen as a highly positive, deterministic theory, much like Lombroso's "born criminal" and Goddard's feeblemindedness theories (see Chapter 4), except that instead of biological or psychological traits causing crime, it is social interaction and learning. Furthermore, Sutherland claimed that individual differences in biological and psychological functioning have little to do with criminality; however, this idea has been discounted by modern research, which shows that such variations do in fact affect criminal behavior, largely because such biopsychological factors influence the learning processes of individuals, thereby directly impacting the basic principles of Sutherland's theory (see Chapters 4 and 5).

▲ **Image 8.1**   Edwin H. Sutherland (1883–1950), University of Chicago and Indiana University, author of differential association theory.

SOURCE: © The Estate of Donald Cressey

Classical Conditioning:
A Learning Theory with Limitations

Sutherland used the dominant psychological theory of learning in his era as the basis for his theory of differential association. This model was **classical conditioning**, which was primarily developed by Ivan Pavlov. Classical conditioning assumes that animals as well as people learn through associations between stimuli and responses.[4] Organisms, animals or people, are somewhat passive actors in this process, meaning that they simply receive and respond in natural ways to various forms of stimuli; over time, they learn to associate certain stimuli with certain responses.

For example, Pavlov showed that dogs, which are naturally afraid of loud noises such as bells, could be quickly conditioned not only to be less afraid of bells but to actually desire and salivate at their sound. A dog naturally salivates when presented with meat, so when this presentation of an unconditioned stimulus (meat) is given, a dog will always salivate (unconditioned response) in anticipation of eating. Pavlov demonstrated through a series of experiments that if a bell (conditioned stimulus) is always rung at the same time the dog is presented with meat then the dog will learn to associate what was previously a negative stimulus with a positive stimulus (food). Thus, the dog will very quickly begin to salivate at the ringing of a bell, even when meat is not presented. When this occurs, it is called a conditioned response because it is not natural; however, it is a very powerful and effective means of learning, and it sometimes takes only a few occurrences of coupling the bell ringing with meat before the conditioned response takes place.

---

[4] For a discussion, see Thomas J. Bernard, Jeffrey B. Snipes, and Alexander L. Gerould, *Vold's Theoretical Criminology*, 6th ed. (Oxford: Oxford University Press, 2010), 156–57 (see chap. 2).

One modern use of this in humans is the administration of drugs that make people ill when they drink alcohol. Alcoholics are often prescribed drugs that make them very sick, often to the point of vomiting, if they ingest any alcohol. The idea is that they will learn to associate feelings of sickness with drinking and thus stop wanting to consume alcohol. One big problem with this strategy is that alcoholics often do not consistently take the drugs, so they quickly slip back into addiction. Still, if they were to maintain their regimen of drugs, it would likely work, because people do tend to learn through association.

This type of learning model was used in the critically acclaimed 1964 novel (and later motion picture) *A Clockwork Orange*. In this novel, the author, Anthony Burgess, told the story of a juvenile murderer who is "rehabilitated" by doctors who force him to watch hour after hour of violent images while simultaneously giving him drugs that make him sick. In the novel, the protagonist is "cured" after only 2 weeks of this treatment, having learned to consistently associate violence with sickness. However, once he is let out, he lacks the ability to choose violence and other antisocial behavior, which is seen as losing his humanity. Therefore, the ethicists order a reversal treatment and make him back into his former self, a violent predator. Although a fictional piece, *A Clockwork Orange* is probably one of the best illustrations of the use of classical conditioning in relation to criminal offending and rehabilitation.

Another example of classical conditioning is the associations we make with certain smells and sounds. For example, all of us can relate good times to smells that were present during those occasions. If a loved one or someone we dated wore a certain perfume or cologne, smelling that scent at a later time can bring back memories. When our partner goes out of town, we can smell his or her pillow, and it will remind us of our partner because we associate his or her smell with his or her being. Or perhaps the smell of a turkey cooking in an oven always reminds us of Thanksgiving or another holiday. Regarding associations of sounds, we can all remember songs that remind us of happy and sad times in our lives. Often these songs will play on the radio, and they take us back to those occasions, whether good or bad. People with post-traumatic stress disorder (PTSD) also experience sound associations; war veterans, for example, may hit the deck when a car backfires. These are all clear examples of classical conditioning and associating stimuli with responses.

▲ **Image 8.2**   The Russian scientist Ivan Petrovich Pavlov (1849–1936). He is best known for his studies of conditioned reflexes and his theory of classical conditioning.

Since Sutherland's theory was published, many of the principles outlined in his model have come under scrutiny. Follow-up research has shown some flaws in, as well as misinterpretations of, his work.[5] Specifically, Sutherland theorized that crime occurs when associations favorable to violation of the law outweigh associations favorable to conforming to the law. However, measuring this type of ratio is nearly impossible for social scientists.[6]

[5]Edwin H. Sutherland and Donald R. Cressey, *Criminology*, 9th ed. (Philadelphia, PA: Lippincott, 1974).

[6]Ross L. Matsueda and Karen Heimer, "Race, Family Structure, and Delinquency: A Test of Differential Association and Social Control Theories," *American Sociological Review* 47 (1987): 489–504; Charles R. Tittle, M. J. Burke, and E. F. Jackson, "Modeling Sutherland's Theory of Differential Association: Toward an Empirical Clarification," *Social Forces* 65 (1986): 405–32.

Another topic of criticism involves Sutherland's claim that all criminals learn the behavior from others before they engage in such activity. However, many theorists have noted that individuals may engage in criminal activity without being taught such behavior, and then seek out others with attitudes and behavior similar to their own.[7] So, do individuals learn to commit crime after they are taught by delinquent peers, or do they start associating with similar delinquents or criminals once they have initiated their offending career (i.e., "birds of a feather flock together")? This exact debate was examined by researchers, and the most recent studies point to the occurrence of both causal processes: Criminal associations cause more crime, and committing crime causes more criminal associations. Both are key in the causal process, so Sutherland was missing half of this equation.[8]

Another key criticism is that if each individual is born with a blank slate and all criminal behavior is learned, then who committed crime in the first place? Who could expose the first criminal to the definitions favorable to violation of law? Furthermore, what factor(s) caused that individual to do the crime if it was not learned? Obviously, if it were due to any factor(s) other than learning—and it must have been because there was no one to teach it—then it obviously was not explained by learning theories. This criticism cannot be addressed, so it is somewhat ignored in the scientific literature.

Despite the criticisms and flaws, much research supports Sutherland's theory. For example, researchers have found that older criminals teach younger delinquents.[9] In addition, delinquents often associate with criminal peers prior to engaging in criminal activity.[10] Furthermore, research has shown that criminal friends, attitudes, and activity are highly associated.[11] Still, Sutherland's principles are quite vague and elusive in terms of measurement, which renders them difficult for social scientists to test.[12] Related to these issues, perhaps one of the biggest problems with Sutherland's formulation of differential association is that he used primarily one type of learning model—classical conditioning—to formulate most of his principles, and thus he neglected other important ways that we learn attitudes and behavior from others. Ultimately, Sutherland's principles are hard to test; more current versions of his framework have incorporated other learning models and thus are easier to test so that empirical validity can be demonstrated.

Differential Identification Theory

Glaser's Concept of Differential Identification

Another reaction to Sutherland's differential association dealt with the influence of movies and television, as well as other reference groups outside of one's significant others. As stated previously, Sutherland claimed that learning of criminal definitions can take place only through social interactions with significant others as opposed to reading a book or watching movies. However, in 1956, Daniel Glaser proposed the idea of **differential identification theory**, which allows for learning to take place not only through people close to us but also through other reference groups, even distant ones, such as sports heroes or movie stars whom we have

---

[7]Tittle et al., "Modeling Sutherland's Theory."

[8]Terence Thornberry, "Toward an Interactional Theory of Delinquency," *Criminology* 25 (1987): 863–87.

[9]Kenneth Tunnell, "Inside the Drug Trade: Trafficking from the Dealer's Perspective," *Qualitative Sociology* 16 (1993): 361–81.

[10]Douglas Smith, Christy Visher, and G. Roger Jarjoura, "Dimensions of Delinquency: Exploring the Correlates of Participation, Frequency, and Persistence of Delinquent Behavior," *Journal of Research in Crime and Delinquency* 28 (1991): 6–32.

[11]Matthew Ploeger, "Youth Employment and Delinquency: Reconsidering a Problematic Relationship," *Criminology* 35 (1997): 659–75.

[12]Reed Adams, "The Adequacy of Differential Association Theory," *Journal of Research in Crime and Delinquency* 1 (1974): 1–8; James F. Short, "Differential Association as a Hypothesis: Problems of Empirical Testing," *Social Problems* 8 (1960): 14–25.

never actually met and with whom we have never corresponded.[13] Glaser claimed that it did not matter much whether an individual had a personal relationship with a reference group; in fact, he argued, a group could be imaginary, such as fictitious characters in a movie or book. The important thing, according to Glaser, was that an individual must identify with a person or character and thus behave in ways that fit the norm set of this reference group or person.

Glaser's proposition has been virtually ignored, with the exception of Kenneth Dawes's study of delinquency in 1973, which found that identification with people other than parents was strong when youths perceived a greater degree of rejection from their parents.[14] Given the profound influence of movies, music, and television on today's youth culture, it is obvious that differential identification was an important addition to Sutherland's framework, and more research should examine the validity of Glaser's theory in contemporary society.

Although Glaser and others modified differential association, the most valid and respected variation is differential reinforcement theory.

Differential Reinforcement Theory

In 1965, C. R. Jeffery provided an extensive critique and reevaluation of Sutherland's differential association theory. He argued that the theory was incomplete without some attention to an updated social psychology of learning (e.g., operant conditioning and modeling theories of learning).[15] He wanted Sutherland to account for the fact that people can be conditioned into behaving in certain ways, such as by being rewarded for conforming behavior. Then, in 1966, Robert Burgess and Akers criticized and responded to Jeffery's criticism by proposing a new theory that incorporated some of these learning models into Sutherland's basic framework.[16] The result was what is now known as **differential reinforcement theory**. Ultimately, Burgess and Akers argued that by integrating Sutherland's work with contributions from the field of social psychology, criminal behavior could be more clearly understood.

In some ways, differential reinforcement theory may appear to be no different than rational choice theory (see Chapter 3). To an extent, this is true, because both models focus on reinforcements and punishments that occur after an individual offends. However, differential reinforcement theory can be distinguished from the rational choice perspective. The latter assumes that humans are born with the capacity for rational decision making, whereas the differential reinforcement perspective assumes people are born with a blank slate and, thus, must be socialized and taught how to behave through various forms of conditioning (e.g., operant and classical) as well as modeling.

Burgess and Akers developed seven propositions to summarize differential reinforcement theory, which largely represent efficient modifications of Sutherland's original nine principles of differential association.[17] The strong influence of social psychologists is illustrated in their first statement as well as throughout the seven principles. Although differential reinforcement incorporates the elements of modeling and classical conditioning learning models in its framework, the first statement clearly states that the essential learning mechanism in

---

[13]Daniel Glaser, "Criminality Theories and Behavioral Images," *American Journal of Sociology* 61 (1956): 433–44.

[14]Kenneth J. Dawes, "Family Relationships, Reference Others, Differential Identification and Their Joint Impact on Juvenile Delinquency" (doctoral dissertation, Ann Arbor, MI: University Mircrofilms, 1973).

[15]C. Ray Jeffery, "Criminal Behavior and Learning Theory," *Journal of Criminal Law, Criminology, and Police Science* 56 (1965): 294–300.

[16]Robert Burgess and Ronald Akers, "A Differential Association-Reinforcement Theory of Criminal Behavior," *Social Problems* 14 (1966): 131.

[17]For a more recent version of these principles, see Ronald Akers, *Deviant Behavior: A Social Learning Approach*, 3rd ed. (Belmont, CA: Wadsworth, 1985). See also Ronald L. Akers and Christine S. Sellers, *Criminological Theories: Introduction, Evaluation, and Application*, 6th ed. (Oxford: Oxford University Press, 2012).

social behavior is operant conditioning, so it is important to understand what operant conditioning is and how it is evident throughout life.

Operant Conditioning

The idea of **operant conditioning** was primarily developed by B. F. Skinner,[18] who ironically was working just across campus from Sutherland when he was developing differential association theory at Indiana University. As in modern times, academia was too intradisciplinary and intradepartmental. Had Sutherland been aware of Skinner's studies and theoretical development, he likely would have included it in his original framework. In his defense, operant conditioning was not well known or researched at the time; as a result, Sutherland incorporated the then-dominant learning model, classical conditioning. Burgess and Akers went on to incorporate operant conditioning into Sutherland's framework.

Operant conditioning concerns how behavior is influenced by reinforcements and punishments. Furthermore, operant conditioning assumes that an animal or human being is a proactive player in seeking out rewards and not just a passive entity that receives stimuli, as classical conditioning assumes. Behavior is strengthened or encouraged through reward (**positive reinforcement**) and avoidance of punishment (**negative reinforcement**). For example, if someone is given a car for graduation from college, that would be a positive reinforcement. On the other hand, if a teenager who has been grounded is allowed to start going out again because he or she has better grades, this would be a negative reinforcement, because he or she is now being rewarded via the avoidance of something negative. Like different types of reinforcement, punishment comes in two forms as well. Behavior is weakened, or discouraged, through adverse stimuli (**positive punishment**) or lack of reward (**negative punishment**). A good example of positive punishment would be a good, old-fashioned spanking, because it is certainly a negative stimulus; anything that directly presents negative sensations or feelings is a positive punishment. On the other hand, if parents take away car privileges from a teenager who broke curfew, that would be an example of negative punishment because the parents are removing a positive aspect or reward.

Some notable examples of operant conditioning include teaching a rat to successfully run a maze. When rats take the correct path and finish the maze quickly, they are either positively reinforced (e.g., rewarded with a piece of cheese) or negatively reinforced (e.g., not zapped with electricity as they were when they chose the wrong path). On the other hand, when rats take wrong turns or do not complete the maze in adequate time, they are either positively punished (e.g., zapped with electricity) or negatively punished (e.g., not given the cheese they expect to receive). The rats, like humans, tend to learn the correct behavior very fast using such consistent implementation of reinforcements and punishments.

In humans, such principles of operant conditioning can be found even at very early ages. In fact, many of us have implemented such techniques (or been subjected to them) without really knowing they were called operant conditioning. For example, during toilet training, children learn to use the bathroom to do their natural duty rather than doing it in their pants. To reinforce the act of going to the bathroom on a toilet, we encourage the correct behavior by presenting positive rewards, which can be as simple as applauding the child or giving him or her a piece of candy for a successful job. While parents (we hope) rarely proactively use spanking in toilet training, there is an inherent positive punishment involved when children go in their pants; namely, they have to be in their dirty diaper for a while, not to mention the embarrassment that most children feel when they do this. Furthermore, negative punishments are present in such situations because the child does not get the applause or candy, so the rewards have been removed.

Of course, this does not apply only to early behavior. An extensive amount of research has shown that humans learn attitudes and behavior best through a mix of reinforcements and punishments throughout life. In terms of

---

[18]B. F. Skinner, *Science and Human Behavior* (New York: Macmillan, 1953).

criminal offending, studies have clearly shown that the rehabilitative programs that appear to work most effectively in reducing recidivism in offenders are those that provide opportunities for reward as well as threats of punishment. Empirical research has combined the findings from hundreds of such studies of rehab programs, showing that the programs that are most successful in changing the attitudes and behavior of previous offenders are those that offer at least four reward opportunities for every one possible punishment.[19] So, whether it is training children to go potty correctly or altering criminals' thinking and behavior, operant conditioning is a well-established form of learning that makes differential reinforcement theory a more valid and specified model of offending than differential association.

Whether deviant or conforming behavior occurs and continues "depends on the past and present rewards or punishment for the behavior, and the rewards and punishment attached to alternative behavior."[20] In contrast to Sutherland's differential association model, which looks only at what happens before an act (i.e., classical conditioning), not at what happens after the act is completed (i.e., operant conditioning), Burgess and Akers's model looks at both. Criminal behavior is likely to occur, Burgess and Akers theorized, when its rewards outweigh the punishments.

▲ **Image 8.3**   B. F. Skinner (1904–1990) was the key proponent of operant conditioning, which emphasized both rewards and punishments in affecting behavior.

SOURCE: © Getty Images / Bettmann / Contributor

Bandura's Theory of Modeling and Imitation

Another learning model that Burgess and Akers emphasized in their formulation of differential reinforcement theory was the element of **modeling and imitation**. Although Sutherland's original formulation of differential association theory was somewhat inspired by Gabriel Tarde's concept of imitation,[21] the nine principles did not adequately emphasize the importance of modeling in the process of learning behavior. Sutherland's failure was likely due to the fact that Albert Bandura's primary work in this area had not occurred when Sutherland was formulating differential association theory.[22]

Through a series of experiments and theoretical development, Bandura demonstrated that a significant amount of learning takes place without any form of conditioning. Specifically, he claimed that individuals can learn even if they are not rewarded or punished for behavior (i.e., operant conditioning) and even if they have not been exposed to associations between stimuli and responses (i.e., classical conditioning). Rather, Bandura proposed that people learn many of their attitudes and behaviors from simply observing the behavior of others, namely

[19]Patricia Van Voorhis and Emily Salisbury, *Correctional Counseling and Rehabilitation*, 8th ed. (Cincinnati: Anderson, 2013).

[20]Ronald L. Akers, *Deviant Behavior: A Social Learning Approach*, 2nd ed. (Belmont, CA: Wadsworth, 1977), 57.

[21]Gabriel Tarde, *Penal Philosophy*, trans. Rapelje Howell (Boston: Little, Brown, 1912).

[22]See Albert Bandura, *Principles of Behavior Modification* (New York: Holt, Rinehart & Winston, 1969); Albert Bandura, *Aggression: A Social Learning Analysis* (Englewood Cliffs, NJ: Prentice Hall, 1973); Albert Bandura, *Social Learning Theory* (Englewood Cliffs, NJ: Prentice Hall, 1977).

through mimicking what others do. This is often referred to as *monkey see, monkey do*, but it is not just monkeys that do this. Like most animal species, humans are biologically hardwired to observe and learn the behavior of others, especially elders, to see what behavior is essential for survival and success.

Bandura showed that simply observing the behavior of others, especially adults, can have profound learning effects on the behavior of children. Specifically, he performed experiments in which a randomized experimental group of children watched a video of adults acting aggressively toward Bobo dolls (which are blow-up plastic dolls); the control group of children did not watch such a video. Both groups of children were then sent into a room containing Bobo dolls, and the experimental group, who had seen the adult behavior, mimicked their elders by acting far more aggressively toward the dolls than the children in the control group. The experimental group had no previous associations of more aggressive behavior toward

▲ **Image 8.4**   On Thursday, May 19, 2016, in the East Room of the White House, President Barack Obama awarded the National Medal of Science to Dr. Albert Bandura, Stanford University, California. He is considered the key proponent of the learning theory of modeling and imitation affecting human behavior.

SOURCE: © Getty Images / NICHOLAS KAMM / Staff

the dolls and no good feelings or motivations, let alone rewards, for such behavior. Rather, the children became more aggressive themselves simply because they were imitating what they had seen older people do.

Bandura's findings have important implications for the modeling behavior of adults (and peers) and for the influence of television, movies, video games, and other factors. Furthermore, the influences demonstrated by Bandura supported a phenomenon commonplace in everyday life. Mimicking is the source of fashion trends—wearing low-slung pants or baseball hats turned a certain way. Styles tend to ebb and flow based on how some respected person (often a celebrity) wears clothing. This can be seen very early in life; parents must be careful what they say and do because their children, as young as 2 years old, imitate what their parents do. This continues throughout life, especially in the teenage years as young persons imitate the cool trends and styles as well as behaviors. Of course, sometimes this behavior is illegal, but individuals are often simply mimicking the way their friends or others are behaving with little regard for potential rewards or punishments. Ultimately, Bandura's theory of modeling and imitation adds a great deal of explanation to a model of learning, and differential reinforcement theory includes such influences, whereas Sutherland's model of differential association does not, largely because the psychological perspective had not yet been developed.

Burgess and Akers's theory of differential reinforcement has also been the target of criticism by theorists and researchers. Perhaps the most important criticism of differential reinforcement theory is that it appears *tautological*, meaning that the variables and measures used to test its validity are true by definition. To clarify, studies testing this theory have been divided into four groups based on variables or factors: associations, reinforcements, definitions, and modeling.

Some critics have noted that if individuals who report that they associate with those who offend are rewarded for offending, believe offending is good, and have seen many of their significant others offend, they will inevitably be more likely to offend. In other words, if your friends and family are doing it, there is little doubt that you will be doing it.[23] For example, critics would argue that a person who primarily hangs out with car thieves knows he will be rewarded for stealing cars, believes stealing cars is good and not immoral, and has observed many respected others stealing cars, will inevitably commit auto theft himself. However, it has been well argued that such criticisms of tautology are not valid because none of these factors necessarily makes offending by the respondent true by definition.[24]

Differential reinforcement theory has also faced the same criticism that was addressed to Sutherland's theory—namely, that delinquent associations may take place after criminal activity rather than before. However, Burgess and Akers's model clearly has this area of criticism covered in the sense that differential reinforcement includes what comes after the activity, not just what happens before it. Specifically, it addresses the rewards or punishments that follow criminal activity and whether those rewards come from friends, parents, or other members or institutions of society.

It is arguable that differential reinforcement theory may have the most empirical validity of any contemporary (nonintegrated) model of criminal offending, especially considering that studies have examined a variety of behaviors, ranging from drug use to property crimes to violence. The theoretical model has also been tested in samples across the United States as well as in other cultures, such as South Korea, with the evidence being quite supportive of the framework. Furthermore, a variety of age groups have been examined, ranging from teenagers to middle-aged adults to the elderly, with all studies providing support for the model.[25]

Specifically, researchers found that the major variables of the theory had a significant effect in explaining marijuana and alcohol use among adolescents.[26] The researchers concluded that the "study demonstrates that central learning concepts are amenable to meaningful questionnaire measurement and that social learning theory can be adequately tested with survey data."[27] Other studies have also supported the theory when attempting to understand delinquency, cigarette smoking, and drug use.[28] Therefore, the inclusion of three psychological learning models—namely, classical conditioning, operant conditioning, and modeling and imitation—appears to have made differential reinforcement one of the most valid theories of human behavior, especially in regard to crime.

---

[23]Mark Warr, "Parents, Peers, and Delinquency," *Social Forces* 72 (1993): 247–64; Mark Warr and Mark Stafford, "The Influence of Delinquent Peers: What They Think or What They Do?" *Criminology* 29 (1991): 851–66.

[24]Akers and Sellers, *Criminological Theories*, 98–101.

[25]See studies including Ronald Akers and Gang Lee, "A Longitudinal Test of Social Learning Theory: Adolescent Smoking," *Journal of Drug Issues* 26 (1996): 317–43; Ronald Akers and Gang Lee, "Age, Social Learning, and Social Bonding in Adolescent Substance Abuse," *Deviant Behavior* 19 (1999): 1–25; Ronald Akers and Anthony J. La Greca, "Alcohol Use among the Elderly: Social Learning, Community Context, and Life Events," in *Society, Culture, and Drinking Patterns Re-examined*, ed. David J. Pittman and Helene Raskin White (New Brunswick, NJ: Rutgers Center of Alcohol Studies, 1991), 242–62; Sunghyun Hwang, "Substance Use in a Sample of South Korean Adolescents: A Test of Alternative Theories" (doctoral dissertation, Ann Arbor, MI: University Microfilms, 2000); and Sunghyun Hwang and Ronald Akers, "Adolescent Substance Use in South Korea: A Cross-Cultural Test of Three Theories," in *Social Learning Theory and the Explanation of Crime: A Guide for the New Century*, ed. Ronald Akers and Gary F. Jensen (New Brunswick, NJ: Transaction, 2003).

[26]Ronald Akers et al., "Social Learning and Deviant Behavior: A Specific Test of a General Theory," *American Sociological Review* 44 (1979): 638.

[27]Akers et al., "Social Learning and Deviant Behavior," 651.

[28]Richard Lawrence, "School Performance, Peers and Delinquency: Implications for Juvenile Justice," *Juvenile and Family Court Journal* 42 (1991): 59–69; Marvin Krohn et al., "Social Learning Theory and Adolescent Cigarette Smoking: A Longitudinal Study," *Social Problems* 32 (1985): 455–71; L. Thomas Winfree, Christine Sellers, and Dennis Clason, "Social Learning and Adolescent Deviance Abstention: Toward Understanding the Reasons for Initiating, Quitting, and Avoiding Drugs," *Journal of Quantitative Criminology* 9 (1993): 101–23; Akers and Lee, "A Longitudinal Test."

Neutralization Theory

Neutralization theory is associated with Gresham Sykes and David Matza's techniques of neutralization[29] and Matza's drift theory.[30] Like Sutherland, both Sykes and Matza thought that social learning influences delinquent behavior, but they also asserted that most criminals hold conventional beliefs and values. Specifically, Sykes and Matza argued that most criminals are still partially committed to the dominant social order. According to Sykes and Matza, youths are not immersed in a subculture that is committed to either extreme: complete conformity or complete nonconformity. Rather, these individuals vacillate, or drift, between these two extremes and are in a state of *transience*.[31]

While remaining partially committed to the conventional social order, youths can drift into criminal activity, Sykes and Matza claimed, and avoid feelings of guilt for these actions by justifying or rationalizing their behavior. This typically occurs in the teenage years, when social controls (parents, family, etc.) are at their weakest point and peer pressures and associations are at their highest level. Why is this called neutralization theory? The answer is that people justify and rationalize behavior through neutralizing it or making it appear not so serious. They make up situational excuses for behavior that they know is wrong to alleviate the guilt they feel for doing such immoral acts. In many ways, this resembles Freud's defense mechanisms, which allow us to forgive ourselves for the bad things we do even when we know they are wrong. The specific techniques of neutralization outlined by Sykes and Matza in 1957 are much like excuses for inappropriate behavior.

Techniques of Neutralization

Sykes and Matza identified methods or techniques of neutralization[32] that people use to justify their criminal behavior. These techniques allow people to neutralize or rationalize their criminal and delinquent acts by making themselves look as though they are conforming to the rules of conventional society. If individuals can create such rationalizations, then they are free to engage in criminal activities without serious damage to their consciences or self-images. According to Sykes and Matza, there are five common techniques of neutralization:

1. *Denial of responsibility*: Individuals may claim they were influenced by forces outside themselves and that they are not responsible or accountable for their behavior. For example, many youths blame their peers for their own behavior.

2. *Denial of injury*: This is the rationalization that no one was actually hurt by the offender's behavior. For instance, if someone steals from a store, he or she may rationalize this by saying that the store has insurance, so there is no direct victim.

3. *Denial of the victim*: Offenders see themselves as avengers and the victims as the wrongdoers. For example, some offenders believe that a person who disrespects or "disses" them deserves what he or she gets, even if it means serious injury.

4. *Condemnation of the condemners*: Offenders claim that the condemners (usually the authorities who catch them) are hypocrites. For instance, one may claim that police speed on the highway all the time, so everyone else is entitled to drive higher than the speed limit.

---

[29]Gresham M. Sykes and David Matza, "Techniques of Neutralization: A Theory of Delinquency," *American Sociological Review* 22 (1957): 664–70.

[30]David Matza, *Delinquency and Drift* (New York: Wiley, 1964).

[31]Ibid., 28.

[32]Sykes and Matza, "Techniques of Neutralization."

5. *Appeal to higher loyalties*: Offenders often overlook the norms of conventional society in favor of the rules of a belief they have or of a group to which they belong. For example, people who kill doctors who perform abortions tend to see their crimes as above the law because they are serving a higher power.

Although Sykes and Matza specifically labeled only five techniques of neutralization, it should be clear that there may be endless excuses people make up to rationalize behaviors they know are wrong. Techniques of neutralization have been applied to white-collar crime, for example. Several studies have examined the tendency to use such excuses to alleviate guilt for engaging in illegal corporate crime; they point out new types of excuses white-collar criminals use to justify their acts, techniques that were not discussed in Sykes and Matza's original formulation.[33]

Studies that have attempted to empirically test neutralization theory are, at best, inconsistent. For example, Agnew argued that there are essentially two general criticisms of studies that support neutralization theory.[34] First, theorists and researchers have noted that some neutralization techniques are much more difficult to measure than commitment to unconventional attitudes or norms.[35] The second major criticism is the concern that criminals may not use techniques of neutralization prior to committing a criminal offense but rather only after committing a crime. As estimated by previous studies, temporal ordering can be problematic in terms of causal implications when neutralization follows a criminal act.[36] This temporal ordering problem results from research conducted at a single point in time. Some would argue that the temporal ordering problem is not a major criticism because individuals may be predisposed to make up such rationalizations for their behavior regardless of whether they do it before or after the act of offending. Such a propensity may be related to low self-control theory, which we will examine later in this chapter.

Summary of Learning Theories

Learning theories tend to emphasize the social processes of how and why individuals learn criminal behavior. These theories also focus on the impact of significant others involved in the socialization process, such as family, friends, and teachers. Ultimately, empirical research has shown that learning theories are key in our understanding of criminal behavior, particularly in terms of whether criminal behavior is rewarded or punished. In summary, if individuals are taught and rewarded for performing criminal acts by the people they interact with on a day-to-day basis, they will in all likelihood engage in illegal activity.

Control Theories

The learning theories discussed in the previous chapter assume that individuals are born with a conforming disposition. By contrast, control theories assume that all people would naturally commit crimes if it weren't for restraints on their innate selfish tendencies. Social control perspectives of criminal behavior thus assume that there is some type

---

[33]For a review and a study on this topic, see Nicole Piquero, Stephen Tibbetts, and Michael Blankenship, "Examining the Role of Differential Association and Techniques of Neutralization in Explaining Corporate Crime," *Deviant Behavior* 26 (2005): 159–88. See also Lynne Vieraitis et al., "Do Women and Men Differ in Their Neutralizations of Corporate Crime?" *Criminal Justice Review* 37 (2012): 478–93.

[34]Robert Agnew, "The Techniques of Neutralization and Violence," *Criminology* 32 (1994): 563–64.

[35]W. William Minor, "The Neutralization of Criminal Offense," *Criminology* 18 (1980): 116; W. William Minor, "Neutralization as a Hardening Process: Considerations in the Modeling of Change," *Social Forces* 62 (1984): 995–1019. See also Roy L. Austin, "Commitment, Neutralization, and Delinquency," in *Juvenile Delinquency: Little Brother Grows Up*, ed. Theodore N. Ferdinand (Beverly Hills, CA: Sage, 1977); and Quint C. Thurman, "Deviance and the Neutralization of Moral Commitment: An Empirical Analysis," *Deviant Behavior* 5 (1984): 291–304.

[36]Travis Hirschi, *Causes of Delinquency* (Berkeley: University of California Press, 1969), 207. See also Mark Pogrebin, Eric Poole, and Amos Martinez, "Accounts of Professional Misdeeds: The Sexual Exploitation of Clients by Psychotherapists," *Deviant Behavior* 13 (1992): 229–52; and John Hamlin, "The Misplaced Concept of Rational Choice in Neutralization Theory," *Criminology* 26 (1988): 425–38.

Figure 8.1 • Frequencies of hitting, biting, and kicking at ages 2 to 12 years

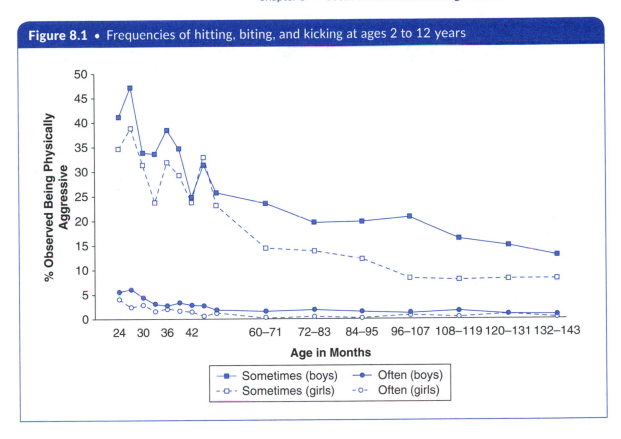

of basic human nature and that all human beings exhibit antisocial tendencies. Such theories are concerned with why individuals don't commit crime or deviant behaviors. Control theorists ask questions like this: What is it about society and human interaction that causes people not to act on their impulses?

The assumption that people have innate antisocial tendencies is a controversial one because it is nearly impossible to test. Nevertheless, some recent evidence supports the idea that human beings are inherently selfish and antisocial by nature. Specifically, researchers have found that most individuals are oriented toward selfish and aggressive behaviors at an early age, with such behaviors peaking at the end of the second year (see Figure 8.1).[37]

An example of antisocial dispositions appearing early in life was reported by Richard Tremblay and David LeMarquand, who found that most young children's (particularly boys') aggressive behaviors peaked at age 27 months. These behaviors included hitting, biting, and kicking others.[38] Their research is not isolated; virtually all developmental experts acknowledge that toddlers exhibit a tendency to show aggressive behavior toward others. This line of research would seem to support the notion that people are predisposed toward antisocial, even criminal, behavior.

---

[37]Michael Lewis, Steven Alessandri, and Margaret Sullivan, "Expectancy, Loss of Control, and Anger in Young Infants," *Developmental Psychology* 25 (1990): 745–51; Albert Restoin et al., "New Data on the Development of Communication Behavior in the Young Child with His Peers," *Recherches de Psychologie Sociale* 5 (1985): 31–56; Richard Tremblay et al., "The Search for the Age of 'Onset' of Physical Aggression: Rousseau and Bandura Revisited," *Criminal Behaviour and Mental Health* 9 (1999): 8–23.

[38]Richard Tremblay and David LeMarquand, "Individual Risk and Protective Factors," in *Child Delinquents: Development, Intervention, and Service Needs*, ed. Rolf Loeber and David Farrington (London: Sage, 2001): 137–64.

Control theorists do not necessarily assume that people are predisposed toward crime in a way that remains constant throughout life. On the contrary, research shows that most individuals begin to desist from such behaviors starting at around age two. This trend continues until approximately age 5, wherein only the most aggressive individuals (i.e., chronic offenders) continue such behavior at higher ages.

It is important to note that, at the same time selfish and aggressive behaviors decline, self-consciousness is formed. In addition, social emotions—such as shame, guilt, empathy, and pride—begin to appear.[39] This observation is critical because it is what separates control theories from the Classical School of criminology and the predispositional theories that we already discussed. According to control theories, without appropriate socialization, people act on their preprogrammed tendency toward crime and deviance.

In short, control theories claim that all individuals have natural tendencies to commit selfish, antisocial, and even criminal behavior. So, what is it that curbs this natural propensity? Many experts believe the best explanation is that individuals are socialized and controlled by social attachments and investments in conventional society. This assumption regarding the vital importance of early socialization is probably the primary reason why control theories are currently the most popular and accepted theories among criminologists.[40] We will now discuss several early examples of these control theories.

Early Control Theories of Human Behavior

Thomas Hobbes

Control theories are found in a variety of disciplines, including biology, psychology, and sociology. Perhaps the earliest significant use of social control in explaining deviant behavior is found in a perspective offered by the 17th-century Enlightenment philosopher Thomas Hobbes (see Chapter 2). Hobbes claimed that the natural state of humanity is one of selfishness and self-centeredness to the point of constant chaos, characterized by a state of warfare between individuals. He stated that all individuals are inherently disposed to take advantage of others in order to improve their own personal well-being.[41]

However, Hobbes also claimed that the constant fear created by such selfishness results in humans rationally coming together to create binding contracts that will keep individuals from violating others' rights. Even with such controlling arrangements, however, Hobbes was clear that the selfish tendencies people exhibit can never be extinguished. In fact, they explain why punishments are necessary to maintain an established social contract among people.

Durkheim's Idea of Awakened Reflection and Collective Conscience

Consistent with Hobbes's view of individuals as naturally selfish, Émile Durkheim later proposed a theory of social control in the late 1800s that suggested that humans have no internal mechanism to let them know when they are fulfilled.[42] To this end, Durkheim coined the terms *automatic spontaneity* and *awakened reflection*. Automatic spontaneity can be understood with reference to animals' eating habits. Specifically, animals stop eating when they are full, and they are content until they are hungry again; they don't start hunting right after they have filled their stomachs with food. In contrast, awakened reflection concerns the fact that humans do not have such

---

[39]For reviews of supporting studies, see June Price Tangney and K. W. Fischer, *Self-Conscious Emotions: The Psychology of Shame, Guilt, Embarrassment, and Pride* (New York: Guilford Press, 1995); and Michael Lewis, *Shame: The Exposed Self* (New York: Macmillan, 1992).

[40]Walsh and Ellis, "Political Ideology."

[41]Thomas Hobbes, *Leviathan* (1651; repr., Cambridge: Cambridge University Press, 1904).

[42]Émile Durkheim, *The Division of Labor in Society* (1893; repr., New York: Free Press, 1965); Émile Durkheim, *Suicide* (1897; repr., New York: Free Press, 1951) (see chap. 6, n. 18).

an internal, regulatory mechanism. That is because people often acquire resources beyond what is immediately required. Durkheim went so far as to say that "our capacity for feeling is in itself an insatiable and bottomless abyss."[43] This is one of the reasons that Durkheim believed crime and deviance are quite normal, even essential, in any society.

Durkheim's awakened reflection has become commonly known as greed. People tend to favor better conditions and additional fulfillment because they apparently have no biological or psychological mechanism to limit such tendencies. As Durkheim noted, the selfish desires of humankind "are unlimited so far as they depend on the individual alone. . . . The more one has, the more one wants."[44] Thus, society must step in and provide the regulative force that keeps humans from acting too selfishly.

One of the primary elements of this regulative force is the *collective conscience*, which is the extent of similarities or likenesses that people share. For example, almost everyone can agree that homicide is a serious and harmful act that should be avoided in any civilized society. The notion of collective conscience can be seen as an early form of the idea of social bonding, which has become one of the dominant theories in criminology.[45]

According to Durkheim, the collective conscience serves many functions in society. One such function is the establishment of rules that keep individuals from following their natural tendencies toward selfish behavior. Durkheim also believed that crime allows people to unite together in opposition against deviants. In other words, crime and deviance allow conforming individuals to be bonded together in opposition against a common enemy, as can be seen in everyday life when groups come together to face opposition. This enemy consists of the deviants who have not internalized the code of the collective conscience.

Many of Durkheim's ideas hold true today. Just recall a traumatic incident you may have experienced with other strangers (e.g., being stuck in an elevator during a power outage, weathering a serious storm, or being involved in a traffic accident). Incidents such as these bring people together and permit a degree of bonding that would not take place in everyday life. Crime, Durkheim argued, serves a similar function.

How is all of this relevant today? Most control theorists claim that individuals commit crime and deviant acts not because they are lacking in any way but because certain controls have been weakened in their development. This assumption is consistent with Durkheim's theory, which we discussed previously (see Chapter 6).

Freud's Concepts of the Id, Superego, and Ego

Although psychoanalytic theory would seem to have few similarities with sociological positivistic theory, in this case, it is extremely complementary. One of Freud's most essential propositions is that all individuals are born with a tendency toward inherent drives and selfishness due to the **id** domain of the psyche (see Figure 8.2).[46] According to Freud, all people are born with equal amounts of id drives (e.g., libido, food) and motivations toward selfishness and greed. Freud said this inherent selfish tendency must be countered by controls produced from the development of the **superego**, which is the subconscious domain of the psyche that contains our conscience. According to Freud, the superego is formed through the interactions between a young infant or child and his or her significant others. As you can see, the control perspective has a long history in many philosophical and scientific disciplines.

---

[43]Durkheim, *Suicide*, 246–47. Also, much of this discussion is adapted from Raymond Paternoster and Ronet Bachman, *Explaining Criminals and Crime* (Los Angeles: Roxbury, 2001) (see chap. 5, n. 10).

[44]Durkheim, *Suicide*, 254.

[45]A good discussion of Durkheim's concepts, particularly that of the collective conscience, can be found in Bernard et al., *Vold's Theoretical Criminology*, 124–39 (see chap. 2).

[46]Sigmund Freud, "The Ego and the Id," in *The Complete Psychological Works of Sigmund Freud*, Vol. 19, ed. James Strachey (1923; repr., London: Hogarth Press, 1959).

Figure 8.2 • Freud's model of the three domains of the psyche

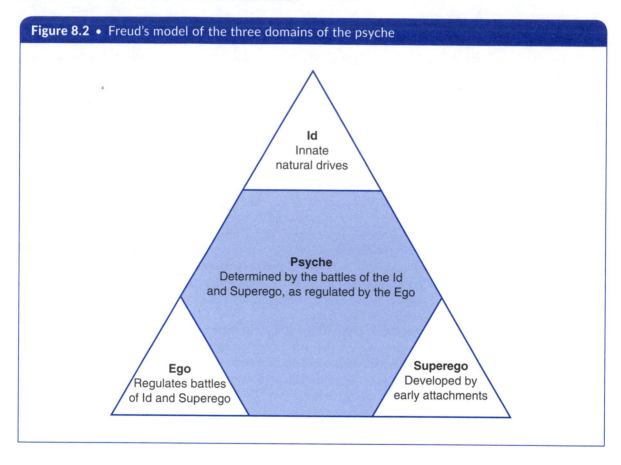

These two drives of the subconscious domains of the id and superego are regulated, Freud thought, by the only conscious domain of the psyche: the **ego**. This ego mediates the battles between our innate drives (id) and our socialized constraints (superego); it represents our personality. There have been a number of applications of Freud's theoretical model to criminality, such as the concept of a deficient superego (due to a lack of early attachments) or a weak ego (which fails to properly regulate the battle between the id and superego). The main point is that Freud was an early control theorist and that his theoretical model was highly influential among psychologists in the early 1900s as they tried to determine why certain individuals committed criminal offenses.[47]

Early Control Theories of Crime

Throughout the 1950s and 1960s, criminologists borrowed and built on some of the ideas just discussed. Until that time, most research in the criminological literature was dominated by the learning theories discussed earlier in this chapter, or social structure theories such as the Chicago School or Merton's strain theory (see Chapters 6 and 7). While early control theories may not be particularly popular in this day and age, they were vitally important in the sense that they laid the groundwork for future theoretical development.

---

[47]Ibid.

Reiss's Control Theory

One of the first control theories of crime was proposed by Albert Reiss in 1951. Reiss claimed that delinquency was a consequence of weak ego or superego controls among juvenile probationers.[48] Reiss found no explicit motivation for delinquent activity. Rather, he thought it would occur in the absence of controls or restraints against such behavior.

Like Freud, Reiss believed that the family was the primary source through which deviant predispositions were discouraged. Furthermore, Reiss claimed that a sound family environment would provide for an individual's needs and the essential emotional bonds that are so important in socializing individuals. Another important factor in Reiss's model was close supervision, not only by the family but also by the community. He said that individuals must be closely monitored for delinquent behavior and adequately disciplined when they break the rules.

Personal factors, such as the ability to restrain one's impulses and delay gratification, were also important in Reiss's framework. These concepts are very similar to later, more modern concepts of control theory, which have been consistently supported by empirical research.[49] For this reason, Reiss was ahead of his time when he first proposed his control theory. Although the direct tests of Reiss's theory have provided only partial support for it, his influence is apparent in many contemporary criminological theories.[50]

Toby's Concept of Stake in Conformity

Soon after Reiss's theory was presented, a similar theory was developed. In 1957, Jackson Toby proposed a theory of delinquency and gangs.[51] He claimed that individuals were more inclined to act on their natural inclinations when the controls on them were weak. Like most other control theorists, Toby claimed that such inclinations toward deviance were distributed equally across all individuals. Furthermore, he emphasized the concept of a **stake in conformity** that supposedly prevents most people from committing crime. The stake in conformity Toby was referring to is the extent to which individuals have investments in conventional society. In other words, how much is a person willing to risk when he or she violates the law?

Studies have shown that stake in conformity is one of the most influential factors in individuals' decisions to offend. People who have nothing to lose are much more likely to take risks and violate others' rights than those who have relatively more invested in social institutions.[52]

One distinguishing feature of Toby's theory is his emphasis on peer influences in terms of both motivating and inhibiting antisocial behavior depending on whether most peers have low or high stakes in conformity. Toby's stake in conformity has been used effectively in subsequent control theories of crime.

Nye's Control Theory

A year after Toby introduced the stake in conformity, F. Ivan Nye proposed a relatively comprehensive control theory that placed a strong focus on the family.[53] Following the assumptions of early control theorists, Nye claimed that

---

[48]Albert Reiss, "Delinquency as the Failure of Personal and Social Controls," *American Sociological Review* 16 (1951): 196–207.

[49]For a comprehensive review of studies of low self-control, see Travis Pratt and Frank Cullen, "The Empirical Status of Gottfredson and Hirschi's General Theory of Crime: A Meta-analysis," *Criminology* 38 (2000): 931–64.

[50]See Bernard et al., *Vold's Theoretical Criminology*, 202–3.

[51]Jackson Toby, "Social Disorganization and Stake in Conformity: Complementary Factors in the Predatory Behavior of Hoodlums," *Journal of Criminal Law, Criminology, and Police Science* 48 (1957): 12–17.

[52]Hirschi, *Causes of Delinquency*; Robert Sampson and John Laub, *Crime in the Making: Pathways and Turning Points in Life* (Cambridge, MA: Harvard University Press, 1993).

[53]F. Ivan Nye, *Family Relationships and Delinquent Behavior* (New York: Wiley, 1958).

there was no significant positive force that caused delinquency because such antisocial tendencies are universal and would be found in virtually everyone if not for certain controls usually found in the home.

Nye's theory consisted of three primary components of control. The first component was internal control, which is formed through social interaction. This socialization, he claimed, assists in the development of a conscience. Nye further claimed that if individuals are not given adequate resources and care, they will follow their natural tendencies toward doing what is necessary to protect their interests.

Nye's second component of control was direct control, which consists of a wide range of constraints on individual propensities to commit deviant acts. Direct control includes numerous types of sanctions, such as jail and ridicule, and the restriction of one's chances to commit criminal activity. Nye's third component of control was indirect control, which occurs when individuals are strongly attached to their early caregivers. For most children, it is through an intense and strong relationship with their parents or guardians that they establish an attachment to conventional society. However, Nye suggested that when the needs of an individual are not met by their caregivers, inappropriate behavior can result.

As shown in Figure 8.3, Nye predicted a U-shaped curve of parental controls in predicting delinquency. Specifically, he argued that either no controls (i.e., complete freedom) or too much control (i.e., no freedom at all) would predict the most chronic delinquency. He believed that a healthy balance of freedom and parental control was the best strategy for inhibiting criminal activity. Some recent research supports Nye's prediction.[54] Contemporary control theories, such as Charles Tittle's control–balance theory, draw heavily on Nye's idea of having a healthy balance of controls and freedom.[55]

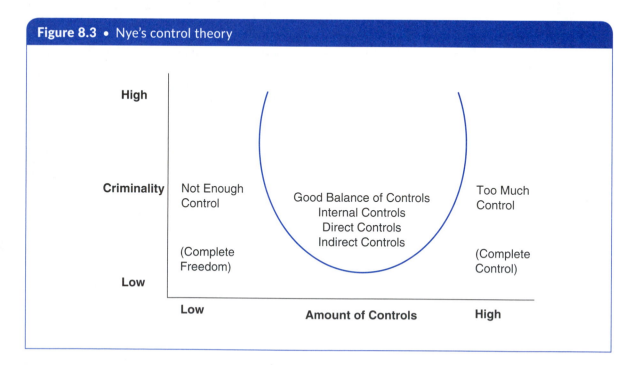

Figure 8.3 • Nye's control theory

---

[54]Ruth Seydlitz, "Complexity in the Relationships among Direct and Indirect Parental Controls and Delinquency," *Youth and Society* 24 (1993): 243–75.

[55]Charles Tittle, *Control Balance: Toward a General Theory of Deviance* (Boulder, CO: Westview, 1995).

Reckless's Containment Theory

Another control theory, known as **containment theory**, has been proposed by Walter Reckless.[56] This theory emphasizes both inner containment and outer containment, which can be viewed as internal and external controls. Reckless broke from traditional assumptions of social control theories by identifying predictive factors that push or pull individuals toward antisocial behavior. However, the focus of his theory remained on the controlling elements, which can be seen in the emphasis placed on containment in the theory's name.

Reckless claimed that individuals can be pushed into delinquency by their social environment, such as by a lack of opportunities for education or employment. Furthermore, he pointed out that some individual factors, such as brain disorders or risk-taking personalities, could push some people to commit criminal behavior. Reckless also noted that some individuals could be pulled into criminal activity by hanging out with delinquent peers, watching too much violence on television, and so on. All told, Reckless went beyond the typical control theory assumption of inborn tendencies. In addition to these natural dispositions toward deviant behavior, containment theory proposes that extra pushes and pulls can motivate people to commit crime.

Reckless further claimed that the pushes and pulls toward criminal behavior could be enough to force individuals into criminal activity unless they are sufficiently contained or controlled. Reckless claimed that such containment should be both internal and external. By *internal containment*, he meant building a person's sense of self, which helps the person resist the temptations of criminal activity. According to Reckless, other forms of internal containment include the ability to internalize societal norms. With respect to *external containment*, Reckless claimed that social organizations, such as school, church, and other institutions, are essential in building bonds that inhibit individuals from being pushed or pulled into criminal activity.

Reckless offered a visual image of containment theory, which we present in Figure 8.4. The outer circle (Circle 1) in the figure represents the social realm of pressures and pulls (e.g., peer pressure), whereas the innermost circle (Circle 4) symbolizes a person's individual-level pushes to commit crime, such as predispositions or personality traits that are linked to crime. In between these two circles are the two layers of controls, external containment (Circle 2) and internal containment (Circle 3). The structure of Figure 8.4 and the examples included in each circle are those specifically noted by Reckless.[57]

While some studies have shown general support for containment theory, others offer more support for some components, such as internalization of rules, than for other factors, such as self-perception, in accounting for variations in delinquency.[58] External factors may be more important than internal ones. Furthermore, some studies have noted weaker support for Reckless's theory among minorities and females, who may be more influenced by their peers or other influences. Thus, the model appears to be most valid for White males—at least according to empirical studies.[59]

One of the problems with containment theory is that it does not go far enough toward specifying the factors that are important in predicting criminality, especially regarding specific groups of individuals. For example, an infinite number of concepts could potentially be categorized either as a push or pull toward criminality or as an inner or outer containment of criminality. Thus, the theory could be considered too broad or vague and not specific enough to be of practical value. To Reckless's credit, however, containment theory has increased the exposure of control

---

[56]Walter Reckless, *The Crime Problem*, 4th ed. (New York: Appleton-Century-Crofts, 1967).

[57]Ibid., 479.

[58]Richard Lawrence, "School Performance, Containment Theory, and Delinquent Behavior," *Youth and Society* 7 (1985): 69–95; Richard A. Dodder and Janet R. Long, "Containment Theory Reevaluated: An Empirical Explication," *Criminal Justice Review* 5 (1980): 74–84.

[59]William E. Thompson and Richard A. Dodder, "Containment Theory and Juvenile Delinquency: A Reevaluation through Factor Analysis," *Adolescence* 21 (1986): 365–76.

Figure 8.4 • Reckless's containment theory

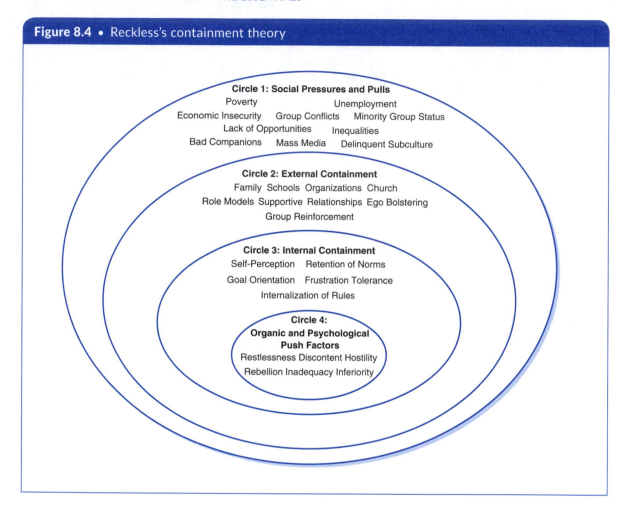

theories of criminal behavior. And although support for containment theory has been mixed, there is no doubt that it has influenced other, more recent control theories.[60]

Modern Social Control Theories

As the previous chapters attest, control theory has been around in various forms for some time. Modern social control theories build on these earlier versions and add levels of depth and sophistication. Two modern social control theories are Matza's drift theory and Hirschi's social bonding theory.

Matza's Drift Theory

The theory of drift, or **drift theory**, presented by Matza in 1964, claims that individuals offend at certain times in their lives when social controls—such as parental supervision, employment, and family ties—are weakened.[61]

---

[60]Akers, *Criminological Theories*, 3rd ed., 103–4.

[61]Matza, *Delinquency and Drift*.

Figure 8.5 • Matza's theory of drift

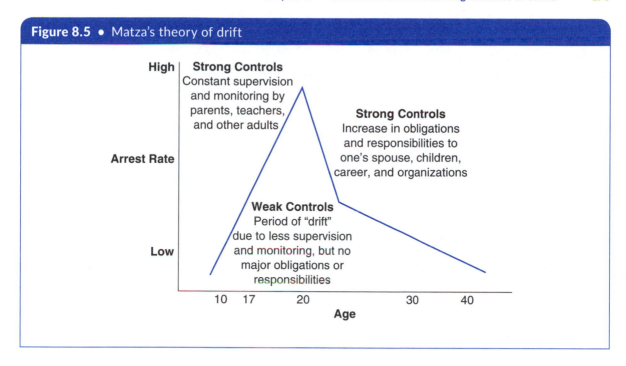

In developing his theory, Matza criticized earlier theories and their tendency to predict too much crime. For example, the Chicago School would incorrectly predict that all individuals in bad neighborhoods will commit crime. Likewise, strain theory predicts that all poor individuals will commit crime. Obviously, this is not true. Thus, Matza claimed, there is a degree of determinism (i.e., Positive School) in human behavior but also a significant amount of free will (i.e., Classical School). He called this perspective **soft determinism**, which is the gray area between free will and determinism. This is illustrated in Figure 8.5.

Returning to the basics of Matza's theory, he claimed that individuals offend at the time in life when social controls are most weakened. As is well known, social controls are most weakened for most individuals during the teenage years. At this time, parents and other caretakers stop having a constant supervisory role, and at the same time, teenagers generally do not have too many responsibilities—such as careers or children—that would inhibit them from experimenting with deviance. This is very consistent with the well-known age–crime relationship; most individuals who are arrested experience this in their teenage years.[62] Once sufficient ties are developed, people tend to mature out of criminal lifestyles.

Matza further claimed that when supervision is absent and ties are minimal, the majority of individuals are the most free to do what they want. Where, then, does the term *drift* come from? During the times when people have few ties and obligations, they will drift in and out of delinquency, Matza proposed. He pointed out that previous theories were unsuccessful in explaining this age–crime relationship:

---

[62]*OJJDP Statistical Briefing Book.* Unpublished arrest data for 1980–1997 from the Federal Bureau of Investigation for 1998, 1999, and 2000 from *Crime in the United States* reports (Washington, DC: Government Printing Office, 1999, 2000, and 2001, respectively).

Most theories of delinquency take no account of maturational reform; those that do often do so at the expense of violating their own assumptions regarding the constrained delinquent.[63]

Matza insisted that drifting is not the same as a commitment to a life of crime. Instead, it is experimenting with questionable behavior and then rationalizing it. The way youths rationalize behavior that they know to be wrong is through learning the techniques of neutralization discussed earlier.

Drift theory goes on to say that individuals do not reject the conventional normative structure. On the contrary, much offending is based on neutralizing or adhering to **subterranean values**, which young people have been socialized to use as a means of circumventing conventional values. This is basically the same as asserting one's independence, which tends to occur with a vengeance during the teenage years.

Subterranean values are quite prevalent and underlie many aspects of our culture, which is why Matza's drift theory is also classified as a learning theory. For example, while it is conventional to believe that violence is wrong, boxing matches and sports that commonly lead to injury are some of the most popular spectator activities. Such phenomena create an atmosphere that readily allows neutralization or rationalization of criminal activity.

We will see other forms of subterranean values when we discuss risk-taking and low self-control later in this chapter. In many contexts, such as business, risk-taking and aggressiveness are seen as desirable characteristics, so many individuals are influenced by such subterranean values. This, according to Matza, adds to individuals' likelihood of drifting into crime and delinquency.

Matza's theory of drift seems sensible on its face, but empirical research examining the theory has shown mixed results.[64] One of the primary criticisms of Matza's theory, which even he acknowledged, is that it does not explain the most chronic offenders, the people who are responsible for the vast majority of serious, violent crimes. Chronic offenders often offend long before and well past their teenage years, which clearly limits the predictive value of Matza's theory.

Despite its shortcomings, Matza's drift theory appears to explain why many people offend exclusively during their teenage and young adult years but then grow out of it. Also, the theory is highly consistent with several of the ideas presented by control theorists, including the assumption that (a) selfish tendencies are universal, (b) these tendencies are inhibited by socialization and social controls, and (c) the selfish tendencies appear at times when controls are weakest. The theory goes beyond previous control theories by adding the concepts of soft determinism, neutralization, and subterranean values as well as the idea that, in many contexts, selfish and aggressive behaviors are not wrong but actually desirable.

Hirschi's Social Bonding Theory

Perhaps the most influential social control theory was presented by Hirschi in 1969.[65] Hirschi's model of **social bonding theory** takes an assumption from Durkheim that "we are all animals, and thus naturally capable of committing criminal acts."[66] However, as Hirschi acknowledged, most humans can be adequately socialized to become tightly bonded to conventional entities, such as families, schools, and communities. Hirschi said that the more strongly a person is bonded to conventional society, the less prone to engaging in crime he or she

---

[63]"Age-Arrest Rate Curve" is loosely based on data provided by the Federal Bureau of Investigation, *Crime in the United States* report (Washington, DC: Government Printing Office, 1997).

[64]See Bernard et al., *Vold's Theoretical Criminology*, 205–7.

[65]Hirschi, *Causes of Delinquency* (see chap. 6, n. 30).

[66]Ibid., 31, in which Hirschi cites Durkheim.

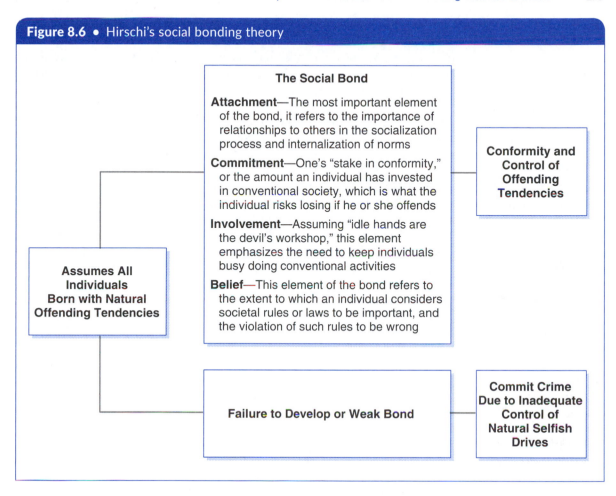

Figure 8.6 ● Hirschi's social bonding theory

The Social Bond

Attachment—The most important element of the bond, it refers to the importance of relationships to others in the socialization process and internalization of norms

Commitment—One's "stake in conformity," or the amount an individual has invested in conventional society, which is what the individual risks losing if he or she offends

Involvement—Assuming "idle hands are the devil's workshop," this element emphasizes the need to keep individuals busy doing conventional activities

Belief—This element of the bond refers to the extent to which an individual considers societal rules or laws to be important, and the violation of such rules to be wrong

Assumes All Individuals Born with Natural Offending Tendencies

Conformity and Control of Offending Tendencies

Failure to Develop or Weak Bond

Commit Crime Due to Inadequate Control of Natural Selfish Drives

will be. More specifically, the stronger the social bond, the lower the likelihood that an individual will commit criminal offenses.

As shown in Figure 8.6, Hirschi's social bond is made up of four elements: (1) attachment, (2) commitment, (3) involvement, and (4) moral belief. The stronger or more developed the person is in each of the four elements, the lower the likelihood that he or she will commit crime. Let us now consider each element in detail.

The most important factor in the social bond is attachment, which consists of affectionate bonds between an individual and his or her significant others. Attachment is vitally important for the internalization of conventional values. Hirschi said, "The essence of internalization of norms, conscience, or superego thus lies in the attachment of the individual to others."[67] Hirschi made it clear, as did Freud, that strong, early attachments are the most important factor in developing a social bond. The other constructs in the social bond—commitment, involvement, and belief—are contingent on adequate attachment to others, he argued. That is, without healthy attachments, especially early in life, the probability of acting inappropriately increases.

Commitment, the second element of Hirschi's social bond, is the investment a person has in conventional society. This has been explained as one's stake in conformity, or what is at risk of being lost if one gets caught

[67]Ibid., 18.

committing crime. If people feel they have much to lose by committing crime, they will probably not do it. In contrast, if someone has nothing to lose, what is to prevent that person from doing something he or she may be punished for? The answer is, of course, not much. And this, some theorists claim, is why it is difficult to control so-called chronic offenders. Trying to instill a commitment to conventional society in such individuals is extremely difficult.

Another element of the social bond is involvement, which is the time spent in conventional activities. The assumption is that time spent in constructive activities will reduce time devoted to illegal behaviors. This element of the bond goes back to the old adage that "idle hands are the devil's workshop."[68] Hirschi claimed that participating in conventional activities can inhibit delinquent and criminal activity.

The last element of the social bond is beliefs, which have generally been interpreted as moral beliefs concerning the laws and rules of society. This is one of the most examined and consistently supported aspects of the social bond. Basically, individuals who feel that a course of action is against their moral beliefs are much less likely to pursue it than individuals who don't see a breach of morality in such behavior. For example, we all probably know some people who see drunk driving as a very serious offense because of the injury and death it can cause. However, we also probably know individuals who don't see a problem with such behavior. The same can be said about speeding in a car, shoplifting from a store, or using marijuana; people differ in their beliefs about most forms of criminal activity.

Hirschi's theory has been tested by numerous researchers and has, for the most part, been supported.[69] However, one criticism is that the components of the social bond may predict criminality only if they are defined in a certain way. For example, with respect to the involvement element of the bond, studies have shown that not all conventional activities are equal when it comes to preventing delinquency. Only academic or religious activities seem to have consistent effects in inhibiting delinquency. In contrast, many studies show that teenagers who date or play sports actually have an increased risk of committing crime.[70]

Another major criticism of Hirschi's theory is that the effect of attachment on crime depends on to whom one is attached. Studies have clearly and consistently shown that attachment to delinquent peers is a strong predictor of criminal activity.

Finally, some evidence indicates that social bonding theory may better explain why individuals start offending than why they continue or escalate in their offending. One reason for this is that Hirschi's theory does not elaborate on what occurs after an individual commits criminal activity. This is likely the primary reason why some of the more complex, integrated theories of crime often attribute the initiation of delinquency to a breakdown in the social bond. However, other theories (such as differential reinforcement) are typically seen as better predictors of what happens after the initial stages of the criminal career.[71]

Despite the criticism it has received, Hirschi's social bonding theory is still one of the most accepted theories of criminal behavior.[72] It is a relatively convincing explanation for criminality because of the consistent support that it has found among samples of people taken from all over the world.[73]

---

[68]Ibid., 22.

[69]For a review, see Akers, *Criminological Theories*, 3rd ed., 105–10.

[70]Ibid.

[71]Delbert Elliott, David Huizinga, and Suzanne Ageton, *Explaining Delinquency and Drug Use* (Beverly Hills, CA: Sage, 1985).

[72]Walsh and Ellis, "Political Ideology."

[73]Dennis Wong, "Pathways to Delinquency in Hong Kong and Guangzhou, South China," *International Journal of Adolescence and Youth* 10 (2001): 91–115; Alexander Vazsonyi and Martin Killias, "Immigration and Crime among Youth in Switzerland," *Criminal Justice and Behavior* 28 (2001): 329–66; Manuel Eisner, "Crime, Problem Drinking, and Drug Use: Patterns of Problem Behavior in Cross-National Perspective," *Annals of the American Academy of Political and Social Science* 580 (2002): 201–25.

Case Study: Jesse Pomeroy

Jesse Pomeroy

Jesse Pomeroy was born on November 29, 1859, in Charlestown, Massachusetts. His father, Thomas, was a violent alcoholic. He would often go on drinking binges and then proceed to beat his two sons, Charles and Jesse. Jesse's mother, Ruth Ann, eventually divorced Thomas in the 1870s; divorce was extremely uncommon during this time. In fact, Ruth Ann revealed that she divorced her husband after one of these brutal beatings:

> Jesse later admitted to his doctors that his father had made him go to his room and strip totally naked, whereupon Thomas had proceeded to lash out with a leather belt. . . . [Jesse] realized the beatings . . . were not that bad, not nearly as horrific as the relentless pummeling he had received almost four years earlier, when his father had taken Jesse, just eight years old, to an abandoned shed in the woods. There Thomas had become so enraged that the blows from a horsewhip had nearly killed his son.[74]

▲ **Image 8.5** Jesse Pomeroy.
SOURCE: © AP Photo

Ruth Ann realized that Jesse was a strong-willed boy. Jesse was often made fun of at school, primarily because of a deformity in his right eye. Jesse's teacher complained of his problem behavior at school. The teacher noted that he was a loner; he preferred to read cheap "dime novels." During this time, these novels were full of violence, sex, battles, and mayhem. Eventually, Ruth Ann was asked to remove her son from school.

Jesse's problems were not restricted to just school. His mother brought home two yellow canaries; she would come home looking forward to their chirping in the wooden cage. One afternoon, she came home to find the two canaries dead—their heads were twisted off their bodies. Prior to this, a neighbor had told Ruth Ann that her little kitten had gone missing. A few days later, Ruth Ann watched Jesse walking down a nearby street with the dead kitten in one hand and a kitchen knife in the other. In 1871, there were reports that children in the next city over, Chelsea, were being beaten by an older boy. Some of these children were sexually assaulted. The victims reported that this boy would offer them money and treats; then he would suggest they go to a remote locale. There he would abuse the children.[75] The newspapers referred to him as "The Boy Torturer" and "The Red Devil." After reading a description of this boy in the *Boston Globe*, Ruth Ann recognized this was her son; she moved her family to South Boston. In August 1872, a young boy was found tortured in South Boston; a month later, a child was found beaten, assaulted, and tied up to a telephone pole. This victim, however, was able to give a very detailed description. This resulted in Jesse Pomeroy being arrested and sentenced to the State Reform School at Westborough for the remainder of his minor-status years (e.g., six years). Ruth Ann, however, diligently worked to have her son released earlier; Jesse was released months after.[76]

(Continued)

---

[74] Roseanne Montillo, *The Wilderness of Ruin: A Tale of Madness, Fire, and the Hunt for America's Youngest Serial Killer* (New York: William Morrow, 2015), 18.

[75] Ibid.

[76] "The Story of Jesse Pomeroy, 14-Year-Old Serial Killer," CBS News, March 13, 2015. http://www.cbsnews.com/news/the-story-of-jesse-pomeroy-14-year-old-serial-killer.

(Continued)

In March 1874, nine-year-old Katie Curran disappeared. During the investigation, it was revealed that the last place she had been seen was at the Pomeroys' shop; Jesse was interrogated, but there was no arrest at that time. In April, the body of four-year-old Horace Millen was found on the beach of Dorchester Bay. His throat had been cut and he had been stabbed 15 times; also, one of his eyes had been torn out. The police recalled the beatings of the other children two years earlier and arrested Jesse Pomeroy; he was 14 years old at the time. In July 1874, Jesse confessed to Horace Millen's murder. Jesse Pomeroy also confessed to the murder of Katie Curran. He had lured her into the basement of his mother's dress shop. He had then cut her throat and buried her body under an ash heap. When he was asked why he committed the murders, he stated, "I couldn't help it."[77] On September 7, 1876, Jesse Pomeroy was sentenced to death. Subsequently, his sentence was commuted to life in prison—solitary confinement. In 1916, he was released from solitary confinement and was allowed to mix with other prisoners at the Charlestown Prison. On September 29, 1932, he died at the age of 73 years.[78]

> *When he was asked why he committed the murders, he stated, "I couldn't help it."*

Think About It

1. So why did he do it? As described by the theories presented in this chapter, specifically various social control theories (such as Hirschi's theory of social bonding) and socialization theories (e.g., differential association theory, differential reinforcement theory), it appears that Jesse Pomeroy never had much of a chance to form strong social bonds with conventional society, nor was he adequately socialized. To clarify, his father was abusive. He was considered a loner at school. He began early in life to demonstrate cruel behavior to animals. Thus, do you think Jesse Pomeroy engaged in such behaviors out of selfishness and personal satisfaction, and without any empathy for his victims, because that was what his experience in the world taught him to do?

2. If you maintain that Jesse had low self-control and therefore engaged in these behaviors, why did he have such low self-control?

3. What types of things could have been done to improve Jesse's low self-control?

Integrated Social Control Theories

Although we will review integrated theories in detail in Chapter 11, it is worthwhile to briefly discuss the two integrated models that most incorporate the control perspective into their frameworks. These two integrated models are control–balance theory and power–control theory. Both have received considerable attention in the criminological literature. Other integrated theories that incorporate control theory to a lesser extent include John Braithwaite's shaming theory and Sampson and Laub's life-course theory. These will be covered in more detail in Chapters 11 and 12.

---

[77]"Jesse Pomeroy: The Boy Fiend," CelebrateBoston.com, n.d. http://www.celebrateboston.com/crime/jesse-pomeroy-serial-killer.htm.

[78]Thomas M. McDade, *The Annals of Murder* (Norman: University of Oklahoma Press, 1961).

Tittle's Control–Balance Theory

Presented by Tittle in 1995, **control–balance theory** proposes that (a) the amount of control to which one is subjected and (b) the amount of control one can exercise determine the probability that deviance will occur. The balance between these two types of control, he argued, can even predict the type of behavior that is likely to be committed.[79]

Tittle argued that a person is least likely to offend when he or she has a balance of controlling and being controlled. Furthermore, the likelihood of offending increases when these become unbalanced. If individuals are more controlled (Tittle called this *control deficit*), then the theory predicts that they will commit predatory or defiant acts. In contrast, if an individual possesses an excessive level of control (Tittle calls this *control surplus*), then he or she will be more likely to commit acts of exploitation or decadence. Note that excessive control is not the same as excessive self-control. Tittle argued that people who are controlling—that is, who have excessive control over others—will be predisposed toward inappropriate activities.

Initial empirical tests of control–balance theory have reported mixed results with both surpluses and deficits predicting the same types of deviance.[80] In addition, researchers have uncovered differing effects of the control–balance ratio on two types of deviance that are contingent on gender. This finding is consistent with the gender-specific support found for Reckless's containment theory, described earlier in this chapter.[81]

Hagan's Power–Control Theory

Power–control theory is an integrated theory that was proposed by John Hagan and his colleagues.[82] The primary focus of this theory is on the level of control and patriarchal attitudes, as well as structure in the household, which are influenced by parental positions in the workforce. Power–control theory assumes that mothers will be less likely to exert control on their daughters in households where the mothers and fathers have relatively similar levels of power at work (i.e., balanced households). These balanced households will be less likely to experience gender differences in the criminal offending of the children. However, households in which mothers and fathers have dissimilar levels of power in the workplace (i.e., unbalanced households) are more likely to suppress criminal activity in daughters. In addition, assertiveness and risky activity among the males in the house will be encouraged. This assertiveness and risky activity may be a precursor to crime.

Most empirical tests of power–control have provided moderate support for the theory, while more recent studies have further specified the validity of the theory in different contexts.[83] For example, one recent study reported that the influence of mothers, not fathers, on sons had the greatest impact on reducing the delinquency of young

---

[79]Tittle, *Control Balance.*

[80]Alex Piquero and Matthew Hickman, "An Empirical Test of Tittle's Control Balance Theory," *Criminology* 37 (1999): 319–42; Matthew Hickman and Alex Piquero, "Exploring the Relationships between Gender, Control Balance, and Deviance," *Deviant Behavior* 22 (2001): 323–51.

[81]Hickman and Piquero, "Exploring the Relationships," 323–51.

[82]John Hagan, *Structural Criminology* (Newark, NJ: Rutgers University Press, 1989); John Hagan, A. Gillis, and J. Simpson, "The Class Structure of Gender and Delinquency: Toward a Power-Control Theory of Common Delinquent Behavior," *American Journal of Sociology* 90 (1985): 1151–78; John Hagan, A. Gillis, and J. Simpson, "Clarifying and Extending Power-Control Theory," *American Journal of Sociology* 95 (1990): 1024–37; John Hagan, J. Simpson, and A. Gillis, "Class in the Household: A Power-Control Theory of Gender and Delinquency," *American Journal of Sociology* 92 (1987): 788–816.

[83]Hagen et al., "Class in the Household," 788–816; B. McCarthy and John Hagan, "Gender, Delinquency, and the Great Depression: A Test of Power-Control Theory," *Canadian Review of Sociology and Anthropology* 24 (1987): 153–77; Merry Morash and Meda Chesney-Lind, "A Reformulation and Partial Test of the Power-Control Theory of Delinquency," *Justice Quarterly* 8 (1991): 347–77; Simon Singer and Murray Levine, "Power-Control Theory, Gender, and Delinquency: A Partial Replication with Additional Evidence on the Effects of Peers," *Criminology* 26 (1988): 627–47.

males.[84] Another researcher found that differences in perceived threats of embarrassment and formal sanctions varied between more patriarchal and less patriarchal households.[85] Finally, studies have also started measuring the effect of patriarchal attitudes on crime and delinquency.[86] Power–control theory is a good example of a social control theory in that it is consistent with the idea that individuals must be socialized and that the gender differences in such socialization make a difference in how people will act throughout life.

A General Theory of Crime: Low Self-Control

In 1990, Hirschi, along with his colleague Michael Gottfredson, proposed a general **theory of low self-control**, which is often referred to as *the general theory of crime*.[87] This theory has led to a significant amount of debate and research in the field since its appearance—more than any other contemporary theory of crime. Like previous control theories of crime, this theory assumes that individuals are born predisposed toward selfish, self-centered activities and that only effective child rearing and socialization can create self-control. Without such adequate socialization (i.e., social controls) and reduction of criminal opportunities, individuals will follow their natural tendencies to become selfish predators. Furthermore, the general theory of crime assumes that self-control must be established by age 10. If it has not formed by that time, then, according to the theory, individuals will forever exhibit low self-control.

Although Gottfredson and Hirschi still attribute the formation of controls to the socialization processes, the distinguishing characteristic of this theory is its emphasis on the individual's ability to control himself or herself. That is, the general theory of crime assumes that people can take a degree of control over their own decisions and, within certain limitations, control themselves.

The general theory of crime is accepted as one of the most valid theories of crime.[88] This is probably because it identifies only one primary factor that causes criminality—low self-control. But low self-control theory may actually implicate a series of personality traits and behavior, including risk-taking, impulsiveness, self-centeredness, short-term orientation, and quick temper. For example, recent research has supported the idea that inadequate child-rearing practices tend to result in lower levels of self-control among children and that these low levels produce various risky behaviors, including criminal activity.[89] Such propensities toward low self-control can manifest in varying forms across an individual's life. For example, teenagers with low self-control will likely hit or steal from peers, and as they grow older, they will be more likely to gamble or cheat on taxes.

---

[84]B. McCarthy, John Hagan, and T. Woodward, "In the Company of Women: Structure and Agency in a Revised Power-Control Theory of Gender and Delinquency," *Criminology* 37 (1999): 761–88.

[85]Brenda Sims Blackwell, "Perceived Sanction Threats, Gender, and Crime: A Test and Elaboration of Power-Control Theory," *Criminology* 38 (2000): 439–88.

[86]Blackwell, "Perceived Sanction Threats," 439–88; Kristin Bates and Chris Bader, "Family Structure, Power-Control Theory, and Deviance: Extending Power-Control Theory to Include Alternate Family Forms," *Western Criminology Review* 4 (2003).

[87]Michael Gottfredson and Travis Hirschi, *A General Theory of Crime* (Palo Alto, CA: Stanford University Press, 1990).

[88]For an excellent review of studies regarding low self-control theory, see Pratt and Cullen, "The Empirical Status," 931–64. For critiques of this theory, see Ronald Akers, "Self-Control as a General Theory of Crime," *Journal of Quantitative Criminology* 7 (1991): 201–11. For a study that demonstrates the high popularity of the theory, see Walsh and Ellis, "Political Ideology."

[89]Carter Hay, "Parenting, Self-Control, and Delinquency: A Test of Self-Control Theory," *Criminology* 39 (2001): 707–36; Karen Hayslett-McCall and Thomas Bernard, "Attachment, Masculinity, and Self-Control: A Theory of Male Crime Rates," *Theoretical Criminology* 6 (2002): 5–33.

Psychological Aspects of Low Self-Control

Criminologists have recently claimed that low self-control may be due to the emotional disposition of individuals. For example, one study showed that the effects of low self-control on intentions to commit drunk driving and shoplifting were tied to individuals' perceptions of pleasure and shame. More specifically, the findings of this study showed that individuals who had low self-control had significantly lower levels of anticipated shame but significantly higher levels of perceived pleasure in committing both drunk driving and shoplifting.[90] These results suggest that individuals who lack self-control will be oriented toward gaining pleasure and taking advantage of resources and toward avoiding negative emotional feelings (e.g., shame) that are primarily induced through socialization.

Physiological Aspects of Low Self-Control

Low self-control can also be tied to physiological factors. Interestingly, research has shown that chronic offenders show greater arousal toward danger and risk-taking than toward the possibility of punishment.[91] This arousal has been measured by monitoring brain activity in response to certain stimuli. The research suggests that individuals are encouraged to commit risky behavior due to physiological mechanisms that reward their risk-taking activities by releasing pleasure chemicals in their brains.[92]

In a similar vein, recent studies show that chronic gamblers tend to get a physiological high (such as a sudden, intense release of brain chemicals similar to that following a small dose of cocaine) from the activity of betting, particularly when they are gambling with their own money and risking a personal loss.[93] Undoubtedly, a minority of individuals thrive off of risk-taking behaviors significantly more than others. This suggests that physiological as well as psychological differences may explain why certain individuals favor risky behaviors.

Researchers have also found that criminal offenders generally perceive a significantly lower level of internal sanctions (e.g., shame, guilt, embarrassment) than do nonoffenders.[94] So, in summary, a select group of individuals appear to derive physiological and psychological pleasure from engaging in risky behaviors while simultaneously being less likely to be inhibited by internal emotional sanctions. Such a combination, Gottfredson and Hirschi claimed, is very dangerous and helps explain why impulsive individuals often end up in prison.

Finally, the psychological and physiological aspects of low self-control may help explain the gender differences observed between males and females. Specifically, studies show that females are significantly more likely than males to experience internal emotional sanctioning for offenses they have committed.[95] In other words, there appears to be something innately different about males and females that helps explain the differing levels of self-control each possesses.

---

[90]Alex Piquero and Stephen Tibbetts, "Specifying the Direct and Indirect Effects of Low Self-Control and Situational Factors in Offenders' Decision Making: Toward a More Complete Model of Rational Offending," *Justice Quarterly* 13 (1996): 481–510.

[91]Adrian Raine, *The Psychopathology of Crime* (San Diego, CA: Academic Press, 1993).

[92]Anthony Walsh, *Biosocial Criminology: Introduction and Integration* (Cincinnati, OH: Anderson, 2002).

[93]Christopher D. Fiorillo, Phillippe N. Tobler, and Wolfram Schultz, "Discrete Coding of Reward Probability and Uncertainty by Dopamine Neurons," *Science* 299 (2003): 1898–1902.

[94]Harold Grasmick and Robert Bursik, "Conscience, Significant Others, and Rational Choice: Extending the Deterrence Model," *Law and Society Review* 24 (1990): 837–61; Stephen Tibbetts, "Shame and Rational Choice in Offending Decisions," *Criminal Justice and Behavior* 24 (1997): 234–55.

[95]Stephen Tibbetts and Denise Herz, "Gender Differences in Factors of Social Control and Rational Choice," *Deviant Behavior* 17 (1996): 183–208.

Summary of Control Theories

Control perspectives are among the oldest and most respected explanations of criminal activity. The fundamental assumption that humans have an inborn, selfish disposition that must be controlled through socialization distinguishes control theories from other theories of crime. The control perspective's longevity as one of the most popular criminological theories demonstrates its legitimacy as an explanation of behavior. This is likely due to the dedication and efforts of criminologists who are constantly developing new and improved versions of control theory—many of which we have discussed here.

Policy Implications

Numerous policy implications can be taken from the various types of social learning and control theories presented here. We will concentrate on those that are likely to be most effective and pragmatic in helping to reduce criminal behavior.

A number of policy implications can be drawn from the various learning models. Perhaps their most important suggestion is to supply many opportunities for positive reinforcements, or rewards, for good behavior. Such reinforcements have been found to be far more effective than punishments, especially among criminal offenders.[96] Furthermore, studies show that the most effective rehabilitation programs for offenders should be based on a cognitive behavioral approach, which teaches individuals to think before they act.[97] Furthermore, evaluation studies have shown that simply grouping offenders together for counseling or peer therapy sessions is not an effective strategy; rather, it appears that such programs often show no effect, or actually increase offending among participants, perhaps because they tend to learn more antisocial attitudes from such sessions.[98] Ultimately, offender programs that emphasize positive reinforcements and are based on a cognitive behavioral approach show the greatest success.

Regarding the policy implications of control theories, we will focus on the early social bonding that must take place and the need for more parental supervision to help an individual develop or learn self-control and create healthy, strong bonds to conventional society. Most control theories assume that individuals are predisposed to criminal behavior, so the primary focus of programs should be to reduce this propensity toward such behavior. According to most control perspectives, the most important factor in preventing or controlling this predisposition involves early parenting and building attachments or ties to prosocial aspects of the individual's environment.

According to the Maryland Report of "What Works" (see previous chapters), evidence consistently supports programs that involve long-term, frequent home visitation combined with preschool as well as family therapy by clinical staff for at-risk youth.[99] Furthermore, the Maryland Report stressed the success of school programs that aim to clarify and communicate norms for various behaviors by establishing school rules and consistently enforcing them through positive reinforcement and schoolwide campaigns.[100] Other effective school programs focus on various competency skills, such as developing self-control, stress management, responsible decision making, problem solving, and communication skills.[101] On the other hand, the Maryland Report noted some school programs that do

---

[96]Van Voorhis and Salisbury, *Correctional Counseling.*

[97]Ibid.

[98]Ibid. See also reviews of such programs in Richard J. Lundman, *Prevention and Control of Juvenile Delinquency* (New York: Oxford University Press, 1993); and Akers and Sellers, *Criminological Theories*, 101–8.

[99]Ibid.

[100]Ibid.

[101]Ibid.

not reduce delinquent behavior, such as those that counsel students in a peer-group context (see reasoning above), as well as substance use programs that simply rely on information dissemination or fear arousal (such as the traditional D.A.R.E. [Drug Abuse Resistance Education] program).[102]

Consistent with the Maryland Report, in a 2017 study that systematically reviewed the extant literature, David Weisburd and his colleagues claimed that there is "good evidence" for the effectiveness of programs designed to strengthen and restore positive social ties with at-risk youth.[103] These researchers also concluded that the most effective programs target specific risk factors and that the key mechanisms underlying effective programs across all dimensions are efforts to enhance supportive and informal social controls and reintegration into the community by repairing social bonds.[104]

Ultimately, programs that teach youths to develop cognitive or thinking skills are beneficial as opposed to those that simply focus on providing information about drugs or criminal offending. The bottom line for successful programs appears to be that they must instruct youths to deal with everyday influences in a healthy way (according to a cognitive behavioral model) as opposed to just giving them information about crime and drugs.

Thus, perhaps the most important policy recommendation is to increase the ties between early caregivers or parents and their children. A variety of programs try to increase the relationship and bonding that takes place between infants and young children and their parents as well as to monitor the supervision that takes place in this dynamic. Such programs have consistently been shown to be effective in preventing and reducing criminality in high-risk children, especially when such programs involve home visitations by health care providers (e.g., nurses) and social care experts (e.g., social workers).[105] By visiting the homes of high-risk children, workers can provide more direct, personal attention in aiding and counseling parents about how best to nurture, monitor, and discipline their young children.[106] These types of programs may lead to more control over behavior while building stronger bonds to society and developing self-control among these high-risk individuals.

Conclusion

In this chapter, we have discussed a wide range of theories that may appear to be quite different. However, all of the criminological theories here share an emphasis on social processes as the primary reason why individuals commit crime. This is true of the learning theories, which propose that people are taught to commit crime, as well as the control theories, which claim that people offend naturally and must be taught not to commit crime. Despite their seemingly opposite assumptions of human behavior, the fact is that learning and control theories both identify socialization, or the lack thereof, as the key cause of criminal behavior.

We also examined some of the key policy recommendations that have been suggested by both of these theoretical perspectives. Specifically, we noted that programs that simply group offenders together only seem to reinforce their tendency to offend, whereas programs that take a cognitive behavioral approach and use many reward opportunities appear to have some effect in reducing recidivism. Also, we concluded that programs that involve home visitations by experts (e.g., nurses, counselors) tend to aid in developing more effective parenting and building social bonds among young individuals, which helps them to build strong attachments to society and develop self-control.

---

[102]Ibid.

[103]David Weisburd, David P. Farrington, and Charlotte Gill, "What Works in Crime Prevention and Rehabilitation: An Assessment of Systematic Reviews," *Criminology & Public Policy* 16 (2017): 415–49.

[104]Ibid.

[105]Joycen Carmouche and Joretta Jones, "Her Children, Their Future," *Federal Prisons Journal* 1 (1989): 23, 26–27.

[106]For a review, see Stephen G. Tibbetts, "Perinatal and Developmental Determinants of Early Onset of Offending: A Two-Peak Model Approach," in *The Development of Persistent Criminality*, ed. Johanna Savage (New York: Oxford University Press, 2009), 179–201.

/// CHAPTER SUMMARY

- First, we discussed what distinguishes learning theories of crime from other perspectives.

- Then we reviewed Glaser's differential identification theory, which emphasizes the learning that takes place via reference groups or role models.

- We then discussed Sutherland's differential association theory and how this framework was improved by Akers's differential reinforcement theory.

- We examined in depth the psychological learning model of classical conditioning as well as its limitations.

- We then explored two other learning models that formed the basis of differential reinforcement theory—namely, operant conditioning and learning according to modeling and imitation.

- We reviewed the theory of neutralization, including the five original techniques of neutralization presented by Sykes and Matza.

- We also reviewed several early forms of social control theory, such as Hobbes's, Freud's, and Durkheim's.

- Then we examined the early social control theories of crime, presented by Reiss, Toby, and Nye along with Reckless's containment theory.

- We then examined more modern social control theories, such as Matza's drift theory and Hirschi's social bonding theory.

- Integrated social control theories were briefly examined, including Tittle's control–balance theory and Hagan's power–control theory.

- Finally, we reviewed low self-control theory from both a psychological and a physiological perspective.

/// KEY TERMS

classical conditioning 155

containment theory 171

control–balance theory 179

control theories 153

differential association theory 154

differential identification
  theory 157

differential reinforcement
  theory 158

drift theory 172

ego 168

id 167

learning theories 153

modeling and imitation 160

negative punishment 159

negative reinforcement 159

neutralization theory 163

operant conditioning 159

positive punishment 159

positive reinforcement 159

power–control theory 179

social bonding theory 174

soft determinism 173

stake in conformity 169

subterranean values 174

superego 167

tabula rasa 153

theory of low self-control 180

DISCUSSION QUESTIONS

1. What distinguishes learning theories from other criminological theories?

2. What distinguishes differential association from differential reinforcement theory?

3. What did differential identification add to learning theories?

4. Which technique of neutralization do you use or relate to the most? Why?

5. Which technique of neutralization do you find least valid? Why?

6. Which element of Hirschi's social bond do you find you have the highest levels of?

7. Which element of Hirschi's social bond do you find you have the lowest levels of?

8. Can you identify someone you know who fits the profile of a person with low self-control?

9. Which aspects of the low self-control personality do you think you fit?

10. Do you think Matza's theory of drift relates to when you or your friends have committed crime in life? Studies show that most people commit crimes or at least know people who do when they are in their teens or 20s (e.g., drinking under age 21, speeding).

WEB RESOURCES

Differential Association Theory

http://study.com/academy/lesson/differential-association-theory-definition-examples.html
https://www.d.umn.edu/~bmork/2306/Theories/BAMdiffassn.htm

Differential Reinforcement Theory

http://study.com/academy/lesson/differential-reinforcement-theory-definition-quiz.html
http://www.sociologyassignments.com/differential-association-theory-and-differential-reinforcement-theory-4795

Social and Self-Control Theory

http://study.com/academy/lesson/social-control-definition-theory-examples.html
http://forensicpsychology.umwblogs.org/organized-crime/the-social-control-theory
http://www.everydaysociologyblog.com/2008/11/gottfredson-and.html

Techniques of Neutralization

http://study.com/academy/lesson/five-techniques-of-neutralization.html
https://www.britannica.com/biography/Gresham-M-Sykes#ref940804

Social Reaction and Critical Models of Crime

T his chapter will discuss the evolution of social reaction and labeling theory, reviewing contributions made by early theorists as well as modern developments in this area. We will then discuss social conflict and reaction models of criminal behavior, emphasizing the foundational assumptions and principles of Karl Marx as well as the more criminological applications of Marxist and conflict theory by Willem Bonger, Austin Turk, George Vold, and others. During the 1960s and early 1970s, social reaction and labeling theories as well as various critical and conflict theories became popular. At the time, society was looking for theories that placed the blame for criminal offending on government authorities—either the police or societal institutions like economic or class structures. Here, we explore these various theories with a special emphasis on how they radically altered the way that crime and law were viewed as well as how these perspectives highly represented the overall climate in the United States at that time. Specifically, many groups of people—particularly the lower class, minorities, and women—were fighting for their rights during this period, and this manifested itself in criminological theory and research.

Labeling and Social Reaction Theory

Social reaction theory, otherwise referred to as **labeling theory**, is primarily concerned with how individuals' personal identities are highly influenced by the way that society or authorities tend to categorize them as offenders. With such categorization or labeling, an offender becomes a self-fulfilling prophecy, from this perspective, and results in individuals confirming their status as criminals or delinquents by increasing the frequency or seriousness of their illegal activity. Furthermore, this perspective assumes that there is a tendency to put negative labels on lower-class individuals or minorities as offenders significantly more often than on middle- or upper-class White people.[1]

   This perspective assumes that people who are labeled offenders have virtually no choice but to conform to the role that they have been "assigned" by society. Thus, social reaction theory claims that recidivism can be reduced by limiting stigmatization by authorities (e.g., law enforcement) and society. This is referred to as the *hands-off policy*,

---

[1]Thomas J. Bernard, Jeffrey B. Snipes, and Alexander L. Gerould, *Vold's Theoretical Criminology*, 6th ed. (Oxford: Oxford University Press, 2010) (see chap. 2).

and it became very popular in the 1960s and early 1970s.[2] Policies that became popular during this period were diversion, decriminalization, and deinstitutionalization (known as the *Ds*). All of these attempted to get youthful or first-time offenders out of the formal justice system as soon as possible to avoid stigmatizing or labeling them as offenders. Today, these very policies have led critics to dismiss labeling theory by claiming that it promotes lenient and ineffective sentencing.[3]

Labeling theory was based on seminal work by George Mead and Charles Cooley, which emphasized the importance of the extreme ways that individuals react to and are influenced by the social reaction to their roles and behavior. Mead, who was a member of the Chicago School (see Chapter 7), said that a person's sense of self is constantly constructed and reconstructed through the various social interactions a person has on a daily basis.[4] Every person is constantly aware of how she or he is judged by others through social interactions.

Readers can probably relate to this in the sense that they have experienced how differently they are treated in stores or restaurants if they are dressed nicely as opposed to being less well dressed; as you have observed, there is a significant difference in the way one is treated. Also, when growing up, you probably heard your parents or guardians warn that you should not hang out with Johnny or Sally because they were "bad" kids. Or perhaps you were a Johnny or Sally at some point. Either way, you can see how certain individuals can be labeled by authorities or society and then ostracized by mainstream groups. This can lead to isolation and typically results in a person having only other bad kids or adults to hang out with. This results in a type of feedback system in which the person begins associating with others who will only increase their propensity for illegal activity.[5]

Many strain theorists claim that certain demographic factors, such as social class or the neighborhood where a certain offense took place, may make it more likely that the offender will be caught and labeled by authorities. This claim is quite likely to be true, especially given recent policing strategies that target areas or neighborhoods that have high rates of crime. This is the side of social reaction and labeling theory that deals with the disproportionate rate at which members of the lower class and minorities are labeled as offenders.

Some of the earliest labeling theorists laid the groundwork for this perspective long before it became popular in the 1960s. For example, in the 1930s, Frank Tannenbaum noted the **dramatization of evil** that occurred when youth were arrested and charged with their first offense.[6] Later, other theorists such as Edwin Lemert contributed a highly important causal sequence to how labeling affects criminality among those who are labeled. Lemert said that individuals, typically youths, commit **primary deviance**, which is not serious (i.e., it is nonviolent) and not frequent, but they happen to be caught by police and are subsequently labeled.[7] The stigma of the label makes them think of themselves as offenders and forces them to associate only with other offenders. This results in what Lemert referred to as **secondary deviance** in which offending is more serious (often violent) and far more frequent. Thus, the causal model that Lemert describes is illustrated as follows:

Primary Deviance → Caught and Labeled → Secondary Deviance

[2]Edwin Schur, *Radical Nonintervention: Rethinking the Delinquency Problem* (Englewood Cliffs, NJ: Prentice Hall, 1973).

[3]Ronald L. Akers and Christine S. Sellers, *Criminological Theories: Introduction, Evaluation, and Application*, 6th ed. (Oxford: Oxford University Press, 2012) (see chap. 8).

[4]George H. Mead, *Mind, Self, and Society* (Chicago: University of Chicago, 1934).

[5]Howard S. Becker, *Outsiders: Studies in the Sociology of Deviance* (New York: Free Press, 1963).

[6]Frank Tannenbaum, *Crime and the Community* (Boston: Ginn, 1938).

[7]Edwin Lemert, *Human Deviance, Social Problems, and Social Control*, 2nd ed. (Englewood Cliffs, NJ: Prentice Hall, 1972).

According to Lemert's model, if the label or stigma is not placed on a young or first-time offender, then the more serious and more frequent offending of secondary deviance will not take place. Therefore, Lemert's model is highly consistent with the labeling approach's hands-off policies, such as diversion, decriminalization, and deinstitutionalization. If you ignore such behavior, Lemert reasoned, it will tend to go away. However, since the mid-1970s, the get-tough approach has become highly dominant, so such policies are not emphasized by society or policy makers today.

Research on labeling theory suffered a significant blow in the 1970s and 1980s when empirical findings consistently showed that formal arrests and sanctions did not tend to have results that supported traditional labeling theory.[8] In fact, most people who are arrested once are never arrested again, which tends to support deterrence theory and does not support labeling theory. In addition, some experts have concluded that "the preponderance of research finds no or very weak evidence of [formal] labeling effects. . . . The soundest conclusion is that official sanctions by themselves have neither strong deterrent nor a substantial labeling effect."[9] Furthermore, some theorists have questioned the basic assumptions of labeling theory, pointing out that the label does not cause the initial (or primary) offending and that labeling theorists largely ignore the issue of what is causing individuals to engage in illegal activity in the first place. Also, labeling theorists do not recognize the fact that offenders who are caught tend to be the ones who are committing more crimes than those who are not caught; in fact, there tends to be a strong relationship between being caught and committing multiple offenses.[10]

However, more contemporary research and theorizing have emphasized more informal forms of labeling, such as labeling by the community, parents, or friends. Studies have shown more support for the influence of this informal labeling on individuals' behavior.[11] After all, it only makes sense that informal labeling by people with whom you interact on a daily basis (i.e., parents, friends, neighbors, employers) will have more impact in terms of how you feel about yourself than labeling by police or other authorities, which tends to be temporary or situational.

▲ **Image 9.1** California Sociologist Dr. Edwin M. Lemert (1912–1996), key proponent of labeling theory, offered a better solution to help delinquents and claimed attempts to rehabilitate juvenile delinquents by putting them in large institutions have failed. He was a consultant to the President's Commission on Law Enforcement and Administration of Justice.

SOURCE: © Getty Images / Ed Maker / Contributor

Marxist Theories of Crime

Based on the writings of Marx, Marxist theories of crime focus on the fact that people from the lower classes (i.e., the poor) are arrested and charged with crimes at a disproportionate rate. Like conflict criminology, Marxist

[8]Marvin Wolfgang, Robert Figlio, and Thorsten Sellin, *Delinquency in a Birth Cohort* (Chicago: University of Chicago Press, 1972).

[9]Akers and Sellers, *Criminological Theories*, 142.

[10]Charles Wellford, "Labeling Theory and Criminology," *Social Problems* 22 (1975): 313–32.

[11]Lening Zhang, "Informal Reactions and Delinquency," *Criminal Justice and Behavior* 24 (1997): 129–50.

▲ **Image 9.2**   Karl Marx (1818–1883), German social theorist and revolutionary, who founded Marxism theory.

theories emphasize the effects of a capitalistic society on how justice is administered, describing how society is divided by money and power.[12] Marx said the law is the tool by which the **bourgeoisie** (the ruling class in a country without a ruling aristocracy, e.g., industrialists and financiers in Western industrialized countries) controls the lower classes (the **proletariat** and the lowest group, the *lumpenproletariat*) and keeps them in a disadvantaged position. In other words, the law is used as a mechanism by which the middle or upper class maintains its dominance over the lower classes. More specifically, Marx claimed that law is used as a tool to protect the economic interests and holdings of the bourgeoisie, as well as to prevent the lower classes from gaining access to financial resources.[13] Thus, Marxist theories propose that economic power can be translated into legal or political power and substantially accounts for the general disempowerment of the majority.

Willem Bonger

One early key theorist who applied Marxist theory to crime was Bonger, who emphasized the relationship between economy and crime but did not believe simply being poor would cause criminal activity. Rather, he thought crime came about because capitalism caused a difference in the way individuals felt about society and their place in it. In the early 1900s, Bonger said that the contemporary economic structure, particularly capitalism, was the cause of crime in the sense that it promoted a system based on selfishness and greed.[14] Such selfishness manifests itself in competition among individuals, which is obvious in interactions and dealings carried out for the purpose of obtaining goods and resources. This competition and selfishness led to more isolation, individualism, and egoistic tendencies, which promote a strong focus on self-interests at the expense of communitarianism and societal well-being. Bonger believed that this strong focus on the individual leads to criminal behavior.[15] He also stressed the association between social conditions (largely the result of economic systems) and criminal offending; because of cultural differences, crime can be a normal, adaptive response to social and economic problems, he argued. The poor often develop a strong feeling of injustice, which also contributes to their entering into illegal activity.[16]

Richard Quinney

Although Bonger's theory did not become popular in the early 1900s, when his book was originally published, his ideas received a lot of attention when a neo-Marxist period began in the early 1970s. This renewed interest in Marxist theory was coupled with harsh criticisms leveled at the existing theoretical frameworks, which is why

---

[12]Karl Marx, *Selected Works of Karl Marx and Frederick Engels* (Moscow: Foreign Languages Publishing House, 1962).

[13]Bernard et al., *Vold's Theoretical Criminology.*

[14]Willem Bonger, *Criminality and Economic Conditions* (1905; repr., Bloomington: Indiana University Press, 1969).

[15]Bernard et al., *Vold's Theoretical Criminology*; Akers and Sellers, *Criminological Theories.*

[16]Bonger, *Criminality and Economic Conditions.*

these neo-Marxist theories are often referred to as critical theories. This time, Marxist theories of crime became quite popular, largely because the social climate desired such perspectives. Whereas notable European theorists in this vein include Ian Taylor, Paul Walton, and Jock Young,[17] one of the key figures in this neo-Marxist perspective in the United States was Richard Quinney.[18]

Like Bonger, Quinney claimed that crime was caused by the capitalistic economic structure and the emphasis on materials that this system produced. One way that Quinney's theory goes beyond Bonger is that Quinney further proposed that even the crimes committed by the upper classes are caused by capitalism. To clarify, Quinney claimed that such acts are crimes of "domination and repression" committed by the elite to keep the lower classes down or to protect their property, wealth, and power.[19] A good example is white-collar crimes, which almost always involve raising profits or income, whether for individual or company advantage; such crimes often result in losses to the relatively lower-income clients or customers.

▲ **Image 9.3**   Richard Quinney, a renowned American sociologist who is best known for his philosophical and critical approach to crime and social justice.

SOURCE: Courtesy of Richard Quinney.

Evidence regarding Marxist Theories of Crime

Many critics noted that these seminal Marxist theories of crime were too simplistic as well as somewhat naive in the sense that they seemed to claim that the capitalistic economic system was the only reason for crime and that socialism or communism was the only sure way to reduce crime in the United States.[20] Now, even most Marxist theorists reject this proposition. Thus, more modern frameworks have been presented that place more emphasis on factors that stem from capitalism. For example, Mark Colvin and John Pauly presented a theoretical model that claims that delinquency and crime are the result of problematic parenting, which results from the degrading and manipulative treatment that parents of lower-class children get in the workplace.[21] However, the empirical tests of this more modern Marxist theory have demonstrated rather weak effects regarding the importance of capitalism (or parenting practices resulting from employment positions or social class).[22] Thus, there does not seem to be much empirical support for Marxist or neo-Marxist theories of crime, which is perhaps why this theoretical framework is not one of the primary models currently accepted by most criminologists.[23]

[17]Ian Taylor, Paul Walton, and Jock Young, *The New Criminology: For a Social Theory of Deviance* (New York: Harper & Row, 1973).

[18]Richard Quinney, *Critique of Legal Order: Crime Control in Capitalist Society* (Boston: Little, Brown, 1974).

[19]Quinney, *Critique of Legal Order*. See also Akers and Sellers, *Criminological Theories*, 224–26, for a discussion.

[20]For a discussion, see Akers and Sellers, *Criminological Theories*, 226–31.

[21]Mark Colvin and John Pauly, "A Critique of Criminology: Toward an Integrated Structural Marxist Theory of Delinquency Production," *American Journal of Sociology* 89 (1983): 513–51.

[22]See Sally Simpson and Lori Elis, "Is Gender Subordinate to Class? An Empirical Assessment of Colvin and Pauly's Structural Marxist Theory of Delinquency," *Journal of Criminal Law and Criminology* 85 (1994): 453–80. See further discussion in Akers and Sellers, *Criminological Theories*.

[23]Lee Ellis and Anthony Walsh, "Criminologists' Opinions about the Causes and Theories of Crime and Delinquency," *The Criminologist* 24 (1999): 1–4.

Conflict Theories of Crime

▲ **Image 9.4**   Thorsten Sellin (1896–1994) was a Swedish American sociologist at the University of Pennsylvania, a penologist, and one of the pioneers of scientific criminology, especially in the area of conflict and subcultural theory.

SOURCE: Courtesy of Thorsten Sellin

Conflict theories of crime assume that all societies are in a process of constant change and that this dynamic process inevitably creates conflicts among various groups.[24] Much of the conflict is due to the competition to have each group's interests promoted, protected, and often put into law. If all groups were equally powerful and had the same amount of resources, such battles would involve much negotiation and compromise; however, groups tend to differ significantly in the amount of power or resources that they have. Thus, laws can be created and enforced such that powerful groups can exert dominance over the weaker groups. So, as in Marxist theories, law is seen as a tool by which some groups gain and maintain dominance over less powerful groups. Furthermore, this state of inequality and resulting oppression creates a sense of injustice and unfairness among members of the less powerful groups, and such feelings are a primary cause of crime.[25]

There are several types of conflict theory, and fittingly, for this framework (as well as inherently supportive of the model), theorists of varying types often give scathing reviews of the other types of conflict theory. Marxist theories are one example. Critics have noted that many communistic countries (e.g., Cuba, Russia) have high rates of crime, whereas some countries that have capitalistic economic structures have very low crime rates, such as Sweden.

Another type of conflict theory is referred to as *pluralistic*; it argues that, instead of one or a few groups holding power over all the other groups, a multitude of groups must compete on a relatively fair playing field.[26] However, this latter type of conflict theory is not one of the more popular versions among critical theorists because it is sometimes seen as rather naive and idealistic.[27] Some of the key theorists in the **pluralistic (conflict) perspective** are Thorsten Sellin, Vold, and Turk.

Thorsten Sellin

Sellin applied Marxist and conflict perspectives, as well as numerous other types of models, to studying the state of cultural diversity in industrial societies. Sellin claimed that separate cultures will diverge from a unitary, mainstream set of norms and values held by the dominant group in society.[28] Thus, these minority groups that break off from the mainstream will establish their own norms. Furthermore, when laws are enacted, they will reflect only the values and interests of the dominant group, which causes what Sellin referred to as *border culture conflict*. This conflict of values, which manifests itself when different cultures interact, can cause a backlash by the weaker groups,

---

[24]William Chambliss and Robert Seidman, *Law, Order, and Power* (Reading, PA: Addison-Wesley, 1971).

[25]Bernard et al., *Vold's Theoretical Criminology.*

[26]Akers and Sellers, *Criminological Theories.*

[27]Quinney, *Critique of Legal Order.*

[28]Thorsten Sellin, *Culture Conflict and Crime* (New York: Social Science Research Council, 1938).

which tend to react defiantly or defensively. According to Sellin, the more unequal the balance of power, the worse the conflict tends to be.[29]

George Vold

Another key conflict theorist was Vold, who presented his model in his widely used textbook, *Theoretical Criminology*.[30] Vold claimed that people are naturally social and inevitably form groups out of shared needs, values, and interests. Because various groups compete with each other for power and to promote their values and interests, each group competes for control of political processes, including the power to create and enforce laws that can suppress the other groups. Some critics have argued that Vold put too much emphasis on the battle for creation of laws as opposed to the power to enforce laws.[31]

Austin Turk

Like the other conflict theorists, Turk assumed that the competition for power among various groups in society is the primary cause of crime.[32] Turk emphasized the idea that a certain level of conflict among groups can be very beneficial because it reminds citizens to consider whether the status quo or conventional standards can be improved. This type of idea is very similar to Émile Durkheim's proposition that a certain level of crime is healthy for society because it defines moral boundaries and sometimes leads to progress (see Chapter 6). Another aspect of Turk's theorizing, which separates him from other conflict theorists, is that he saw conflict among the various components of the criminal justice system. For example, the police often are at odds with the courts and district attorney's office. Such tension or conflict among formal agencies that should be on the same side of the playing field leads to even more frustration and inefficiency when it comes to fighting crime and ensuring that justice is served.

Case Study: Ted "the Unabomber" Kaczynski

Ted Kaczynski

In 1978, the explosion of what was considered a primitive homemade bomb sent to a Chicago university started Theodore Kaczynski's "reign of terror." Over the next 17 years, these bombs were either hand-delivered or mailed, resulting in three deaths and 24 injuries. In 1979, a Federal Bureau of Investigation (FBI) task force, including the Bureau of Alcohol, Tobacco, Firearms, and Explosives and the U.S. Postal Inspection Service, was formed to investigate what was designated as the UNABOM (university and airline bombing targets) case. This task force, which grew to more than 150 full-time investigators, analysts, and others, attempted to recover bomb components and examined the lives of the victims in an effort to identify the bomber.[33]

(Continued)

---

[29]Ibid.

[30]George Vold, *Theoretical Criminology* (New York: Oxford University Press, 1958).

[31]Akers and Sellers, *Criminological Theories.*

[32]Austin Turk, *Criminality and Legal Order* (Chicago: Rand McNally, 1969).

[33]"FBI 100: The Unabomber," FBI.gov, April 24, 2008, http://www.fbi.gov/news/stories/2008/april/unabomber_042408.

(Continued)

In 1995, the unidentified "Unabomber" sent the FBI a 35,000-word essay that explained, from his perspective, the reasons for these bombs as well as his views on the ills of modern society. The following is just one item among the 232 listed in the manifesto:

4. We therefore advocate a revolution against the industrial system. This revolution may or may not make use of violence; it may be sudden or it may be a relatively gradual process spanning a few decades. We can't predict any of that. But we do outline in a very general way the measures that those who hate the industrial system should take in order to prepare the way for a revolution against that form of society. This is not to be a POLITICAL revolution. Its object will be to overthrow not governments but the economic and technological basis of the present society.[34]

> *Its object will be to overthrow not governments but the economic and technological basis of the present society.*

▲ **Image 9.5**   Mug shot of Theodore "Ted" Kaczynski. Federal Bureau of Investigation.

SOURCE: Federal Bureau of Investigation, via Wikimedia Commons

FBI director Louis Freeh and Attorney General Janet Reno agreed with the task force's recommendation to publish the essay, hoping that a reader could identify the author. This manifesto was printed in the *Washington Post* and the *New York Times*.

While thousands of people offered various suspects, one stood out. In January 1996, in his family home in Illinois, David Kaczynski found papers, written by his brother Theodore (Ted), that contained Unabomber-like rhetoric. David Kaczynski notified the FBI. Linguistic analysis revealed that the author of these documents was most likely the author of the manifesto as well. On April 3, 1996, Ted Kaczynski was arrested in his remote mountain cabin in Stemple Pass, Montana. During the search of his cabin, investigators found a large number of bomb components, 40,000 handwritten journal pages, descriptions of Unabomber crimes, and one live bomb ready for mailing. Following his guilty plea in January of 1998, Ted Kaczynski was incarcerated in an isolated cell in a Colorado supermax prison.[35]

Think About It

1.   Are any features of this type of offense reflected in the various theories that have been discussed?

---

[34]See "The Unabomber Trial: The Manifesto," *Washington Post*, 1997, http://www.washingtonpost.com/wp-srv/national/longterm/unabomber/manifesto.text.htm.

[35]"FBI 100."

Evidence regarding Conflict Theories of Crime

Empirical tests of conflict theories are rare, likely because of the nature of the framework, which lends itself to a global view of societal structure and a perhaps infinite number of interest groups who are constantly in play for power.[36]

However, one notable study found evidence of a relationship between U.S. states that had large numbers of interest groups and violent crime but not property crime.[37] The authors concluded that these findings demonstrated the need for more discussion about how competitiveness in the United States affects criminal behavior, but no other studies have examined the influence of political interest groups on criminal behavior. It is rather difficult to test conflict theory in other ways. Perhaps conflict theory researchers should build an agenda of more rigorous ways to test the propositions of their theoretical perspective; as it stands, it remains quite vague. The few studies there are do not seem rigorous enough to persuade other criminologists or readers toward accepting the validity of this model.[38]

Despite the lack of empirical research supporting the conflict (and Marxist or critical) theories of crime, there is little doubt that such perspectives have contributed much to the theorizing and empirical studies of criminologists regarding this framework. In fact, the American Society of Criminology (ASC)—which is probably the largest and best-known professional society in the discipline—has a special division made up of experts devoted to this area of study. Thus, it is likely that theorizing and empirical research will be greatly enhanced in the near future. Furthermore, it is clear that criminologists have acknowledged the need to explore the various issues presented by the conflict and Marxist perspectives in research in criminal justice and offending.

Policy Implications

A variety of policy implications have come from the theoretical perspectives reviewed in this chapter. Regarding social reaction and labeling theory, several policies have evolved, known as the *Ds*: diversion, decriminalization, and deinstitutionalization. **Diversion**, which is now commonly used, involves trying to get cases out of the formal justice system as soon as possible. Courts try to get many juvenile cases and, in recent times, drug possession cases diverted to a less formal, more administrative process (e.g., drug courts, youth accountability boards or teams). Such diversion programs appear to have saved many billions of dollars, since the offenders would otherwise have been incarcerated, while providing a way for first-time or relatively nonserious offenders not to experience the stigmatizing effects of being incarcerated. Although empirical evaluations of such diversion programs are mixed and suffer from methodological problems (i.e., the individuals who volunteer or qualify for such programs are likely the better cases among the sample population), some studies have shown their potential promise.[39]

There have also been numerous examples of **decriminalization**, which refers to reducing the criminality of certain illegal activities. A good example is the legal approach to marijuana possession in California. Unlike other jurisdictions, California does not incarcerate individuals for possessing less than an ounce of marijuana; rather, they receive a citation, similar to a parking ticket. There are many other forms of decriminalization (which is distinguished from legalization, which makes an act completely legal and not subject to legal sanction). The purpose of decriminalization is to de-emphasize less dangerous crimes and decrease the resources devoted to offenders who pose less danger to society. In terms of social reaction and labeling theory, decriminalization also reduces the

---

[36]See discussion by Akers and Sellers, *Criminological Theories*, 210–12.

[37]Gregory G. Brunk and Laura A. Wilson, "Interest Groups and Criminal Behavior," *Journal of Research in Crime and Delinquency* 28 (1991): 157–73.

[38]Ellis and Walsh, "Criminologists' Opinions."

[39]For a review, see John Worrall, *Crime Control in America: What Works?* 2nd ed. (Boston: Allyn & Bacon, 2008): 228–29.

stigmatization of individuals who are relatively minor offenders but would likely become more serious offenders if they were incarcerated with more chronic offenders.

Another policy implication of this chapter is **deinstitutionalization**. In the early 1970s, federal laws were passed that ordered all youth status offenders to be removed from incarceration facilities. This has not been accomplished; some are still being placed in such facilities. However, the number and rate of status offenders being placed in incarceration facilities has declined, avoiding any further stigmatization and integration into further criminality. Overall, this deinstitutionalization has kept relatively minor, often first-time offenders from experiencing the ordeals of incarceration.

Additional policy implications that can be inferred from this chapter involve providing more economic and employment opportunities to those who do not typically have access to such options. From a historical perspective, such as the New Deal, which was meant to deal with the effects of the Great Depression of the 1930s, providing more employment opportunities can greatly enhance the well-being of the population, and in that period, there was a very significant decrease in crime and homicide rates (see Chapter 1). Today, perhaps nothing could be more important in our nation than creating jobs; the ability to do this will largely determine future crime rates.

The bulk of policies that have been derived from conflict theories have emphasized attempting to make laws, enforcement, and processing through the justice system more equitable in terms of social class. For example, the federal sentencing guidelines were recently reviewed for drug possession because it became clear that they were unfair in how they punished drug possession offenders. Specifically, according to the 1980s guidelines, possession of an ounce of crack cocaine earned a defendant a sentence 100 times longer than an offender who possessed an ounce of powder cocaine. Not surprisingly, crack cocaine is typically used and sold by lower-class minorities, whereas cocaine powder is typically used and sold by upper- or middle-class Whites. The disparity in this form of sentencing, which clearly penalizes a certain group of people more than another, has recently become a target for reform by the Obama administration, so there are current efforts to address this issue. This is just one example of how laws and processing are significantly disproportionate in the sense that certain groups (typically lower-class minorities) are arrested, punished, and locked up far more than well-to-do offenders. Studies showing higher conviction rates and longer sentences for offenders who must rely on public defenders to represent them consistently support the high degree of disparities in the criminal justice system, which policies derived from conflict theory attempt to address.

Recently, these hands-off policies have been less attractive to authorities and politicians who want to be seen as hard on criminal offenders so they will be elected or retained in office. Still, due to recent economic crises in many state and local communities, it is likely that many jurisdictions will reconsider these approaches and find alternative strategies for dealing with nonviolent offenders.

Conclusion

This chapter examined the theories that place responsibility for individuals' criminal behavior on societal factors, particularly factors that are unjust or discriminatory. Specifically, this chapter discussed theories of social reaction or labeling as well as critical perspectives of criminal behavior. All of these theories have a common theme: They emphasize the use of legal or criminal justice systems to target or label certain groups of people (the poor, women, etc.) as criminals while protecting the interests of those who have power (typically White males). Given the evidence discussed here, you will have enough evidence to make objective conclusions about whether this perspective is valid as well as which aspects of these theories are more supported by empirical research and which are more in question.

We also examined Marxist perspectives of society as explanations of crime. Other theories were examined that are similar to Marxist theory but also include other types of group conflict than those just based on economic factors, such as cultural and political. Most of these latter types of group conflict theories claim that there are a multitude of groups constantly competing for power and influence over the other groups, especially by trying to enact or enforce laws favorable to their group.

//// CHAPTER SUMMARY

- First, we explored the basic assumptions of social reaction and labeling theory.

- We then reviewed the primary theoretical concepts and propositions of labeling theory, especially the importance of distinguishing primary deviance from secondary deviance.

- We discussed the current state of labeling theory, which emphasizes informal sources of social reaction, not just the formal sources as in traditional models.

- Then we examined Marx's perspective on reasons for class conflict, particularly the conflict between the bourgeoisie and the proletariat.

- We then discussed numerous subsequent versions of Marxist theory that attempted to directly explain crime.

- One of these was developed by Bonger, who claimed that the contemporary economic structure, particularly capitalism, was the cause of crime in the sense that it promoted a system based on selfishness, individualism, and greed rather than more communitarian values and goals.

- Another Marxist perspective of crime was presented by Quinney, who went a bit further than Bonger in proposing that even the crimes committed by the upper classes are caused by capitalism, such as crimes of "domination and repression" committed by the elite to keep the lower classes down or to protect their property, wealth, and power.

- We also examined conflict theories that were not based only on Marxist principles or limited to economic factors but rather emphasize that there are multiple groups that are constantly competing for influence and power, which results in crime.

- One key culture conflict theory was proposed by Sellin, who claimed that when laws are enacted, they will reflect only the cultural values and interests of the dominant group, which can cause a backlash by the weaker groups that tend to react defiantly or defensively.

- Vold presented a theory that various groups compete with each other for power and to promote their values and interests via control of political processes and enacting laws that can suppress the other groups.

- Also, Turk proposed a theory that emphasized the idea that a certain level of conflict among groups can be very beneficial because it reminds citizens to consider whether the status quo or conventional standards can be improved and also applied group conflict to the various agencies in the criminal justice system.

//// KEY TERMS

bourgeoisie 190

decriminalization 195

deinstitutionalization 196

diversion 195

dramatization of evil 188

labeling theory 187

pluralistic (conflict)
    perspective 192

primary deviance 188

proletariat 190

secondary deviance 188

DISCUSSION QUESTIONS

1. What are the major assumptions of labeling and social reaction theory, and how do they differ significantly from other traditional theories of crime?

2. According to Lemert, what is the difference between primary deviance and secondary deviance?

3. How can you relate personally to being labeled, even if not for offending?

4. How do Marx's ideas relate to the study of crime? Provide some examples.

5. Which conflict theory do you buy into the most? The least? Why?

WEB RESOURCES

Conflict Theories

https://www.khanacademy.org/test-prep/mcat/society-and-culture/social-structures/v/conflict-theory
https://www.thoughtco.com/conflict-theory-3026622
http://study.com/academy/lesson/social-conflict-theory-in-sociology-definition-lesson-quiz.html

Labeling Theory

http://study.com/academy/lesson/labeling-theory-of-deviance-definition-examples-quiz.html
https://www.thoughtco.com/labeling-theory-3026627
https://www.youtube.com/watch?v=lrQ454s0mgo

Marxist Theory

http://law.jrank.org/pages/819/Crime-Causation-Sociological-Theories-Critical-theories.html
http://www.allaboutphilosophy.org/what-is-marxism-faq.htm
https://www.nyu.edu/projects/ollman/docs/what_is_marxism.php

CHAPTER 10

Feminist Models of Crime

I n this chapter, we will examine the importance of feminist perspectives of crime. Feminist criminology evolved when various assumptions and stereotypes about women in criminal justice were being questioned. Such questions included women as both offenders and victims. It is important to note up front that there is no single feminist perspective, and they often seem to be at odds with each other. However, the overall goal of this perspective is agreed on: to further advance the importance of understanding and furthering research regarding females in the realm of crime and criminal justice. After all, given that far fewer females commit serious violence than males, if we could better explain why women have much lower rates of criminality, then perhaps we could apply this in order to significantly reduce male offending. We will also review feminist critiques of previous research as well as policy implications of feminist perspectives of crime.

Feminist Theories of Crime

About the same time that Marxist theories of crime were becoming popular in the early 1970s, the feminist perspective began to receive attention; this was a key period in the women's rights movement. The Feminist School of criminology began largely as a reaction to the lack of rational theorizing about why females commit crime and why they tend to be treated far differently by the criminal justice system.[1] Prior to the 1970s, theories of why girls and women engage in illegal activities were primarily based on false stereotypes.

Key Terms in the Feminist Perspective

Before discussing the various feminist perspectives, it is essential for readers to appreciate key terms associated with these perspectives. A few of these key terms are *chivalry*, *paternalism*, and *patriarchy*.

Chivalry pertains to behaviors and attitudes toward certain individuals that treat them as though they are on a pedestal.[2] Chivalrous behavior is more complex than just preferential treatment. Engaging in a chivalrous relationship usually entails a bartering system in which men hold a more powerful status than do women. Social class

---

[1]Meda Chesney-Lind and Lisa Pasko, *The Female Offender: Girls, Women, and Crime* (Thousand Oaks, CA: Sage, 2004).

[2]Joanne Belknap, *The Invisible Woman: Gender, Crime, and Justice*, 3rd ed. (Belmont, CA: Wadsworth, 2007), 150–51; Elizabeth F. Moulds, "Chivalry and Paternalism: Disparities of Treatment in the Criminal Justice System," in *Women, Crime, and Justice*, ed. Susan K. Datesman and Frank R. Scarpitti (New York: Oxford University Press, 1980), 279.

and race or ethnicity are also intertwined with such treatment. Women of certain social classes and racial or ethnic backgrounds are considered more worthy of chivalrous treatment than other women. This is best illustrated by Sojourner Truth's speech "Ain't I a Woman?" The idea of **paternalism** denotes that women need to be protected for their own good. In a broader social context, paternalism implies independence for men and dependence for women. Both chivalry and paternalism suggest that certain individuals or groups need protection because they are weak and helpless. This protection can also lead to various types of control.

The Latin word *pater* refers to the social role of a father as opposed to the biological role of a father. Patriarchal societies exclude women from the exercise of political responsibilities; **patriarchy** refers to the subordinate role of women and male dominance.[3] Thus, patriarchy is a social, legal, and political climate based on male dominance and hierarchy. A key aspect to this ideology is that women's nature is biologically, not culturally, determined.[4]

Key Issues in Research on Gender Differences in Offending

Much of the attention of theorists in the feminist area can be broken into two categories: the *gender ratio* issue and the *generalizability* issue. The gender ratio issue refers to theorizing and research that examines why females so often commit less serious, less violent offenses than males. Some experts feel that this does not matter; however, if we understood why females commit far less violence, then perhaps we could apply such knowledge to reducing male offending.[5] The generalizability argument is consistent with the ideas some have about the gender ratio issue; specifically, many of the same critics argue that theorists should simply take the findings found for male offending and generalize them to females. However, given the numerous differences found between males and females in what predicts their offending patterns, simply generalizing across gender is not a wise thing to do.[6] It is far more complicated than that.

Another important issue in feminist research on crime is that women today have more freedom and rights than those in past generations. Seminal theories of female crime in the 1970s predicted that this would result in far higher offending rates for women.[7] However, this has not been seen in serious, violent crimes. Rather, increases have been observed in property and public order crimes, but they are typically committed by girls or women who have not benefited from such freedom and rights—for example, those who do not have much education, are poor, or who lack strong employment records.

Types of Feminism

Also, there are numerous forms of feminism and, thus, many types of feminist theories of crime, as pointed out by Daly and Chesney-Lind.[8] One of the earliest was **liberal feminism**, which assumed that differences between males and females in offending were due to the lack of opportunities for females in education and employment and that, as more females were given such opportunities, they would come to resemble males in terms of offending. Liberal

---

[3]Janet K. Boles and Diane Long Hoeveler, *Historical Dictionary of Feminism* (Lanham, MD: Scarecrow Press, 2004), 253.

[4]Belknap, *The Invisible Woman*, 10; see also Anne Edwards, "Male Violence in Feminist Theory: An Analysis of the Changing Conception of Sex/Gender Violence and Male Dominance," in *Women, Violence, and Social Control*, ed. Jalna Hanmer and Mary Maynard (Atlantic Highlands, NJ: Humanities Press International, 1987), 13–29.

[5]For a discussion, see Stephen Tibbetts and Denise Herz, "Gender Differences in Factors of Social Control and Rational Choice," *Deviant Behavior* 17 (1996): 183–208.

[6]Tibbetts and Herz, "Gender Differences."

[7]Freda Adler, *Sisters in Crime: The Rise of the New Female Criminal* (New York: McGraw-Hill, 1975).

[8]Kathleen Daly and Meda Chesney-Lind, "Feminism and Criminology," *Justice Quarterly* 5 (1988): 536–58.

feminism, also termed *mainstream feminism*, is founded on political liberalism, which holds a positive view of human nature as well as the ideals of liberty, equality, justice, dignity, and individual rights. A major feature of liberal feminism is that women should receive the same rights and treatment as men.[9] This perspective purports that gender inequality is due to women's blocked opportunities to participate in various aspects of the public sphere, such as education, employment, and political activity.[10] Strategies for social change are devised to free women from oppressive gender roles—for instance, performing only those jobs associated with the traditional feminine personality (e.g., nursing, teaching, child care).[11]

There are generally two types of liberal feminists: classical and welfare. Both approaches rely a great deal on legal remedies to address gender inequality. Classical liberal feminists support limited government and a free market as well as political and legal rights. Central facets of this approach are freedom of expression, religion, and conscience. Welfare liberal feminists favor government involvement in providing citizens, particularly underprivileged individuals, with housing, education, health care, and social security. They also maintain that the market should be limited through significant taxes and restricting profits.[12]

A major criticism of the liberal feminist perspective is that it primarily focuses "on the interests of white, middle-class, heterosexual women."[13] Specifically, within the area of feminist criminology, some argue that the liberal perspective poses "men as the criminal yardstick." This results in equating justice with equality and not considering other influential standpoints such as race/ethnicity and social class.[14] Joanne Belknap maintains this:

> Prison reform for women would not be nearly as effective in achieving equality with men's prisons if the only goal was to allow the same access to health care, vocational, educational, legal, and treatment programs. While these would be significant advances, it is also necessary to request reforms that address women prisoners' experiences, needs, and histories that differ from male prisoners.[15]

Another area where the "equal treatment" doctrine is problematic is in sentencing. Specifically, sentencing reforms aimed at reducing race- and class-based disparities in sentencing for male offenders "may yield equality with a vengeance" for female offenders.[16] Thus, "equality defined as equal treatment of men and women . . . forestalls more fundamental change and in some instances may worsen women's circumstances."[17]

Another major feminist perspective of crime is **critical feminism** or **radical feminism**, which emphasizes the idea that many societies (such as the United States) are based on a structure of patriarchy wherein males dominate virtually every aspect of society, including politics, family structure, and the economy. Radical feminism evolved from the women's liberation movement of the 1960s. This perspective emphasizes the importance of personal feelings, experiences, and relationships. Gender is a system of male dominance, and women's biology is the main cause of patriarchy.[18]

---

[9]Boles and Hoeveler, *Historical Dictionary of Feminism*, 192.

[10]Daly and Chesney-Lind, "Feminism and Criminology," 537.

[11]Rosemarie Tong, *Feminist Thought: A More Comprehensive Introduction*, 3rd ed. (Boulder, CO: Westview Press, 2009), 34.

[12]Ibid., 35.

[13]Ibid., 43.

[14]Dana M. Britton, "Feminism in Criminology: Engendering the Outlaw," *Annals of the American Academy of Political and Social Science* 571 (2000): 57–76.

[15]Belknap, *The Invisible Woman*, 13.

[16]Daly and Chesney-Lind, "Feminism and Criminology," 525.

[17]Ibid., 526.

[18]Boles and Hoeveler, *Historical Dictionary of Feminism*, 270–71.

▲ **Image 10.1**   Female gang member.

SOURCE: © istockphoto.com / Bluberries

The cause of gender inequality, according to this perspective, is based on men's need or desire to control women's sexuality and reproductive potential. Further, the process of gender formation is founded on the power relations between men and women wherein boys and men view themselves as superior to and having a right to control girls and women. These relations are further intensified through heterosexual sexuality, as defined by men.[19]

Radical feminists maintain, in principle, that sexism is the first, most widespread form of human oppression. They do not, however, agree on the nature or function of this sexism or on what strategies are needed for social change. Rosemarie Tong identified two types of radical feminism: libertarian and cultural.[20] Radical-libertarian feminists assert that an exclusively feminine gender identity will most often limit a woman's development as a full human person. They encourage women to become androgynous individuals who embody both (good) masculine and (good) feminine characteristics. Radical-cultural feminists argue that women should be strictly female or feminine. They should not try to be like men. Women should emphasize such values and virtues as interdependence, community, connection, sharing, emotion, body, trust, absence of hierarchy, nature, immanence, process, joy, peace, and life. Alternatively, women should not emphasize such values as independence, autonomy, intellect, will, wariness, hierarchy, domination, culture, transcendence, product, asceticism, war, and death.

Tong noted that this distinction, while not perfect, does the following:

[It] helps explain not only why some radical feminists embrace the concept of androgyny and others eschew it, but also why some radical feminists view both sex and reproduction as oppressive, even dangerous for women and why others view these aspects as liberating, even empowering for women. . . . *Radical feminists are not afraid to take exception to each other's views* [emphasis added].[21]

Suggested strategies for social change among some radical feminists include overthrowing patriarchal relations, developing methods of biological reproduction to permit women's sexual autonomy, and establishing women-centered social institutions and women-only organizations. Other radical feminists celebrate gender differences, particularly women's special capacities or talents; however, these feminists do not pose gender differences in the framework of power relations.[22]

One of the criticisms of radical-libertarian and radical-cultural feminism is that they need to reconcile the split between themselves in an effort to avoid polarization, particularly in the area of sexuality. Even though radical-libertarian feminists are hesitant about consensual heterosexuality, they maintain that these relationships can be pleasurable for women. Radical-cultural feminists warn against the dangers of heterosexuality and have implied that there is no such thing as consensual heterosexuality. Thus, according to this view, "only lesbians are capable of

[19]Daly and Chesney-Lind, "Feminism and Criminology," 538.

[20]Tong, *Feminist Thought*, 48–51.

[21]Ibid., 51.

[22]Daly and Chesney-Lind, "Feminism and Criminology," 538.

consensual sex in a patriarchal society."[23] Citing Ann Ferguson, a socialist feminist, Tong noted that there is no one universal "function" for human sexuality.[24]

It is hard to contest the primary assumption of this theory. Despite the fact that more women than ever hold professional, white-collar jobs, men still get paid a significant amount more than women for the same positions, on average. Furthermore, the U.S. Senate and House of Representatives—and other high political offices, such as president, vice president, cabinet posts, and U.S. Supreme Court justices—are still held primarily (or exclusively) by men. So the United States, like most other countries in the world, appears to be based in patriarchy.

The extent to which this model explains female criminality, however, remains to be seen. Regarding serious crimes, it is not clear why this perspective would expect higher or lower rates of female criminal behavior. Regarding some delinquent offenses, it may partially explain the greater tendency to arrest females. For example, virtually every self-report study ever conducted shows that males run away far more than females; however, Federal Bureau of Investigation (FBI) data show that female juveniles are arrested for running away far more often than males. Critical feminism may provide the best explanation for this difference. Females are more protected—that is, reported and arrested for running away—because they are considered to be more like property in our patriarchal society. This is just one explanation, but it appears to be somewhat valid.

Similar to critical or radical feminism is **Marxist feminism**, which emphasizes men's ownership and control of the means of economic production, thus focusing solely on the economic structure. Marxist feminists point out that men control economic success in our country—as well as in virtually every country in the world—and that this flows from capitalism. One of the primary assumptions of capitalism is *survival of the fittest* or *the best person for the job*, which would seem to favor women. Studies have found that women in the United States do far better, despite our capitalistic system, than those in most other countries. Furthermore, women in countries based on Marxism have a less favorable lifestyle and are no better off economically than those in the United States. Whether or not one believes in a Marxist economic structure, it does not readily explain female criminality.

Another feminist perspective is that of **socialist feminism**, which moved away from focusing on economic structure (e.g., Marxism) as the primary detriment for females and instead emphasized control of reproductive systems. This model believes that women should take control of their own bodies and their reproductive functions in order to control their criminality. It is not entirely clear how females' taking charge of their reproductive destinies can increase or reduce their crime rates. Although no one can deny that data show that females who reproduce frequently, especially in inner-city, poor environments, tend to offend more often than other females, it appears that other factors mediate these effects. Women who want good futures tend to take more precautions against becoming pregnant; on the other hand, the very females who most need to take precautions against getting pregnant are the least likely to do so, despite the availability of numerous forms of contraception. This is one of the many paradoxes in our field. It is unclear how much socialist feminism has contributed to an understanding of female criminality.

Some scholars maintain that while it is possible to distinguish between Marxist feminism and socialist feminism, it is difficult, particularly because these two perspectives' differences are more an issue of emphasis than of substance.[25] Marxist feminism places gender in the context of production methods. The burdens of physical and social reproduction in the home are operated and reinforced in a male-dominated economic and political order.[26] The causes of gender inequality are due to hierarchical relations of control with the increase of private property

---

[23]Tong, *Feminist Thought*, 92–93; see also Ann Ferguson, "Sex War: The Debate between Radical and Libertarian Feminists," *Signs: The Journal of Women in Culture and Society* 10 (1984): 106–12.

[24]Tong, *Feminist Thought*, 93.

[25]Ibid., 96.

[26]Boles and Hoeveler, *Historical Dictionary of Feminism*, 204–5.

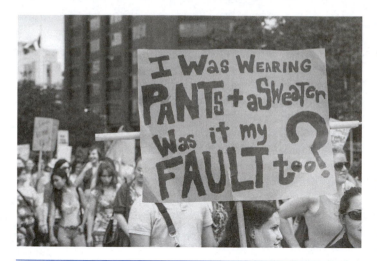

▲ **Image 10.2** Feminist protests and influence have done much to alter how females are viewed and valued in our traditional patriarchal society as well as in most other developed countries around the world.

SOURCE: © istockphoto.com / Jen Grantham

and ownership among men. Class relations are primary, and gender relations are secondary.[27] An insightful example of such gender and class relations is housework. Traditionally, housework has been delegated to women; however, housework does not produce surplus value or profit. Thus, some do not consider this labor. Jenny van Hooff conducted semistructured interviews to examine dual-career heterosexual couples' explanations and justifications for the division of housework that followed more traditional gender roles. Marxist feminism focuses essentially on work-related inequalities as well as enhancing our understanding of the trivialization of women's work in the home (e.g., raising children, doing housework) and the tedious, poorly paid jobs predominately occupied by women.[28] The General Social Survey reveals that when asking males and females regarding their perceptions as to who does most of the cleaning in the household, there is an overwhelming response of either "always female" or "usually female."

Socialist feminism attempts to synthesize radical and Marxist feminism. This perspective attempts to integrate concepts such as male domination and political–economic relations. Social feminists focus on gender, class, and racial relations of domination. They differ from Marxist feminists in that both class and gender relations are deemed primary.[29] Within the socialist feminism perspective, there are two general themes: (1) two-system explanations of women's oppression and (2) interactive-system explanations of women's oppression. Under the two-system explanations, these emphases are less committed to the Marxist-founded framework. Rather, they maintain that patriarchy, not capitalism, may be women's ultimate worst enemy.[30] The interactive-system explanations attempt to illustrate that both capitalism and patriarchy are equal contributors to women's oppression; they are interdependent. These feminists use terms such as *capitalist patriarchy* or *patriarchal capitalism*.[31]

An additional perspective of feminist criminology is that of **postmodern feminism**, which holds that an understanding of women as a group, even by other women, is impossible because every person's experience is unique. If this is true, we should give up discussing female criminal theory and theories of criminality in general—along with all studies of medicine, astronomy, psychology, and so on—because every person interprets each observation

---

[27]Daly and Chesney-Lind, "Feminism and Criminology," 537.

[28]Belknap, *The Invisible Woman*, 13; see also Sandra Harding, "Can Men Be Subjects of Feminist Thought?," in *Feminist Perspectives on Social Research*, ed. Sharlene Hesse-Biber and Michelle Y. Yaiser (New York: Oxford University Press, 2004); Heidi I. Hartmann, "The Family as the Locus of Gender, Class, and Political Struggle: The Example of Housework," in *Feminism and Methodology*, ed. Sandra Harding (Bloomington: Indiana University Press, 1987), 109–134.

[29]Belknap, *The Invisible Woman*, 538.

[30]Tong, *Feminist Thought*, 111.

[31]Ibid., 115.

subjectively. This perspective rejects the traditional assumptions about truth and reality; the emphasis is more on the plurality, diversity, and multiplicity of women as distinct from men.[32] Tong argued that the relationship between postmodernists and feminists is "uneasy."[33] For instance, similar to all postmodernists, postmodern feminists reject ideas centered on an absolute world that is "male" in style (i.e., phallogocentric). They also reject any attempts to provide a single explanation or steps women must take to achieve liberation (i.e., a feminist "to-do list"). Those who identify themselves as postmodern feminists "invite each woman who reflects on their writings to become the kind of feminist she wants to be. There is, in their estimation, no single formula for being a 'good feminist.'"[34] The bottom line is that, according to postmodern feminists, there is no point in measuring anything. Thus, this model is based on anti-science and has contributed very little to the study of understanding or explaining female criminality or gaining some useful information about females as victims.

In all these variations of feminist perspectives, it is interesting that little emphasis is placed on parental differences in how children are disciplined and raised. Studies have clearly and consistently shown that parents, often without realizing it, tend to globally reward young boys for completing a task (e.g., "You are such a good boy"), whereas they tend to tell a young girl that she did a good job. On the other hand, when young boys do not successfully complete a task, most parents tend to excuse the failure (e.g., "It was a hard thing to do; don't worry"), whereas for young girls, the parents will often globally evaluate them for the task (e.g., "Why couldn't you do it?").[35] Although numerous psychological studies have found this tendency, it has yet to make it into the mainstream criminological theories of crime.

Case Study: Gertrude Baniszewski

When the police arrived at the home of Gertrude Baniszewski in October 1965, they found the lifeless body of 16-year-old Sylvia Likens. Sylvia's parents had found employment as carnival workers. This required them to move around, so Gertrude Baniszewski agreed to board Sylvia and her sister Jenny for $20 a week. When one of the checks arrived late, Baniszewski lashed out at the two girls. This was followed by 3 weeks of violent and sadistic attacks, especially on Sylvia. A number of Baniszewski's seven children, along with some neighborhood children, watched or actually joined in the torture. This was all done under the supervision of Baniszewski. No one reported the abuse.[36]

Sylvia's emaciated corpse was covered with more than 150 wounds ranging from burns to cuts. Sylvia was burned with cigarettes numerous times, was forced to dance naked in front of the other children, took

Do we as a society perceive such offenses committed by a mother differently than similar offenses committed by a father?

(Continued)

[32]Boles and Hoeveler, *Historical Dictionary of Feminism*, 262–63.

[33]Tong, *Feminist Thought*; see also Toril Moi, *Sexual/Textual Politics* (London: Methuen, 1985).

[34]Tong, *Feminist Thought*, 270.

[35]June Price Tangney and Kurt W. Fischer, *Self-Conscious Emotions: The Psychology of Shame, Guilt, Embarrassment, and Pride* (New York: Guilford Press, 1995).

[36]Sam Stall, "Looking Back on Indiana's Most Infamous Crime, 50 Years Later," *Indianapolis Monthly*, October 21, 2015, http://www.indianapolismonthly.com/features/looking-back-indianas-infamous-crime-50-years-later.

(Continued)

▲ **Image 10.3**   A 1965 photograph of Sylvia Likens.

baths in scalding water, and was constantly beaten and starved. On one horrible night, Baniszewski took a sewing needle and carved an "I" in Sylvia's abdomen. She then gave the needle to a neighbor boy and instructed him to spell the word *prostitute.*

After this incident, Sylvia was dead, and Baniszewski was arrested along with eight youthful offenders ranging in age from 11 to 17 years. The children stated that they participated in the torture of Sylvia because "Gertie" told them to. In 1966, Gertrude Baniszewski was convicted of first-degree murder; her daughter, Paula, was convicted of second-degree murder; and the remaining offenders were found guilty of lesser homicide charges.[37]

Think About It

1. After reading this case, one may ask, How could a mother do that to another child? How could a mother ask her children to engage in torturing another child? Do we as a society perceive such offenses committed by a mother differently than similar offenses committed by a father?

2. If so, we need to explore how gender influences our attitudes about criminal behavior as well as criminal offenders.

Evidence regarding Feminist Theories of Crime

As discussed previously, there is no doubt that female offenders were highly neglected by traditional models of criminological theory, and given that females make up at least 50% of the population of the world, it is important that they be covered and explained by such theories. Furthermore, we also discussed the fact that if we knew why females everywhere commit far less violence than men, it would likely go a long way toward devising policies to reduce the extremely higher rates of violence among males. However, in other ways, the feminist theories of crime have not been supported.

For instance, as noted previously, the seminal feminist crime theories specifically proposed that, as women became liberated, their rates of crime would become consistent with the rates of male offending.[38] Not only did this fail to occur, but the evidence actually supports the opposite trend; specifically, the females who were given the most opportunities (e.g., education, employment, status) were the *least* likely to offend, whereas the women who were not liberated or given such opportunities were the *most* likely to engage in criminal behavior.[39]

---

[37]Mara Bovsun, "Teen Girl Fatally Bullied in Indiana House of Horrors," *New York Daily News*, April 6, 2013, http://www.nydailynews.com/news/justice-story/teen-girl-fatally-bullied-indiana-house-horrors-article-1.1309751.

[38]Adler, *Sisters in Crime.*

[39]For a discussion, see Ronald L. Akers and Christine S. Sellers, *Criminological Theories: Introduction, Evaluation, and Application*, 6th ed. (Oxford: Oxford University Press, 2012). See also the discussion in Thomas J. Bernard, Jeffrey B. Snipes, and Alexander L. Gerould, *Vold's Theoretical Criminology*, 6th ed. (Oxford: Oxford University Press, 2010), 117–22 (see chap. 1).

On the other hand, one major strength of feminist theories of crime is that they have led to a number of studies showing that the factors causing crime in males are different than those for females. For example, females appear to be far more influenced by internal, emotional factors; they are more inhibited by moral emotions, such as shame, guilt, and embarrassment.[40] Ultimately, there is no doubt that feminist theories of crime have contributed much to the discourse and empirical research regarding why females (as well as males) commit crime. In fact, some highly respected criminology and criminal justice journals have been created to deal with that very subject. So, in that sense, the field has recognized and accepted the need to examine feminist theorizing and research on offending and the justice system and explore the various issues involved.

▲ **Image 10.4**   Female delinquency has become more common in recent decades.

SOURCE: © istockphoto.com / Daxus

Feminist criminology evolved, primarily from liberal feminists, with the realization and objection that gender was essentially ignored and excluded from criminological theory.[41] This exclusion was difficult to understand given that gender was such a strong predictor of criminal behavior.[42] Further, feminists recognized the limitations of critical and radical criminological perspectives given the primary focus on economic disparities without examining the issues of race and gender. Thus, "early feminist criminologists demanded that analyses of crime include consideration of gender in ways that had not occurred before."[43] Twenty years after her essay on female crime, Dorie Klein included an afterword; she maintained that feminist criminologists need to address three major challenges: They must (1) continue to search for the scientific basis of theories of men's and women's criminal behavior, (2) reexamine gender and racial/ethnic biases in the social sciences, and (3) develop a new definition of crime.[44] Joanne Belknap gave an overview of the potential of various traditional criminological theories to provide insight in examining gender differences and similarities in understanding criminal behavior. Some of the traditional criminological theories that do have some promise in this area of understanding include differential association theory and strain and general strain theory.[45]

---

[40]For a review, see Tibbetts and Herz, "Gender Differences."

[41]Amanda Burgess-Proctor, "Intersections of Race, Class, Gender, and Crime: Future Directions for Feminist Criminology," *Feminist Criminology* 1 (2006): 30.

[42]Ibid.; see also Alfred Blumstein et al., "Introduction: Studying Criminal Careers," in *Criminal Careers and "Career Criminals,"* ed. Alfred Blumstein et al. (Washington, DC: National Academy Press, 1986), 12–30; Darrell Steffensmeier and Emilie Allan, "Gender and Crime: Toward a Gendered Theory of Female Offending," *Annual Review of Sociology* 22 (2006): 459–87.

[43]Burgess-Proctor, "Intersections of Race, Class, and Crime," 31.

[44]Dorie Klein, "The Etiology of Female Crime: A Review of the Literature," in *The Criminal Justice System and Women: Offenders, Victims, and Workers,* 2nd ed., ed. Barbara Raffel Price and Natalie Sokoloff (New York: McGraw-Hill, 1995), 48–52.

[45]Belknap, *The Invisible Woman,* 36–56.

Kathleen Daly and Meda Chesney-Lind identified the following five elements that distinguish feminist thought from other forms of social and political thought:

1. Gender is not a natural fact but a complex social, historical, and cultural product; it is related to but not simply derived from biological sex differences and reproductive capacities.

2. Gender and gender relations order social life and social institutions in fundamental ways.

3. Gender relations are constructs of masculinity and femininity and are not symmetrical but are based on an organizing principle of men's superiority and social and political–economic dominance over women.

4. Systems of knowledge reflect men's views of the natural and social world; the production of knowledge is gendered.

5. Women should be at the center of intellectual inquiry, not peripheral, invisible, or appendages to men.[46]

When addressing whether there can be a feminist criminology, Daly and Chesney-Lind maintained that feminist theories and research should be incorporated in any criminologist's study of crime. Incorporating such perspectives entails more than just a focus on women or sexism. Rather, these approaches provide an opportunity to study unexplored aspects of men's crime and forms of justice as well as forms of theory construction and verification. Thus, they argued that the promise of feminist thought has barely been realized.[47]

Almost 20 years after Daly and Chesney-Lind's article on feminist criminology, Amanda Burgess-Proctor argued that for contemporary third-wave feminist criminologists, it is essential to build on the foundation laid by previous feminist criminologists.[48] Specifically, she maintained that feminist criminology needs to embrace all sources of oppression without prioritizing gender. Thus, feminist criminology should incorporate an intersectional framework, informed by multiracial feminism, which includes such defining social characteristics as race, class, gender, sexuality, nationality, and age.[49]

One feminist framework that has been used to explore the experiences of women in the criminal justice system is pathways research:

A feminist approach to understanding the etiology of females' (and sometimes males') offending is termed by some as "pathways to crime." . . . [T]his approach attempts to determine life experiences, particularly childhood ones, that place one at risk of offending. The pathways research indicates that traumas such as physical and sexual abuse and child neglect are not only defining features in the lives of many female offenders, but also these traumas are often related to one's likelihood of committing crimes.[50]

Critiques of Feminist Theories

A number of criticisms concerning feminist theories have been raised by feminist scholars. In the 1960s, women of color challenged feminism by arguing that these perspectives essentially focused on the experiences of White

---

[46]Daly and Chesney-Lind, "Feminism and Criminology," 504.

[47]Ibid., 504.

[48]Burgess-Proctor, "Intersections of Race, Class, Gender, and Crime," 27–47.

[49]Ibid., 43.

[50]Emily Gaarder and Joanne Belknap, "Tenuous Borders: Girls Transferred to Adult Court," *Criminology* 40 (2002): 484.

middle-class women.[51] After reviewing feminist theory in sociology, Janet Saltzman Chafetz argued that the current topic among feminist scholars is the intersection of race, class, and gender.[52] A number of feminist scholars maintain that examining difference, rather than equality, is a major emphasis of current feminist studies.

While some feminist scholars maintain that this shift in focus has revitalized feminist theory,[53] others assert that it has introduced new conflicts in feminist studies.[54] Maxine Baca Zinn and Bonnie Thornton Dill stressed, however, that while there may be problems when focusing on difference,

> our perspectives take their bearings from social relations. Race and class difference are crucial, we argue, not as individual characteristics . . . but insofar as they are primary organizing principles of a society which locates and positions groups within that society's opportunity structures.[55]

Some feminist scholars emphasize the importance of examining the interlocking, or intersection, of race, class, and gender.[56] The development of an intersectional perspective on gender and race is rooted in the work of scholars focusing on women of color.[57]

Burgess-Proctor identified key conceptual factors that distinguish multiracial feminism from other feminist perspectives.[58] First, multiracial feminism claims that gender relations do not exist in a vacuum; rather, men and women are also characterized by their race, class, sexuality, age, physical ability, and other social locations of inequality. Second, multiracial feminism stresses the importance of recognizing the ways intersecting systems of power and privilege interact on all social–structural levels. Third, multiracial feminism is founded on the concept of *relationality*; this "assumes that groups of people are socially situated in relation to other groups of people based on their differences."[59] Other key conceptual facets to multiracial feminism include appreciating the interaction of social structure and women's agency, implementing various methodological approaches, and an emphasis on understandings founded on the lived experiences of women. This evolving perspective uses various terms such as *multiracial feminism, multicultural feminism,* and *U.S. Third World feminism.*[60] Another issue that has been raised by feminist scholars is that, when conducting research on women, it is essential that one avoid placing these women as *either* offenders *or* victims. This has been referred to as the "blurred boundaries" theory of victimization and criminalization. As Mary Gilfus noted, "Criminalization is connected to women's subordinate position in society where victimization by violence coupled with economic marginality related to race, class, and gender all too often blur the

---

[51]Maxine Baca Zinn and Bonnie Thornton Dill, "Theorizing Difference from Multiracial Feminism," *Feminist Studies* 22 (2006): 321–31.

[52]Janet Saltzman Chafetz, "Feminist Theory and Sociology: Underutilized Contributions for Mainstream Theory," *Annual Review of Sociology* 23 (1997): 97–120. See also Burgess-Proctor, "Intersections of Race, Class, Gender, and Crime."

[53]Faye Ginsberg and Anna Lowenhaupt Tsing, "Introduction," in *Uncertain Terms, Negotiating Gender in American Culture*, ed. Faye Ginsberg and Anna Lowenhaupt Tsing (Boston: Beacon Press, 1990), 1–32.

[54]Susan E. Martin, "Outsider within" the Station House: The Impact of Race and Gender on Black Women Police," *Social Problems* 41 (1994): 383–400.

[55]Zinn and Thornton Dill, "Theorizing Difference from Multiracial Feminism."

[56]Patricia Hill Collins, *Black Feminist Thought: Knowledge, Consciousness and the Politics of Empowerment*, 2nd ed. (London: HarperCollins, 1999).

[57]Irene Browne and Joya Misra, "The Intersection of Gender and Race in the Labor Market," *Annual Review of Sociology* 29 (2003): 487–513.

[58]Burgess-Proctor, "Intersections of Race, Class, Gender, and Crime," 36–7.

[59]Ibid., p. 37.

[60]See Alison M. Jaggar and Paula S. Rothenberg, *Feminist Frameworks: Alternative Theoretical Accounts of the Relations between Women and Men*, 3rd ed. (New York: McGraw-Hill, 1993); Chela Sandoval, "U.S. Third World Feminism: The Theory and Method of Oppositional Consciousness in the Postmodern World," *Genders* 10 (Spring 1991): 1–24; Zinn and Thornton Dill, "Theorizing Difference from Multiracial Feminism."

boundaries between victims and offenders."[61] This false categorization of women as *either* offenders *or* victims does not provide an enhanced understanding about women who commit crime.

Policy Implications

There are numerous policy implications regarding feminist theory and feminist perspectives of crime. A key aspect to understanding policies based on feminist theories of crime is that some policies are not always directly related to crime. Rather, feminist perspectives also incorporate broader social issues that are connected to criminal behavior.[62] Thus, aspects of policies related to feminist theories of crime are reflected in broader concepts of feminism. For instance, feminist researchers emphasize the importance of *reflexivity*.[63] This is when research empowers women; this form of research takes women's experiences seriously and centers on the idea that "the personal is the political":

> Feminist work has demonstrated that even the most apparently private interactions have political consequences and motivations. The inextricable connections between the personal and the political means that what happens to "the individual" is not merely the result of individual processes. As a consequence, it is unsatisfactory to treat individuals as if they were isolated from society—at the very least because this cannot give an accurate picture of people and their lives.[64]

This phrase—"The personal is the political"—refers to the notion that the "private sphere" (e.g., sexuality and domestic life) is as structured by power relations involving gender, sexuality, race, class, and age as the "public sphere" (e.g., waged work outside the home, party politics, and state institutions).[65]

Another aspect related to feminism is praxis. According to Josephine Donovan, praxis does not refer just to consciousness raising. Rather, praxis also refers to "the development of alternative arrangements that will themselves provide models for change and will in the process change consciousness."[66] Praxis also implies building alternative institutions, such as the establishment of rape crisis centers and shelters as well as changes in personal relationships. Generally, praxis is when theory translates into action. One of the most essential opportunities for praxis centers on the pursuit of social justice.[67]

Influenced by the women's movement (i.e., the second wave of feminism), our understanding of and the legal response to rape have undergone substantial changes.[68] For instance, Julia and Herman Schwendinger theorized how rape myths have pervaded the legal sphere of society, as exemplified by the belief that if a rape victim did not "fight back" or resist, as well as demonstrate physical evidence of such a confrontation, then she must have initially

---

[61]Mary E. Gilfus, "From Victims to Survivors to Offenders: Women's Routes of Entry and Immersion into Street Crime," *Women and Criminal Justice* 4 (1992): 86.

[62]Franklin P. Williams and Marilyn D. McShane, *Criminological Theory*, 3rd ed. (Upper Saddle River, NJ: Prentice Hall, 1999), 260.

[63]Christine Griffin and Ann Phoenix, "The Relationship between Qualitative and Quantitative Research: Lessons from Feminist Psychology," *Journal of Community & Applied Social Psychology* 4 (1994): 290.

[64]Ibid.

[65]Ibid.

[66]Josephine Donovan, *Feminist Theory: The Intellectual Traditions of American Feminism* (New York: Frederick Ungar, 1985), 88.

[67]Burgess-Proctor, "Intersections of Race, Class, Gender, and Crime," 42. See also Margaret L. Andersen and Patricia Hill Collins, *Race, Class, and Gender*, 5th ed. (Belmont, CA: Wadsworth, 2004); Lynn Weber, *Understanding Race, Class, Gender, and Sexuality: A Conceptual Framework* (Boston: McGraw-Hill, 2001).

[68]Katherine van Wormer and Clemens Bartollas, *Women and the Criminal Justice System* (Boston: Allyn & Bacon, 2000).

given her consent and afterward "changed her mind."[69] In the past, this myth has been significant in laws that required a demonstration of resistance. However, the Schwendingers provided the following analogy to elucidate the misconceptions associated with this myth:

> Businessmen may forcibly resist theft of their property. But no law *demands* this kind of personal resistance as a condition for the lawful protection of his property rights. Women's rights, on the other hand, seem to be another matter [italics in original].[70]

Legislative reforms were enacted in an effort to modify state rape statutes. Patricia Searles and Ronald Berger asserted that the five major goals of the legislative reforms included (1) increasing the reporting of rape and enhancing the prosecution and conviction in rape cases, (2) improving the treatment of rape victims involved in the criminal justice process, (3) achieving comparability between the legal treatment of rape and other violent offenses, (4) prohibiting a broader range of coercive sexual conduct, and (5) expanding the range of persons protected by the law.[71] Four major types of legislative reforms were identified: (1) redefinition of the offense, (2) evidentiary reforms, (3) statutory offenses, and (4) penal structure.[72]

Another example of how feminist criminologists have informed policies is in the area of gender-specific programming. The Office of Juvenile Justice and Delinquency Prevention established a funding opportunity to enhance programs specifically targeted to juvenile girls.[73] Such programming gives females an increased sense of community. This sense of community has been associated with juveniles developing and integrating a healthy identity.[74]

There have been efforts to incorporate these key factors of gender-specific services for female juvenile offenders. For instance, Lisa Bond-Maupin and her colleagues argued that intake officials recognized an appreciation of how gender, class, and race influence the lives of female juveniles.[75] Other studies have also recommended that agencies providing services to female juveniles incorporate gender-specific or gender-responsive programs.[76] Such programming has also been recommended for adult female offenders with substance abuse problems[77] as well as for adult female prisoners.[78]

---

[69]Julia R. Schwendinger and Herman Schwendinger, "Rape Myths: In Legal, Theoretical, and Everyday Practice," *Crime and Social Justice* 1 (1974): 18–26.

[70]Ibid., 21.

[71]Patricia Searles and Ronald J. Berger, "The Current Status of Rape Reform Legislation: An Examination of State Statutes," *Women's Rights Law Reporter* 10 (1987): 25.

[72]Ibid., 25–27.

[73]Donna Bownes and Rodney L. Albert, "State Challenge Activities," in *OJJDP Juvenile Justice Bulletin* (Washington, DC: Office of Juvenile Justice and Delinquency Prevention, September 1996); Kimberly Kempf-Leonard and Lisa L. Sample, "Disparity Based on Sex: Is Gender-Specific Treatment Warranted?" *Justice Quarterly* 17 (2000): 89–128.

[74]Paula Smith and William A. Smith, "Experiencing Community through the Eyes of Young Female Offenders," *Journal of Contemporary Criminal Justice* 21 (2005): 364–85.

[75]Lisa Bond-Maupin, James R. Maupin, and Amy Leisenring, "Girls' Delinquency and the Justice Implications of Intake Workers' Perspectives," *Women & Criminal Justice* 13 (2002): 51–77.

[76]Suman Kakar, Marie-Luse Friedemann, and Linda Peck, "Girls in Detention: The Results of Focus Group Discussion Interviews and Official Records Review," *Journal of Contemporary Criminal Justice* 18 (2002): 57–73; Wansley Walters, "The Miami-Dade Juvenile Assessment Center National Demonstration Project: An Overview," *Journal of Offender Rehabilitation* 41 (2005): 1–37.

[77]Michael Fendrich, Amy Hubbell, and Arthur J. Lurigio, "Providers' Perceptions of Gender-Specific Drug Treatment," *Journal of Drug Issues* 36 (2006): 667–86.

[78]Katherine van Wormer and Laura E. Kaplan, "Results of a National Survey of Wardens in Women's Prisons: The Case for Gender Specific Treatment," *Women and Therapy* 29 (2006): 133–51.

Conclusion

In this chapter introduction, we discussed the reasons for why it is so very important to examine the feminist perspective of crime. Importantly, we examined a wide variety of types of feminist perspectives and the factors that each of them focus on. We also examined the evidence that empirical research has shown for the feminist perspectives as well as the critiques of such theories in this realm. We also discussed some of the policy implications that can be derived from these models. Ultimately, it is of primary importance to include such feminist perspectives in future research and theoretical developments. Furthermore, it is important to realize that females offend far less than males; if criminologists could figure out why, this could be a landmark finding in efforts to reduce crime, especially if we could apply some of the findings of research on this perspective to chronic male offending.

 CHAPTER SUMMARY

- An emphasis on the feminist perspective on crime grew out of a long history of females being neglected in the history of criminological research as well as concern for them as victims in the criminal justice system.

- Various concepts are key in the feminist perspective, such as chivalry, patriarchy, and paternalism—all essentially diminish the status of females in society.

- One primary research question in this area is about why females are universally less likely to commit serious violent crime than males, called the gender-ratio issue.

- The other primary research area deals with whether or not the same key factors (e.g., peers, unemployment, poverty) apply in the same way for females as they do for males, which is referred to as the generalizability issue.

- We examined five different key types of feminism and what each of them focus on regarding why females are discriminated against and what leads them to commit crime.

- Evidence regarding feminist models of crime are mixed with some showing clear support and others showing the opposite of what was predicted.

- Daly and Chesney-Lind's list of the elements of feminist thought were discussed and presented as one of the key propositions of the feminist perspective on not just criminology but also society and social life.

- Critiques of feminist theories showed that many women take issue with what other feminist scholars have proposed, particularly by neglecting the issues of race and social class and focusing only on gender.

- It is notable that the critiques mentioned led to much research and discussion on the intersection of these various classes of people, which has advanced the understanding of feminism, racism, classism, etc., across the board.

- Policy implications based on the feminist perspective were also examined with the ultimate conclusion that if we could truly understand and explain why females commit so many fewer serious violent crimes, then we could likely reduce our crime rate dramatically by applying such knowledge to males.

KEY TERMS

chivalry 199

critical feminism 201

liberal feminism 200

Marxist feminism 203

paternalism 200

patriarchy 200

postmodern feminism 205

radical feminism 201

socialist feminism 203

/// DISCUSSION QUESTIONS

1. What are some of the key concepts of the feminist perspective?

2. What are the key assumptions and features of the various types of feminist perspectives?

3. Which type of feminist theory do you believe is the most helpful for explaining crime?

4. Do you believe the "generalizability" hypothesis is accurate and that key factors or causes of crime are the same for males and females? In other words, do the same factors (e.g., unemployment, peers, emotions) have the same influence across gender?

5. What are the primary critiques of feminist criminological theories?

6. Which of the policy implications based on the feminist perspective do you most agree with? Least agree with?

/// WEB RESOURCES

Feminist Theories of Crime

http://www.youtube.com/watch?v=wldzD8kpYwk
http://faculty.washington.edu/matsueda/courses/517/Readings/Daly%20Chesney-Lind%20Feminism%201988.pdf
http://now.org
http://www.historylearningsite.co.uk/sociology/crime-and-deviance/feminism-and-crime
https://www.google.com/#q=feminist+theories+of+crime
http://www.oxfordbibliographies.com/view/document/obo-9780195396607/obo-9780195396607-0013.xml

CHAPTER 11

Life-Course Perspectives of Criminality

This chapter will discuss the development of the life-course perspective in the late 1970s and its influence on modern research on criminal trajectories. We will explain the various concepts in the life-course perspective, such as onset, desistence, and frequency as well as the arguments against this perspective. Finally, we will review the current state of research regarding this perspective.

This chapter will present one of the most current and progressive approaches to explaining why individuals engage in criminal activity—namely, **developmental theories** of criminal behavior. Developmental theories are explanatory models of criminal behavior that follow individuals throughout their life courses of offending, thus explaining the development of offending over time. Such developmental theories represent a break with traditional theoretical frameworks, which typically focused on the effects of constructs and variables on behavior at a given point in time. Virtually no theories attempted to explain the various stages (e.g., onset, desistence) of individuals' criminal careers, and certainly no models differentiated the varying factors that are important at each stage. Developmental theories have been prominent in modern times, and we believe that readers will agree that developmental theories have added a great deal to our understanding of and thinking about why people commit criminal behavior.

Developmental Theories

Developmental theories, which are also to some extent integrated, are distinguished by their emphasis on the evolution of individuals' criminality over time. Developmental theories tend to look at the individual as the unit of analysis, and such models focus on the onset, frequency, seriousness or intensity, duration, persistence or consistency, desistence, and other aspects of the individual's criminal career. The onset of offending is when the offender first begins offending, and desistence is when an individual stops committing crime. Frequency refers to how often the individual offends, whereas intensity is the degree of seriousness of the offenses he or she commits. Persistence is the concept of how consistent the individual's offending rate is over time. Finally, duration is the length of an individual's criminal career.[1]

---

[1]Matt DeLisi and Kevin M. Beaver, eds., *Criminological Theory: A Life-Course Approach*, 2nd ed. (Burlington, MA: Jones & Bartlett, 2014). See also Alex R. Piquero, David P. Farrington, and Alfred Blumstein, "Criminal Career Paradigm: Background, Recent Developments, and the Way Forward," *International Annals of Criminology* 41 (2003): 243–69; and Brame et al., "Cumulative Prevalence of Arrest."

Experts have long debated and examined these various aspects of the development of criminal behavior. For example, virtually all studies show an escalation from minor status offending (e.g., truancy, underage drinking, tobacco use) to petty crimes (e.g., shoplifting, smoking marijuana) to far more serious criminal activity, such as robbery and aggravated assault, and then murder and rape. This development of criminality is shown across every study that has ever been performed and demonstrates that, with very few exceptions, people begin with relatively minor offending and progress toward more serious, violent offenses.

Although this trend is undisputed, other issues are not yet resolved. For example, studies have not yet determined when police contact or an arrest becomes **early onset**. Most empirical studies draw the line at age 14, so that any arrest or contact prior to this time is considered early onset.[2] However, other experts would disagree and say that this line should be drawn earlier (say, 12 years old) or even later (such as 16 years old). Still, however it is defined, early onset is one of the most important predictors of any of the measures we have in determining who is most at risk for developing serious, violent offending behavior.

Perhaps the most discussed and researched aspect of developmental theory is *offender frequency*, which has been referred to as **lambda**. Estimates of lambda (or λ), or average frequency of offending by criminals over a year's time, vary greatly.[3] Some estimates of lambda are in the high single digits, and some are in the triple digits. Given this large range, it does not do much good to estimate what the frequency of most offenders is. Rather, the frequency depends on many, many variables, such as what type of offenses the individual commits. Perhaps if we were studying only drug users or rapists, it would make sense to determine lambda, but given the general nature of most examinations of crime, such estimates are not useful. Even within the same crime type, the frequency of offending varies so widely across individuals that we question its use in understanding criminal careers.

Before we discuss the dominant models of developmental theory, it is important to discuss the opposing viewpoint, which is that of complete stability in offending. Such counterpoint views assume that the developmental approach is a waste of time because the same individuals who show antisocial behavior at early ages (before age 10) are those who will exhibit the most criminality in their teenage years, 20s, 30s, 40s, and so on. This framework is most notably represented by the theoretical perspective proposed by Michael Gottfredson and Travis Hirschi in their model of low self-control.

Case Study: Henry Earl

Henry Earl is, according to all available sources, the most arrested individual on record, at least in recent times. Hailing from the area of Lexington, Kentucky (Fayette County), Earl was born in 1949 and has since done quite an impressive job of getting himself arrested, especially after he turned 21. Specifically, Earl is on record for being arrested well over 1,300 times since 1970. Although the actual number is disputed, and likely growing every month, recent official reports from the local jurisdictions show that Earl has been arrested for more than 1,352 offenses and has spent more than 15 years in jail. Despite being jailed for much of his life, Earl appears to make up for lost time when he is not incarcerated, as the data show.

---

[2]For more discussion, see Stephen G. Tibbetts, "Perinatal and Developmental Determinants of Early Onset of Offending: A Biosocial Approach for Explaining the Two Peaks of Early Antisocial Behavior," in *The Development of Persistent Criminality*, ed., Joanne Savage (New York: Oxford University Press, 2009), 179–201; Matt DeLisi, "Zeroing In on Early Arrest Onset: Results from a Population of Extreme Career Criminals," *Journal of Criminal Justice* 34 (2006): 17–26; Stephen Tibbetts and Alex Piquero, "The Influence of Gender, Low Birth Weight, and Disadvantaged Environment in Predicting Early Onset of Offending: A Test of Moffitt's Interactional Hypothesis," *Criminology* 37 (1999): 843–78; and Chris L. Gibson and Stephen Tibbetts, "A Biosocial Interaction in Predicting Early Onset of Offending," *Psychological Reports* 86 (2000): 509–18.

[3]For a review, see Samuel Walker, *Sense and Nonsense about Crime and Drugs: A Policy Guide*, 7th ed. (Belmont, CA: Cengage, 2011). See also Piquero et al., "Criminal Career Paradigm."

Although many of his arrests were for public intoxication, he also had a number of more serious charges, including third-degree trespassing and various charges of disorderly conduct. Readers are probably wondering how this man could still be on the streets, but the most likely explanation is that virtually all his arrests were for nonviolent, nontheft, and nondrug (except alcohol) violations, which tend not to get much jail time. However, one would think that after the first hundred arrests, not to mention the first thousand, the judges would try to put this public nuisance away for a long time. Apparently, that is not the case. Earl's last publicly documented arrest was in November 2013, so he is seemingly still active and perhaps trying to achieve a record of arrests that may be hard for anyone to beat. According to developmental theory, he clearly is the "poster child" for the definition of persistent or consistency in offending.

> *... If someone is highly motivated to commit crime, he or she can easily find ways to do so.*

This goes to show a couple of things that relate to this chapter. First, if someone is highly motivated to commit crime, he or she can easily find ways to do so. After all, anyone can simply leave the house and commit numerous felonies against neighbors, people driving by on the street, and so forth—not to mention what that person is capable of outside of his or her neighborhood. Second, there is virtually no way to deter or stop a person from committing a crime he or she is highly motivated to commit, especially if that person has nothing to lose. Obviously, Earl has nothing at stake in terms of conventional society.

This case is notable in the context of developmental/life-course criminology. Although a highly extreme case study, it reveals that normal development, such as key transitions in life, as noted by Robert Sampson and John Laub's theory, clearly don't apply in this case. Some individuals have an extremely high predisposition to offend, an even higher predisposition than Gottfredson and Hirschi's theory of low self-control may have imag-

▲ **Image 11.1** Henry Earl, arrested more than 1,300 times, is widely considered the most arrested individual in U.S. history.

SOURCE: Lexington-Fayette Urban County Government Community Corrections / United States Department of Justice

ined possible. Regardless, this amazingly strong predisposition toward such antisocial behavior is likely due to major failures in all areas of development throughout Earl's life course, beginning with his genetics, early development, and adolescence.

Think About It

1. Can you apply the life-course persistent label from Terrie Moffitt's theory to Henry Earl?

2. Can you think of any intervention or policy that would help Mr. Earl reduce his consistent arrests?

SOURCES: "Henry Earl: Setting the Record Straight," SmokingGun.com, September 25, 2008, http://www.thesmokinggun.com/documents/crime/henry-earl-setting-record-straight; Lexington-Fayette Urban County Government, Division of Community Corrections, JailWebsite.com, n.d., http://jail.lfucg.com/Secure/Account/Login.aspx?ReturnUrl=%2fQueryProfile.aspx%3foid%3d137&oid=137. "Henry Earl, Arrested More than 1500 Times, in Jail Again," *HuffPost*, November 27, 2013, http://www.huffingtonpost.com/2013/11/27/henry-earl-arrest-1500-thanksgiving-in-jail_n_4352833.html.

Antidevelopmental Theory: Low Self-Control Theory

In 1990, Hirschi, along with his colleague Gottfredson, proposed a general theory of low self-control as the primary cause of all crime and deviance (see prior discussion in Chapter 8); this is often referred to as *the general theory of crime*.[4] This theory has led to a significant amount of debate and research in the field since its appearance, more than any other contemporary theory of crime.

Like other control theories of crime, this theory (see Figure 11.1) assumes that individuals are born predisposed toward selfish, self-centered activities and that only effective child rearing and socialization can create self-control. Without such adequate socialization (i.e., social controls) and reduction of criminal opportunities, individuals will follow their natural tendencies to become selfish predators. The general theory of crime assumes that self-control must be established by age 10. If it has not formed by that time, then according to the theory, individuals will forever exhibit low self-control. The assumption that self-control must be formed by age 10 is the feature of this theory that opposes the developmental perspective. The authors assert that once low self-control is set by age 10, there is no way to develop it afterward. In contrast, developmental theory assumes that people can indeed change over time.

Like others, Gottfredson and Hirschi attribute the formation of controls to socialization processes in the first years of life; the distinguishing characteristic of this theory is its emphasis on the individual's ability to control himself or herself. That is, the general theory of crime assumes that people can take a degree of control over their own decisions and, within certain limitations, control themselves. The general theory of crime is accepted as one of the most valid theories of crime.[5] This is probably due to the parsimony, or simplicity, of the theory, as it identifies only one primary cause of criminality—low self-control. However, low self-control may actually consist of a series of personality traits, including risk-taking, impulsiveness, self-centeredness, short-term orientation, and quick temper. Recent research has supported the idea that inadequate child-rearing practices tend to result in lower levels of self-control among children and that these low levels produce various risky behaviors, including criminal activity.[6] It is important to note that this theory has a developmental component in the sense that it proposes that self-control develops during early years from parenting practices; thus, even this most notable antidevelopment theory actually includes a strong developmental aspect.

In contrast to Gottfredson and Hirschi's model, one of the most dominant and researched frameworks of the past 20 years, another sound theoretical model shows that individuals can change their life trajectories in terms of crime. Research shows that events or realizations can occur that lead people to alter their frequency or incidence of offending, sometimes to zero. To account for such extreme **transitions**, we must turn to the dominant life-course model of offending, which is **Sampson and Laub's developmental model**.

[4]Michael Gottfredson and Travis Hirschi, *A General Theory of Crime* (Palo Alto, CA: Stanford University Press, 1990).

[5]For reviews of studies regarding low self-control theory, see John P. Wright, Stephen G. Tibbetts, and Leah Daigle, *Criminals in the Making: Criminality across the Life Course*, 2nd ed. (Thousand Oaks, CA: Sage, 2015) (see chap. 1); George E. Higgins and Margaret Mahoney, "Self-Control Theory and Antisocial Behavior," in *Criminological Theory: A Life-Course Approach*, 2nd ed., ed. Matt DeLisi and Kevin M. Beaver (Burlington, MA: Jones & Bartlett, 2014), 249–60; and Travis Pratt and Frank Cullen, "The Empirical Status of Gottfredson and Hirschi's General Theory of Crime: A Meta-analysis," *Criminology* 38 (2000): 931–64. For critiques of this theory, see Ronald Akers, "Self-Control as a General Theory of Crime," *Journal of Quantitative Criminology* 7 (1991): 201–11. For a study that demonstrates the high popularity of the theory, see Anthony Walsh and Lee Ellis, "Political Ideology and American Criminologists' Explanations for Criminal Behavior," *The Criminologist* 24 (1999): 1, 14 (see chap. 1, n. 13).

[6]Carter Hay, "Parenting, Self-Control, and Delinquency: A Test of Self-Control Theory," *Criminology* 39 (2001): 707–36; K. Hayslett-McCall and T. Bernard, "Attachment, Masculinity, and Self-Control: A Theory of Male Crime Rates," *Theoretical Criminology* 6 (2002): 5–33.

Figure 11.1 ● Gottfredson and Hirschi's theory of low self-control

Bad Child-Rearing

- Inconsistent discipline
- Neglect/lack of supervision
- Physical abuse
- Providing bad models of behavior
- Emotional/mental abuse

Low Self-Control
(identifiable before age 10)

- Self-centeredness
- Short-term orientation
- Failure to consider future consequences of actions
- Avoidance of difficult tasks and hard work
- Short temper/impulsive
- Risk taking
- Gives in readily when opportunities for crime arise

Criminal offending and all forms of deviant behavior

Assumes all individuals are born lacking self-control and are selfish

Good Child-Rearing

- Fair and consistent discipline
- Consistent monitoring
- Emotional support
- Building responsibility and accountability
- Good role models

High Self-Control
(must be established by age 10)

- Ability to work hard and delay gratification
- Inhibited by potential consequences of actions
- Long-term orientation
- Not as tempted by opportunities to commit crime

Able to resist temptations to commit crime and other forms of deviance

Sampson and Laub's Developmental Model

Perhaps the best-known and best-researched developmental theoretical model to date is that of Sampson and Laub.[7] Sampson and Laub have proposed a developmental framework that is largely based on a reanalysis of original data collected by Sheldon and Eleanor Glueck in the 1940s. As a prototypical developmental model, this theoretical perspective focuses primarily on individual stability and change.

Most significantly, Sampson and Laub emphasized the importance of certain events and life changes, which can alter an individual's decisions to commit (or not commit) criminal activity. Although based on a social control framework, this model contains elements of other theoretical perspectives. First, Sampson and Laub's model assumes, like other developmental perspectives, that early antisocial tendencies among individuals, regardless of social variables, are often linked to later adult criminal offending. Furthermore, some social structure factors (e.g., family structure, poverty) also tend to lead to problems in social and educational development, which then lead to crime. Another key factor in this development of criminality is the influence of delinquent peers or siblings, which further increases an individual's likelihood for delinquency.

▲ **Image 11.2**   Robert Sampson (1956–) and John Laub (1954–), who proposed one of the most researched theoretical frameworks, largely based on transitions and trajectories in life.

SOURCE: Courtesy of Robert Sampson and John Laub

However, Sampson and Laub also strongly emphasized the importance of transitions, or events that are important in altering life trajectories, such as marriage, employment, or military service, drastically changing a person's criminal career. Sampson and Laub showed sound evidence that many individuals who were once on a path toward a consistent form of behavior—in this case, serious, violent crime—suddenly (or gradually) halted due to such a transition or series of transitions. In some ways, this model is a more specified form of David Matza's theory of drift, which we discussed in Chapter 8, in which individuals tend to grow out of crime and deviance due to the social controls imposed by marriage, employment, and so on. Still, Sampson and Laub's framework contributed much to the knowledge of criminal offending by providing a more specified and grounded framework that identified the ability of individuals to change their criminal trajectories via life-altering transitions. In fact, recent research has consistently shown that marriage and full-time employment significantly reduce the recidivism of California parolees, and other recent studies have shown similar results from employment in later years.[8]

---

[7]Robert Sampson and John Laub, "Crime and Deviance over the Life Course: The Salience of Adult Social Bonds," *American Sociological Review* 55 (1990): 609–27; Robert Sampson and John Laub, "Turning Points in the Life Course: Why Change Matters to the Study of Crime," *Criminology* 31 (1993): 301–26; Robert Sampson and John Laub, *Crime in the Making: Pathways and Turning Points through Life* (Cambridge: Harvard University Press, 1993).

[8] Alex Piquero, Robert Brame, Paul Mazzerole, and Rudy Haapanen, "Crime in Emerging Adulthood," *Criminology* 40 (2002): 137–70; Chris Uggen, "Work as a Turning Point in the Life Course of Criminals: A Duration Model of Age, Employment, and Recidivism," *American Sociological Review* 65 (2000): 529–46.

Case Study: Teen Burglar

The Teen Burglar

A news story from the spring of 2012 reported that a 14-year-old boy had been arrested in Tennessee in connection with nearly 100 burglaries in the north Nashville area of Tennessee.[9] Officers said the teen was linked to these burglaries over the previous 2 years (making him 12 when he started offending). According to police, he had a specific and consistent modus operandi, or method of operation (MO). Specifically, he would kick in back doors, enter, and steal whatever he could grab quickly, such

> *. . . One must wonder what inspired him to commit more than 100 residential burglaries, starting when he was 12 years old!*

as flat-screen TVs or video games. Officers noted his creativity and innovation, which included using a go-kart as his getaway vehicle, driving from house to house through back alleys. The police also mentioned that he had lost both parents and likely didn't have much guidance or anyone looking out for him. They had evidence tying him to the burglaries, such as fingerprints and items found inside his home, which likely is the reason he admitted to many of the break-ins. It is unfortunate that this boy had such a poor family life and so little parental supervision, but one must wonder what inspired him to commit more than 100 residential burglaries, starting when he was 12 years old! We will revisit this case in our conclusion, with additional insight into why he may have committed these crimes.

Think About It

1. Have you ever met or known about a child this young in your neighborhood doing so many crimes before the age of 14? If so, what do you think were the causes?

2. How much do you think having poor parental supervision contributed to his crimes? Do you think he would have been prevented, or do you think he was driven to commit these crimes regardless of family supervision?

3. What do you think of his MO in how he committed his burglaries? Do you see some intellectual skill in how he did it, given that he wasn't caught for 2 years?

Moffitt's Developmental Taxonomy

Another primary developmental model that has had a profound effect on the current state of criminological thought and theorizing is **Moffitt's developmental theory (taxonomy)**, proposed in 1993.[10] Moffitt's framework distinguishes two types of offenders: **adolescence-limited offenders** and **life-course-persistent offenders.** Adolescence-limited offenders make up most of the general public and include all persons who committed offenses when they were teenagers or young adults. Their offending is largely caused by association with peers and a desire to engage in activities exhibited by the adults that they are trying to be. Such activities are a type of rite of passage

---

[9]"14-Year-Old Suspected in Nearly 100 Nashville Burglaries," WSMV.com, May 18, 2012, http://www.wsmv.com/story/18151966/14-year-old-suspected-in-north-nashville-burglaries.

[10]Terrie Moffitt, "Adolescence Limited and Life Course Persistent Antisocial Behavioral: A Developmental Taxonomy," *Psychological Review* 100 (1993): 674–701. For a review, see Savage, *Development of Persistent Criminality*.

▲ **Image 11.3**   Life-course theories attempt to uncover points of desistence, critical events that may change a person's life path from deviant behavior back to law-abiding status. Getting married and being employed are considered some of the most significant events. Once one is married or gains steady employment, free time to hang out with one's friends tends to disappear.

SOURCE: © istockphoto.com / simonkr

and quite normal among all people who have normal social interactions with their peers in their teenage or young adult years. It should be noted that a very small percentage of the population (about 1% to 3%) are nonoffenders who quite frankly do not have normal relations with their peers and therefore do not offend at all, even in adolescence.

On the other hand, there exists another small group of offenders, referred to in this model as life-course-persistent offenders. This small group, estimated to be 4% to 8% of offenders—albeit the most violent and chronic—commit the vast majority of the serious, violent offenses in any society, such as murder, rape, and armed robbery. In contrast to the adolescence-limited offenders, the disposition of life-course-persistent offenders toward offending is caused by an entirely different model: an interaction between neurological problems and the disadvantaged or criminological environments in which they are raised.

For example, if an individual has only neurological problems or only a poor, disadvantaged environment, then that individual will be unlikely to develop a life-course-persistent **trajectory** toward crime. However, if a person has both neurological problems and a disadvantaged environment, then that individual will have a very high likelihood of becoming a chronic, serious, violent offender. This proposition, which has been supported by empirical studies,[11] suggests that it is important to pay attention to what happens early in life. Because illegal behaviors are normal among teenagers or young adults, more insight can be gained by looking at the years prior to age 12 to determine who is most likely to become a chronic, violent offender. Life-course-persistent offenders begin offending very early in life and continue to commit crime far into adulthood, even to middle age, whereas adolescence-limited offenders tend to engage in criminal activity only during their teenage and young adult years. Moffitt's model suggests that more than one type of development explains criminality. Furthermore, this framework shows that different types of offenders commit crime due to entirely different causes and factors.

Policy Implications

There are many, perhaps an infinite number of, policy implications that can be derived from developmental theories of criminality. In a 2017 systematic review of the extant literature on developmental programs, David Weisburd and his colleagues concluded that there are positive findings for a wide range of prevention strategies, including individual and family programs as well as school-based programs.[12] Thus, we will focus on one of the most important, which concerns the prenatal and perinatal stages of life, because the most significant and effective interventions

---

[11]See Tibbetts and Piquero, "Influence of Gender." For a recent review of such studies, see Wright et al., *Criminals in the Making* (see chap. 1). See also Savage, *Development of Persistent Criminality*.

[12]David Weisburd, David P. Farrington, and Charlotte Gill, "What Works in Crime Prevention and Rehabilitation: An Assessment of Systematic Reviews," *Criminology & Public Policy* 16 (2017): 415–49.

can occur during this time. If policy makers hope to reduce early risk factors for criminality, they must insist on universal health care for pregnant women as well as their newborn infants through the first few years of life. The United States is one of the few developed nations that does not guarantee this type of maternal and infant medical care and supervision. Doing so would go a long way toward avoiding the costly (in many ways) damages of criminal behavior among youths at risk.[13]

Furthermore, there should be legally mandated interventions for pregnant women who are addicted to drugs or alcohol. Although this is a highly controversial topic, it appears to be a no-brainer that women who suffer from such addictions may become highly toxic to the child(ren) they carry and should receive closer supervision and more health care. There may be no policy implementation that would have as much influence on reducing future criminality in children as making sure their mothers do not take toxic substances while they are pregnant.[14]

Other policy implications include assigning special caseworkers to high-risk infants, such as those with low birth weight or low Apgar scores. Another advised intervention would be to have a centralized medical system that provides a flag for high-risk infants who have numerous birth or delivery complications so that the doctors who are seeing them for the first time are aware of their vulnerabilities.[15] Finally, universal preschool should be funded and provided to all young children; studies have shown that this leads to better performance once they enter school, both academically and socially.[16]

Ultimately, as the many developmental theories have shown, there are many concepts and stages of life that can have a profound effect on the criminological trajectories that lives can take. However, virtually all of these models propose that the earlier stages of life are likely the most important in determining whether an individual will engage in criminal activity throughout life or not. Therefore, policy makers should focus their efforts on providing care and interventions in this time period.

▲ **Image 11.4**   Terrie Moffitt (1955–), who proposed one of the most researched frameworks in developmental criminology.

SOURCE: Courtesy of Terrie Moffitt

Conclusion

This chapter presented a brief discussion of the importance of developmental or life-course theories of criminal behavior. This perspective, having become popular in the 1970s, is relatively new compared to other traditional theories explored in this text. Ultimately, this is one of the most cutting-edge areas of theoretical development, and life-course theories are likely to be the most important frameworks in the future of the field of criminological theory.

We discussed the various concepts of developmental theory, including those of offending onset, frequency, seriousness, duration, and desistance. We also examined the importance of early onset and how it is considered one of the most important predictors of any of the measures we have in determining who is most at risk for developing serious, violent offending behavior yet has issues regarding where researchers draw the line in what constitutes

[13]Wright et al., *Criminals in the Making*, 260–62.

[14]Ibid., 184–86, 258.

[15]Ibid., 259–62.

[16]Ibid.

"early" onset versus normal or late onset. Additionally, we discussed frequency of offending, often presented as an estimate called lambda (or λ), and the problematic issue of making such estimates—especially for different types of offenders.

Then we examined the policy implications of this developmental approach, emphasizing the need to provide universal care for pregnant mothers as well as their newborn children. Other policy implications include legally mandated interventions for mothers who are addicted to toxic substances (e.g., alcohol, drugs) and assignment of caseworkers to high-risk infants and children, such as those with a history of complications at birth. Such interventions would go a long way toward saving society the many problems (e.g., financial difficulties, victimization) that will persist without such interventions. Ultimately, a focus on the earliest stages of intervention will provide "the biggest bang for the buck."

/// CHAPTER SUMMARY

- Developmental or life-course theory focuses on the individual, following people throughout life to examine their offending careers. In-depth consideration of changes during the life course are of highest concern, especially regarding general conclusions that can be made about the factors that tend to increase or decrease the risk that individuals will continue offending.

- Life-course perspectives emphasize onset of offending, frequency of offending, duration of offending, seriousness of offending, persistence or consistency in offending rate, desistence of offending, and other factors that play key roles in when individuals offend and why they do so—or don't do so—at certain times of their lives.

- Early onset is one of the most important predictors of any of the measures we have in determining who is most at risk for developing serious, violent offending behavior.

- The criteria of determining what early onset is varies much based on the researchers making the decision, the type of offense(s) being studied, and the type of data being used in the study (e.g., self-reports vs. official police data).

- Lambda (or λ) is used to represent the average rate of offending by offenders in a given period of time, typically a year.

- Problems exist with using estimates of lambda, given how drastically different the estimates are across studies of various types of offenses as well as across different types of measures (e.g., official arrest data as compared to self-report data [SRD]).

- There are many critics of the developmental or life-course perspective, particularly those who buy into the low self-control model, which is antidevelopmental in the sense that it assumes that propensities for crime do not change over time but rather remain unchanged across life.

- One of the developmental models that has received the most attention is that of Sampson and Laub, which emphasizes transitions in life (e.g., marriage, military service, employment) that alter trajectories either toward or away from crime.

- Moffitt's developmental theory of chronic offenders (whom she labeled *life-course-persistent offenders*) versus more normal offenders (whom she labeled *adolescence-limited offenders*) is the developmental model that has received the most attention over the last decade, and much of this research is supportive of the interactive effects of biology and environment that combine to create chronic, habitual offenders.

/// KEY TERMS

adolescence-limited offenders   221

developmental theories   215

early onset   216

lambda (offender frequency)   216

life-course-persistent
  offenders   221

Moffitt's developmental theory
  (taxonomy)   221

Sampson and Laub's
  developmental model   218

trajectory   222

transitions   218

/// DISCUSSION QUESTIONS

1. What characteristic distinguishes developmental theories from traditional theoretical frameworks?

2. What aspects of a criminal career do experts consider important in such a model? Describe all of the aspects they look at in a person's criminal career.

3. Discuss the primary criticisms of the developmental perspective, particularly as it was presented by Gottfredson and Hirschi. Which theoretical paradigm do you consider most valid? Why?

4. What transitions or trajectories have you seen in your life or your friends' lives that support Sampson and Laub's developmental model? What events encouraged offending or inhibited it?

5. Given Moffitt's dichotomy of life-course-persistent offenders and adolescence-limited offenders, which of these should be given more attention by research? Why do you feel this way?

6. Do you think the use of lambda as an estimate of offending rates is useful for comparison across studies, given the large range and differences in the estimates that have been reported for different types of offenses and different types of measures?

/// WEB RESOURCES

Developmental Theories of Crime

https://quizlet.com/15249226/flashcards
http://www.cram.com/flashcards/criminology-chapter-9-developmental-theories-life-course-latent-trait-and-trajectory-3470365
https://benthamopen.com/contents/pdf/TOCRIJ/TOCRIJ-4-13.pdf

Sampson and Laub's Model

http://www.everydaysociologyblog.com/2008/12/sampson-laubs-a.html
https://scholar.harvard.edu/sampson/content/crime-and-life-course
http://harvardmagazine.com/2004/03/twigs-bent-trees-go-stra.html

Moffitt's Theory

http://www.colorado.edu/ibs/jessor/psych7536-805/readings/moffitt-1993_674-701.pdf
https://www.ncbi.nlm.nih.gov/pmc/articles/PMC4465023
http://www.wpic.pitt.edu/research/famhist/PDF_Articles/APA/BF16.pdf

CHAPTER 12

Integrated Theoretical Models and New Perspectives of Crime

This chapter will introduce **integrated theories**: those in which two or more traditional theories are merged into one cohesive model. We will then discuss the pros and cons of integrating theories and explain the various ways theories can be integrated. A review of integrated theories will demonstrate the many ways different theories have been merged to form more empirically valid explanations for criminal behavior.

This chapter examines relatively recent changes in criminological development; virtually all of these advances have taken place in the past few decades. Specifically, we discuss the types of models that modern explanatory formulations seem to have adopted, namely integrated theories. Of course, other unique theoretical frameworks have been presented in the past 30 years, but most of the dominant models presented during this time fall into the category of integrated theories.

Integrated theories attempt to put together two or more traditionally separate models of offending to form one unified explanatory theory. Given the empirical validity of most of the theories discussed in previous chapters, as well as the failure of these previously examined theories to explain all variation in offending behavior, it makes sense that theorists would try to combine the best of several theories while disregarding or de-emphasizing the concepts and propositions that don't seem to be as scientifically valid. Furthermore, some forms of theoretical integration deal with only concepts or propositions, while others vary by level of analysis (micro vs. macro, or both). Although such integrated formulations sound attractive and appear to be surefire ways to develop sounder explanatory models of behavior, they have a number of weaknesses and criticisms. Here, we explore these issues as well as the best-known and most accepted integrated theories that are currently being examined and tested in the criminological literature.

Integrated Theories

About 30 years ago at a conference at the State University of New York at Albany, leading scholars in criminological theory development and research came together to discuss the most important issues in the growing area of theoretical integration.[1] Some integrated theories go well beyond formulating relationships between two or more

---

[1] For a compilation of the papers presented at this conference, see Steven F. Messner, Marvin D. Krohn, and Allen E. Liska, eds., *Theoretical Integration in the Study of Deviance and Crime: Problems and Prospects* (Albany: State University of New York Press, 1989).

traditionally separate explanatory models; they actually fuse the theories into one all-encompassing framework. The following sections will examine why integrated theories became popular over the past several decades while discussing different types of integrated theories, the strengths and weaknesses of theoretical integration, and several of the better-known and better-respected integrated theories.

The Need for Integrated Theories in Criminology

The emphasis on theoretical integration is a relatively recent development that has evolved due to the need to improve the empirical validity of traditional theories, which suffer from lack of input from various disciplines.[2] This was the result of the history of criminological theory, which we discussed in prior chapters of this book. Specifically, most 19th-century theories of criminal behavior are best described as based on single-factor (e.g., intelligence quotient, or IQ) or limited-factor (e.g., stigmata) reductionism. Later, in the early 1900s, a second stage of theoretical development involved the examination of various social, biological, and psychological factors, which became known as the multiple-factor approach and is most commonly linked with the work of Sheldon and Eleanor Glueck.

Finally, in the latter half of the 20th century, a third stage of theoretical development and research in criminology became dominant, which represented a backlash against the multiple-factor approach. This stage has been called *systemic reductionism*, which refers to pervasive attempts to explain criminal behavior in terms of a particular system of knowledge.[3] For example, a biologist who examines only individuals' genotypes will likely not be able to explain much criminal behavior because he is missing a lot of information about the environment in which the people live, such as their levels of poverty or unemployment. For the past 60 years, the criminological discipline in the United States has been dominated by sociologists, which is largely due to the efforts and influence of Edwin Sutherland (see Chapter 8). Thus, as one expert has observed,

> It is not surprising to find that most current explanations of criminal behavior are sociologically based and are attempts to explain variations in the rates of criminal behavior as opposed to individual instances of that behavior. . . . Even when the effort is to explain individual behavior, the attempt is to use exposure to or belief in cultural or social factors to explain individual instances or patterns of criminal behavior. . . . We find ourselves at the stage of development in criminology where a variety of sociological systemic reductionistic explanations dominate, all of which have proven to be relatively inadequate (to the standard of total explanation, prediction, or control) in explaining the individual occurrence or the distribution of crime through time or space.[4]

Other criminologists have also noted this sociological dominance, with some going as far to claim that

> Sutherland and the sociologists were intent on turning the study of crime into an exclusively sociological enterprise and . . . they overreacted to the efforts of potential intruders to capture some of what they regarded as their intellectual turf.[5]

---

[2] This discussion is largely drawn from Charles F. Wellford, "Towards an Integrated Theory of Criminal Behavior," in Messner et al., *Theoretical Integration*, 119–27.

[3] Ibid., 120.

[4] Ibid., 120–21.

[5] This quote is taken from Stephen E. Brown, Finn-Aage Esbensen, and Gilbert Geis, *Criminology: Explaining Crime and Its Context*, 8th ed. (Cincinnati: Anderson, 2013), 251 (see chap. 6), regarding claims made by Robert Sampson and John Laub, "Crime and Deviance over the Life Course: The Salience of Adult Social Bonds," *American Sociological Review* 55 (1990): 609–27. See also discussion in Richard A. Wright, "Edwin H. Sutherland," *Encyclopedia of Criminology*, Vol. 1, ed. Richard A. Wright and J. Mitchell Miller (New York: Routledge, 2005).

This dominance of sociology over the discipline is manifested in many obvious ways. For example, virtually all professors of criminology have doctorates of philosophy (PhDs) in sociology or criminal justice, and virtually no professors have a degree in biology, neuropsychology, or other fields that obviously have important influence on human behavior. Furthermore, virtually no undergraduate (or even graduate) programs in criminal justice and criminology currently require students to take a course that covers principles in biology, psychology, anthropology, or economics; rather, virtually all the training is sociology based. In fact, most criminal justice programs in the United States do not even offer a course in biopsychological approaches to understanding criminal behavior, despite the obvious need for and relevance of such perspectives.

Many modern criminologists now acknowledge the limitations of this state of systemic reductionism, which limits theories to only one system of knowledge, in this case sociology.[6] What resulted is a period of relative stagnation in theoretical development; experts regarded the 1970s as "one of the least creative periods in criminological history."[7] In addition, the mainstream theories that were introduced for most of the 1900s (such as differential association, strain, social bonding, and labeling, which we reviewed in previous chapters) received limited empirical support, which should not be too much of a surprise given that they were based on principles of only one discipline—namely, sociology. Thus, it has been proposed that integrated theories evolved as a response to such limitations and the need to revitalize progress in the area of criminological theory building.[8] After reviewing some of the many integrated theories that have been proposed in the past two decades, we think readers will agree that combining explanatory models has indeed helped stimulate much growth in the area of criminological theory development. But, before examining these theories, it is important to discuss the varying forms they take.

Different Forms of Integrated Theories

There are several different types of integrated theories, which are typically categorized by the way that their creators propose that the theories should be fused together. The three most common forms of propositional theoretical integration, meaning synthesis of theories based on their postulates, are known as end-to-end, side-by-side, and up-and-down integration.[9] We will first explore each of these types before discussing a few more variations of combining theoretical concepts and propositions.

End-to-End Integration

The first type, **end-to-end (or sequential) integration**, typically is used when theorists expect that one theory will come before or after another in terms of temporal ordering of causal factors. This type of integration is more developmental in the sense that it tends to propose a certain ordering of the component theories that are being merged. For example, an integrated theory may claim that most paths toward delinquency and crime have their early roots in the breakdown of social attachments and controls (i.e., social bonding theory), but later, the influence of negative peers (i.e., differential association) becomes more emphasized. Thus, such a model would look like this:

Weak Social Bond → Negative Peer Associations → Crime

---

[6] Wellford, "Towards an Integrated Theory"; Sampson and Laub, "Crime and Deviance."

[7] Wellford, "Towards an Integrated Theory," 120, citing Frank P. Williams III, "The Demise of Criminological Imagination: A Critique of Recent Criminology," *Justice Quarterly* 1 (1984): 91–106.

[8] Wellford, "Towards an Integrated Theory."

[9] This typology is largely based on Travis Hirschi, "Separate and Unequal Is Better," *Journal of Research in Crime and Delinquency* 16 (1979): 34–37.

▲ **Image 12.1**   This image of very different and unique threads coming together forms a much stronger fabric, which similarly mimics how various different strands (i.e., theories) come together to form a more unified, stronger piece. Integrated theories are the same in the sense that the combining of various different strands of theoretical frameworks can come together to form a much stronger, more robust understanding of criminal behavior.

SOURCE: © istockphoto.com / JamesBrey

Such an integrated model is referred to as an end-to-end (or sequential) integration, which is appropriately named because it conveys the linkage of the theories based on the temporal ordering of two or more theories in their causal timing.[10] Specifically, the breakdown of social bonds comes first, followed by the negative peer relations. Another way of saying this is that the breakdown of social bonds is expected to have a more remote or indirect influence on crime, which is mediated by differential peer influences; on the other hand, according to this model, peer influences are expected to have a more immediate or direct effect on crime, with no mediating influences of other variables. This model is hypothetical and presented to illustrate the end-to-end form of integration, but we will see that some established frameworks have incorporated similar propositions regarding social bonding and differential association and reinforcement theories.

Many of the traditionally separate theories that we have examined in previous chapters tend to differ in their focus on either remote or immediate causal factors.[11] For instance, one of the assumptions of differential association theory is that psychological learning of crime is based on day-to-day (or even moment-to-moment) learning, so the emphasis is on more immediate causes of crime—namely, interactions with peers and significant others. On the other hand, other theories tend to focus more on remote causes of crime, such as social disorganization and strain theory, which place the emphasis on social structure factors (e.g., relative deprivation or industrialization) that most experts would agree are typically not directly implicated in situational decisions to engage in an actual criminal act but are extremely important nonetheless.

This situation seems conducive to the use of end-to-end integration, and often, the theories seem to complement each other quite well, as in our hypothetical example in which social control theory proposes the remote cause (i.e., weakened bonds) and differential association theory contributes the more direct, proximate cause (i.e., negative peer influence). On the other hand, two or more theories that focus only on more immediate causes of crime would be harder to combine because they both claim they are working at the same time, each in a sense competing against the other for being the primary direct cause of criminal activity; thus, they would be unlikely to fuse together as nicely and would not complement one another. Also, some theorists have argued that end-to-end integration is simply a form of **theoretical elaboration**, which we will discuss later. Another major limitation of end-to-end integration is the issue of whether the basic assumptions of the included theories are consistent with one another. We will investigate this in the following section, which discusses criticism of integration. But first, we must examine the other forms of theoretical integration.

---

[10] Allen E. Liska, Marvin D. Krohn, and Steven F. Messner, "Strategies and Requisites for Theoretical Integration in the Study of Crime and Deviance," in Messner et al., *Theoretical Integration*, 1–19.

[11] Much of our discussion of these forms of integration is taken from Liska et al., "Strategies and Requisites."

Side-by-Side Integration

Another type of integrated theory is called **side-by-side (or horizontal) integration**. In the most common form of side-by-side integration, cases are classified by a certain criterion (e.g., impulsive vs. planned), and two or more theories are considered parallel explanations depending on what type of case is being considered. So, when the assumptions or target offenses of two or more theories are different, a side-by-side integration is often the most natural way to integrate them. For example, low self-control theory may be used to explain impulsive criminal activity, whereas rational choice theory may be used to explain criminal behavior that involves planning, such as white-collar crime. Traditionally, many theorists would likely argue that low self-control and rational choice theory are quite different, almost inherently opposing perspectives of crime. However, contemporary studies and theorizing have shown that the two models complement and fill gaps in each other.[12] Specifically, the rational choice and deterrence framework has always had a rather hard time explaining and predicting why individuals often do very stupid things for which there is little payoff and a high likelihood of getting in serious trouble, so the low self-control perspective helps fill in this gap by explaining that some individuals are far more impulsive and are more concerned about the immediate payoff (albeit often small) than they are about any long-term consequences.

An illustration of side-by-side integration of these two theories might thus look something like this:

For most typical individuals

High Self-Control → Consideration of Potential Negative Consequences →
Deterred from Committing Crime

For more impulsive individuals or activities

Low Self-Control → Desire for Immediate Payoff → Failure to Consider Consequences →
Decision to Commit Criminal Act

This side-by-side integration shows how two different theories can each be accurate, depending on what type of individual or criminal activity is being considered. As some scholars have concluded, rational choice theory is likely not a good explanation for homicides between intimates (which tend to be spontaneous acts), but it may be very applicable to corporate crime.[13]

---

[12] Daniel Nagin and Raymond Paternoster, "Enduring Individual Differences and Rational Choice Theories of Crime," *Law and Society Review* 27 (1993): 467–96; Alex Piquero and Stephen Tibbetts, "Specifying the Direct and Indirect Effects of Low Self-Control and Situational Factors in Offenders' Decision Making: Toward a More Complete Model of Rational Offending," *Justice Quarterly* 13 (1996): 481–510; Stephen Tibbetts and Denise Herz, "Gender Differences in Factors of Social Control and Rational Choice," *Deviant Behavior* 17 (1996): 183–208 (chap. 8, n. 90); Stephen Tibbetts and David Myers, "Low Self-Control, Rational Choice, and Student Test Cheating," *American Journal of Criminal Justice* 23 (1999): 179–200; Bradley Wright, Avshalom Caspi, and Terrie Moffitt, "Does the Perceived Risk of Punishment Deter Criminally Prone Individuals? Rational Choice, Self-Control, and Crime," *Journal of Research in Crime and Delinquency* 41 (2004): 180–213. For a review, see Stephen Tibbetts, "Individual Propensities and Rational Decision-Making: Recent Findings and Promising Approaches," in *Rational Choice and Criminal Behavior: Recent Research and Future Challenges*, ed. Alex Piquero and Stephen Tibbetts (New York: Routledge, 2002), 3–24.

[13] Liska et al., "Strategies and Requisites." For a review, see Brown et al., *Criminology: Explaining Crime*. For a recent study of rational choice applied to corporate crime, see Nicole Leeper Piquero, M. Lyn Exum, and Sally S. Simpson, "Integrating the Desire-for-Control and Rational Choice in a Corporate Crime Context," *Justice Quarterly* 22 (2005): 252–81.

Up-and-Down Integration

Another way of combining two or more theories is referred to as **up-and-down (or deductive) integration**. It is generally considered the classic form of theoretical integration because it has been done relatively often in the history of criminological theory development—even before it was considered integration. It often involves increasing the level of abstraction of a single theory so that postulates seem to follow from a conceptually broader theory. Up-and-down integration can take two prevalent forms: (1) theoretical reduction and (2) theoretical synthesis.

Theoretical reduction is typically done when it becomes evident "that theory A contains more abstract or general assumptions than theory B and, therefore, that key parts of theory B can be accommodated within the structure of theory A."[14] We have discussed this form of integration previously in this book without actually calling it by name. For example, in Chapter 8, we discussed how differential reinforcement theory subsumed Sutherland's differential association theory. By equating concepts contained in both theories, the authors of differential reinforcement argued somewhat effectively that the learning that takes place through interactions with primary groups is one type of conditioning.[15] As you will recall, the main point is that the concepts and propositions of differential reinforcement theory are more general than—but entirely consistent with—those of differential association theory, such that the latter is typically a specific form of the former model. In other words, differential reinforcement is a much more broad, general theory, which accounts for not only differential association (i.e., classical conditioning) but also many other theoretical concepts and propositions (operant conditioning, modeling, or imitation).

This same type of theoretical reduction was also discussed in Chapter 6 when we noted that general strain theory subsumed Robert Merton's traditional strain theory. Specifically, traditional strain theory focused on only one type of strain: failure to achieve positively valued goals. While general strain theory also places an emphasis on failure to achieve positively valued goals, it is more general and broader because it also focuses on two other forms of strain: loss of positively valued stimuli and exposure to noxious stimuli. Therefore, it seems to make sense that general strain theory would subsume traditional strain theory, because the concepts and principles of traditional strain appear to simply represent a specific type of general strain and can be fully accounted for by the more general version of the theory.[16]

Despite the obvious efficiency in theoretical reduction, many theorists have criticized such subsuming of theories by another. Specifically, many experts in the social sciences view such reduction as a form of theoretical imperialism, because the theory being reduced essentially loses its unique identity.[17] Therefore, the very phrase *theoretical reduction* generally has a negative connotation among scholars. In fact, one of the most accepted reductions in 20th-century criminological literature, the differential association-differential reinforcement synthesis we referred to previously, has been condemned as a "revisionist takeover . . . a travesty of Sutherland's position."[18] So, even the most widely known and cited forms of theoretical reduction have been harshly criticized, which gives readers some idea of how much social scientists can frown upon the subsuming of one theory by another.

The other form of up-and-down integration is referred to as *theoretical synthesis*, which is "done by abstracting more general assumptions from theories A and B, allowing parts of both theories to be incorporated in a new

---

[14] Liska et al., "Strategies and Requisites," 10.

[15] Liska et al., "Strategies and Requisites," 13; Robert L. Burgess and Ronald Akers, "Differential Association-Reinforcement Theory of Criminal Behavior," *Social Problems* 14 (1966): 128–46; Ronald Akers, *Deviant Behavior: A Social Learning Approach*, 3rd ed. (Belmont, CA: Wadsworth, 1985) (see chap. 8).

[16] Robert Agnew, "Foundation for a General Strain Theory of Crime and Delinquency," *Criminology* 30 (1992): 47–87; Robert Agnew and Helen R. White, "An Empirical Test of General Strain Theory," *Criminology* 30 (1992): 475–99.

[17] Liska et al., "Strategies and Requisites."

[18] This quote is from Ian Taylor, Paul Walton, and Jock Young, *The New Criminology* (New York: Harper & Row, 1973), 131–32. See discussion in Liska et al., "Strategies and Requisites," 13.

theory C."[19] This form of up-and-down integration is more uncommon in social science than theoretical reduction, perhaps because it is more difficult to achieve successfully, since by definition it requires the formulation of a new theory with new concepts or hypotheses that are not already found in the original component models. Furthermore, if the constituent theories are competing explanations, then it is quite likely that new terminology will have to be created or incorporated to resolve these differences.[20] However, if theoretical synthesis can be done correctly, it is perhaps the type of integration that provides the most advancement of theory development because, in addition to bringing together previously independent models, it also results in a new theory with predictions and propositions that go beyond the original frameworks.

One of the best-known and most accepted (despite its critics) examples of theoretical synthesis is **Elliott's integrated model**, which we review in detail later in this chapter.[21] For our purposes here, it is important only to understand why Delbert Elliott's model is considered theoretical synthesis. This is because Elliott's model integrates the concepts and propositions of various theories (e.g., social control and differential association) and contributes additional propositions that did not exist in the component theories.

Levels of Analysis of Integrated Theories

Beyond the variation in types of propositional theoretical integration discussed previously, such synthesis of explanatory models also differs in terms of the level of analysis that is being considered. Specifically, the integrated models can include component theories of micro–micro, macro–macro, or even micro–macro (called *cross-level*) combinations. For example, Elliott's integrated theory is a micro–micro level theory, which means that all of the component theories that make up the synthesized model refer to the individual as the unit of analysis. Although these models can provide sound understanding for why certain individuals behave in certain ways, they typically do not account for differences in criminality across groups (gender, socioeconomic groups, etc.).

On the other hand, some integrated models include theories from only macro levels. A good example of this type of integration is seen in Robert Bursik's synthesis of conflict theory and the social disorganization framework.[22] Both of these component theories focus only on the macro (group) level of analysis, thus neglecting the individual level; for example, they would fail to explain why some individuals do or do not commit crime even in the same structural environment.

The most complicated integrated theories, at least in terms of levels of analysis, are those that include both micro and macro models. Such models are likely the most difficult to synthesize successfully because this involves bringing together rather unnatural relationships between individual-based propositions and group-level postulates. However, when done effectively, such a model can be rather profound in terms of explanation of crime. After all, one of the primary objectives of a good theory is to explain behavior across as many circumstances as possible. Thus, a theory that can effectively explain why crime occurs in certain individuals as well as certain groups would be better than a theory that explains crime across only individuals or only groups.

---

[19] Liska et al., "Strategies and Requisites," 10.

[20] David Wagner and Joseph Berger, "Do Sociological Theories Grow?" *American Journal of Sociology* 90 (1985): 697–728.

[21] Delbert Elliott, Suzanne S. Ageton, and Rachelle J. Canter, "An Integrated Theoretical Perspective on Delinquent Behavior," *Journal of Research in Crime and Delinquency* 16 (1979): 3–27. See also discussion in Delbert Elliott, "The Assumption That Theories Can Be Combined with Increased Explanatory Power: Theoretical Integrations," in *Theoretical Methods in Criminology*, ed. Robert F. Meier (Beverly Hills, CA: Sage, 1985), 123–49. Discussion of Elliott's model as an example of theoretical synthesis can be found in Charles R. Tittle, "Prospects for Synthetic Theory: A Consideration of Macrolevel Criminological Activity," in Messner et al., *Theoretical Integration*, 161–78.

[22] Robert J. Bursik, "Political Decision Making and Ecological Models of Delinquency, Conflict and Consensus," in Messner et al., *Theoretical Integration*, 105–18.

An example of such a theory is **Braithwaite's reintegrative shaming theory**, which begins with an individual (or micro) level theory of social control and bonding—which he refers to as **interdependency**—and then relates levels of this concept to a group or community (or macro) level theory of bonding—which he refers to as **communitarianism**.[23] This theory will be discussed in far more detail later, but it is important here to acknowledge the advantages of explaining both the micro (individual) and macro (group) level of analysis in explanations of criminal behavior, such as in the theory of reintegrative shaming.

Ultimately, the levels of analysis of any component theories are important considerations in the creation of integrated models of crime. It is particularly important to ensure that the merging of certain theories from within or across particular levels makes rational sense and, most important, advances our knowledge and understanding of the causes of crime.

Additional Considerations regarding Types of Integration

Beyond the basic forms of propositional integration models and levels of analysis, there are two additional types of integration—conceptual integration and theoretical elaboration—that are quite common, perhaps even more common than the traditional forms discussed previously. **Conceptual integration** involves the synthesis of models in which "the theorist equates concepts in different theories, arguing that while the words and terms are different, the theoretical meanings and operations of measurement are similar."[24] Essentially, the goal in such a formulation is to take the primary constructs of two or more theories and merge them into a more general framework that aids understanding in explaining behavior by unifying terms that represent fundamentally similar phenomena or issues. Such formulations are considered less intrusive on the component theories than the propositional integrations we discussed previously.

One of the first and most cited examples of conceptual integration was provided by Frank Pearson and Neil Weiner in 1985.[25] As shown in Table 12.1, Pearson and Weiner attempted to map the various concepts of numerous criminological theories. This was done by creating categories that numerous concepts from various theories would appear to fit into through their inclusion in explanatory models of criminal behavior and across levels of explanation. Although based on a social learning and differential reinforcement perspective, Pearson and Weiner's model attempts to include concepts of virtually all existing theories of crime and delinquency. A particular strength is that this model includes feedback or behavioral consequence elements as well as classifying each model by unit of measurement and analysis.

For example, as illustrated in Table 12.1, the conceptual model shows that differential association theory has concepts that apply to all internal aspects and one of the two concepts under consequences or feedback at the micro level but none of the aspects under the external micro level or any of the four macro-level concepts. On the other hand, Marxist-critical theory is shown to apply to three of the internal micro and one of the consequences or feedback level concepts and to most of the macro-level concepts as well. Although only some of the theories that we have discussed in this book are included, largely because Pearson and Weiner's conceptual integration was done in the mid-1980s, this model includes most of the dominant theoretical frameworks that were prevalent in the criminological literature at the time of their formulation. Thus, this conceptual model remains as a sort of prototype for future attempts to conceptually integrate established theories explaining criminal conduct.

---

[23] John Braithwaite, *Crime, Shame and Reintegration* (Cambridge: Cambridge University, 1989).

[24] Liska et al., "Strategies and Requisites," 15; definition adapted from Frank S. Pearson and Neil Alan Weiner, "Toward an Integration of Criminological Theories," *Journal of Criminal Law and Criminology* 76 (1985): 116–50.

[25] Pearson and Weiner, "Toward an Integration." See review in Thomas J. Bernard and Jeffrey B. Snipes, "Theoretical Integration in Criminology," in *Crime and Justice Review*, Vol. 20, ed. Michael Tonry (Chicago: University of Chicago Press, 1996), 301–48.

Table 12.1 ● Mapping of the Selected Criminological Theories into the Integrative Structure

Selected Criminological Theories	INTEGRATIVE CONSTRUCTS											
	Micro Level								Macro Level			
	Antecedent						Consequences or Feedback		Social Structural Production and Distribution of:			
	Internal				External							
	Utility Demand (Deprivation)	Behavioral Skill	Rules of Expedience	Rules of Morality	Signs of Favorable Opportunities (Descriminative Stimuli)	Behavioral Resources	Utility Reception	Information Acquisition	Utilities	Opportunities	Rules of Expedience and Morality	Belief about Sanctioning Practices
Differential association	✓	✓	✓	✓			✓					
Negative labeling	✓	✓		✓			✓					
Social control:												
1. Attachment	✓		✓				✓					
2. Commitment	✓		✓		✓			✓				
3. Involvement					✓			✓				
4. Belief				✓								
Deterrence	✓		✓		✓		✓	✓	✓			✓
Economic	✓		✓		✓		✓	✓	✓		✓	
Routine activities	✓	✓	✓		✓	✓			✓	✓		
Neutralization		✓		✓							✓	
Relative deprivation	✓		✓	✓			✓		✓	✓		
Strain	✓	✓	✓	✓	✓		✓	✓	✓	✓	✓	
Normative (culture) conflict				✓							✓	
Generalized strain and normative (culture) conflict	✓		✓	✓	✓	✓	✓	✓	✓	✓	✓	
Marxist-critical/group conflict	✓		✓	✓					✓	✓	✓	

SOURCE: Frank S. Pearson and Neil Alan Weiner, "Toward an Integration of Criminological Theories," *Journal of Criminal Law and Criminology* 76 (1985): 116–50 (table p. 130). Copyright © 2004–2008 *The Journal of Criminal Law and Criminology*—Northwestern University School of Law.

One notable strength of Pearson and Weiner's conceptual integration is the inclusion of most mainstream theories—differential association, labeling, social control, deterrence, economic, routine activities, neutralization, strain, normative (culture) conflict, generalized strain, and Marxist-critical group conflict—in existence at the time in which they created their integrated framework. Another strength of their integrated framework is the fact that they account for concepts at different levels of analysis, namely the micro (individual) and macro (group) levels, as shown in Table 12.1. So, the framework clearly does a good job at creating links between the most prominent theories in terms of the concepts they propose as the primary causes of crime.

However, Pearson and Weiner's conceptually integrated framework does have several notable weaknesses. One of the most prominent criticisms of the conceptual model is that it is based on a single theory, specifically social learning theory (tied to Akers's differential reinforcement and social learning theory, discussed in Chapter 8), and the authors never really provide a strong argument for why they chose this particular base framework for their model. Another major weakness of this conceptual framework is that it completely neglects many biological and biosocial factors—hormones, neurotransmitters, toxins—that have been consistently shown to have profound effects on human behavior. Still, despite the criticisms of this integrated framework, respected theorists have noted that Pearson and Weiner's "integration of these concepts into a consistent, coherent framework is impressive," but the model has never received much attention in the criminological literature.[26]

However, despite the obvious tendency to simplify formulations through conceptual integration, many critics have claimed that such attempts are simply a means toward propositional integration. Thus, despite its categorization as conceptual, this type of integration is not necessarily seen as such, and it may be seen by many as a form of deductive integration. However, many experts have noted that conceptual integration is actually not a form of side-by-side integration, nor is it end-to-end integration. Rather, it is what it says it is: conceptual integration. It is nothing more and nothing less.[27] Therefore, it appears that conceptual integration is a distinct derivative form of integration and that it can and should occur independently if it helps to advance understanding of why people commit crime. As the most knowledgeable experts recently concluded, "establishing some conceptual equivalence is necessary for deductive integration."[28]

An additional variation of integration is theoretical elaboration, which is a strategy that takes an existing theory that is arguably underdeveloped and then further develops it by adding concepts and propositions from other theories. Many critics of traditional theoretical integration have argued that theoretical elaboration is a more attractive strategy because existing theories of offending are not developed enough to fully integrate them.[29] An example of theoretical integration can be seen in the expansion of rational choice theory, which had traditionally focused on ratios of perceived costs and benefits, to include deontological constructs, such as moral beliefs. Specifically, studies have consistently shown that ethical constraints condition the influence of expected consequences on

---

[26] Ronald L. Akers and Christine S. Sellers, *Criminological Theories: Introduction, Evaluation, and Application*, 6th ed. (Oxford: Oxford University Press, 2012), 288 (see chap. 8).

[27] Liska et al., "Strategies and Requisites," 15.

[28] Ibid., 16.

[29] Liska et al., "Strategies and Requisites," 16; Travis Hirschi, "Exploring Alternatives to Integrated Theory," in Messner et al., *Theoretical Integration*, 37–50; Terence P. Thornberry, "Reflections on the Advantages and Disadvantages of Theoretical Integration," in Messner et al., *Theoretical Integration*, 51–60; Robert F. Meier, "Deviance and Differentiation," in Messner et al., *Theoretical Integration*, 199–212.

criminal behavior ranging from violence to academic dishonesty to white-collar crime.[30] Although they are not without critics, most rational choice scholars appear to agree that such elaboration advanced the theoretical framework and made it a more accurate explanation of human behavior. In sum, theoretical integration, like conceptual integration, is an option for merging and improving theoretical models without completely synthesizing two or more entire paradigms.

Criticisms and Weaknesses of Integrated Theories

A number of criticisms have been leveled at theoretical integration. Perhaps one of the most obvious and prevalent, not to mention extremely valid, criticisms is the argument that caution should be taken in attempting to integrate theories that have apparent contradictions or inconsistencies in their postulates.[31] As we have seen, different theories are based on varying, often opposite, perspectives of human nature. While most versions of strain theory (e.g., Merton's theory) assume that human beings are born with a natural tendency toward being good, most variations of control theory (e.g., Hirschi's social bonding and self-control theories) assume that humans are innately selfish and hedonistic. At the same time, most versions of learning theory (e.g., Sutherland's theory of differential association and Akers's differential reinforcement theory) assume that humans are born with a blank slate; in other words, people are born with neither good nor bad tendencies but rather learn their morality moment to moment from social interaction.

Obviously, attempts to integrate these theories face the hurdles of dealing with such obvious contradictions, and many formulations that do merge some of these perspectives simply do not deal with this issue. The failure to acknowledge, let alone explain, such inconsistencies is likely to result in regression of theoretical development instead of leading to progress in understanding, which is the primary goal of integrating theories in the first place.

Other experts have argued that any attempts to integrate theories must unite three different levels of analysis, including individual (micro), group (macro), and microsituational, which merges the micro level with the spontaneous context.[32] While we agree that this would be the ideal for theory formulation, we know of no theory that does so. Therefore, this proposition is more of an ideal that has not yet been attempted. Thus, we are inclined to go with the best that has been offered by expert theorists. Still, it is hoped that in the future, such an integrated model will be offered that addresses all of these aspects in an explanatory model.

Another argument against theoretical integration is the stance that explanatory perspectives of crime are meant to stand alone. This is the position taken by Travis Hirschi, who has been one of the most cited and respected scholars in criminology over the last 40 years.[33] As others have noted, Hirschi confirmed his position on this debate unequivocally when he stated that "separate and unequal is better" than integrating traditionally independent theoretical models.[34]

---

[30] Amitai Etzioni, *The Moral Dimension: Toward a New Economics* (New York: Free Press, 1988); Ronet Bachman, Raymond Paternoster, and Sally Ward, "The Rationality of Sexual Offending: Testing a Deterrence/Rational Choice Conception of Sexual Assault," *Law and Society Review* 26 (1992): 401–19; Raymond Paternoster and Sally Simpson, "Sanction Threats and Appeals to Morality: Testing a Rational Choice Model of Corporate Crime," *Law and Society Review* 30 (1996): 378–99; Stephen G. Tibbetts, "College Student Perceptions of Utility and Intentions of Test Cheating," doctoral dissertation, University of Maryland–College Park (Ann Arbor: UMI, 1997). For a review and discussion, see Sally Simpson, Nicole Leeper Piquero, and Raymond Paternoster, "Rationality and Corporate Offending Decisions," in Piquero and Tibbetts, *Rational Choice*, 25–40.

[31] Much of this discussion is taken from Brown et al., *Criminology: Explaining Crime*; and Messner et al., *Theoretical Integration*.

[32] James Short, "The Level of Explanation Problem in Criminology," in *Theoretical Methods in Criminology*, ed. Robert Meier (Beverly Hills, CA: Sage, 1985), 42–71. See also James Short, "On the Etiology of Delinquent Behavior," *Journal of Research in Crime and Delinquency* 16 (1979): 28–33.

[33] Bernard and Snipes, "Theoretical Integration"; Hirschi, "Exploring Alternatives."

[34] Hirschi, "Separate but Unequal."

This type of perspective is also called *oppositional tradition* or *theoretical competition*, because the separate theories are essentially pitted against one another in a form of battle or opposition. Although scientists are trained to always be skeptical of their own beliefs and open to other possibilities, especially the desire to refine theoretical models that are shown to be invalid, it is surprising that such a position exists. Despite the rather unscientific nature of this stance, such a position of oppositional tradition has many supporters. Specifically, one of the most respected and cited criminologists, Hirschi, claimed the following:

> The first purpose of oppositional theory construction is to make the world safe for a theory contrary to currently accepted views. Unless this task is accomplished, there will be little hope for the survival of the theory and less hope for its development. Therefore, oppositional theorists should not make life easy for those interested in preserving the status quo. They should instead remain at all times blind to the weaknesses of their own position and stubborn in its defense. Finally, they should never smile.[35]

Unfortunately, this position against theoretical integration is presented in a very unscientific tone. After all, scientists should always be critical of their own views and theories. By stating that theorists should be "blind" to opposing viewpoints and "stubborn" in their own perspective's defense, Hirschi advocates a position that is absolutely against science. Still, this statement, albeit flawed, demonstrates the extreme position against theoretical integration that is favorable toward having each independent theory standing opposed to others. It is our position that this stand does not have much defense, which is shown by Hirschi's lack of rational argument. Furthermore, it is generally acceptable to smile when presenting any theoretical or empirical conclusions, even when they involve opposition to or acceptance of integrated theoretical models of criminal behavior.

Perhaps one of the most important criticisms against Hirschi's and others' criticisms of integrated models is that most traditional models alone explain only a limited amount of variation in criminal activity. Elliott and colleagues have claimed the following:

> Stated simply, the level of explained variance attributable to separate theories is embarrassingly low, and, if sociological explanations for crime and delinquency are to have any significant impact upon future planning and policy, they must be able to demonstrate greater predictive power.[36]

While some put this estimate at 10% to 20% of the variance in illegal activities, this is simply an average across different theories and various forms of deviant behavior.[37] However, this range is an overestimate based on many studies investigating the accuracy of separate theories, which tend to show weak support (explaining well under 10% of the variation in offending), particularly social bonding and strain models.[38]

On the other hand, this estimated range of explained variance underestimates the empirical validity of some theoretical frameworks that consistently show high levels of explained variation in certain criminal behaviors. For example, a large number of studies investigating Akers's differential reinforcement and social learning theory (discussed in Chapter 8), which examine not only a wide range of samples (in terms of age, nationality, and other demographic characteristics) but also a large range of deviant activities (e.g., cigarette smoking, drug usage, violent sexual

---

[35] Hirschi, "Exploring Alternatives," 45.

[36] Delbert Elliott, David Huizinga, and Suzanne Ageton, *Explaining Delinquency and Drug Use* (Beverly Hills, CA: Sage, 1985), 125, as quoted in Bernard and Snipes, "Theoretical Integration," 306.

[37] This estimate can be found in Bernard and Snipes, "Theoretical Integration," 306, but is based on the estimates of others, as discussed in this work.

[38] See review in Akers and Sellers, *Criminological Theories*.

crimes), consistently account for more than 20% of variation in such behaviors.[39] Specifically, most of these studies estimate that Akers's social learning model explains up to 68% or more of the variation in certain deviant behaviors, with the lowest estimate being around 30%.

Obviously, not all independent theories of crime lack empirical validity, so this does not support critics' claims that traditionally separate theories of crime do not do a good job of explaining criminal behavior. However, it is also true that many of the theories that do the best job in empirical tests for validity are those that are somewhat integrated in the sense that they often have been formed by merging traditional theories with other constructs and propositions, much like Akers's differential reinforcement theory, which added more modern psychological concepts and principles (e.g., operant conditioning and modeling) to Sutherland's traditional theory of differential association (see Chapter 8). So, in a sense, an argument can be made that theoretical integration (or at least theoretical elaboration) had already occurred, which made this theory far more empirically valid than the earlier model.

Another example of the high level of empirical validity of existing models of offending can be found in some models of rational choice, which have been revised through theoretical elaboration and have explained more than 60% of the explained variation in deviant behavior.[40] However, much of the explanatory power of such frameworks relies on incorporating the constructs and principles of other theoretical models, which is what science is based on; specifically, they revise and improve theory based on what is evident from empirical testing. After all, even some of the harshest critics of theoretical integration admit that traditional theories do not own variables or constructs.[41] For example, Hirschi claimed the following:

Integrationists somehow conclude that variables appear . . . with opposition theory labels attached to them. This allows them to list variables by the theory that owns them. Social disorganization theory . . . might own economic status, cultural heterogeneity, and mobility. . . . Each of the many variables is measured and . . . the theories are ranked in terms of the success of their variables in explaining variation in delinquency . . . such that integration is in effect *required* by the evidence and surprisingly easily accomplished.[42]

This is the way that science and theoretical development and revision are supposed to work, so in our opinion, this is exactly as it should be. All scientists and theoreticians should constantly be seeking to improve their explanatory models and be open to ways to do so as opposed to being staunch supporters of one position and blind to existing evidence.

Despite the criticisms against theoretical integration, a strong argument has been made that theoretical competition and oppositional tradition are generally pointless.[43] A big reason for this belief among proponents of

---

[39] Ronald Akers et al., "Social Learning and Deviant Behavior: A Specific Test of a General Theory," *American Sociological Review* 44 (1979): 635–55; Marvin Krohn and Lonn Lanza-Kaduce, "Community Context and Theories of Deviant Behavior: An Examination of Social Learning and Social Bonding Theories," *Sociological Quarterly* 25 (1984): 353–71; Lonn Lanza-Kaduce et al., "Cessation of Alcohol and Drug Use among Adolescents: A Social Learning Model," *Deviant Behavior* 5 (1984): 79–96; Ronald Akers and John Cochran, "Adolescent Marijuana Use: A Test of Three Theories of Deviant Behavior," *Deviant Behavior* 6 (1985): 323–46; Ronald Akers and Gang Lee, "Age, Social Learning, and Social Bonding in Adolescent Substance Use," *Deviant Behavior* 19 (1999): 1–25; Marvin Krohn et al., "Social Learning Theory and Adolescent Cigarette Smoking: A Longitudinal Study," *Social Problems* 32 (1985): 455–73; Ronald Akers and Gang Lee, "A Longitudinal Test of Social Learning Theory: Adolescent Smoking," *Journal of Drug Issues* 26 (1996): 317–43; Ronald Akers et al., "Social Learning Theory and Alcohol Behavior among the Elderly," *Sociological Quarterly* 30 (1989): 625–38; Scot Boeringer, Constance Shehan, and Ronald Akers, "Social Contexts and Social Learning in Sexual Coercion and Aggression: Assessing the Contribution of Fraternity Membership," *Family Relations* 40 (1991): 558–64; Sunghyun Hwang and Ronald Akers, "Adolescent Substance Use in South Korea: A Cross-Cultural Test of Three Theories," in *Social Learning Theory and the Explanation of Crime: A Guide for the New Century*, ed. Ronald Akers and Gary Jensen (New Brunswick, NJ: Transaction, 2003), 39–64.

[40] For example, see Tibbetts, "College Student Perceptions," which showed that an elaborated rational choice model explained more than 60% of variation in test cheating among college students.

[41] See discussion in Bernard and Snipes, "Theoretical Integration," 306–7.

[42] Hirschi, "Exploring Alternatives," 41, as cited (revised) in Bernard and Snipes, "Theoretical Integration," 307.

[43] Bernard and Snipes, "Theoretical Integration," 306, based on the rationale provided by Elliott et al., *Explaining Delinquency*.

▲ **Image 12.2** Delbert Elliott proposed one of the most widely known and researched integrated theories, which combines elements of strain, social disorganization, bonding or control, and learning or socialization theories into one causal model of offending.

SOURCE: Courtesy of Delbert Elliott.

theoretical integration is that various theories tend to explain different types of crime and varying portions of the causal processes for behavior. For example, some theories focus more on property crimes while others focus on violent crimes, and some theories emphasize the antecedent or root causes of crime (e.g., genetics, poverty) while others emphasize more immediate causes (e.g., current social context at the scene). Given that there are multiple factors that contribute to crime and that different factors are more important for different types of crime, it only makes sense that a synthesis of traditionally separate theories must come together to explain the wide range of criminal activity that occurs in the real world.

Ultimately, there are both pros and cons of integrating theories. It is our belief that theoretical integration is generally a good thing as long as there is caution and attention given to merging models that have opposing assumptions, such as those regarding the natural state of human beings (e.g., good vs. bad vs. blank slate). But only after considerable empirical research will the true validity of integrated models be tested, and many have already been put to the test. We will now examine a handful of integrated theories that have been proposed over the past couple of decades as well as the studies that have examined their empirical validity. Not surprisingly, some integrated and elaborated theories appear to be more valid than others—with most adding considerably to our understanding of human behavior and contributing to explaining the reasons why certain individuals or groups commit criminal behavior more than others.

Examples of Integrated Criminological Theory

We have already discussed the advantages and disadvantages of theoretical integration as well as the ways in which traditionally separate explanatory models are combined to form new, synthesized frameworks. We will now review a number of the most prominent examples of theoretical integration that have been proposed in the past 35 years, which is largely the time period when most attempts at integration have been presented. We hope that readers will critique each theory based on the criteria that we have already discussed, particularly noting the empirical validity of each model based on scientific observation and the logical consistency of its propositions.

Elliott's Integrated Model

Perhaps the first and certainly the most prominent integrated model is that proposed by Elliott and his colleagues in 1979, which has become known as Elliott's integrated model.[44] In fact, this model "opened the current round of debate on integration," because it was essentially the first major perspective proposed that clearly attempted to merge various traditionally separate theories of crime.[45] Elliott's integrated framework attempts to merge strain, social disorganization, control, and social learning and differential association-reinforcement perspectives for the

---

[44] Elliott et al., "An Integrated Theoretical Perspective." For further elaboration and refinement of this theory, see Elliott et al., *Explaining Delinquency*.

[45] Bernard and Snipes, "Theoretical Integration," 310.

Figure 12.1 • Elliott et al.'s integrated theoretical model

SOURCE: Delbert S. Elliott, David Huizinga, and Suzanne S. Ageton, *Explaining Delinquency and Drug Use* (Beverly Hills, CA: SAGE, 1985), pg. 66. Copyright © 1985 SAGE Publications, Inc. Reprinted by permission of SAGE Publications, Inc.

purpose of explaining delinquency, particularly in terms of drug use but also for other forms of deviant behavior (see Figure 12.1).

As can be seen in Figure 12.1, the concepts and propositions of strain and social disorganization, as well as inadequate socialization, are considered antecedent (or root) causes of delinquency. In other words, failing to achieve one's goals (i.e., strain theory) and coming from a disadvantaged neighborhood (i.e., social disorganization) are key factors predisposing people to criminal behavior. Furthermore, the fact that many low-income households tend to lack adequate socialization, such as when a single parent has to work two or three jobs to make ends meet, is also a major root cause of delinquency.

Because this model clearly shows some constructs that lead to criminality as coming first (e.g., strain, social disorganization) and others as coming later (e.g., weak bonding and then affiliations with delinquents), this is a good example of end-to-end theoretical integration. In other words, this is an end-to-end form of integration because some models or concepts, such as strain, occur first, which then lead chronologically to other models and concepts, such as weak conventional bonding or strong delinquent bonding, which then lead to crime.

The notable ways in which this perspective becomes a true integrated model is seen in the mediating or intervening variables. Although some antecedent variables (such as strain) can lead directly to delinquent activity, most of the criminal activity is theoretically predicted through a process that would include a breakdown of conventional bonding (i.e., social control and bonding theory), which occurs in many individuals who experience strain or social disorganization in their neighborhoods along with inadequate socialization. Furthermore, individuals who have such a breakdown in conventional bonding tend to be more highly influenced by the associations that they make in the streets among their peers (i.e., differential association-reinforcement and social learning theory). According to Elliott's integrated theory, this factor—strong delinquent bonding—most directly results in delinquent behavior among most juvenile offenders.

One of the notable features of this theoretical model is that it allows for various types of individuals to become criminal. In other words, unlike traditionally separate frameworks that assume that offenders expect not to achieve their goals (e.g., strain theory) or come from bad neighborhoods (e.g., Chicago or social disorganization theory), Elliott's integrated theory allows for a variety of possibilities when it comes to causal paths that explain how crime and delinquency develop in certain people and groups. This is what makes integrated models so much more powerful; namely, they bring several valid explanations together and allow for various possibilities to occur, all of which explain some criminality. Whereas traditional theories largely provide for only one causal process, Elliott and his colleagues showed right from the first major integrated theory that different types of trajectories, or paths to crime, are possible.

One of the major criticisms of merging such theories, particularly strain (which assumes individuals are born relatively good) and control or social bonding (which clearly assumes that people are born relatively bad [i.e., selfish, greedy, aggressive]), is that they tend to have extremely different, even opposite, assumptions of human behavior. As a recent review of theoretical integration noted, Elliott and his colleagues attempted to circumvent this obvious contrast in basic assumptions by claiming that the model allows for variation in individual motivations for why people engage in delinquency and crime.[46] For example, they claimed that failure to achieve one's goals (i.e., strain theory) is not always the motivation for crime; rather, crime can result from inadequate socialization or from coming from a disadvantaged neighborhood.

Furthermore, Elliott's integrated model allows for different forms of control or social bonding with not all of the delinquents being required to have weak social bonds with conventional society. For instance, as can be seen in Figure 12.1, a person who has experienced strain (or failure to achieve her or his goals) can move directly to the social learning and differential association-reinforcement variables of strong delinquent bonding so that the weak conventional bonding construct is not a required causal process in this theoretical model. So, while some critics claim that Elliott and his colleagues have combined theories that simply cannot be synthesized due to contrasting assumptions, we believe that this integrated theory did, in fact, find a logical and consistent way of showing how both models can be merged in a way that makes a lot of sense in the real world. On the other hand, the model does indeed claim that strain directly causes weak conventional bonding, and the theoretical framework implies that the probability of delinquency is highest when an individual experiences both strain and weak conventional bonding, so to some extent, the critics make an important point regarding the logical consistency of the full model, which Elliott and his colleagues have not adequately addressed.[47]

Despite the presence of elements of four traditionally separate theories (strain, social disorganization, social control or bonding, and social learning or differential association-reinforcement), Elliott and his colleagues identified this integrated theory with social control, as opposed to any of the other perspectives, which they argue is a more general theory and can explain crime and delinquency across different levels of explanation. They also noted that the social control perspective is more sociological in the sense that it places more importance on the role of institutional structures in controlling criminal behavior.[48] Perhaps another reason why they identified their model with social control or bonding theory was because both intervening constructs represent types of bonds formed or not formed with others: weak conventional bonding and strong delinquent bonding. However, it is important to keep in mind that these constructs actually represent two traditionally separate theories—namely, social bonding theory and differential association-reinforcement or social learning, respectively.

The author of this textbook believes that when an integrated theory (which claims to be such an integrated model) chooses a primary or dominant theory as its basis, this does not help in selling it to the scientific community, let alone others. A similar problem was seen in Pearson and Weiner's conceptual integration in their identifying a single traditionally separate theory—social learning or differential association-reinforcement—as the foundation or basis for their framework. Obviously, the first reaction by many theorists, even those that are not inherently against theoretical integration, would be somewhat cautious or even resistant. After all, why would a theory that claims to be integrated outright claim a single explanatory framework as its basis?

Rather, such models may be seen more as examples of theoretical elaboration, which tends to start with the assumptions and concepts of one theory and draw from other models to improve the base model. Still, despite

---

[46] Ibid.

[47] Ibid.

[48] Ibid., 311–12.

the criticisms against identifying a single model as a basis for developing an integrated framework for explaining criminality, it is apparent that latitude has been granted. It is important to note that Elliott's model is considered the first true attempt at theoretical integration and is still widely respected as the prototype and example of what an integrated model could and should be.

Much of the empirical evidence supporting Elliott's integrated model has been provided by Elliott and his colleagues themselves through their testing of the theory. Specifically, much of the testing they have done has been via the National Youth Survey (NYS), a national survey collected and synthesized by criminologists at the University of Colorado Boulder, which is where Elliott and most of the colleagues with whom he works are professors. This longitudinal measure of delinquency has been administered and analyzed for several decades, and it represents perhaps the most systematic collection of information from youths regarding key developmental variables and delinquency rates that has ever existed.

Most of the evidence from the NYS shows general strong support for Elliott's model.[49] However, some evidence has shown few direct effects of the strain and social control concepts, which is surprising given that the basis of the model was the social control and bonding elements of the theory.[50] In fact, the original hypothesis in the model—that strain and social control or bonding would have a direct effect on delinquency—was not observed.[51] Rather, only bonding to delinquent peers had a significant and strong effect on future criminality, which supports social learning and differential association-reinforcement theory. This strongly supports the social learning variables in the model and diminishes the claim made by Elliott and his colleagues about the fundamental theoretical perspective of social control and bonding.

Furthermore, a critical review of Elliott's framework, as presented in his 1985 book (with David Huizinga and Suzanne Ageton), noted that a major problem is that its "most puzzling feature . . . is the inclusion of social disorganization in it as a causal factor, in the absence of any attempt to measure or test the importance of this factor. Presumably, the authors wished to claim that their theory was 'more sociological than psychological.'"[52]

This point is particularly important, given that virtually none of the tests of Elliott's integrated model have included social disorganization factors in their studies, even after this critical review was published more than 25 years ago. So, Elliott and his colleagues should either drop this portion from consideration in the model or provide an adequate test of it in relation to the rest of the framework. Although we would opt for the latter, one of these two alternatives must be chosen.

However, from the presentation that Elliott gave as his presidential address to the American Society of Criminology (ASC) in 1993, it appears that the former alternative was chosen. Specifically, in his model of the onset of serious violent offending, all of the antecedent variables could be explained by the other traditionally separate theoretical models in his framework. He included two bonding constructs (family and school), parental sanctions, stressful life events (i.e., strain), and early exposure to crime and victimization. Perhaps the last factor could be construed as related to social disorganization theory, but it is probably regarded more as a social learning and differential association-reinforcement variable, as is suggested from the original model.

In addition, this critique noted that the existing evidence shows that most delinquent activity is committed among groups of juveniles, and, thus, youths who tend to commit illegal acts naturally associate with delinquents. Yet, the affiliation with delinquent peers is not considered the basic foundation of the theory—as tests of this model demonstrated—but rather an intervening variable in the model. The author of this critique claims that Elliott's

---

[49] See review in Akers and Sellers, *Criminological Theories*, 273–76.

[50] Elliott et al., *Explaining Delinquency*.

[51] Akers and Sellers, *Criminological Theories*, 275.

[52] David Farrington, book review of *Explaining Delinquency*, by Elliott et al., *British Journal of Addiction* 81 (1986): 433; embedded quote taken from p. 67 in Elliott et al.'s book.

model does not emphasize this point strongly enough and thereby does not provide convincing evidence that delinquent peers cause or facilitate offending.[53]

In light of these findings, even Elliott and his colleagues acknowledged that their integrated model best fit the data as a social learning and differential association-reinforcement framework of delinquency.[54] However, they chose to retain social control and bonding theory as the primary foundation of their integrated model, stating that "it is not clear that a social learning model would have predicted a conditional relationship between conventional bonding . . . and deviant bonding."[55] Elliott and colleagues went on to say that they did not attribute most of the explained variation in the model to social learning and differential reinforcement as being the most important construct because they claimed that such variables did not play a strong enough part in the indirect effects that were seen in the estimated models.

This is actually a logical position, given the fact that their integrated framework would, in fact, predict that social learning and differential association-reinforcement variables were the primary direct effects on delinquency, and social control, strain, and social disorganization variables were considered primarily indirect all along, according to their model. However, some critics, especially the proponents of social learning and differential reinforcement theory, have claimed the following:

> Even with the addition of the interactive effects of conventional bonding, the final model reported by Elliott et al. is more of a variation on social learning theory (with bonding modifications) than it is a variation on social bonding theory (with learning modifications).[56]

After all, the measures of delinquent peer bonds used by Elliott and his colleagues are essentially measures that have been used by theorists and researchers of social learning theory over the past few decades regarding differential associations, reinforcements, and modeling.[57]

Additional analyses using the NYS have tended to agree with the critics regarding the importance of social learning and differential reinforcement variables in predicting crime and delinquency. Specifically, one relatively recent reanalysis of NYS data showed that social learning variables appeared to predict more variation in deviance than did the other models or constructs in the model.[58] The assumption that strong attachments to others, regardless of who they are, reduces offending, has been shown by empirical research to be false (see Chapter 8). This is true, and all future integrated models must address this issue if they include social control or bonding propositions or constructs in their models.

Despite these criticisms and empirical observations, it appears that Elliott's integrated model has contributed to our understanding of the development of delinquent behavior. In the least, it inspired other theoretical frameworks, some of which we review here. However, it should also be obvious that there are some valid criticisms of this model, such as the claim that it is based on social control and bonding theory while depending heavily on the strong delinquent bonding that takes place in most cases of criminality, clearly implicating social learning and differential reinforcement theory. Again, we want to stress that a true integrated model should not place any emphasis on a

---

[53] Farrington, book review, 433.

[54] Ibid.

[55] Ibid., based on a quote from Elliott et al., *Explaining Delinquency*, 137.

[56] Akers and Sellers, *Criminological Theories*, 275.

[57] Ibid., 276.

[58] Robert Agnew, "Why Do They Do It? An Examination of the Intervening Mechanisms between 'Social Control' Variables and Delinquency," *Journal of Research in Crime and Delinquency* 30 (1993): 245–66.

particular theory; otherwise, the critics will have a sound argument when findings show that one theory is more influential than another.

Thornberry's Interactional Theory

After Elliott's integrated model, presented in 1979, the next major integrated framework was that of Terrence Thornberry in 1987.[59] This model incorporated empirical evidence drawn since Elliott's presentation to create a unique and insightful model of criminality, which addressed an extremely important aspect that had never been addressed previously in criminological theory. Specifically, Thornberry's interactional theory was the first to emphasize reciprocal, or feedback, effects in the causal modeling of the theoretical framework.

As a basis for his model, Thornberry combined social control and social learning models. According to Thornberry, both of these theories try to explain criminality in a straightforward, causal process and are largely targeted toward a certain age population.[60] Thornberry uniquely claimed that the processes of both social control and social learning theory affect each other in a type of feedback process.

Thornberry's integrated model incorporates five primary theoretical constructs, which are synthesized in a comprehensive framework to explain criminal behavior. These five concepts include the following: (1) commitment to school, (2) attachment to parents, (3) belief in conventional values (these first three are taken from social control and bonding theory), (4) adoption of delinquent values, and (5) association with delinquent peers (these last two are drawn from social learning and differential association-reinforcement theory). These five constructs, which most criminologists would agree are important in the development of criminality, are obviously important in a rational model of crime, so at first it does not appear that Thornberry has added much to our understanding of criminal behavior. Furthermore, Thornberry's model clearly points out that different variables will have greater effects at certain times; for example, he claims that association with delinquent peers will have more effect in the midteenage years than at other ages.

What Thornberry adds beyond other theories is the idea of reciprocity or feedback loops, which no previous theory had mentioned, much less emphasized. In fact, much of the previous criminological literature had spent much time debating whether individuals become delinquent and then start hanging out with similar peers or whether individuals start hanging out with delinquent peers and then begin engaging in criminal activity. This has been the traditional chicken-or-egg question in criminology for most of the 20th century; namely, which came first, delinquency or bad friends? It has often been referred to as the *self-selection* versus *social learning* debate; in other words, do certain individuals decide to hang out with delinquents based on their own previous behavior, or do they learn criminality from delinquents with whom they start associating? One of the major contributions of **Thornberry's interactional model** is that he directly answered this question.

Specifically, Thornberry noted that most, if not all, contributors to delinquency (and criminal behavior itself) are related reciprocally. Thus, Thornberry postulated that engaging in crime leads to hanging out with other delinquents and that hanging out with delinquents leads to committing crimes. It is quite common for individuals to commit crime and start hanging out with other peers who are doing the same, and it is also quite common for people to start hanging out with delinquent peers and then start committing offenses. Furthermore, it is perhaps the most likely scenario for a person who is offending to be dealing with both the influences of past experiences and peer effects as well.

---

[59] Terrence Thornberry, "Toward an Interactional Theory of Delinquency," *Criminology* 25 (1987): 863–87. See also Thornberry, "Reflections"; Terrence Thornberry et al., "Testing Interactional Theory: An Examination of Reciprocal Causal Relationships among Family, School and Delinquency," *Journal of Criminal Law and Criminology* 82 (1991): 3–35; Terrence Thornberry et al., "Delinquent Peers, Beliefs, and Delinquent Behavior: A Longitudinal Test of Interactional Theory," *Criminology* 32 (1994): 47–83.

[60] Much of this discussion is taken from Bernard and Snipes, "Theoretical Integration," 314–16; and also Akers and Sellers, *Criminological Theories*, 278.

As mentioned previously, Thornberry considered the social control and bonding constructs, such as attachment to parents and commitment to school, the most essential predictors of delinquency. Like previous theoretical models of social bonding and control, Thornberry's model puts the level of attachment and commitment to conventional society ahead of the degree of moral beliefs that individuals have regarding criminal offending. However, lack of such moral beliefs leads to delinquent behavior, which in turn negatively affects the level of commitment or attachments an individual may have built in her or his development. Thornberry claimed the following:

> While the weakening of the bond to conventional society may be an initial cause of delinquency, delinquency eventually becomes its own indirect cause precisely because of its ability to weaken further the person's bonds to family, school, and conventional beliefs.[61]

Thus, the implications of this model are that variables relating to social control or bonding and other sources cause delinquency, which then becomes, in itself, a predictor and cause for the breakdown of other important causes of delinquency and crime.

Such a model, although complex and hard to measure, is logically consistent, and the postulates are sound. However, the value of any theory has to be determined by the empirical evidence that is found regarding its validity. Much of the scientific evidence regarding Thornberry's empirical model has been contributed by Thornberry and his colleagues.

Case Study: Thornberry's Interactional Model

As an example, consider a person we shall call Johnny who has an absent father and a mother who uses inconsistent discipline and sometimes harsh physical abuse of her son. He sees his mother's state of constant neglect and abuse as proof that belief in conventional values is wrong, and he becomes indifferent toward governmental laws; after all, his main goal is to survive and be successful. Because of his mother's psychological and physical neglect, Johnny pays no attention to school and rather turns to his older peers for guidance and support. These peers guide him toward behavior that gives him both financial reward (selling what they steal) and status in their group (respect for performing well in illegal acts). At some point, Johnny gets caught, and this makes the peers who taught him how to engage in crime very proud, while alienating him from the previous bonds he had with his school, from which he is suspended, and with his mother, who further distances herself from him. This creates a reciprocal effect or feedback loop to the previous factors, which were lack of attachment to his mother and lack of commitment to school. The lowered level of social bonding and control with conventional institutions and factors (mother, school) and increased influence by delinquent peers then leads Johnny to commit more frequent and more serious crimes.

The lowered level of social bonding and control with conventional institutions and factors (mother, school) and increased influence by delinquent peers then leads Johnny to commit more frequent and more serious crimes.

---

[61] Thornberry, "Toward an Interactional Theory," 876, as quoted by Bernard and Snipes, "Theoretical Integration," 315.

Figure 12.2 ● Thornberry's interactional model of delinquent involvement at middle adolescence

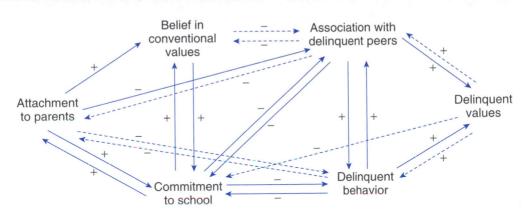

Thornberry's theoretical model is based on reciprocal effects, meaning that what is an outcome variable (e.g., association with delinquent peers) also becomes a predictive variable in that it influences previous variables (e.g., commitment to school). This figure shows how such relationships function with negative signs (−) meaning that there is an inverse relationship between the two variables (e.g., more association with delinquent peers is associated with less commitment to school) or positive (+) signs meaning that there is a direct positive association between two variables (e.g., belief in conventional values is associated with commitment to school). These variables tend to have a feedback loop, as represented in the figure.

Although the full model has yet to be tested, the researchers "have found general support for the reciprocal relationships between both control concepts and learning concepts with delinquent behavior."[62] One test of Thornberry's model used the longitudinal Rochester Youth Development Study to test its postulates.[63] This study found that the estimates of previous unidirectional models (nonreciprocal models) did not adequately explain the variation in the data. Rather, the results supported the interactional model, with delinquent associations leading to increases in delinquency, delinquency leading to reinforcing peer networks, and both directional processes working through the social environment. In fact, this longitudinal study demonstrated that, once the participants had acquired delinquent beliefs from their peers, the effects of these beliefs had further effects on their future behavior and associations, which is exactly what Thornberry's theory predicts (see Figure 12.2).[64]

Perhaps the most recent test of Thornberry's interactional model examined the age-varying effects of the theory.[65] This study incorporated hierarchical linear modeling in investigating a sample of the NYS. The results showed that, while the effects of delinquent peers were relatively close to predictions, peaking in the midteen-age years, the predictions regarding the effects of family on delinquency were not found to be significant in the periods that were expected although family was important during adolescence.

[62] Bernard and Snipes, "Theoretical Integration," 316.

[63] Thornberry et al., "Delinquent Peers."

[64] Ibid.

[65] Sung Joon Jang, "Age-Varying Effects of Family, School, and Peers on Delinquency: A Multilevel Modeling Test of Interactional Theory," *Criminology* 37 (1999): 643–85.

Unlike other authors of integrated theories, Thornberry specifically noted that he prefers to see his approach as theoretical elaboration and not full theoretical integration. While we commend Thornberry for addressing this concern, virtually all criminologists still consider his framework a fully integrated model. And, in many ways, Thornberry's interactional model is far more integrated than others discussed here because it gives equal weight to the traditionally separate theoretical frameworks that are combined into his model in the sense that both are considered antecedent and reciprocal in their effects on criminal behavior.

Braithwaite's Theory of Reintegrative Shaming

A unique integrated model that proposed the synthesis of several traditionally separate theories was presented in 1989 in a book titled *Crime, Shame and Reintegration.*[66] The theory of reintegrative shaming merges constructs and principles from several theories, primarily social control or bonding theory and labeling theory with elements of strain theory, subculture and gang theory, and differential association theory. All of these theories are synthesized in a clear and coherent framework that is presented in both descriptive and graphic form. We will spend extra time discussing John Braithwaite's theory because it addresses not only U.S. culture but also cultural and justice tendencies in Japanese culture.

Braithwaite's idea for the theory was obviously inspired by the cultural differences he observed in Eastern (particularly Japanese) culture, in terms of both socialization practices and the justice system, as compared to the Western world. (Note that Braithwaite is from Australia, which uses the same Western practices as England and the United States.) Specifically, he emphasized the Japanese focus on the aggregate, such as the family, school, or business, to which the individual belongs. In contrast, in many Western cultures, epitomized by U.S. culture, the emphasis is clearly placed on the individual.

This contrast has often been referred to as the *we* culture versus the *me* culture (Eastern vs. Western emphases, respectively). Although this is seen in virtually all aspects of culture and policy practices, it is quite evident in people's names. In most Eastern cultures, people are known by their family name, which is placed first in the ordering. This shows the importance that is placed on the group to which they belong. In contrast, Western societies list individual names first, implying a focus on the individual herself or himself. These naming practices are a manifestation of a virtually all-encompassing cultural difference regarding group dynamics and social expectations across societies, especially in their justice systems. For example, it is quite common in Japan to receive a sentence of apologizing in public, even for the most serious violent crimes.[67] In his book, Braithwaite pointed out that, after World War II, Japan was the only highly industrialized society that showed a dramatic decrease in its crime rate.

Criminological theory would predict an increasing crime rate in Japan, given the extremely high density of urban areas due to rapid industrialization, especially on such a small amount of land—Japan being a large island. As Braithwaite described it, the Japanese suffered from anomie after the war in the sense of a general breakdown of cultural norms, but the nation was able to deal with this anomic state despite the odds. Japan definitively decided not to follow the Western model of justice after the war; rather, it rejected the Western system of stigmatizing convicted felons. Instead, the Japanese implemented a system in which offenders are reintroduced (hence *reintegration*) via a formal ceremony in which citizens accept the offenders back into conventional society. In contrast, in the United States, we typically give our ex-cons about $200 on average and make them promise always to identify themselves as felons on legal documents.

Japan is also extremely lenient in sentencing offenders to prison. In contrast, by rate of incarceration, the United States is the most punitive developed nation. In Japan, Braithwaite noted the following:

---

[66] Braithwaite, *Crime, Shame and Reintegration.*

[67] Ibid., 62.

Prosecution only proceeds in major cases . . . where the normal process of apology, compensation, and forgiveness by the victim breaks down. Fewer than 10 percent of those offenders who are convicted receive prison sentences, and for two-thirds of these, prison sentences are suspended. Whereas 45 percent of those convicted of a crime serve a jail sentence in the U.S., in Japan the percentage is under two.[68]

Public apology is the most common punishment among the Japanese, which strongly reflects the nature of honor in Japanese society, as well as pointing out the fundamental differences between how we deal with offenders. Braithwaite claimed that this cultural and political difference has a huge impact on why crime rates in both nations have experienced such different trends.

Most developing Western nations, including the United States, experienced a rising crime rate in the 1950s, 1960s, and 1970s. Braithwaite argued that this was likely due to culture and the differential treatment of its offenders:

It might be argued that this [the downward trend in crime rates after World War II in Japan] was a result of the re-establishment of cultural traditions of shaming wrongdoers, including the effective coupling of shame and punishment. . . . One contention . . . is that the uncoupling of shame and punishment manifested in a wide variety of ways in many Western countries is an important factor in explaining the rising crime rates in those countries.[69]

Furthermore, in contrast to American society, the Japanese are typically less confrontational with authority. For example, some scholars have noted that the Japanese accept the authority of law, and police officers are considered similar to "elder brothers" who rely "on positive rather than negative reinforcement" when it comes to crime control.[70] This difference in the way officers and other authority figures are considered is likely due to the way that the Japanese view society in terms of neighborhood, community, school, and work—the informal institutions of control that we have mentioned earlier in this book as having more effect on the crime rate than formal institutions (i.e., police, courts, prisons).

Beyond discussing the cultural differences, Braithwaite's integrated theory addresses some of the most notable scientific observations regarding which types of individuals and groups are likely to commit crime. Specifically, Braithwaite stated that most crime is committed by young, poor, single males who live in urban communities that have high levels of residential mobility; they are likely to be unattached to or to do poorly in school, have low educational or occupational aspirations, are not strongly attached to their parents, associate with delinquent peers, and do not have moral beliefs against violating the law.[71]

It is obvious from this list that Braithwaite incorporated some of the major theories and corresponding variables into his theoretical perspective. The emphasis on poor people who do not have high educational or occupational aspirations obviously supports strain theory, whereas the inclusion of urban individuals who live in communities with high residential mobility reflects the Chicago School or social disorganization theory. At the same time, Braithwaite clearly highlighted the predisposition of people who have limited moral beliefs and weak attachments, which conjures up images of social bonding and control theory; individuals having delinquent peers obviously

---

[68] Ibid., citing findings from J. Haley, "Sheathing the Sword of Justice in Japan: An Essay on Law without Sanctions," *Journal of Japanese Studies* 8 (1982): 265–81.

[69] Braithwaite, *Crime, Shame and Reintegration*, 61; brackets are authors' paraphrasing.

[70] David H. Bayley, *Forces of Order: Police Behavior in Japan and the United States* (Berkeley: University of California Press, 1976).

[71] Braithwaite, *Crime, Shame and Reintegration*, 44–53.

▲ **Image 12.3**   John Braithwaite, a highly respected scholar, proposed the theory of reintegrative shaming, which has led to many successful policy implementations, especially regarding the use of restorative programs for more minor offenders.

SOURCE: Courtesy of John Braithwaite

supports differential association and reinforcement theory. Thus, a handful of theories are important in the construction of Braithwaite's integrated theory.

Braithwaite noted that much of the effectiveness of the Japanese system of crime control depends on two constructs: (1) interdependency and (2) communitarianism. Interdependency is the level of bonding of an individual to conventional society, such as the degree to which she or he is involved with or attached to conventional groups in society, which would include employment, family, church, and organizations. According to Braithwaite, interdependency is the building block of the other major theoretical construct in his integrated model: communitarianism. Communitarianism is the macro (group) level of interdependency, meaning that it is the cumulative degree of the bonds that individuals have with conventional groups and institutions (e.g., family, employment, organizations, church) in a given society. Obviously, these theoretical constructs are mostly based on the theory of social bonding and control in the sense that they are based on attachments, commitment, and involvement in conventional society.

Braithwaite's model has a causal ordering that starts with largely demographic variables, such as age, gender, marital status, employment, and aspirations, on the individual level and urbanization and residential mobility on the macro (group) level. All of these factors are predicted to influence the level of interdependency and communitarianism in the model, which, as we previously discussed, is largely based on social control and bonding theory. Depending on which type of culture is considered, or what forms of shaming are used in a given jurisdiction, the various types of shaming that are administered are key in this integrated model.

According to Braithwaite, societies that emphasize reintegrative shaming, such as Japan, will reduce the rates of crime in their societies. When an offender in Japan completes her or his sentence or punishment for committing a crime, the government will often sponsor a formal ceremony in which the offender is reintroduced or reintegrated into conventional society. According to Braithwaite, we in the United States do not reintegrate offenders into our society after shaming them but rather stigmatize them, which leads them to associate only with people from criminal subcultures (e.g., drug users, gang members). Braithwaite claimed that this leads to the formation of criminal groups and the grasping of illegitimate opportunities offered in the local community. Ultimately, this means that people who are not reintegrated into conventional society will inevitably be stigmatized and labeled as offenders, preventing them from becoming productive members of the community, even if their intentions are to do such.

Most empirical studies of Braithwaite's theory show mixed results, with most being in favor of this theory, especially regarding its implementation for policy. Some tests have shown that reintegrative ideology regarding violations of law can have a positive impact on future compliance with the law; others have found that high levels of shaming in parental practices do not increase offending.[72] Studies in other countries, such as China and Iceland,

---

[72] Toni Makkai and John Braithwaite, "Reintegrative Shaming and Compliance with Regulatory Standards," *Criminology* 32 (1994): 361–86; Carter Hay, "An Exploratory Test of Braithwaite's Reintegrative Shaming Theory," *Journal of Research in Crime and Delinquency* 38 (2001): 132–53.

show partial support for Braithwaite's theory.[73] While some studies have found encouraging results,[74] other recent studies have also found weak or no support for the theory.[75]

The most recent reports regarding the effects of shame show that outcomes largely depend on how shame is measured, which Braithwaite's theory largely ignores. There are, for example, episodic or situational shame states as well as long-term shame traits or propensities. Recent reviews of the literature and studies of how different types of shame are measured show that certain forms of shame are positively correlated with offending, whereas other forms of shame tend to inhibit criminal behavior.[76] If individuals persistently feel shame, they are more likely to commit criminal activity, but if persons who are not predisposed to feel shame perceive that they would feel shame for doing a given illegal activity, then they would be strongly inhibited from engaging in such activity.[77] This is consistent with findings from another recent study that demonstrated that the effect of reintegrative shaming had an interactive effect on delinquency.[78]

Furthermore, Braithwaite's theory does not take into account other important self-conscious emotions, such as guilt, pride, embarrassment, and empathy, that are important when individuals are deciding whether to commit criminal behavior. Although some theorists claim that shame is the key social emotion, studies show that they are clearly wrong. Rather, many emotions, such as guilt and embarrassment, are based on social interaction and self-consciousness; in many ways, they are just as inhibitory or rehabilitating as shame.[79] The literature examining rational choice theory is also an indication of the effects of emotions other than shame in influencing decisions on offending.[80]

Still, Braithwaite's reintegrative theory provides an important step ahead in theoretical development, particularly in terms of combining explanatory models to address crime rates, as well as correctional policies and philosophies, across various cultures. Specifically, Braithwaite's theory makes a strong argument that Eastern (particularly Japanese) policies of reintegration and apology for convicted offenders are beneficial for that culture. Would this system work in Western culture, especially the United States? The answer is definitely unknown, but it is unlikely that such a model would work well in the United States. After all, most of the chronic, serious offenders in the United States would not be highly deterred by having to apologize to the public, and many might consider such an apology or reintegration ceremony an honor, or a way to show that they really hadn't been punished. This may not be true,

---

[73] Lu Hong, Zhang Lening, and Terance Miethe, "Interdependency, Communitarianism, and Reintegrative Shaming in China," *Social Science Journal* 39 (2002): 189–202; Eric Baumer et al., "Crime, Shame, and Recidivism: The Case of Iceland," *British Journal of Criminology* 42 (2002): 40–60.

[74] Nathan Harris, Lode Walgrave, and John Braithwaite, "Emotional Dynamics in Restorative Conferences," *Theoretical Criminology* 8 (2004): 191–210; Eliza Ahmed and Valerie Braithwaite, "'What, Me Ashamed'? Shame Management and School Bullying," *Journal of Research in Crime and Delinquency* 41 (2004): 269–94.

[75] Bas Van Stokkom, "Moral Emotions in Restorative Justice Conferences: Managing Shame, Designing Empathy," *Theoretical Criminology* 6 (2002): 339–61; Charles Tittle, Jason Bratton, and Marc Gertz, "A Test of a Microlevel Application of Shaming Theory," *Social Problems* 50 (2003): 592–617; Lening Zhang and Sheldon Zhang, "Reintegrative Shaming and Predatory Delinquency," *Journal of Research in Crime and Delinquency* 41 (2004): 433–53.

[76] Stephen Tibbetts, "Shame and Rational Choice in Offending Decisions," *Criminal Justice and Behavior* 24 (1996): 234–55.

[77] Stephen Tibbetts, "Self-Conscious Emotions and Criminal Offending," *Psychological Reports* 93 (2003): 201–31; Stephen G. Tibbetts, "Traits and States of Self-Conscious Emotions in Criminal Decision Making," in *Affect and Cognition in Criminal Decision Making*, ed. Jean-Louis Van Gelder et al. (London: Routledge, 2014), 221–38.

[78] Hay, "An Exploratory Test."

[79] For an excellent review, see June Price Tangney and Kurt Fischer, *Self-Conscious Emotions: The Psychology of Shame, Guilt, Embarrassment, and Pride* (New York: Guilford Press, 1995).

[80] See Harold Grasmick, Brenda Sims Blackwell, and Robert Bursik, "Changes over Time in Gender Differences in Perceived Risk of Sanctions," *Law and Society Review* 27 (1993): 679–705; Harold Grasmick, Robert Bursik, and Bruce Arneklev, "Reduction in Drunk Driving as a Response to Increased Threats of Shame, Embarrassment, and Legal Sanctions," *Criminology* 31 (1993): 41–67; and Tibbetts, "College Student Perceptions."

but we would not know this until such policies were implemented fully in our system. However, programs along these lines have been implemented in our country, and some of these programs will be reviewed later in this book.

Tittle's Control–Balance Theory

One of the more recently proposed models of theoretical integration is Charles **Tittle's control–balance theory**. Presented by Tittle in 1995, control–balance integrated theory proposes that (a) the amount of control to which one is subjected and (b) the amount of control that one can exercise determine the probability of deviance occurring. In other words, the balance between these two types of control, he argued, can predict the type of behavior that is likely to be committed.[81]

In this integrated theoretical framework, Tittle claimed that a person is least likely to offend when she or he has a balance of controlling and being controlled. On the other hand, the likelihood of offending will increase when these become unbalanced. If individuals are more controlled by external forces, which Tittle calls *control deficit*, then the theory predicts that they will commit predatory or defiant criminal behavior. In contrast, if an individual possesses an excessive level of control by external forces, which Tittle refers to as *control surplus*, then that individual will be more likely to commit acts of exploitation or decadence. It is important to realize that this excessive control is not the same as excessive self-control, which would be covered by other theories examined in this chapter. Rather, Tittle argued that people who are controlling—that is, who have excessive control over others—will be predisposed toward inappropriate activities.

Early empirical tests of control–balance theory have reported mixed results with both surpluses and deficits predicting the same types of deviance.[82] Furthermore, researchers have uncovered differing effects of the control–balance ratio on two types of deviance that are contingent on gender. This finding is consistent with the gender-specific support found for Walter Reckless's containment theory and with the gender differences found in other theoretical models.[83] Despite the mixed findings for Tittle's control–balance theory of crime, this model of criminal offending still gets a lot of attention, and most of the empirical evidence has been in favor of this theory.

Hagan's Power–Control Theory

The final integrated theory that we will cover in this chapter deals with the influence of familial control and how this relates to criminality across gender. Power–control theory is another integrated theory that was proposed by John Hagan and his colleagues.[84] The primary focus of this theory is on the level of patriarchal attitudes and structure in the household, which are influenced by parental positions in the workforce.

Power–control theory assumes that, in households where the mother and father have relatively similar levels of power at work (i.e., balanced households), mothers will be less likely to exert control on their daughters. These balanced households will be less likely to experience gender differences in the criminal offending

---

[81] Charles Tittle, *Control Balance: Toward a General Theory of Deviance* (Boulder, CO: Westview, 1995) (see chap. 8, n. 55).

[82] Alex Piquero and Matthew Hickman, "An Empirical Test of Tittle's Control Balance Theory," *Criminology* 37 (1999): 319–42 (see chap. 8, n. 75); Matthew Hickman and Alex Piquero, "Exploring the Relationships between Gender, Control Balance, and Deviance," *Deviant Behavior* 22 (2001): 323–51 (see chap. 8, n. 75).

[83] Hickman and Piquero, "Exploring the Relationships." For contrast and comparison, see Grasmick et al., "Changes over Time"; Grasmick et al., "Reduction in Drunk Driving"; and Tibbetts, "College Student Perceptions."

[84] John Hagan, *Structural Criminology* (Newark, NJ: Rutgers University Press, 1989) (see chap. 8, n. 77); John Hagan, A. Gillis, and J. Simpson, "The Class Structure of Gender and Delinquency: Toward a Power-Control Theory of Common Delinquent Behavior," *American Journal of Sociology* 90 (1985): 1151–78 (see chap. 8, n. 77); John Hagan, A. Gillis, and J. Simpson, "Clarifying and Extending Power-Control Theory," *American Journal of Sociology* 95 (1990): 1024–37 (see chap. 8, n. 77); John Hagan, J. Simpson, and A. Gillis, "Class in the Household: A Power-Control Theory of Gender and Delinquency," *American Journal of Sociology* 92 (1987): 788–816 (see chap. 8, n. 77).

of the children. However, households in which mothers and fathers have dissimilar levels of power in the workplace (i.e., unbalanced households) are more likely to suppress criminal activity in daughters. In such families, it is assumed that daughters will be taught to be less risk-taking than the males in the family. In addition, assertiveness and risky activity among the males in the house will be encouraged. This assertiveness and risky activity may be precursors to crime, which is highly consistent with the empirical evidence regarding trends in crime related to gender. Thus, Hagan's integrated theory seems to have a considerable amount of face validity.

Most empirical tests of power–control theory have provided moderate support, while more recent studies have further specified the validity of the theory in different contexts.[85] For example, one recent study reported that the influence of mothers, not fathers, on sons had the greatest impact on reducing the delinquency of young males.[86] Another researcher has found that differences in perceived threats of embarrassment and formal sanctions vary between more patriarchal and less patriarchal households.[87] Finally, studies have also started measuring the effect of patriarchal attitudes on crime and delinquency.[88] However, most of the empirical studies that have shown support for the theory have been done by Hagan or his colleagues. Still, power–control theory is a good example of a social control theory in that it is consistent with the idea that individuals must be socialized and that the gender differences in such socialization make a difference in how people will act throughout life.

Policy Implications

Few policy strategies have actually been derived from integrated or developmental theories, probably because most policy makers are either unaware of such theoretical frameworks or because the theories are so complicated that it is difficult for practitioners to apply them. However, one exception to this rule is Braithwaite's theory of shaming and reintegration. Braithwaite and others have gone to great lengths to apply his theory in Australia, and some evaluations of this approach have shown promise, even if not commonly incorporated in the United States. Interventions stress the restorative concepts of his theory, particularly the idea of reintegrating offenders into society as opposed to stigmatizing them.[89]

This strategy emphasizes holding offenders accountable, yet it tries to bring them back into conventional society as quickly and efficiently as possible. In contrast, the U.S. system typically gives prisoners a nominal sum of money (in most jurisdictions, about $200), and they must report themselves as convicted felons for the rest of their lives on all job applications. Would Braithwaite's model work here in the United States? We don't know yet, but it seems that there could be a better way to incorporate offenders back into society in such a way that they are not automatically set up to fail.

---

[85] Hagan et al., "Class in the Household"; B. McCarthy and John Hagan, "Gender, Delinquency, and the Great Depression: A Test of Power-Control Theory," *Canadian Review of Sociology and Anthropology* 24 (1987): 153–77 (see chap. 8, n. 78); Merry Morash and Meda Chesney-Lind, "A Reformulation and Partial Test of the Power-Control Theory of Delinquency," *Justice Quarterly* 8 (1991): 347–77 (see chap. 8, n. 78); Simon Singer and Murray Levine, "Power-Control Theory, Gender, and Delinquency: A Partial Replication with Additional Evidence on the Effects of Peers," *Criminology* 26 (1988): 627–47 (see chap. 8, n. 78).

[86] B. McCarthy, John Hagan, and T. Woodward, "In the Company of Women: Structure and Agency in a Revised Power-Control Theory of Gender and Delinquency," *Criminology* 37 (1999): 761–88 (see chap. 8, n. 79).

[87] Brenda Sims Blackwell, "Perceived Sanction Threats, Gender, and Crime: A Test and Elaboration of Power-Control Theory," *Criminology* 38 (2000): 439–88 (see chap. 8, n. 80).

[88] Blackwell, "Perceived Sanction Threats"; Kristin Bates and Chris Bader, "Family Structure, Power-Control Theory, and Deviance: Extending Power-Control Theory to Include Alternate Family Forms," *Western Criminology Review* 4 (2003): 170–90 (see chap. 8, n. 81).

[89] John Braithwaite, "Restorative Justice: Assessing Optimistic and Pessimistic Accounts," in *Crime and Justice: A Review of Research*, Vol. 25, ed. Michael Tonry (Chicago: University of Chicago Press, 1999), 1–27.

Other policy implications can be drawn from the various integrated theoretical models that we have discussed in this chapter. We will focus on the concepts that were most prominent, which are parenting and peer influences. Regarding the former, numerous empirical studies have examined programs for improving the ability of parents and expecting parents to be effective.[90] Such programs typically involve training high school students—or individuals or couples who are already parents—on how to be better parents. Additional programs include Head Start and other preschool programs that attempt to prepare high-risk youth for starting school; these have been found to be effective in reducing disciplinary problems.[91]

Regarding peer influences, numerous programs and evaluations have examined the effects of reducing negative peer influences regarding crime.[92] Programs that emphasize prosocial peer groups are often successful, whereas others show little or no success.[93] The conclusion from most of these studies is that the most successful programs of this type are those that focus on learning life skills and prosocial skills and use a curriculum based on a cognitive behavioral approach.[94] This strategy includes reinforcing positive behavior; clarifying rules of behavior in social settings; teaching life and thinking skills; and, perhaps most important, thinking about the consequences of a given behavior before acting (hence, the cognitive behavioral approach). Studies consistently show that programs using a cognitive behavioral approach (i.e., think before you act) are far more successful than programs that emphasize interactions among peers or use psychoanalysis or other forms of therapy.[95]

Many other policy implications can be derived from integrated theories explaining criminal behavior, but parenting practices and peer influences are the primary constructs in most integrated models. Thus, these are the two areas that should be targeted for policy interventions, but this must be done correctly. For a start, policy makers could review the findings from empirical studies and evaluations and see that the earlier parenting programs start, particularly for high-risk children, the more effective they can be. Regarding the peer influence programs, a combination of cognitive behavioral therapy and training in life skills appears to be more effective than other approaches.

Conclusion

In this chapter, we have reviewed which factors determine the types of integrated theories and which criteria make an integrated theory a good explanation of human behavior. We have also examined examples of integrated theories that have been proposed in the criminological literature in the past 30 years. All of the examples represent the most researched and discussed integrated theories, and they demonstrate both the advantages and disadvantages of theoretical integration or elaboration. We hope that readers will be able to determine for themselves which of these integrated theories are the best in explaining criminal activity.

In this chapter, we have examined the various ways in which theoretical integration can be done, including forms of conceptual integration and theoretical elaboration. Furthermore, the criticisms of the different variations of integration and elaboration have been discussed. In addition, numerous examples of theoretical integration have been presented along with the empirical studies that have been performed to examine their validity. Such examples included Elliott's seminal integrated theory as well as Pearson and Weiner's conceptual integration framework. We also examined other integrated theoretical models, such as Braithwaite's theory of reintegration, Tittle's model of

---

[90] See review in Brown et al., *Criminology: Explaining Crime*, 425.

[91] Ibid.

[92] For a review, see Akers and Sellers, *Criminological Theories*, 102–8.

[93] Ibid.

[94] Ibid., 108.

[95] Ibid.

control balance, and **Hagan's power–control theory**. All have received much attention and research in order to test the propositions proposed by each integrated perspective—with mixed results.

Finally, we discussed the policy implications that can be recommended from such integrated theories. Specifically, we concluded that early parenting and peer influences are the two most important influences across these theoretical models. Furthermore, we concluded that when it comes to parenting programs, the earlier, the better. We also concluded that a cognitive behavioral approach that includes the teaching of life skills is most effective for peer influence programs.

/// CHAPTER SUMMARY

- Theoretical integration is one of the more contemporary developments in criminological theorizing.

- This approach brings with it many criticisms yet arguably many advantages because these models tend to merge separate theories that have very different assumptions about criminal behavior.

- Types of theoretical integration include end-to-end, side-by-side, and up-and-down, which vary greatly and are typically based on the types of theories they are merging or integrating.

- Conceptual integration appears to be a useful, albeit rarely explored, form of theoretical integration.

- Pearson and Weiner presented what is considered the most comprehensive and detailed framework regarding conceptual integration.

- Theoretical elaboration is another form of integration, which involves using one theory as the base or primary model and then incorporating concepts and propositions from other theories to make the primary model stronger.

- A number of seminal integrated theories have been examined using empirical evidence and appear to have enhanced our understanding of criminal behavior.

- Some of the theoretical models that have been proposed, such as the first notable model by Elliott et al., have been supported by empirical research.

- Thornberry's interactive model of criminality was unique in claiming that certain causal variables act as both predictive and consequential variables, which give feedback to other predictive variables and create a type of feedback loop in which the cumulative effects are difficult to measure because variables are acting cumulatively over time as both a consequence and then as a predictor in affecting other key variables as an individual ages over time.

- We also discussed following integrated frameworks, such as Braithwaite's reintegrative model, Tittle's control–balance theory, and Hagan's power–control model of criminality.

- Theoretical integration models have many critics who claim that the assumptions, concepts, and propositions of the mixed theories are counterintuitive.

- Despite the criticisms, integrated theoretical models of crime provide more understanding about criminal activity of individuals because human behavior is highly complex, and the combination of theories is likely more robust and valid than more simple, separate theories on their own.

/// KEY TERMS

Braithwaite's reintegrative
   shaming theory   234

communitarianism   234

conceptual integration   234

Elliott's integrated model   233

end-to-end (or sequential)
   integration   229

Hagan's power–control theory   255

integrated theories   227

interdependency   234

side-by-side (or horizontal)
   integration   231

theoretical elaboration   230

Thornberry's interactional
   model   245

Tittle's control–balance theory   252

up-and-down (or deductive)
   integration   232

/// DISCUSSION QUESTIONS

1.   What is the definition of theoretical integration, and why can such theories be beneficial?

2.   Describe what end-to-end theoretical integration is, and provide an example of such integration.

3.   Describe what side-by-side theoretical integration is, and provide an example of such integration.

4.   Describe what up-and-down theoretical integration is, and provide an example of such integration.

5.   Discuss the differences among theoretical elaboration, theoretical integration, and conceptual integration.

6.   What are the major strengths and weaknesses of theoretical integration?

7.   In your opinion, what is the best of the integrated models? Why do you believe this is the best integrated model?

8.   What do you believe is the weakest integrated model? Why?

/// WEB RESOURCES

Integrated Theories of Crime

   http://onlinelibrary.wiley.com/doi/10.1002/9781118517390.wbetc028/full
   http://law.jrank.org/pages/821/Crime-Causation-Sociological-Theories-Integrated-theories.html

John Braithwaite/Reintegrative Theory

   https://www.anu.edu.au/fellows/jbraithwaite/_documents/Chapters/Shame_Restorative_2005.pdf
   https://learn.bu.edu/bbcswebdav/pid-1942479-dt-content-rid-6162758_1/courses/14sprgmetcj602_ol/week06/
   metcj602_W06L01T04_Reintegrative.html

Hagan's Power–Control Theory

   http://www.westerncriminology.org/documents/WCR/v04n3/article_pdfs/bates.pdf

Glossary

actus reus: In legal terms, this is whether the offender actually engaged in a given criminal act. This concept can be contrasted with *mens rea,* which is a concept regarding whether the offender had the intent to commit a given act. This concept is important, especially in situations in which juveniles or mentally disabled individuals engage in offending.

adaptations to strain: As proposed by Robert Merton, these are the five ways that individuals deal with feelings of strain; see *conformity, innovation, rebellion, retreatism,* and *ritualism.*

adolescence-limited offenders: These types of offenders are labeled in Terrie Moffitt's developmental theory; such offenders commit crimes only during adolescence and desist from offending once they reach their 20s or adulthood.

adoption studies: Adoption studies examine the criminality of adoptees as compared to the criminality of their biological and adoptive parents; such studies consistently show that biological parents have more influence on children's criminal behavior than the adoptive parents who raised them.

Age of Enlightenment: This was a period of the late 17th to 18th century in which philosophers and scholars began to emphasize the rights of individuals in society. This movement emphasized the rights of individuals to have a voice in their government and to exercise free choice; it also included the idea of the social contract and other important assumptions that influenced our current government and criminal justice system.

anomie: This is a concept originally proposed by Émile Durkheim, which meant "normlessness" or the chaos that takes place when a society (e.g., economic structure) changes very rapidly. This concept was later used by Robert Merton in his strain theory of crime, where he redefined it as a disjunction between the emphasis placed on conventional goals and the conventional means used to achieve such goals.

atavism: This is the belief that certain characteristics or behaviors of a person are a throwback to an earlier stage of evolutionary development.

autonomic nervous system (ANS): This is the portion of the nervous system that consists of our anxiety levels, such as the fight or flight response, as well as our involuntary motor activities (e.g., heart rate). Studies consistently show that lower levels of ANS functioning are linked to criminality.

bourgeoisie: This is a class or status that Karl Marx assigned to the dominant, oppressing owners of production, who are considered the elite class due to ownership of companies, factories, and so on. Marx proposed that this group created and implemented laws that helped retain the dominance of this class over the proletariat or working class.

Braithwaite's reintegrative shaming theory: This integrated theoretical model merges constructs and principles from several theories, primarily social control or bonding theory and labeling theory with elements of strain theory, subculture or gang theory, and differential association theory.

brutalization effect: This is the predicted tendency of homicides to increase after an execution, particularly after high-profile executions.

central nervous system (CNS): This is the portion of the nervous system that largely consists of the brain and spinal column and is responsible for our voluntary motor activities; studies consistently show that low functioning of the CNS (e.g., slower brain wave patterns) is linked to criminal behavior.

cerebrotonic: This is the type of temperament or personality associated with an ectomorphic (thin) body type; these people tend to be introverted and shy.

certainty of punishment: Certainty of punishment is one of the key elements of deterrence; the assumption is that when people commit a crime, they will perceive a high likelihood of being caught and punished.

Chicago School of Criminology: This is a theoretical framework of criminal behavior that is often referred to as the Ecological School or the theory of social disorganization; it emphasizes the environmental impact of living in a high-crime neighborhood and asserts that this increases criminal activity. This model applies ecological principles of invasion, domination, and succession in explaining how cities grow and the implications this has on crime rates. Also, this model emphasizes the level of organization (or lack thereof) in explaining crime rates in a given neighborhood.

classical conditioning: This is a learning model that assumes that animals as well as people learn through associations between stimuli and responses; this model was primarily promoted by Ivan Pavlov.

Classical School: The Classical School of criminological theory is a perspective that is considered the first rational model of crime, one that was based on logic rather than supernatural or demonic factors. It assumes that crime occurs after a rational individual mentally weighs the potential good and bad consequences of crime and then makes a decision about whether or not to engage in a given behavior. This model is directly tied to the formation of deterrence theory and assumes that people have free will to control their behavior

clearance rate: This is the percentage of crimes reported to police that result in an arrest or an identification of a suspect who cannot be apprehended (due to death of suspect, or fleeing, etc.). In other words, the authorities essentially have a very good idea of who committed the crime, so it is considered "solved." The clearance rate can be seen as a rough estimate of the rate at which crimes are solved.

collective conscience: According to Émile Durkheim, this is the extent of similarities or likeness that people in a society share. The theory assumes that the stronger the collective conscience, the less crime in that community.

college boy: This is a type of lower-class male youth identified by Albert Cohen who has experienced the same strains and status frustration as his peers but responds to his disadvantaged situation by dedicating himself to overcoming the odds and competing in the middle-class schools despite his unlikely chances for success.

communitarianism: This is a concept in John Braithwaite's theory of reintegration, which is a macro-level measure of the degree to which the individuals are connected or interdependent on mainstream society (via organizations or groups).

conceptual integration: This is a type of theoretical integration in which a theoretical perspective consumes or uses concepts from many other theoretical models.

concordance rates: Concordance rates are rates at which twin pairs either share a trait (e.g., criminality) or the lack of the trait. For example, either both twins are criminal or neither is criminal; discordant would be if one of the pair is criminal, and the other is not.

conflict gangs: This is a type of gang identified by Richard Cloward and Lloyd Ohlin that tends to develop in neighborhoods with weak stability and little or no organization. Gangs are typically relatively disorganized and lack the skills and knowledge to make a profit through criminal activity; thus, their primary illegal activity is violence, which is used to gain prominence and respect among themselves and the neighborhood.

conflict theories: These are theories of criminal behavior that assume that most people disagree on what the law should be and/or that law is used as a tool by those in power to keep down other groups.

conformity: In strain theory, this is an adaptation to strain in which an individual buys into the conventional means of success and also buys into the conventional goals.

consensual perspective: Consensual perspective encompasses theories that assume virtually everyone is in agreement on the laws and therefore assume no conflict in attitudes regarding the laws/rules of society.

containment theory: Containment theory is a control theory proposed by Walter Reckless in the 1960s. It presented a model that emphasized internal and social pressures to commit crime, which range from personality predispositions to peer influences as well as internal and external constraints, ranging from personal self-control to parental control, that determine whether an individual will engage in criminal activity. This theory is often criticized as being too vague or general, but it advanced criminological theory by providing a framework in which many internal and external factors were emphasized.

control–balance theory: An integrated theory originally presented by Charles Tittle, it assumes that the amount of control to which one is subjected, as compared to the amount of control that one can exercise, determines the probability of deviant behavior and the types of deviance that are committed by that individual. In other words, the balance or imbalance between these two types of control can predict the amount and type of behavior likely to be committed.

control theories: These are a group of theories of criminal behavior that emphasize the assumption that humans are born selfish and have tendencies to be aggressive and offend and that individuals must be controlled typically by socialization and discipline or from internalized self-control that has been developed in their upbringing.

corner boy: This is a type of lower-class male youth identified by Albert Cohen who has experienced the same strains and status frustration as others but responds to his disadvantaged situation by accepting his place in society as someone who will somewhat passively make the best of life at the bottom of the social order. As the label describes, they often "hang out" on corners.

correlation, or covariation: This is a criterion of causality that requires a change in a predictor variable (X) to be consistently associated with some change (either positive or negative) in the explanatory variable (Y). An example would be unemployment (X) being related to criminal activity (Y).

craniometry: This is the field of study that emphasized the belief that the size of the brain or skull reflected superiority or inferiority, with larger brains or skulls being considered superior.

criminal gangs: This is a type of gang identified by Richard Cloward and Lloyd Ohlin that forms in lower-class neighborhoods with an organized structure of adult criminal behavior. Such neighborhoods are so organized and stable that their criminal networks are often known and accepted by the conventional citizens. In these neighborhoods, the adult gangsters mentor neighborhood youth and take them under their wing. Such gangs tend to be highly organized and stable.

criminology: Criminology is the scientific study of crime and the reasons why people engage (or don't engage) in criminal behavior as well as the study of why certain trends occur or groups of people seem to engage in criminal behavior more than others.

cross-sectional studies: This is a form of research design modeling in which a collection of data is taken at one point in time (often in survey format).

cultural and subcultural theories: This is a perspective of criminal offending that assumes that many offenders believe in a normative system that is distinctly different than, and often at odds with, the norms accepted by conventional society.

cytogenetic studies: These are studies of crime that focus on the genetic makeup of individuals, having a specific focus on abnormalities in their chromosomal makeup. An example is XYY instead of the normal XX (females) and normal XY (males).

dark figure: This is the vast majority of major crime incidents that never get reported to police due to the failure of victims to file a police report; covers most criminal offending, with the exception of homicide and motor vehicle theft, which are almost always reported to police.

decriminalization: This is a policy related to labeling theory, which proposes less harsh punishments for some minor offenses, such as the possession of small amounts of marijuana; for example, in California, an offender gets a ticket or fine for this offense rather than being officially charged and prosecuted.

deinstitutionalization: This is a policy related to labeling theory. It proposes that juveniles or those accused of relatively minor offenses should not be locked up in jail or prison.

delinquent boy: Identified by Albert Cohen, this is a type of lower-class male youth who responds to strains and status frustration by joining with similar others in a group to commit a crime.

determinism: Determinism is the assumption that human behavior is caused by factors outside of free will and rational decision making (e.g., biology, peer influence, poverty, bad parenting). It is the distinctive, primary assumption of positivism (as opposed to the Classical School of criminological theory, which assumes free will/free choice).

deterrence theory: The theory of crime associated with the Classical School, it proposes that individuals will make rational decisions regarding their behavior. This theory focuses on three concepts: the individual's perception of (1) swiftness of punishment, (2) certainty of punishment, and (3) severity of punishment.

developmental theories: Developmental theories are perspectives of criminal behavior that are also to some extent integrated but are distinguished by their emphasis on the evolution of individuals' criminality over time. Specifically, developmental theories tend to look at the individual as the unit of analysis, and such models focus on the various aspects of the onset, frequency, intensity, duration, desistence, and other aspects of the individual's criminal career.

deviance: Deviance involves behaviors that are not normal. It includes many illegal acts as well as activities that are not necessarily criminal but are unusual and often violate social norms, such as burping loudly at a formal dinner or wearing inappropriate clothing.

differential association theory: This is a theory of criminal behavior that emphasizes the association with significant others (peers, parents, etc.) in learning criminal behavior. This theory was originally presented by Edwin Sutherland.

differential identification theory: This is a theory of criminal behavior that is very similar to differential association theory; the major

difference is that differential identification theory takes into account associations with persons or images that are presented in the media (e.g., movies, TV, sports). This model was originally proposed by Daniel Glaser.

differential reinforcement theory: This is a theory of criminal behavior that emphasizes various types of social learning, specifically classical conditioning, operant conditioning, and imitation or modeling. This theory was originally presented by Robert Burgess and Ronald Akers and is one of the most supported theories according to empirical studies.

diversion: Diversion is a set of policies related to labeling theory that attempt to get an offender out of the formal justice system as quickly as possible; an offender might perform a service or enter a rehabilitation program instead of serving time in jail or prison. Often, if an offender successfully completes the contract, the official charge or conviction for the crime is expunged or eliminated from the official record.

dizygotic (DZ) twins: Also referred to as fraternal or nonidentical twins, these are twin pairs that come from two separate eggs (zygotes) and thus share only 50% of the genetic makeup that can vary.

dopamine: This is a neurotransmitter that is largely responsible for "good feelings" in the brain; it is increased by many illicit drugs (e.g., cocaine).

dramatization of evil: A concept proposed by Frank Tannenbaum in relation to labeling theory, it states that often when relatively minor laws are broken, the community tends to overreact and make a rather large deal out of it ("dramatizing" it). A good example is when a very young offender sprays graffiti on a street sign, and the neighborhood ostracizes that youth.

drift theory: This is a theory of criminal behavior in which the lack of social controls in the teenage years allows for individuals to experiment in various criminal offending, often due to peer influence, without the individuals buying into a criminal lifestyle; this theory was introduced by David Matza.

early onset: This is a key criterion that developmental researchers use as a vital predictor of which individuals are most likely to become chronic, persistent offenders throughout life; despite this criterion varying by study or offense, most researchers mark early onset as an arrest occurring before age 14.

Ecological School: See *Chicago School of Criminology.*

ectoderm: This is a medical term for the outer layer of tissue in our bodies (e.g., skin, nervous system).

ectomorphic: This is the type of body shape associated with an emphasis on the outer layer of tissue (ectoderm) during development; these people are disposed to be thin.

ego: This is the only conscious domain of the psyche; according to Sigmund Freud, it functions to mediate the battle between id and superego.

Elliott's integrated model: This is perhaps the first major integrated perspective proposed that clearly attempted to merge various traditionally separate theories of crime. Delbert Elliott's integrated framework attempts to merge strain, social disorganization, control, and social learning or differential association–reinforcement perspectives for the purpose of explaining delinquency, particularly in terms of drug use, as well as other forms of deviant behavior.

empirical validity: This refers to the extent to which a theoretical model is supported by scientific research. Empirical research has consistently supported a number of theories and consistently refuted others.

endoderm: This is the medical term for the inner layer of tissue in our bodies (e.g., digestive organs).

endomorphic: This is the type of body shape associated with an emphasis on the inner layer of tissue (endoderm) during development. These people are disposed to be obese.

end-to-end (or sequential) integration: This is a type of theoretical integration that conveys the linkage of the theories based on the temporal ordering of two or more theories in their causal timing. This means that one theory (or concepts from one theory) precedes another theory (or concepts from another theory) in terms of causal ordering or timing.

equivalency hypothesis: This is a "mirror-image" tendency, which is the observed phenomenon that virtually all studies have shown. The characteristics, such as young, male, urban, poor, or minority, tend to have the highest rates of criminal offending *and* the highest rates of victimization. One important exception is, namely, lower-class offenders tend to have higher rates of theft against middle- to upper-class households/individuals.

eugenics: This is the study of and policies related to the improvement of the human race via discriminatory control over reproduction.

experiential effect: This is the extent to which individuals' previous experience has an effect on their perceptions of how certain or severe criminal punishment will be when they are deciding whether or not to offend again.

family studies: Studies that examine the clustering of criminality in a given family.

feeblemindedness: This was a technical, scientific term in the early 1900s meaning those who had significantly below average levels of intelligence.

focal concerns: This is the primary concept of Walter Miller's theory, which asserts that all members of the lower class focus on a number of concepts they deem important: fate, autonomy, trouble, toughness, excitement, and smartness.

formal controls: These are factors that involve the official aspects of criminal justice, such as police, courts, and corrections (e.g., prisons, parole, probation)

frontal lobes: This is a region of the brain that is, as its name suggests, located in the frontal portion of the brain; most of the "executive functions" of the brain, such as problem solving, take place here, so it is perhaps the most vital portion of the brain and what makes us human.

general deterrence: Punishments given to an individual that are meant to prevent or deter other potential offenders from engaging in such criminal activity in the future.

general strain theory: Although derived from traditional strain theory, this theoretical framework assumes that people of all social classes and economic positions deal with frustrations in routine daily life to which virtually everyone can relate; it includes more sources of strain than traditional strain theory.

Hagan's power–control theory: This integrated theory deals with the influence of familial control and how this relates to criminality across gender; the primary focus of this theory is on the level of patriarchal attitudes and structure in the household, which are influenced by parental positions in the workforce.

hot spots: These are specific locations, such as businesses, residences, or parks, that experience a high concentration of crime incidents. This is a key concept in routine activities theory.

hypotheses: Hypotheses are specific predictions that are based on a scientific theoretical framework and tested via observation.

id: This is a subconscious domain of the psyche, according to Sigmund Freud, with which we are all born; it is responsible for our innate desires and drives (such as libido [sex drive]); it battles the moral conscience of the superego.

index offenses: Also known as Part I offenses, according to the Federal Bureau of Investigation (FBI) Uniform Crime Report (UCR), these are eight common offenses: murder, forcible rape, aggravated assault, robbery, burglary, motor vehicle theft, larceny, and arson. All reports of these crimes, even when they do not result in an arrest, are recorded to estimate crime in the nation and various states or regions.

informal controls: Informal controls are factors like family, church, or friends that do not involve official aspects of criminal justice, such as police, courts, and corrections (e.g., prisons).

innovation: In strain theory, this is an adaptation to strain in which an individual buys into the conventional goals of success but does not buy into the conventional means for getting to the goals.

integrated theories: Integrated theories combine two or more traditional theories into one combined model.

interdependency: A concept in John Braithwaite's theory of reintegration, it is a micro-level measure of the degree to which the individuals are connected or interdependent on mainstream society (via organizations or groups).

interracial: This is a description of when an occurrence (such as a crime event) involves people of a different race or ethnicity, such as a White person committing crime against a Black person.

intraracial: This is when an occurrence (such as a crime event) involves people of the same race or ethnicity, such as a White person committing crime against another White person.

labeling theory: Labeling theory is a theoretical perspective that assumes that criminal behavior increases because certain individuals are caught and labeled as offenders; their offending increases because they have been stigmatized as "offenders." Most versions of this perspective also assume that certain people (e.g., lower class or minorities) are more likely to be caught and punished. Another assumption of most versions is that if such labeling did not occur, the behavior would stop; this assumption led to numerous policy implications, such as diversion, decriminalization, and deinstitutionalization.

lambda (offender frequency): The Greek letter lambda is used by developmental perspective researchers to denote offending frequency by one individual or an average offending rate by a group of offenders, typically over the period of 1 year; the estimate of lambda ranges drastically across estimates for different individuals or groups, especially regarding the type of offense and whether based on self-reports or official data.

learning theories: Learning theories are theoretical models that assume criminal behavior of individuals due to a process of learning from others the motivations and techniques for engaging in such behavior. Virtually all of the variations of the learning perspective propose that the processes involved in a person learning how and why to commit crimes are the same as those involved in learning to engage in conventional activities (e.g., riding a bike, playing basketball).

legalistic approach: A way of defining behaviors as crime, it includes only acts that are specifically against the legal codes of a given jurisdiction. The problem with such a definition is that what is a crime in one jurisdiction is not necessarily a crime in other jurisdictions.

life-course-persistent offenders: These types of offenders, as labeled by Terrie Moffitt's developmental theory, start offending early and persist in offending through adulthood.

logical consistency: This refers to the extent to which concepts and propositions of a theoretical model make sense both in terms of face value and regarding the extent to which the model is consistent with what is readily known about crime rates or trends.

macro level of analysis: These are theories that focus on group or aggregated scores and measures as the unit of analysis, as opposed to individual rates.

mala in se: These are acts that are considered inherently evil and that virtually all societies consider to be serious crimes; an example is murder.

mala prohibita: These are the many acts that are considered crimes primarily because they have been declared bad by the legal codes in that jurisdiction. In other places and times, they are not illegal; examples are gambling, prostitution, and drug usage.

mechanical societies: In Émile Durkheim's theory, these societies were rather primitive with a simple distribution of labor (e.g., hunters and gatherers) and thus a high level of agreement regarding social norms and rules because nearly everyone is engaged in the same roles.

mens rea: In legal terms, this means "guilty mind" or intent. This concept involves whether or not offenders actually knew what they were doing and meant to do it.

mesoderm: This is the medical term for the middle layer of tissue in our bodies (e.g., muscles, tendons, bone structure).

mesomorphic: This is the type of body shape associated with an emphasis on the middle layer of tissue (mesoderm) during development. These people are disposed to be athletic or muscular.

micro level of analysis: This encompasses theories that focus on individual scores and measures as the unit of analysis, as opposed to group or aggregate rates.

minor physical anomalies (MPAs): MPAs are physical features, such as asymmetrical or low-seated ears, which are believed to indicate developmental problems—typically problems in the prenatal stage in the womb.

modeling and imitation: A major factor in differential reinforcement theory, modeling and imitation propose that much social learning takes place via imitation or modeling of behavior; for example, when adults or parents say "bad" words, their children begin using those words.

Moffitt's developmental theory (taxonomy): In this theoretical perspective proposed by Terrie Moffitt, criminal behavior is believed to be caused by two different causal paths: (1) adolescence-limited offenders commit their crimes during their teenage years due to peer pressure, whereas (2) life-course-persistent offenders commit antisocial behavior throughout life, starting very early and continuing on throughout their lives, because of the interaction between their neuropsychological deficits and criminogenic environments in their upbringing.

monozygotic (MZ) twins: Also referred to as identical twins, these are twin pairs that come from a single egg (zygote) and thus share 100% of their genetic makeup.

National Crime Victimization Survey (NCVS): The NCVS is one of the primary measures of crime in the United States collected by the U.S. Department of Justice (DOJ) and the U.S. Census Bureau based on interviews with victims of crime. This measure started in the early 1970s.

natural areas: This is the Chicago School's idea that all cities naturally contain identifiable clusters, such as a Chinatown or Little Italy, and neighborhoods that have low or high crime rates.

negative punishment: This is a concept in social learning in which people are given a punishment by removing something that they enjoy or like (e.g., taking away driving privileges for a teenager).

negative reinforcement: This is a concept in social learning in which people are given a reward by removing something that they dislike (e.g., not being on curfew or not having to do their "chores").

Neoclassical School: The Neoclassical School of criminological theory is virtually identical to the Classical School (both assume free will, rationality, the social contract, deterrence, etc.) except that it assumes that aggravating and mitigating circumstances should be taken into account for purposes of sentencing or punishing an offender.

neurotransmitters: These are nervous system chemicals in the brain and body that help transmit electric signals from one neuron to another, thus allowing healthy communication in the brain and to the body.

neutralization theory: This is a theory of criminal behavior that emphasizes the excuses or neutralization techniques that are used by offenders to alleviate their guilt or to excuse their behavior, when they know that their behavior is immoral; this theory was originally presented by Gresham Sykes and David Matza. In their theory, they presented five key "techniques"— ways that offenders alleviate their guilt or excuse their behavior, which they know is wrong; since they presented this idea in the 1960s, other techniques have been added, especially regarding white-collar crime.

nonindex offenses: Also known as Part II offenses, these are more than two dozen crimes that are considered relatively less serious than index crimes and must result in an arrest to be recorded by the Federal Bureau of Investigation (FBI). Therefore, the data on such results are far less reliable because the vast majority of reports of these crimes do not result in an arrest and are not in the annual FBI report.

operant conditioning: This is the learning model that takes place in organisms (such as humans) based on association between an action and feedback that occurs after it has taken place; for example, a rat running a maze can be trained to run the maze faster based on rewards (reinforcement), such as cheese, as well as punishments, such as electric shocks; introduced and promoted by B. F. Skinner.

organic societies: In the Durkheimian model, those societies have a high division of labor and thus a low level of agreement about societal norms, largely because everyone has such different roles in society, leading to very different attitudes about the rules and norms of behavior.

paradigms: A unique perspective of a phenomenon, it has an essential set of assumptions that significantly oppose those of other existing paradigms or explanations of the same phenomenon.

parsimony: Essentially meaning "simple," this is a characteristic of a good theory, meaning that it explains a certain phenomenon, in our case criminal behavior, with the fewest possible propositions or concepts.

phenotype: A phenotype is an observed manifestation of the interaction of genotypical traits with the environment, such as height (which depends largely on genetic disposition and diet, as exhibited by Asians or Mexicans who are raised in the United States and thus grow taller).

phrenology: This is the science of determining human dispositions based on distinctions (e.g., bumps) in the skull, which was believed to conform to the shape of the brain.

physiognomy: This is the study of facial and other bodily aspects to identify developmental problems, such as criminality.

pluralistic (conflict) perspective: This is a theoretical assumption that instead of one dominant and other inferior groups in society, there are a variety of groups that lobby and compete to influence changes in law; most are linked to George Vold's theoretical model.

policy implications: Policy implications are the extent to which a theory can be used to inform authorities about how to address a given phenomenon—in this case, ways to help law enforcement, court, and prison officials reduce crime or recidivism.

positive punishment: Positive punishment is a concept in social learning in which an individual is given a punishment by doing something he or she dislikes (e.g., spanking, sending to time-out, grounding).

positive reinforcement: Positive reinforcement is a concept in social learning in which an individual is given a reward by providing something he or she likes (e.g., money, curfew extended).

Positive School: The Positive School of criminological theory is a perspective that assumes individuals have no free will to control their behavior. Rather, the theories of the Positive School assume that criminal behavior is "determined" by factors outside of free choices made by the individual, such as peers, bad parenting, poverty, or biology.

power–control theory: Power–control theory is an integrated theory of crime that assumes that in households where the mother and father have relatively similar levels of power at work (i.e., balanced households), the mothers will be less likely to exert control on their daughters. These balanced households will be less likely to experience gender differences in the criminal offending of their children. However, households in which mothers and fathers have dissimilar levels of power in the workplace (i.e., unbalanced households) are more likely to suppress criminal activity in daughters, but more criminal activity is likely in the boys of the household.

primary deviance: A concept in labeling theory originally presented by Edwin Lemert, this is the type of minor, infrequent offending that people commit before they are caught and labeled as offenders. Most normal individuals commit this type of offending due to peer pressure and normal social behavior in their teenage years.

proletariat: In Karl Marx's conflict theory, the proletariat is the oppressed group of workers who are exploited by the bourgeoisie, an elite class that owns the means of production. According to Marx, the proletariat will never truly profit from their efforts because the upper class owns and controls the means of production.

rational choice theory (or lifestyle theory): This is a modern, Classical School–based framework for explaining crime that includes the traditional formal deterrence aspects, such as police, courts, and corrections and adds other informal factors that studies show consistently and strongly influence behavior, specifically informal deterrence factors (such as friends, family, community, etc.) and also the benefits of offending, whether they be monetary, peer status, or physiological (the "rush" of engaging in deviance).

reaction formation: A Freudian defense mechanism applied to Albert Cohen's theory of youth offending, it involves adopting attitudes or committing behaviors that are opposite of what is expected, for example, by engaging in malicious behavior as a form of defiance. Youth buy into this antinormative belief system so that they will feel less guilt for not living up to the standards they are failing to achieve and so they can achieve status among their delinquent peers.

rebellion: In strain theory, this is an adaptation to strain in which an individual buys into the idea of conventional means and goals of success but does not buy into the current conventional means or goals.

relative deprivation: This perception results when relatively poor people live in close proximity to relatively wealthy people. This concept is distinct from poverty in the sense that a poor area could mean that nearly everyone is poor, but relative deprivation inherently suggests that there is a notable amount of wealth and poor in a given area.

retreatism: In strain theory, this is an adaptation to strain in which an individual does not buy into the conventional goals of success and also does not buy into the conventional means.

retreatist gangs: This type of gang identified by Richard Cloward and Lloyd Ohlin tends to attract individuals who have failed to succeed in both the conventional world and the criminal or conflict gangs of their neighborhoods. Members of retreatist gangs are no good at making a profit from crime, nor are they good at using violence to achieve status, so the primary form of offending in retreatist gangs is usually drug usage.

ritualism: In strain theory, this is an adaptation to strain in which an individual buys into the conventional means of success (e.g., work, school) but does not buy into the conventional goals.

routine activities theory: This is an explanation of crime that assumes that most crimes are committed during the normal daily activities of people's lives. It assumes that crime or victimization is highest in places where three factors come together in time and place: motivated offenders, suitable or attractive targets, and absence of guardian. This perspective assumes a rational offender who picks targets due to opportunity.

Sampson and Laub's developmental model: One of the most known and researched developmental frameworks, this model focuses on the various life transitions (e.g., marriage, stable employment) in influencing the long-term trajectory of an individual and whether that trajectory makes him or her more or less likely to commit crime.

scenario (vignette) research: These are studies that involve providing participants with specific hypothetical scenarios and then asking them what they would do in that situation. Typically, they are also asked about their perceptions of punishment and other factors related to that particular situation.

scientific method: This is the method used in all scientific fields to determine the most objective results and conclusions regarding empirical observations. This method involves testing hypotheses via observation or data collection and then making conclusions based on the findings.

scope: Scope refers to the range of criminal behavior that a theory attempts to explain, which in our case can be seen as the amount of criminal activity a theory can account for, such as only violent crime or only property crime, or only drug usage. If a theory has a very large scope, it would attempt to explain all types of offending.

secondary deviance: A concept in labeling theory originally presented by Edwin Lemert, it is the type of more serious, frequent offending that people commit after they get caught and are labeled offenders. Individuals commit this type of offending because they have internalized their status as offenders and often have resorted to hanging out with other offenders.

selective placement: This is a criticism of adoption studies, arguing that adoptees tend to be placed in households that resemble those of their biological parents; thus, adoptees from rich biological parents are placed in rich adoptive households.

self-report data (SRD): This is one of the primary ways that crime data are collected, typically by asking offenders about their own offending; the most useful data for examining key causal factors in explaining crime (e.g., personality, attitudes).

serotonin: It is a neurotransmitter that is key in information processing; low levels are linked to depression and other mental illnesses. This is the neurotransmitter most consistently linked to criminal behavior in its deficiency.

severity of punishment: One of the key elements of deterrence, the assumption is that a given punishment must be serious enough to outweigh any potential benefits gained from a crime (but not too severe, so that it causes people to commit far more severe offenses to avoid apprehension). In other words, this theoretical concept advises graded penalties that increase as the offender recidivates or reoffends.

side-by-side (or horizontal) integration: This is a type of theoretical integration in which cases are classified by a certain criteria (e.g., impulsive vs. planned), and two or more theories are considered parallel explanations based on what type of case is being considered. Thus, there are two different paths in which a case is predicted to go, typically based on an initial variable (such as low or high self-control).

social bonding theory: This control theory proposed by Travis Hirschi in 1969 assumes that individuals are predisposed to commit crime and that the conventional bond that is formed with the individual prevents or reduces his or her offending. This bond is made up of four constructs: attachments, commitment, involvement, and moral beliefs regarding committing crime.

social contract: This is an Enlightenment ideal or assumption that stipulates there is an unspecified arrangement among citizens of a society in which they promise the state or government not to commit offenses against other citizens (to follow the rules of a society), and in turn, they gain protection from being violated by other citizens; violators will be punished.

social Darwinism: This is the belief that only the beneficial (or "fittest") societal institutions or groups of people survive or thrive in society.

social disorganization: See *Chicago School of Criminology*.

social dynamics: This is a concept proposed by Auguste Comte that describes aspects of social life that alter how societies are structured and that pattern the development of societal institutions.

social sciences: This is a category of scientific disciplines or fields of study that focus on various aspects of human behavior, such as criminology, psychology, economics, sociology, or anthropology. The scientific method is typically used for gaining knowledge.

social statics: This concept was proposed by Auguste Comte to describe aspects of society that relate to stability and social order, which allow societies to continue and endure.

soft determinism: This is the assumption that both determinism (the fundamental assumption of the Positive School of criminology) and free will or free choice (the fundamental assumption of the Classical School) play a role in offenders' decisions to engage in criminal behavior. This perspective can be seen as a type of compromise or "middle-road" concept.

somatotyping: This is the area of study, primarily linked to William Sheldon, that links body type to risk for delinquent or criminal behavior. Also, as a methodology, it is a way of ranking body types based on three categories: ectomorphic, endomorphic, and mesomorphic (see other entries).

somotonic: This is the type of temperament or personality associated with a mesomorphic (muscular) body type. These people tend to be risk-taking and aggressive.

specific deterrence: Punishments given to an individual that are meant to prevent or deter that particular individual from committing crime in the future.

spuriousness: This is when other factors (often referred to as Z factors) are actually causing two variables (X and Y) to occur at the same time; it may appear as if X causes Y when in fact they are both being caused by (an)other Z factor(s). To account for spuriousness, which is required for determining causality, researchers must ensure that no other factors are causing the observed correlation between X and Y. An example is when ice cream sales (X) are related to crime rates (Y); the Z variable is warm weather, which increases the opportunity for crime because more people and offenders are interacting.

stake in conformity: This significant portion of Jackson Toby's control theory applies to virtually all control theories, which refers to the extent to which individuals have investments in conventional society. It is believed—and supported by empirical studies—that the higher the stake in conformity an individual has, the less likely he or she will engage in criminal offending.

stigmata: The physical manifestations of atavism (biological inferiority); according to Lombroso, if a person had more than 5, he or she was a born criminal, meaning that a person or feature of an individual is a throwback to an earlier stage of evolutionary development and inevitably would be a chronic offender. An example is very large ears or very small ears.

strain theory: This is a category of theories of criminal behavior in which the emphasis is placed on a sense of frustration (e.g., economy) in crime causation—hence, "strain" theories.

subterranean values: These are the norms that individuals have been socialized to accept (e.g., violence) in certain contexts in a given society; an example would be the popularity of boxing or Ultimate Fighting Championship events in American society, even though violence is generally viewed negatively. Another example is the romanticized nature and popularity of crime movies, such as *The Godfather* and *Pulp Fiction*.

superego: This is a subconscious domain of the psyche, according to Sigmund Freud; it is not part of our nature but must be developed through early social attachments. It is responsible for our morality and conscience and battles the subconscious drives of the id.

swiftness of punishment: Swiftness of punishment is one of the key elements of deterrence. The assumption is that the faster punishment occurs after a crime is committed, the more an individual will be deterred in the future.

tabula rasa: This is the assumption that when people are born, they have a "blank slate" regarding morality and that every portion of their ethical or moral beliefs is determined by the interactions that occur in the way they are raised and socialized. This is a key assumption of virtually all learning theories.

telescoping: This is a human tendency in which events are perceived to occur much more recently in the past than they actually did, causing estimates of crime events to be overreported. In the National Crime Victimization Survey (NCVS) measure asking respondents to estimate their victimization over the past 6 months, respondents often report victimization that happened before the 6-month cutoff date.

temporal lobes: This is the region of the brain located above our ears, which is responsible for a variety of functions. It is located right above many primary limbic structures, which govern our emotional and memory functions.

temporal ordering: The criterion for determining causality, it requires that the predictor variable (X) precede the explanatory variable (Y) in time.

testability: This refers to the extent to which a theoretical model can be empirically or scientifically tested through observation and empirical research.

theoretical elaboration: This is a form of theoretical integration that uses a traditional theory as the framework for the theoretical model but also adds concepts or propositions from other theories.

theory: This is a set of concepts linked together by a series of propositions in an organized way to explain a phenomenon.

theory of concentric circles: This is a model proposed by Chicago School theorists; it assumes that all cities grow in a natural way that universally has the same five zones (or circles or areas). For example, all cities have a central Zone I, which contains basic government buildings, as well as a Zone II, which was once residential but is being "invaded" by factories. The outer three zones involve various forms of residential areas.

theory of low self-control: This is a theory that proposes that individuals either develop self-control by the time they are about age 10 or do not. Those who do not develop self-control will manifest criminal or deviant behaviors throughout life. This perspective was originally proposed by Michael Gottfredson and Travis Hirschi.

Thornberry's interactional model: This integrated model of crime was the first major perspective to emphasize reciprocal, or feedback, effects in the causal modeling of the theoretical framework.

Tittle's control–balance theory: This integrated theory was proposed in 1995; it claims (a) the amount of control to which one is subjected and (b) the amount of control that one can exercise determine the probability of deviance occurring. This theory proposes that the balance between these two types of control can predict the type of behavior that is likely to be committed.

trajectory: This is the path that someone takes in life, often due to the transitions (see *transitions*).

transitions: These are events that are important in altering trajectories toward or against crime, such as marriage, employment, or military service.

twins-separated-at-birth studies: These are studies that examine the similarities between identical twins who are separated in infancy; research indicates that such twins are often extremely similar even though they grew up in completely different environments.

twin studies: These are studies that examine the relative concordance rates for monozygotic (MZ) versus dizygotic (DZ) twins with virtually every study showing that identical twins (MZ) tend to be far more concordant for criminality than fraternal (DZ) twins.

Uniform Crime Report (UCR): This is an annual report published by the Federal Bureau of Investigation (FBI) in the U.S. Department of Justice (DOJ), which is meant to estimate most of the major street crimes in the United States. It is based on police reports or arrests throughout the nation, and started in the 1930s.

up-and-down (or deductive) integration: This type of theoretical integration is generally considered the classic form of theoretical integration because it has been done relatively often in the history of criminological theory development. This often involves increasing the level of abstraction of a single theory so that postulates seem to follow from a conceptually broader theory, such as differential reinforcement theory assuming virtually all of the concepts and assumptions of differential association theory.

utilitarianism: This is a philosophical concept that is often applied to social policies of the Classical School of criminology, which relates to the "greatest good for the greatest number."

viscerotonic: This is the type of temperament or personality associated with an endomorphic (obese) body type. These people tend to be jolly, lazy, and happy-go-lucky.

zone in transition: In the Chicago School or social disorganization theory, this zone (labeled Zone II) was once residential but is becoming more industrial because it is being invaded by the factories; this area of a city tends to have the highest crime rates due to the chaotic effect that the invasion of factories has on the area.

Index

About the Author

Stephen G. Tibbetts has been pursuing an understanding of criminal offending for the past two decades. He has attempted to discover the extent to which individuals' inherent dispositions and attitudinal traits contribute to their offending decisions, especially in relation to other factors, such as demographic, developmental, and situational considerations. Dr. Tibbetts's research has included work on the differences between men and women in their decisions to commit deviant behavior, as well as their perceptions of risk and consequences of getting caught. His additional research interests include the effects of perinatal disorders as an influence in future criminality, the etiology of white-collar crime, gang intervention, and citizens' attitudes regarding various forms of pornography. Dr. Tibbetts has published nine books and more than 50 scholarly papers examining various issues in criminology. He received the annual Outstanding Professor Award at California State University, San Bernardino (CSUSB), in 2011. Dr. Tibbetts taught at East Tennessee State University for four years prior to coming to CSUSB. He served as a court-appointed special advocate in Washington County, Tennessee, for several years, where he directed the disposition of numerous juvenile court cases. He continued this work as a child advocate in San Bernardino County from 2000 to 2006.